MznLnx

Missing Links Exam Preps

Exam Prep for

Introduction To Environmental Geology

Keller, 3rd Edition

The MznLnx Exam Prep is your link from the texbook and lecture to your exams.
The MznLnx Exam Preps are unauthorized and comprehensive reviews of your textbooks.

All material provided by MznLnx and Rico Publications (c) 2010
Textbook publishers and textbook authors do not particpate in or contribute to these reviews.

MznLnx

Rico
Publications

Exam Prep for Introduction To Environmental Geology
3rd Edition
Keller

Publisher: Raymond Houge
Assistant Editor: Michael Rouger
Text and Cover Designer: Lisa Buckner
Marketing Manager: Sara Swagger
Project Manager, Editorial Production: Jerry Emerson
Art Director: Vernon Lowerui

Product Manager: Dave Mason
Editorial Assitant: Rachel Guzmanji
Pedagogy: Debra Long
Cover Image: Jim Reed/Getty Images
Text and Cover Printer: City Printing, Inc.
Compositor: Media Mix, Inc.

(c) 2010 Rico Publications
ALL RIGHTS RESERVED. No part of this work covered by the copyright may be reproduced or used in any form or by an means--graphic, electronic, or mechanical, including photocopying, recording, taping, Web distribution, information storage, and retrieval systems, or in any other manner--without the written permission of the publisher.

Printed in the United States
ISBN:

For more information about our products, contact us at:
Dave.Mason@RicoPublications.com

For permission to use material from this text or product, submit a request online to:
Dave.Mason@RicoPublications.com

Contents

CHAPTER 1
Philosophy and Fundamental Concepts — 1

CHAPTER 2
Internal Structure of the Earth and Plate Tectonics — 19

CHAPTER 3
Minerals and Rocks — 33

CHAPTER 4
Introduction to Natural Hazards — 54

CHAPTER 5
Earthquakes and Related Phenomena — 64

CHAPTER 6
Volcanic Activity — 81

CHAPTER 7
Rivers and Flooding — 94

CHAPTER 8
Slope Processes, Landslides, and Subsidence — 104

CHAPTER 9
Coastal Processes — 115

CHAPTER 10
Impact of Extraterrestrial Objects — 126

CHAPTER 11
Water Resources — 140

CHAPTER 12
Water Pollution — 156

CHAPTER 13
Mineral Resources — 173

CHAPTER 14
Energy and Resources — 187

CHAPTER 15
Soils and Environment — 211

CHAPTER 16
Waste as a Resource: Waste Management — 225

CHAPTER 17
Air Pollution — 235

CHAPTER 18
Global Climate Change — 250

CHAPTER 19
Geology, Society, and the Future — 267

ANSWER KEY — 279

TO THE STUDENT

COMPREHENSIVE

The *MznLnx* Exam Prep series is designed to help you pass your exams. Editors at MznLnx review your textbooks and then prepare these practice exams to help you master the textbook material. Unlike study guides, workbooks, and practice tests provided by the texbook publisher and textbook authors, *MznLnx* gives you **all** of the material in each chapter in exam form, not just samples, so you can be sure to nail your exam.

MECHANICAL

The MznLnx Exam Prep series creates exams that will help you learn the subject matter as well as test you on your understanding. Each question is designed to help you master the concept. Just working through the exams, you gain an understanding of the subject--its a simple mechanical process that produces success.

INTEGRATED STUDY GUIDE AND REVIEW

MznLnx is not just a set of exams designed to test you, its also a comprehensive review of the subject content. Each exam question is also a review of the concept, making sure that you will get the answer correct without having to go to other sources of material. You learn as you go! Its the easiest way to pass an exam.

HUMOR

Studying can be tedious and dry. MznLnx's instructional design includes moderate humor within the exam questions on occassion, to break the tedium and revitalize the brain

Chapter 1. Philosophy and Fundamental Concepts 1

1. _____s, alternatively referred to as _____ matter (PM) or fine particles, are tiny particles of solid or liquid suspended in a gas or liquid. In contrast, aerosol refers to particles and the gas together. Sources of _____ matter can be man made or natural.
   a. 1509 Istanbul earthquake
   b. 1703 Genroku earthquake
   c. 1700 Cascadia earthquake
   d. Particulate

2. _____ are tiny particles of solid or liquid suspended in a gas. They range in size from less than 10 nanometres to more than 100 micrometres in diameter.
   a. 1703 Genroku earthquake
   b. 1700 Cascadia earthquake
   c. 1509 Istanbul earthquake
   d. Particulates

3. Technically, an _____ is a suspension of fine solid or liquid droplets in a gas. Contrast with a smoke which is a suspension of solid particles in a gas. In general conversation, _____ usually refers to an _____ spray can or the output of such a can.
   a. AL 129-1
   b. Aerosol
   c. AASHTO Soil Classification System
   d. AL 333

4. _____ is the substance of which physical objects are composed. _____ can be solid, liquid, plasma or gas. It constitutes the observable universe.
   a. 1700 Cascadia earthquake
   b. Matter
   c. 1509 Istanbul earthquake
   d. 1703 Genroku earthquake

5. _____ is an island in the south Pacific Ocean belonging to Chile. The island is famous for its numerous moai, the stone statues located along the coastlines.
   a. AASHTO Soil Classification System
   b. AL 333
   c. AL 129-1
   d. Easter Island

6. _____ were vertebrate animals that dominated terrestrial ecosystems for over 160 million years, first appearing approximately 230 million years ago. At the end of the Cretaceous Period, approximately 65 million years ago, a catastrophic extinction event ended _____' dominance on land.
   a. Dinosaurs
   b. 1509 Istanbul earthquake
   c. 1703 Genroku earthquake
   d. 1700 Cascadia earthquake

7. _____ involves the study of the interaction of humans with the geologic environment including the biosphere, the lithosphere, the hydrosphere, and to some extent the atmosphere.
   a. Ubehebe Crater
   b. Engineering geology
   c. Isostasy
   d. Environmental geology

8. _____ is the science and study of the solid matter that constitute the Earth. Encompassing such things as rocks, soil, and gemstones, _____ studies the composition, structure, physical properties, history, and the processes that shape Earth's components.
   a. Geology
   b. Glaciology
   c. 1509 Istanbul earthquake
   d. Glacial motion

9. _____ is the discipline concerned with the questions of how one should live ; what sorts of things exist and what are their essential natures ; what counts as genuine knowledge; and what are the correct principles of reasoning.

a. 1509 Istanbul earthquake
b. 1703 Genroku earthquake
c. Philosophy
d. 1700 Cascadia earthquake

10. The _____ is believed to be a gaseous cloud from which Earth's solar system formed. This was first proposed by Emanuel Swedenborg. Immanuel Kant, who was familiar with Swedenborg's work, developed the theory further. He argued that nebulae slowly rotate, gradually collapsing and flattening due to gravity and eventually forming stars and planets.
   a. 1703 Genroku earthquake
   b. 1509 Istanbul earthquake
   c. 1700 Cascadia earthquake
   d. Solar nebula

11. _____ is the study of the past, particularly using written records. New technology, such as photography, and computer text files now sometimes complement traditional archival sources. _____ is a field of research producing a continuous narrative and a systematic analysis of past events of importance to the human race.
   a. 1700 Cascadia earthquake
   b. 1509 Istanbul earthquake
   c. Absolute time
   d. History

12. A _____ is an interstellar cloud of dust, hydrogen gas and plasma. It is the first stage of a star's cycle.
   a. 1700 Cascadia earthquake
   b. 1509 Istanbul earthquake
   c. Nebula
   d. 1703 Genroku earthquake

13. _____ are a class of astronomical objects. The term is generally used to indicate a diverse group of small celestial bodies that drift in the solar system in orbit around the Sun.
   a. AL 333
   b. AASHTO Soil Classification System
   c. Asteroids
   d. AL 129-1

14. The _____ is a cosmological model in which the universe has been expanding for around 13.7 billion years, starting from a tremendously dense and hot state. It is also used in a narrower sense to describe the fundamental 'fireball' that erupted at or close to time t=0 in the history of the universe.
   a. 1703 Genroku earthquake
   b. 1700 Cascadia earthquake
   c. Big bang
   d. 1509 Istanbul earthquake

15. '_____' is an inspirational prose poem about attaining happiness in life. It was first copyrighted in 1927 by Max Ehrmann.

The poem begins: Go placidly amid the noise and the haste, and remember what peace there may be in silence.

In the 1960s, it was widely circulated without attribution to Ehrmann, sometimes with the claim that it was found in Saint Paul's Church, Baltimore, Maryland, and that it had been written in 1692 (the year of the founding of Saint Paul's.)

   a. 1703 Genroku earthquake
   b. 1509 Istanbul earthquake
   c. 1700 Cascadia earthquake
   d. Desiderata

16. In biology and ecology, _____ is the cessation of existence of a species or group of taxa, reducing biodiversity. The moment of _____ is generally considered to be the death of the last individual of that species.

Chapter 1. Philosophy and Fundamental Concepts

a. AASHTO Soil Classification System
b. AL 129-1
c. AL 333
d. Extinction

17. The _____ is used by geologists and other scientists to describe the timing and relationships between events that have occurred during the history of Earth.
   a. 1703 Genroku earthquake
   b. 1700 Cascadia earthquake
   c. 1509 Istanbul earthquake
   d. Geological time scale

18. _____ is a sharp decrease in the number of species in a relatively short period of time. It has sometimes accelerated the evolution of life on earth. Global warming is one of the causes of _____.
   a. Mass extinction
   b. 1700 Cascadia earthquake
   c. 1703 Genroku earthquake
   d. 1509 Istanbul earthquake

19. The _____ is one of three geologic eras of the Phanerozoic eon. The _____ was a time of tectonic, climatic and evolutionary activity, shifting from a state of connectedness into their present configuration. The climate was exceptionally warm throughout the period, also playing an important role in the evolution and diversification of new animal species. By the end of the era, the basis of modern life was in place.
   a. 1703 Genroku earthquake
   b. 1509 Istanbul earthquake
   c. 1700 Cascadia earthquake
   d. Mesozoic

20. _____ is the slow release of a gas that was trapped, frozen, absorbed or adsorbed in some material. It can include sublimation and evaporation which are phase transitions of a substance into a gas, as well as desorption, seepage from cracks or internal volumes and gaseous products of slow chemical reactions.
   a. Outgassing
   b. AL 333
   c. AASHTO Soil Classification System
   d. AL 129-1

21. _____ is a triatomic molecule, consisting of three oxygen atoms. It is an allotrope of oxygen that is much less stable than the diatomic species O2. Ground-level _____ is an air pollutant with harmful effects on the respiratory systems of animals. On the other hand, _____ in the upper atmosphere protects living organisms by preventing damaging ultraviolet light from reaching the Earth's surface.
   a. AL 333
   b. Ozone
   c. AL 129-1
   d. AASHTO Soil Classification System

22. The _____ is the part of the Earth's atmosphere which contains relatively high concentrations of ozone.
   a. AASHTO Soil Classification System
   b. Ozone layer
   c. AL 129-1
   d. AL 333

23. _____ is a theory of geology that has been developed to explain the observed evidence for large scale motions of the Earth's lithosphere. The theory encompassed and superseded the older theory of continental drift.
   a. Plate tectonics
   b. 1703 Genroku earthquake
   c. 1700 Cascadia earthquake
   d. 1509 Istanbul earthquake

24. A _____ is a stellar explosion that creates an extremely luminous object that is initially made of plasma—an ionized form of matter. A _____ may briefly out-shine its entire host galaxy before fading from view over several weeks or months. During this brief period of time, the _____ radiates as much energy as the Sun would emit over about 10 billion years.

Chapter 1. Philosophy and Fundamental Concepts

a. Supernova
b. 1703 Genroku earthquake
c. 1509 Istanbul earthquake
d. 1700 Cascadia earthquake

25. _____ is a characteristic of a process or state that can be maintained at a certain level indefinitely. The term, in its environmental usage, refers to the potential longevity of vital human ecological support systems.
   a. 1703 Genroku earthquake
   b. 1509 Istanbul earthquake
   c. Sustainability
   d. 1700 Cascadia earthquake

26. An _____ is a long period of time with different technical and colloquial meanings, and usages in language. It begins with some beginning event known as an epoch, epochal date, epochal event or epochal moment.
   a. AL 129-1
   b. Era
   c. AASHTO Soil Classification System
   d. AL 333

27. _____ is a field of study within geology concerned generally with the structures within the crust of the Earth, or other planets, and particularly with the forces and movements that have operated in a region to create these structures.
   a. 1700 Cascadia earthquake
   b. 1509 Istanbul earthquake
   c. 1703 Genroku earthquake
   d. Tectonics

28. There are two distinct views on the meaning of _____. One view is that _____ is part of the fundamental structure of the universe, a dimension in which events occur in sequence, and _____ itself is something that can be measured. A contrasting view is that _____ is part of the fundamental intellectual structure in which _____, rather than being an objective thing to be measured, is part of the mental measuring system.
   a. 1509 Istanbul earthquake
   b. Time
   c. 1700 Cascadia earthquake
   d. 1703 Genroku earthquake

29. The _____ Era meaning "new life", is the most recent of the three classic geological eras. It covers the 65.5 million years since the Cretaceous-Tertiary extinction event at the end of the Cretaceous that marked the demise of the last non-avian dinosaurs and the end of the Mesozoic Era. The _____ era is ongoing.
   a. 1703 Genroku earthquake
   b. Cenozoic
   c. 1700 Cascadia earthquake
   d. 1509 Istanbul earthquake

30. The _____ is the most recent of the three classic geological eras. It covers the 65.5 million years since the Cretaceous-Tertiary extinction event at the end of the Cretaceous that marked the demise of the last non-avian dinosaurs and the end of the Mesozoic Era.
   a. 1703 Genroku earthquake
   b. 1700 Cascadia earthquake
   c. 1509 Istanbul earthquake
   d. Cenozoic era

31. The _____ is the earliest of three geologic eras of the Phanerozoic eon. The _____ is subdivided into six geologic periods; from oldest to youngest they are: the Cambrian, Ordovician, Silurian, Devonian, Carboniferous, and Permian.
   a. 1703 Genroku earthquake
   b. Paleozoic
   c. 1509 Istanbul earthquake
   d. 1700 Cascadia earthquake

32. The _____ is an informal name for the eons of the geologic timescale that came before the current Phanerozoic eon. It spans from the formation of Earth around 4500 Ma to the evolution of abundant macroscopic hard-shelled animals, which marked the beginning of the Cambrian, the first period of the first era of the Phanerozoic eon, some 542 Ma.

Chapter 1. Philosophy and Fundamental Concepts 5

a. 1700 Cascadia earthquake
b. 1703 Genroku earthquake
c. Precambrian
d. 1509 Istanbul earthquake

33. The _____ is defined as the summation of all particles and energy that exist and the space-time in which all events occur.
a. AL 129-1
b. AASHTO Soil Classification System
c. AL 333
d. Universe

34. In biology, _____ is the process of change in the inherited traits of a population of organisms from one generation to the next. An area of current investigation in evolutionary developmental biology is the developmental basis of adaptations and exaptations. Adaptations are structures or behaviors that enhance a specific function, causing organisms to become better at surviving and reproducing.
a. Eye of a storm
b. Evolution
c. Antarctica
d. Ediacaran biota

35. _____ is the variation of taxonomic life forms within a given ecosystem, biome or for the entire Earth. _____ is often a measure of the health of biological systems.
a. Biodiversity
b. 1509 Istanbul earthquake
c. 1703 Genroku earthquake
d. 1700 Cascadia earthquake

36. A _____ is an extended period of months or years when a region notes a deficiency in its water supply. Generally, this occurs when a region receives consistently below average precipitation.
a. Drought
b. 1703 Genroku earthquake
c. 1509 Istanbul earthquake
d. 1700 Cascadia earthquake

37. _____ is a general term that includes rocks and materials that are not by definition rocks but are commonly regarded as rocks.
a. Earth materials
b. AASHTO Soil Classification System
c. AL 333
d. AL 129-1

38. An _____ is the result from the sudden release of stored energy in the Earth's crust that creates seismic waves. At the Earth's surface, _____s may manifest themselves by a shaking or displacement of the ground. An _____ is caused by tectonic plates getting stuck and putting a strain on the ground. The strain becomes so great that rocks give way by breaking and sliding along fault planes.
a. AL 333
b. Earthquake
c. AL 129-1
d. AASHTO Soil Classification System

39. An _____ is an assessment of the likely influence a project may have on the environment. The purpose of the assessment is to ensure that decision-makers consider _____s before deciding whether to proceed with new projects.
a. AASHTO Soil Classification System
b. Environmental impact
c. AL 333
d. AL 129-1

40. An _____ is an assessment of the likely influence a project may have on the environment. It is the process of identifying, predicting, evaluating and mitigating the biophysical, social, and other relevant effects of development proposals prior to major decisions being taken and commitments made, to ensure that decision-makers consider environmental impacts before deciding whether to proceed with new projects.

Chapter 1. Philosophy and Fundamental Concepts

    a. AL 333
    b. Environmental Impact Report
    c. AASHTO Soil Classification System
    d. AL 129-1

41. _____ is the study of physical or virtual environment of objects; and in Nature, it is the study of interactions among physical, chemical, and biological components of the environment.
    a. AL 129-1
    b. Environmental science
    c. AL 333
    d. AASHTO Soil Classification System

42. A _____ is a bipedal primate belonging to the mammalian species Homo sapiens in the family Hominidae. Compared to other living organisms on Earth, a _____ has a highly developed brain capable of abstract reasoning, language, and introspection.
    a. 1509 Istanbul earthquake
    b. 1700 Cascadia earthquake
    c. 1703 Genroku earthquake
    d. Human

43. A _____ is a storm system characterized by a low pressure center and numerous thunderstorms that produce strong winds and flooding rain. _____s feed on heat released when moist air rises, resulting in condensation of water vapour contained in the moist air. They are fueled by a different heat mechanism than other cyclonic windstorms such as nor'easters, European windstorms, and polar lows, leading to their classification as 'warm core' storm systems. Depending on its location and strength, a _____ is referred to by many other names, such as hurricane, typhoon, tropical storm, cyclonic storm, tropical depression, and simply cyclone.
    a. Kenya
    b. Persia
    c. Khmer Empire
    d. Tropical cyclone

44. _____ is the human modification of natural environment or wilderness into built environment such as fields, pastures, and settlements. The major effect of _____ on land cover since 1750 has been deforestation of temperate regions. More recent significant effects of _____ include urban sprawl, soil erosion, soil degradation, salinization, and desertification.
    a. 1509 Istanbul earthquake
    b. 1703 Genroku earthquake
    c. 1700 Cascadia earthquake
    d. Land use

45. _____ is the term used for a branch of public policy which encompasses various disciplines which seek to order and regulate the use of land in an efficient and ethical way.
    a. 1700 Cascadia earthquake
    b. 1703 Genroku earthquake
    c. 1509 Istanbul earthquake
    d. Land use planning

46. In biology a _____ is the collection of inter-breeding organisms of a particular species; in sociology, a collection of human beings. A _____ shares a particular characteristic of interest, most often that of living in a given geographic area. In taxonomy _____ is a low-level taxonomic rank.
    a. Metapopulation
    b. 1700 Cascadia earthquake
    c. 1509 Istanbul earthquake
    d. Population

47. _____ is the change in population over time, and can be quantified as the change in the number of individuals in a population per unit time. The term _____ can technically refer to any species, but almost always refers to humans, and it is often used informally for the more specific demographic term _____ rate, and is often used to refer specifically to the growth of the population of the world.

Chapter 1. Philosophy and Fundamental Concepts 7

   a. 1700 Cascadia earthquake
   b. 1703 Genroku earthquake
   c. 1509 Istanbul earthquake
   d. Population growth

48. A _____ is an opening in a planet's surface or crust, which allows hot, molten rock, ash, and gases to escape from below the surface. Volcanic activity involving the extrusion of rock tends to form mountains or features like mountains over a period of time.

_____es are generally found where tectonic plates are diverging or converging.

   a. 1700 Cascadia earthquake
   b. 1703 Genroku earthquake
   c. 1509 Istanbul earthquake
   d. Volcano

49. _____ usually commence with phreatomagmatic eruptions which can be extremely noisy due the rising magma heating water in the ground. This is usually followed by the explosive throat clearing of the vent and the eruption column is dirty grey to black as old weathered rocks are blasted out of the vent. As the vent clears, further ash clouds become grey-white and creamy in colour, with convulations of the ash similar to those of plinian eruptions.
   a. Vulcanian eruptions
   b. 1509 Istanbul earthquake
   c. 1703 Genroku earthquake
   d. 1700 Cascadia earthquake

50. _____ is the process of breaking a complex topic or substance into smaller parts to gain a better understanding of it. The technique has been applied in the study of mathematics and logic since before Aristotle, though _____ as a formal concept is a relatively recent development.

As a formal concept, the method has variously been ascribed by Ibn al-Haytham, Descartes (Discourse on the Method), Galileo, and Isaac Newton, as a practical method of physical discovery.

   a. AASHTO Soil Classification System
   b. AL 129-1
   c. AL 333
   d. Analysis

51. In materials science, _____ is a change in the shape or size of an object due to an applied force. This can be a result of tensile (pulling) forces, compressive (pushing) forces, shear, bending or torsion (twisting.) _____ is often described as strain.
   a. 1703 Genroku earthquake
   b. 1700 Cascadia earthquake
   c. 1509 Istanbul earthquake
   d. Deformation

52. _____ is the degradation of land in arid, semi arid and dry sub-humid areas resulting from various climatic variations, but primarily human activities. Current _____ is taking place much faster worldwide than historically and usually arises from the demands of increased populations that settle on the land in order to grow crops and graze animals.
   a. 1700 Cascadia earthquake
   b. 1509 Istanbul earthquake
   c. 1703 Genroku earthquake
   d. Desertification

53. The _____ is the period of time required for a quantity to double in size or value. It is applied to population growth, inflation, resource extraction, consumption of goods, compound interest, the volume of malignant tumours, and many other things which tend to grow over time. When the relative growth rate (not the absolute growth rate) is constant, the quantity undergoes exponential growth (also known as geometric growth) and has a constant _____ or period which can be calculated directly from the growth rate.

Chapter 1. Philosophy and Fundamental Concepts

   a. 1509 Istanbul earthquake
   c. 1703 Genroku earthquake
   b. Doubling time
   d. 1700 Cascadia earthquake

54. _____, officially the Federal Democratic Republic of _____, is a landlocked country situated in the Horn of Africa. _____ is bordered by Eritrea to the north, Sudan to the west, Kenya to the south, Somalia to the east and Djibouti to the north-east.

_____ is one of the oldest countries in the world and Africa's second-most populous nation.

   a. AL 129-1
   c. AL 333
   b. AASHTO Soil Classification System
   d. Ethiopia

55. In mathematics, _____ occurs when the growth rate of a function is always proportional to the function's current size. Such growth is said to follow an exponential law; the simple-_____ model is known as the Malthusian growth model.
   a. AASHTO Soil Classification System
   c. AL 333
   b. AL 129-1
   d. Exponential growth

56. _____ is the fifth planet from the Sun and the largest planet within the solar system. It is two and a half times as massive as all of the other planets in our solar system combined. _____, along with Saturn, Uranus and Neptune, is classified as a gas giant.
   a. 1703 Genroku earthquake
   c. 1700 Cascadia earthquake
   b. 1509 Istanbul earthquake
   d. Jupiter

57. _____ is a condition where an organism's numbers exceed the carrying capacity of its habitat. In common parlance, the term usually refers to the relationship between the human population and its environment, the Earth.

_____ does not depend only on the size or density of the population, but on the ratio of population to available sustainable resources, and on the means of resource use and distribution used by that population.

   a. Overpopulation
   c. Amblypoda
   b. Ambulocetus
   d. Andrija Mohorovičić

58. The _____ (1968) is a book written by Paul R. Ehrlich. A best-selling work, it predicted disaster for humanity due to overpopulation and the 'population explosion'. The book predicted that 'in the 1970s and 1980s hundreds of millions of people will starve to death', that nothing can be done to avoid mass famine greater than any in the history, and radical action is needed to limit the overpopulation.
   a. Amblypoda
   c. Ambulocetus
   b. Andrija Mohorovičić
   d. Population bomb

59. _____ is the supportable population of an organism, given the food, habitat, water and other necessities available. For the human population other variables such as sanitation and medical care are sometimes considered as infrastructure.
   a. Carrying capacity
   c. 1703 Genroku earthquake
   b. 1509 Istanbul earthquake
   d. 1700 Cascadia earthquake

Chapter 1. Philosophy and Fundamental Concepts 9

60. _____, officially the Republic of _____, is a country in South Asia. It is the seventh-largest country by geographical area, the second-most populous country, and the most populous democracy in the world. Bounded by the Indian Ocean on the south, the Arabian Sea on the west, and the Bay of Bengal on the east, _____ has a coastline of 7,517 kilometers.
   a. Imam
   b. Informal sector
   c. Isthmus
   d. India

61. The _____ was a major shift of technological, socioeconomic, and cultural conditions that occurred in the late 18th century and early 19th century in some Western countries. It began in Britain and spread throughout the world, a process that continues.
   a. AL 129-1
   b. AASHTO Soil Classification System
   c. AL 333
   d. Industrial Revolution

62. A _____ is a fundamental change in power or organizational structures that takes place in a relatively short period of time. Aristotle described two types of political _____:

   1. Complete change from one constitution to another
   2. Modification of an existing constitution.

   _____s have occurred throughout human history and vary widely in terms of methods, duration, and motivating ideology. Their results include major changes in culture, economy, and socio-political institutions.

   Scholarly debates about what does and does not constitute a _____ center around several issues.

   a. 1700 Cascadia earthquake
   b. 1703 Genroku earthquake
   c. Revolution
   d. 1509 Istanbul earthquake

63. _____ is the use of statistics to analyze characteristics or changes to a population. It is related to social demography and demography.
   a. 1703 Genroku earthquake
   b. 1700 Cascadia earthquake
   c. 1509 Istanbul earthquake
   d. Global population statistics

64. In physics, _____ is a scalar physical quantity that describes the amount of work that can be performed by a force. _____ is an attribute of objects and systems that is subject to a conservation law. Several different forms of _____ exist to explain all known natural phenomena.
   a. AL 129-1
   b. AASHTO Soil Classification System
   c. AL 333
   d. Energy

65. Consumption of a _____ requires resources and contributes to air and water pollution. In the industrialized world the development of a _____ has become essential for agriculture, transportation, waste collection, information technology, communications that have become prerequisites of a developed society.
   a. AL 129-1
   b. AASHTO Soil Classification System
   c. AL 333
   d. Energy resource

Chapter 1. Philosophy and Fundamental Concepts

66. A _____ is a naturally occurring substance formed through geological processes that has a characteristic chemical composition, a highly ordered atomic structure and specific physical properties. A rock, by comparison, is an aggregate of _____s and need not have a specific chemical composition. _____s range in composition from pure elements and simple salts to very complex silicates with thousands of known forms.
   a. 1703 Genroku earthquake
   b. 1509 Istanbul earthquake
   c. Mineral
   d. 1700 Cascadia earthquake

67. _____ is the extraction of valuable minerals or other geological materials from the earth, usually from an ore body, vein, or seam. Any material that cannot be grown from agricultural processes, or created artificially in a laboratory or factory, is usually extracted from the earth by this method.
   a. Mining
   b. 1703 Genroku earthquake
   c. 1509 Istanbul earthquake
   d. 1700 Cascadia earthquake

68. _____ is the reprocessing of materials into new products. It prevents useful material resources being wasted, reduces the consumption of raw materials and reduces energy usage, and hence greenhouse gas emissions, compared to virgin production.
   a. 1703 Genroku earthquake
   b. 1700 Cascadia earthquake
   c. Recycling
   d. 1509 Istanbul earthquake

69. _____ are sources of water that are useful or potentially useful to humans. It is important because it is needed for life to exist. Many uses of water include agricultural, industrial, household, recreational and environmental activities.
   a. 1703 Genroku earthquake
   b. Water resources
   c. 1509 Istanbul earthquake
   d. 1700 Cascadia earthquake

70. _____ is the conversion of forested areas to non-forest land use such as arable land, pasture, urban use, logged area or wasteland. _____ results from removal of trees without sufficient reforestation and results in declines in: habitat and biodiversity, wood for fuel and industrial use and decline in quality of life.
   a. 1509 Istanbul earthquake
   b. 1703 Genroku earthquake
   c. 1700 Cascadia earthquake
   d. Deforestation

71. _____ is water located beneath the ground surface in soil pore spaces and in the fractures of geologic formations. _____ is recharged from, and eventually flows to, the surface naturally; natural discharge often occurs at springs and seeps, streams and can often form oases or wetlands.
   a. Groundwater
   b. 1703 Genroku earthquake
   c. 1700 Cascadia earthquake
   d. 1509 Istanbul earthquake

72. _____ is the process in which trees are cut down usually as part of a timber harvest. _____ can also remove wood for forest management goals. _____ is controversial due to its environmental and aesthetic impacts.
   a. 1509 Istanbul earthquake
   b. Logging
   c. 1703 Genroku earthquake
   d. 1700 Cascadia earthquake

73. _____ refers to a method of extracting rock or minerals from the earth by their removal from an open pit or borrow. The term is used to differentiate this form of mining from extractive methods that require tunneling into the earth.
   a. AL 333
   b. AASHTO Soil Classification System
   c. AL 129-1
   d. Open-pit mining

Chapter 1. Philosophy and Fundamental Concepts 11

74. _____ is the practice of mining a seam of mineral by first removing a long strip of overlying soil and rock.
   a. 1703 Genroku earthquake
   b. 1509 Istanbul earthquake
   c. 1700 Cascadia earthquake
   d. Strip mining

75. Water collecting on the ground or in a stream, river, lake, or wetland is called _____; as opposed to groundwater. _____ is naturally replenished by precipitation and naturally lost through discharge to the oceans, evaporation, and subsurface seepage into the groundwater. _____ is the largest source of fresh water.
   a. 1700 Cascadia earthquake
   b. 1509 Istanbul earthquake
   c. 1703 Genroku earthquake
   d. Surface water

76. In agriculture, _____ is the process of gathering mature crops from the fields. Reaping is the _____ of grain crops. The harvest marks the end of the growing season, or the growing cycle for a particular crop. _____ in general usage includes an immediate post-harvest handling, all of the actions taken immediately after removing the crop—cooling, sorting, cleaning, packing—up to the point of further on-farm processing, or shipping to the wholesale or consumer market.
   a. 1509 Istanbul earthquake
   b. Harvesting
   c. 1703 Genroku earthquake
   d. 1700 Cascadia earthquake

77. The _____ of South America is the largest river in the world by volume, with greater total river flow than the next eight largest rivers combined, and with the largest drainage basin in the world. Because of its vast dimensions it is sometimes called The River Sea.
   a. AL 333
   b. AL 129-1
   c. AASHTO Soil Classification System
   d. Amazon River

78. The _____ is made up of the tributaries of The Amazon River, the largest river in the world by volume, with greater total river flow than the next eight largest rivers combined, and with the largest drainage basin in the world.
   a. AL 129-1
   b. AASHTO Soil Classification System
   c. AL 333
   d. Amazon River system

79. The _____ is an ecological hypothesis that proposes that living and nonliving parts of the earth are viewed as a complex interacting system that can be thought of as a single organism.
   a. 1700 Cascadia earthquake
   b. Gaia hypothesis
   c. 1509 Istanbul earthquake
   d. 1703 Genroku earthquake

80. The _____ of economics uses a matrix representation of a nation's (or a region's) economy to predict the effect of changes in one industry on others and by consumers, government, and foreign suppliers on the economy. Wassily Leontief (1905-1999) is credited with the development of this analysis. Francois Quesnay developed a cruder version of this technique called Tableau économique.
   a. AL 129-1
   b. Input-output model
   c. AL 333
   d. AASHTO Soil Classification System

81. A _____ consists either of a suggested explanation for a phenomenon or of a reasoned proposal suggesting a possible correlation between multiple phenomena.
   a. Hypothesis
   b. 1700 Cascadia earthquake
   c. 1509 Istanbul earthquake
   d. 1703 Genroku earthquake

Chapter 1. Philosophy and Fundamental Concepts

82. _____ is a broadly useful concept that expresses how fast something moves through a system in equilibrium. It is the average time a substance spends within a specified region of space, such as a reservoir.
   a. 1509 Istanbul earthquake
   b. 1700 Cascadia earthquake
   c. 1703 Genroku earthquake
   d. Residence time

83. _____ refers to the principle that the same processes that shape the universe occurred in the past as they do now, and that the same laws of physics apply in all parts of the knowable universe.
   a. AASHTO Soil Classification System
   b. Uniformitarianism
   c. AL 333
   d. AL 129-1

84. _____ is a province located in the central part of Canada, the largest by population and second largest, after Quebec, in total area. _____ is bordered by the provinces of Manitoba to the west and Quebec to the east, and the U.S. states of Minnesota, Michigan, Ohio, Pennsylvania, and New York to the south. Most of _____'s borders with the United States are natural, starting at the Lake of the Woods and continuing through four of the Great Lakes: Superior, Huron, Erie, and _____, then along the Saint Lawrence River near Cornwall.
   a. Andrija Mohorovi Ä‡
   b. Ambulocetus
   c. Ontario
   d. Amblypoda

85. A _____ is a geological phenomenon which includes a wide range of ground movement, such as rock falls, deep failure of slopes and shallow debris flows. Although gravity's action on an over-steepened slope is the primary reason for a _____, there are other contributing factors affecting the original slope stability.
   a. 1509 Istanbul earthquake
   b. 1700 Cascadia earthquake
   c. 1703 Genroku earthquake
   d. Landslide

86. _____ is the production of food, feed, fiber, fuel and other goods by the systematic raizing of plants and animals.
   a. AL 129-1
   b. AL 333
   c. AASHTO Soil Classification System
   d. Agriculture

87. The _____ is a landlocked endorheic sea in Central Asia; it lies between Kazakhstan in the north and Karakalpakstan, an autonomous region of Uzbekistan, in the south
   a. AL 129-1
   b. AL 333
   c. AASHTO Soil Classification System
   d. Aral Sea

Chapter 1. Philosophy and Fundamental Concepts 13

88. An interbasin _____ is a hydrological project undertaken to divert water from one drainage basin into another. This is usually to boost water levels for hydroelectricity, or to supply drinking water nearby.

- Campbell-Heber Diversion
- Coquitlam-Buntzen Diversion
- Kemano Diversion
- Vernon Irrigation District Diversion

- Churchill Diversion-Southern Indian Lake

- Saint John Water Supply

- Bay d'Espoir Diversions
- Deer Lake Diversion
- Smallwood Reservoir-Julian Diversion
- Smallwood Reservoir-Kanairiktok Diversion
- Smallwood Reservoir-Naskaupi Diversion

- Wellington Lake Hydro Project Diversion (with Saskatchewan)

- Ingram Diversion
- Jordan Diversion
- Wreck Cove Diversions

- Long Lake Diversion
- Ogoki Diversion
- Opasatika Diversion
- Root River Diversion

- Barrière Diversion
- Boyd-Sakami Diversion
- Lac de la Frégate Diversion
- Laforge Diversion
- Manouane Diversion
- Mégiscane Diversion
- Sault aux Cochons Diversion

- Cypress Lake Diversion (with Alberta)
- Pasquia Land Resettlement Diversion (with Manitoba)
- Swift Current Diversion

a. 1700 Cascadia earthquake
b. 1703 Genroku earthquake
c. 1509 Istanbul earthquake
d. Water diversion

Chapter 1. Philosophy and Fundamental Concepts

89. _____ is the artificial application of water to the soil usually for assisting in growing crops. In crop production it is mainly used to replace missing rainfall in periods of drought, but also to protect plants against frost.
   a. AASHTO Soil Classification System
   b. AL 333
   c. AL 129-1
   d. Irrigation

90. _____ are compounds containing chlorine, fluorine and carbon only, that is they contain no hydrogen. They were formerly used widely in industry, for example as refrigerants, propellants, and cleaning solvents. Their use has been regularly prohibited by the Montreal Protocol, because of effects on the ozone layer.
   a. 1703 Genroku earthquake
   b. 1509 Istanbul earthquake
   c. Chlorofluorocarbons CFCs
   d. 1700 Cascadia earthquake

91. _____ seeks to integrate various fields of academic study to understand the Earth as a system. It looks at interaction between the the atmosphere, hydrosphere, lithosphere and biosphere.

In 1996, the American Geophysical Union, in cooperation with the Keck Geology Consortium and with support from five divisions within the National Science Foundation, convened a workshop 'to define common educational goals among all disciplines in the Earth sciences.' In its report, participants noted that, 'The fields that make up the Earth and space sciences are currently undergoing a major advancement that promotes understanding the Earth as a number of interrelated systems.' Recognizing the rise of this systems approach, the workshop report recommended that an _____ curriculum be developed with support from the National Science Foundation.

   a. AL 333
   b. AASHTO Soil Classification System
   c. Earth system science
   d. AL 129-1

92. A _____ or geophysical hazards is a threat of an event that will have a negative effect on people or the environment. Many _____s are related, e.g. earthquakes can result in tsunamis, drought can lead directly to famine and disease. A concrete example of the division between hazard and disaster is that the 1906 San Francisco earthquake was a disaster, whereas earthquakes are a hazard.
   a. 1700 Cascadia earthquake
   b. 1509 Istanbul earthquake
   c. 1703 Genroku earthquake
   d. Natural hazard

93. A hypothesis consists either of a suggested explanation for a phenomenon or of a reasoned proposal suggesting a possible correlation between multiple phenomena. The scientific method requires that one can test a scientific hypothesis. Scientists generally base such _____ on previous observations or on extensions of scientific theories. Even though the words "hypothesis" and "theory" are often used synonymously in common and informal usage, a scientific hypothesis is not the same as a scientific theory.
   a. 1700 Cascadia earthquake
   b. 1703 Genroku earthquake
   c. 1509 Istanbul earthquake
   d. Hypotheses

94. _____ is a concept that denotes the precise probability of specific eventualities. Technically, the notion of _____ is independent from the notion of value and, as such, eventualities may have both beneficial and adverse consequences. However, in general usage the convention is to focus only on potential negative impact to some characteristic of value that may arise from a future event.
   a. 1700 Cascadia earthquake
   b. 1509 Istanbul earthquake
   c. 1703 Genroku earthquake
   d. Risk

Chapter 1. Philosophy and Fundamental Concepts

95. _____ is a body of techniques for investigating phenomena and acquiring new knowledge, as well as for correcting and integrating previous knowledge. It is based on gathering observable, empirical and measurable evidence subject to specific principles of reasoning,
   a. 1700 Cascadia earthquake
   b. 1703 Genroku earthquake
   c. 1509 Istanbul earthquake
   d. Scientific method

96. _____ are very large slides of snow or rock down a mountainside, caused when a buildup of snow is released down a slope, and is one of the major dangers faced in the mountains.
   a. AL 333
   b. AASHTO Soil Classification System
   c. Avalanches
   d. AL 129-1

97. The _____ is defined as the part of the land adjoining or near the ocean. A coastline is properly a line on a map indicating the disposition of a _____, but the word is often used to refer to the _____ itself. The adjective coastal describes something as being on, near to, or associated with a _____.
   a. 1700 Cascadia earthquake
   b. 1509 Istanbul earthquake
   c. 1703 Genroku earthquake
   d. Coast

98. _____, is the slow downward progression of rock and soil down a low grade slope; it can also refer to slow deformation of such materials as a result of prolonged pressure and stress.
   a. 1700 Cascadia earthquake
   b. Creep
   c. 1509 Istanbul earthquake
   d. 1703 Genroku earthquake

99. _____ is displacement of solids by the agents of ocean currents, wind, water, or ice by downward or down-slope movement in response to gravity or by living organisms.
   a. AL 333
   b. AASHTO Soil Classification System
   c. AL 129-1
   d. Erosion

100. A _____ is a special-purpose map made to show geological features. The stratigraphic contour lines are drawn on the surface of a selected deep stratum, so that they can show the topographic trends of the strata under the ground. It is not always possible to properly show this when the strata are extremely fractured, mixed, in some discontinuities, or where they are otherwise disturbed.
   a. 1700 Cascadia earthquake
   b. 1703 Genroku earthquake
   c. 1509 Istanbul earthquake
   d. Geologic map

101. _____ is molten rock expelled by a volcano during an eruption. When first extruded from a volcanic vent, it is a liquid at temperatures from 700 °C to 1,200 °C.
   a. 1509 Istanbul earthquake
   b. Lava
   c. 1703 Genroku earthquake
   d. 1700 Cascadia earthquake

102. _____ is the wearing away of land or the removal of beach or dune sediments by wave action, tidal currents, wave currents, or drainage. Waves, generated by storms or fast moving moter craft, cause _____, which may take the form of long-term losses of sediment and rocks, or merely in the temporary redistribution of coastal sediments; erosion in one location may result in accretion nearby.
   a. 1700 Cascadia earthquake
   b. 1509 Istanbul earthquake
   c. Beach erosion
   d. 1703 Genroku earthquake

Chapter 1. Philosophy and Fundamental Concepts

103. The _____ of an edge is $c_f(u,v) = c(u,v) - f(u,v)$. This defines a residual network denoted $G_f(V, E_f)$, giving the amount of available capacity. See that there can be an edge from u to v in the residual network, even though there is no edge from u to v in the original network.
   a. 1703 Genroku earthquake
   b. 1509 Istanbul earthquake
   c. 1700 Cascadia earthquake
   d. Residual capacity

104. A _____ is a visual representation of an area--a symbolic depiction highlighting relationships between elements of that space such as objects, regions, and themes.

Many _____s are static two-dimensional, geometrically accurate representations of three-dimensional space, while others are dynamic or interactive, even three-dimensional. Although most commonly used to depict geography, _____s may represent any space, real or imagined, without regard to context or scale; e.g. Brain mapping, DNA mapping, and extraterrestrial mapping.

   a. Cartography
   b. 1509 Istanbul earthquake
   c. 1700 Cascadia earthquake
   d. Map

105. _____ can refer to: a period of time; a distinctive historical period or era, a unit of the geologic time scale, less than a period and greater than an age, or a phase in the development of the universe with distinctive properties.
   a. AASHTO Soil Classification System
   b. Epoch
   c. AL 333
   d. AL 129-1

106. The _____ is part of the Neogene and Quaternary periods. Human civilization dates entirely within the _____. The _____ was preceded by the Younger Dryas cold period, the final part of the Pleistocene epoch. The _____ starts late in the retreat of the Pleistocene glaciers. It can be considered an interglacial in the current ice age.
   a. 1509 Istanbul earthquake
   b. 1703 Genroku earthquake
   c. 1700 Cascadia earthquake
   d. Holocene

107. The _____ on the geologic timescale had been intended to cover the world's recent period of repeated glaciations. The _____ follows the Pliocene and is followed by the Holocene. The _____ is the third epoch of the Neogene period or 6th epoch of the Cenozoic era. The end of the _____ corresponds with the end of the Paleolithic age used in archaeology. The _____ is divided into the Early _____, Middle _____ and Late _____, and numerous faunal stages.
   a. Pleistocene
   b. 1509 Istanbul earthquake
   c. 1703 Genroku earthquake
   d. 1700 Cascadia earthquake

108. _____ generally refers to patterns of human activity and the symbolic structures that give such activities significance and importance. _____s can be 'understood as systems of symbols and meanings that even their creators contest, that lack fixed boundaries, that are constantly in flux, and that interact and compete with one another'.

_____ can be defined as all the ways of life including arts, beliefs and institutions of a population that are passed down from generation to generation.

Chapter 1. Philosophy and Fundamental Concepts 17

    a. 1509 Istanbul earthquake
    c. 1700 Cascadia earthquake
    b. Culture
    d. Nationality

109. _____ concerns approaches to ethics and morality based on the role of evolution in shaping human psychology and behavior.
    a. Evolutionary ethics
    c. AASHTO Soil Classification System
    b. AL 129-1
    d. AL 333

110. _____ is the increase in the average temperature of the Earth's near-surface air and oceans in recent decades and its projected continuation. An increase in global temperatures can in turn cause other changes, including sea level rise, and changes in the amount and pattern of precipitation resulting in floods and drought. There may also be changes in the frequency and intensity of extreme weather events.
    a. 1700 Cascadia earthquake
    c. 1703 Genroku earthquake
    b. Global warming
    d. 1509 Istanbul earthquake

111. A _____ is a building where plants are cultivated.
    a. Greenhouse
    c. 1700 Cascadia earthquake
    b. 1703 Genroku earthquake
    d. 1509 Istanbul earthquake

112. The _____ refers to the change in the steady state temperature of a planet or moon by the presence of an atmosphere containing gas that absorbs and emits infrared radiation. Greenhouse gases, which include water vapor, carbon dioxide and methane, warm the atmosphere by efficiently absorbing thermal infrared radiation emitted by the Earth's surface, by the atmosphere itself, and by clouds. As a result of its warmth, the atmosphere also radiates thermal infrared in all directions, including downward to the Earth's surface.
    a. General circulation model
    c. Glacier
    b. Radiative forcing
    d. Greenhouse effect

113. The _____ is a perspective on environmental ethics first championed by Aldo Leopold in his book A Sand County Almanac. In it he wrote that there was a need for a 'new ethic', an 'ethic dealing with man's relation to land and to the animals and plants which grow upon it'.

The prevailing ethos for the US Forest Service in his day, from the founder of the USFS, Gifford Pinchot, was economic and utilitarian, while Leopold argued for an ecological approach, one of the earliest popularizers of this term created by Henry Chandler Cowles of the University of Chicago during his early 1900's research at the Indiana Dunes.

    a. 1703 Genroku earthquake
    c. 1700 Cascadia earthquake
    b. 1509 Istanbul earthquake
    d. Land ethic

114. _____ is any of a number of similar colors evoked by light consisting predominantly of the longest wavelengths of light discernible by the human eye, in the wavelength range of roughly 625-740 nm. Longer wavelengths than this are called infrared, or below _____ and cannot be seen by the naked human eye. _____ is used as one of the additive primary colors of light, complementary to cyan, in RGB color systems.
    a. 1703 Genroku earthquake
    c. 1700 Cascadia earthquake
    b. 1509 Istanbul earthquake
    d. Red

Chapter 1. Philosophy and Fundamental Concepts

115. The _____ is the centerpiece of the Greater Yellowstone Ecosystem, the largest intact ecosystem in the Earth's northern temperate zone. Located mostly in the U.S. state of Wyoming, the park extends into Montana and Idaho. The park is known for its wildlife and geothermal features; Old Faithful Geyser is one of the most popular features in the park.
   a. 1700 Cascadia earthquake
   b. 1703 Genroku earthquake
   c. 1509 Istanbul earthquake
   d. Yellowstone National Park

116. _____ is a cape on the coast of North Carolina. It is the point that protrudes the farthest to the southeast along the northeast-to-southwest line of the Atlantic coast of North America. Two major Atlantic currents collide just off _____, the southerly-flowing cold water Labrador Current and the northerly-flowing warm water Florida Current (Gulf Stream), creating turbulent waters and a large expanse of shallow sandbars extending up to 14 miles offshore.
   a. Cape Hatteras
   b. 1703 Genroku earthquake
   c. 1509 Istanbul earthquake
   d. 1700 Cascadia earthquake

117. Due to shore erosion in the Outer Bank of North Carolina a navagational lighthouse had to be moved leading to the _____.
   a. 1700 Cascadia earthquake
   b. 1703 Genroku earthquake
   c. 1509 Istanbul earthquake
   d. Cape Hatteras Lighthouse controversy

Chapter 2. Internal Structure of the Earth and Plate Tectonics   19

1. _____ is the largest city in the state of California and the American West as well as second largest in the United States. Often abbreviated as L.A. and nicknamed The City of Angels, _____ is rated an alpha world city, has an estimated population of 3.8 million and spans over 498.3 square miles (1,290.6 km who hail from all over the globe and speak 224 different languages. _____ is the seat of _____ County, the most populated and one of the most diverse counties in the United States.
  a. 1700 Cascadia earthquake
  b. Coachella Valley
  c. 1509 Istanbul earthquake
  d. Los Angeles

2. The _____ is a tectonic plate covering most of North America, extending eastward to the Mid-Atlantic Ridge and westward to the Cherskiy Range in East Siberia.
  a. 1509 Istanbul earthquake
  b. 1700 Cascadia earthquake
  c. 1703 Genroku earthquake
  d. North American plate

3. The _____ is an oceanic tectonic plate beneath the Pacific Ocean.
  a. Pacific plate
  b. 1700 Cascadia earthquake
  c. 1509 Istanbul earthquake
  d. 1703 Genroku earthquake

4. The _____ is a geologic transform fault that runs a length of roughly 800 miles (1,300 km) through California in the United States. The fault's motion is right-lateral strike-slip (horizontal motion.) It forms the tectonic boundary between the Pacific Plate and the North American Plate.
  a. 1509 Istanbul earthquake
  b. 1703 Genroku earthquake
  c. 1700 Cascadia earthquake
  d. San Andreas fault

5. The _____ is the fourth most populous city in California and the 14th most populous city in the United States, with a 2007 estimated population of 764,976. Among the most densely populated cities in the country, San Francisco is part of the San Francisco Bay Area, which is home to more than 7.1 million people. The city is located at the tip of the San Francisco Peninsula, with the Pacific Ocean to the west, San Francisco Bay to the east, and the Golden Gate to the north.
  a. Ambulocetus
  b. Amblypoda
  c. Coachella Valley
  d. City and County of San Francisco

6. _____s are planar rock fractures, which show evidence of relative movement. Large _____s within the Earth's crust are the result of shear motion and active _____ zones are the causal locations of most earthquakes. Earthquakes are caused by energy release during rapid slippage along _____s.
  a. 1700 Cascadia earthquake
  b. 1703 Genroku earthquake
  c. 1509 Istanbul earthquake
  d. Fault

7. _____ is a primarily solid sphere about 1220 km in radius situated at the planets center.
  a. AL 333
  b. Earth's inner core
  c. AASHTO Soil Classification System
  d. AL 129-1

8. Earth's _____ is a ~2,900 km thick rocky shell comprizing approximately 70% of Earth's volume. It is predominantly solid and overlies the Earth's iron-rich core, which occupies about 30% of Earth's volume. Past episodes of melting and volcanism at the shallower levels of the _____ have produced a very thin crust of crystallized melt products near the surface, upon which we live.
  a. 1703 Genroku earthquake
  b. 1509 Istanbul earthquake
  c. 1700 Cascadia earthquake
  d. Mantle

Chapter 2. Internal Structure of the Earth and Plate Tectonics

9. _____ is a theory of geology that has been developed to explain the observed evidence for large scale motions of the Earth's lithosphere. The theory encompassed and superseded the older theory of continental drift.
   a. 1700 Cascadia earthquake
   b. 1703 Genroku earthquake
   c. 1509 Istanbul earthquake
   d. Plate tectonics

10. A _____ is an area of highland, usually consisting of relatively flat rural area.
    a. 1703 Genroku earthquake
    b. 1509 Istanbul earthquake
    c. Plateau
    d. 1700 Cascadia earthquake

11. In geology, _____ is a naturally occurring aggregate of minerals and/or mineraloids.

The Earth's outer solid layer, the lithosphere, is made of _____. In general _____s are of three types, namely, igneous, sedimentary, and metamorphic.

   a. 1700 Cascadia earthquake
   b. 1509 Istanbul earthquake
   c. 1703 Genroku earthquake
   d. Rock

12. The _____ is a vast, elevated plateau in East Asia covering most of the Tibet Autonomous Region and Qinghai Province in the People's Republic of China and Ladakh in Kashmir.
    a. 1509 Istanbul earthquake
    b. 1703 Genroku earthquake
    c. Tibetan Plateau
    d. 1700 Cascadia earthquake

13. The _____ is a primarily solid sphere about 1220 km in radius situated at Earth's center. The existence of an _____ that is different from the liquid outer core was discovered in 1936 by seismologist Inge Lehman using observations of earthquake-generated seismic waves that partly reflect from its boundary and can be detected by sensitive instruments at Earth's surface called seismographs.
    a. Inner Core
    b. AASHTO Soil Classification System
    c. AL 333
    d. AL 129-1

14. The _____ of the Earth is a liquid layer composed of iron and nickel above the solid inner core. Sulphur and oxygen could also be present. Its outer boundary lies approximately 2,890 km (1,800 mi) beneath the Earth's surface, below the mantle.
    a. AL 129-1
    b. AASHTO Soil Classification System
    c. AL 333
    d. Outer Core

15. _____ is a field of study within geology concerned generally with the structures within the crust of the Earth, or other planets, and particularly with the forces and movements that have operated in a region to create these structures.
    a. 1703 Genroku earthquake
    b. 1700 Cascadia earthquake
    c. 1509 Istanbul earthquake
    d. Tectonics

16. In geology, a _____ is the outermost layer of a planet, part of its lithosphere. They are generally composed of a less dense material than its deeper layers. Earths' is composed mainly of basalt and granite. It is cooler and more rigid than the deeper layers of the mantle and core.
    a. 1703 Genroku earthquake
    b. 1700 Cascadia earthquake
    c. 1509 Istanbul earthquake
    d. Crust

Chapter 2. Internal Structure of the Earth and Plate Tectonics   21

17. The _____ is the rigid outermost shell of a rocky planet.

In the Earth, the _____ includes the crust and the uppermost mantle, which constitute the hard and rigid outer layer of the planet. The _____ is underlain by the asthenosphere, the weaker, hotter, and deeper part of the upper mantle.

- a. 1700 Cascadia earthquake
- b. 1509 Istanbul earthquake
- c. 1703 Genroku earthquake
- d. Lithosphere

18. The _____ is the boundary between the Earth's crust and the mantle. The _____ serves to separate both oceanic crust and continental crust from underlying mantle. It mostly lies entirely within the lithosphere; only beneath mid-ocean ridges does the _____ also define the mesosphere-asthenosphere boundary.

- a. 1703 Genroku earthquake
- b. 1700 Cascadia earthquake
- c. Mohorovicic discontinuity
- d. 1509 Istanbul earthquake

19. A _____ is any local separation or discontinuous plane in a geologic formation, such as joints or faults into two or more pieces under the action of stress.

- a. 1700 Cascadia earthquake
- b. 1703 Genroku earthquake
- c. 1509 Istanbul earthquake
- d. Rock fracture

20. The _____ is the mechanically weak ductily-deforming region of the upper mantle of the Earth. It lies below the lithosphere, at depths between 100 and 200 km (~ 62 and 124 miles) below the surface, but perhaps extending as deep as 400 km (~ 249 miles.)

The _____ is a portion of the upper mantle just below the lithosphere that is involved in plate movements and isostatic adjustments.

- a. Asthenosphere
- b. AL 129-1
- c. AL 333
- d. AASHTO Soil Classification System

21. The _____ is the layer of granitic, sedimentary, and metamorphic rocks which form the continents and the areas of shallow seabed close to their shores, known as continental shelves. It is less dense than the material of the Earth's mantle and thus 'floats' on top of it. _____ is also less dense than oceanic crust, though it is considerably thicker. About 40% of the Earth's surface is now underlain by _____.

- a. 1703 Genroku earthquake
- b. 1509 Istanbul earthquake
- c. 1700 Cascadia earthquake
- d. Continental crust

22. _____ in the most general terms refers to the movement of currents within fluids. _____ is one of the major modes of Heat and mass transfer. In fluids, convective heat and mass transfer take place through both diffusion and by advection, in which matter or heat is transported by the larger-scale motion of currents in the fluid.

- a. 1700 Cascadia earthquake
- b. 1703 Genroku earthquake
- c. 1509 Istanbul earthquake
- d. Convection

Chapter 2. Internal Structure of the Earth and Plate Tectonics

23. An _____ is the result from the sudden release of stored energy in the Earth's crust that creates seismic waves. At the Earth's surface, _____s may manifest themselves by a shaking or displacement of the ground. An _____ is caused by tectonic plates getting stuck and putting a strain on the ground. The strain becomes so great that rocks give way by breaking and sliding along fault planes.
   a. AL 129-1
   b. AL 333
   c. AASHTO Soil Classification System
   d. Earthquake

24. _____ is the part of Earth's lithosphere that surfaces in the ocean basins. _____ is primarily composed of mafic rocks, or sima. It is thinner than continental crust, or sial, generally less than 10 kilometers thick, however it is more dense, having a mean density of about 3.3 grams per cubic centimeter.
   a. AASHTO Soil Classification System
   b. Oceanic crust
   c. Interplate earthquake
   d. AL 129-1

25. The _____ is one of the two main types of elastic body waves, so named because they move through the body of an object, unlike surface waves. It moves as a shear or transverse wave, so motion is perpendicular to the direction of wave propagation: S-shaped, like waves in a rope, as opposed to waves moving through a slinky, the P-wave.
   a. 1509 Istanbul earthquake
   b. S waves
   c. 1700 Cascadia earthquake
   d. 1703 Genroku earthquake

26. Seismology is the scientific study of earthquakes and the propagation of elastic waves through the Earth. The field also includes studies of earthquake effects, such as tsunamis as well as diverse _____ sources such as volcanic, tectonic, oceanic, atmospheric, and artificial processes (such as explosions.) A related field that uses geology to infer information regarding past earthquakes is paleoseismology.
   a. 1509 Istanbul earthquake
   b. 1703 Genroku earthquake
   c. Seismic
   d. 1700 Cascadia earthquake

27. A _____ travels through the Earth, most often as the result of a tectonic earthquake, sometimes from an explosion. They are also continually excited by the pounding of ocean waves and the wind.
   a. 1700 Cascadia earthquake
   b. 1509 Istanbul earthquake
   c. 1703 Genroku earthquake
   d. Seismic wave

28. _____ is the scientific study of earthquakes and the propagation of elastic waves through the Earth.
   a. 1700 Cascadia earthquake
   b. Seismology
   c. 1703 Genroku earthquake
   d. 1509 Istanbul earthquake

29. A type of seismic wave is one of the two main types of elastic body waves, so named because they move through the body of an object, unlike surface waves. The _____ moves as a shear or transverse wave, so motion is perpendicular to the direction of wave propagation. The wave moves through elastic mediums, and the main restoring force comes from shear effects.
   a. 1703 Genroku earthquake
   b. 1700 Cascadia earthquake
   c. 1509 Istanbul earthquake
   d. S-wave

30. In physics, _____ is defined as the rate of change of displacement or the rate of displacement. Simply put, it is distance per units of time.

Chapter 2. Internal Structure of the Earth and Plate Tectonics

a. Synthetic aperture radar
b. Velocity
c. Tension
d. Supercritical fluid

31. A _____ is a disturbance that propagates through space or spacetime, transferring energy and momentum and sometimes angular momentum.
   a. 1509 Istanbul earthquake
   b. 1703 Genroku earthquake
   c. Wave
   d. 1700 Cascadia earthquake

32. _____ refers to the movement of the Earth's continents relative to each other. _____ is a concept that said the shapes of continents on either side of the Atlantic Ocean seem to fit together and the similarity of southern continent fossil faunae could mean that all the continents had once been joined into a supercontinent. It was suggested that the continents had been pulled apart by the centrifugal pseudoforce of the Earth's rotation.
   a. 1509 Istanbul earthquake
   b. 1703 Genroku earthquake
   c. 1700 Cascadia earthquake
   d. Continental drift

33. _____ is molten rock located beneath the surface of the Earth, and which often collects in a _____ chamber. _____ is a complex high-temperature fluid substance. Most are silicate solutions. It is capable of intrusion into adjacent rocks or of extrusion onto the surface as lava or ejected explosively as tephra to form pyroclastic rock. Environments of _____ formation include subduction zones, continental rift zones, mid-oceanic ridges, and hotspots, some of which are interpreted as mantle plumes.
   a. 1700 Cascadia earthquake
   b. 1509 Istanbul earthquake
   c. 1703 Genroku earthquake
   d. Magma

34. _____ are an underwater mountain range, formed by plate tectonics. This uplifting of the ocean floor occurs when convection currents rise in the mantle beneath the oceanic crust and create magma where two tectonic plates meet at a divergent boundary. The _____ of the world are connected and form a system that is part of every ocean, making it the longest mountain range in the world.
   a. 1700 Cascadia earthquake
   b. 1703 Genroku earthquake
   c. 1509 Istanbul earthquake
   d. Mid-ocean ridges

35. The _____ the bottom of the ocean. At the bottom of the continental slope is the continental rise, which is caused by sediment cascading down the continental slope.
   a. Seafloor
   b. 1509 Istanbul earthquake
   c. 1703 Genroku earthquake
   d. 1700 Cascadia earthquake

36. _____ occurs at mid-ocean ridges, where new oceanic crust is formed through volcanic activity and then gradually moves away from the ridge. _____ helps explain continental drift in the theory of plate tectonics.
   a. 1700 Cascadia earthquake
   b. 1509 Istanbul earthquake
   c. 1703 Genroku earthquake
   d. Seafloor spreading

37. A mid-ocean ridge or mid-oceanic ridge is an underwater mountain range, typically having a valley known as a rift running along its axis, formed by plate tectonics. This type of oceanic ridge is characteristic of what is known as an oceanic _____. The uplifted sea floor results from convection currents which rise in the mantle as magma at a linear weakness in the oceanic crust, and emerge as lava, creating new crust upon cooling.

a. Spreading center
b. 1509 Istanbul earthquake
c. 1700 Cascadia earthquake
d. 1703 Genroku earthquake

38. In geology, a _____ zone is an area on Earth where two tectonic plates meet and move towards one another, with one sliding underneath the other and moving down into the mantle, at rates typically measured in centimeters per year. An oceanic plate ordinarily slides underneath a continental plate; this often creates an orogenic zone with many volcanoes and earthquakes.
   a. 1703 Genroku earthquake
   b. 1700 Cascadia earthquake
   c. Subduction
   d. 1509 Istanbul earthquake

39. A _____ is an area on Earth where two tectonic plates meet and move towards one another, with one sliding underneath the other and moving down into the mantle, at rates typically measured in centimeters per year. In a sense, _____s are the opposite of divergent boundaries, areas where material rises up from the mantle and plates are moving apart.
   a. Subduction zone
   b. 1703 Genroku earthquake
   c. 1700 Cascadia earthquake
   d. 1509 Istanbul earthquake

40. A _____ is a geological feature that is also known as a Rip in the earth causing magma to flow out and forming an undersea volcano, it also has geological features, a continuous elevational crest for some distance. _____s are usually termed hills or mountains as well, depending on size.
   a. 1703 Genroku earthquake
   b. 1700 Cascadia earthquake
   c. 1509 Istanbul earthquake
   d. Ridge

41. _____ was a Greek captain employed by Spain to sail northward from Mexico and look for a northern passage from the Pacific Ocean to the Atlantic Ocean. In 1592, his exploration took him into the body of water, the Strait of _____.
   a. Juan de Fuca
   b. Ambulocetus
   c. Andrija Mohorovičić
   d. Amblypoda

42. The _____ is a tectonic plate arizing from the Juan de Fuca Ridge, and subducting under the northerly portion of the western side of the North American Plate. It is bounded on the south by the Blanco Fracture Zone, on the north by the Nootka Fault, and along the west by the Pacific Plate.
   a. 1700 Cascadia earthquake
   b. 1703 Genroku earthquake
   c. Juan de Fuca plate
   d. 1509 Istanbul earthquake

43. A _____ is a visual representation of an area--a symbolic depiction highlighting relationships between elements of that space such as objects, regions, and themes.

Many _____s are static two-dimensional, geometrically accurate representations of three-dimensional space, while others are dynamic or interactive, even three-dimensional. Although most commonly used to depict geography, _____s may represent any space, real or imagined, without regard to context or scale; e.g. Brain mapping, DNA mapping, and extraterrestrial mapping.

   a. 1509 Istanbul earthquake
   b. 1700 Cascadia earthquake
   c. Map
   d. Cartography

Chapter 2. Internal Structure of the Earth and Plate Tectonics   25

44. A _____ is a deep active seismic area in a subduction zone. Differential motion along the zone produces deep seated earthquakes, the foci of which may be as deep as about 700 km. They develop beneath volcanic island arcs and continental margins above active subduction zones.
   a. 1703 Genroku earthquake
   b. 1509 Istanbul earthquake
   c. Wadati-Benioff zone
   d. 1700 Cascadia earthquake

45. In plate tectonics, a _____ a linear feature that exists between two tectonic plates that are moving away from each other. These areas can form in the middle of continents but eventually form ocean basins.
   a. 1509 Istanbul earthquake
   b. 1700 Cascadia earthquake
   c. 1703 Genroku earthquake
   d. Divergent plate boundary

46. _____ is the supercontinent that existed during the Paleozoic and Mesozoic eras before each of the component continents were separated into their current configuration.
   a. 1509 Istanbul earthquake
   b. 1703 Genroku earthquake
   c. Pangaea
   d. 1700 Cascadia earthquake

47. In geology, a _____ is a place where the Earth's crust and lithosphere are being pulled apart.
   a. 1703 Genroku earthquake
   b. 1509 Istanbul earthquake
   c. 1700 Cascadia earthquake
   d. Rift

48. A _____ in geology is a valley created by the formation of a rift.
   a. 1509 Istanbul earthquake
   b. 1700 Cascadia earthquake
   c. 1703 Genroku earthquake
   d. Rift valley

49. In geology, a _____ is a depression with predominant extent in one direction. The terms U-shaped and V-shaped are descriptive terms of geography to characterize the form of _____s. Most _____s belong to one of these two main types or a mixture of them, at least with respect of the cross section of the slopes or hillsides.
   a. 1509 Istanbul earthquake
   b. Valley
   c. 1700 Cascadia earthquake
   d. 1703 Genroku earthquake

50. The _____ are South America's longest mountain range, forming a continuous chain of highland along the western coast of South America.
   a. AASHTO Soil Classification System
   b. AL 129-1
   c. Andes Mountains
   d. AL 333

51. In geology the term _____ refers to the system of forces that tend to decrease the volume of or shorten rocks. Compressive strength refers to the maximum compressive stress that can be applied to a material before failure occurs.
   a. 1703 Genroku earthquake
   b. 1509 Istanbul earthquake
   c. 1700 Cascadia earthquake
   d. Compression

52. _____ is the stress applied to materials resulting in their compaction, decrease of volume.
   a. 1703 Genroku earthquake
   b. 1700 Cascadia earthquake
   c. Compression stress
   d. 1509 Istanbul earthquake

53. _____ is a phenomenon of the plate tectonics of Earth. _____ is a variation on the fundamental process of subduction, whereby the subduction zone is destroyed, mountains produced, and two continents sutured together. _____ is known only from this planet and is an interesting example of how our different crusts, oceanic and continental, behave during subduction.
   a. 1703 Genroku earthquake
   b. 1700 Cascadia earthquake
   c. 1509 Istanbul earthquake
   d. Continental collision

54. The _____ is a mostly underwater mountain range of the Atlantic Ocean and Arctic Ocean that runs from South of the North Pole to subantarctic Bouvet Island. The _____ forms part of the global mid-oceanic ridge system and is thought to result from a divergent boundary that separates tectonic plates. These plates are still moving apart, so the Atlantic is growing at the ridge, at a rate of about 5–10 centimeters per year in East-West direction.
   a. 1703 Genroku earthquake
   b. Mid-Atlantic Ridge
   c. 1509 Istanbul earthquake
   d. 1700 Cascadia earthquake

55. The _____ are a chain of more than 300 small volcanic islands forming an island arc in the Northern Pacific Ocean, occupying an area of 6,821 sq mi westward from the Alaska Peninsula toward the Kamchatka Peninsula.
   a. AL 129-1
   b. AL 333
   c. AASHTO Soil Classification System
   d. Aleutian Islands

56. The _____ is a subduction zone and oceanic trench which runs along the southern coastline of Alaska and the adjacent waters of northeastern Siberia off the coast of Kamchatka Peninsula. It is classified as a 'marginal trench' in the east as it runs along the margin of the continent, and as an island arc where it runs through the open sea. The trench extends for 3,400 km from a triple junction in the west with the Ulakhan Fault and the northern end of the Kuril-Kamchatka Trench, to a junction with the northern end of the Queen Charlotte Fault system in the east.
   a. AL 129-1
   b. AASHTO Soil Classification System
   c. Aleutian trench
   d. Interplate earthquake

57. _____ climate is the average weather for a region above the tree line. The climate becomes colder at high elevations—this characteristic is described by the lapse rate of air: air will tend to get colder as it rises, since it expands.
   a. AL 129-1
   b. AASHTO Soil Classification System
   c. AL 333
   d. Alpine

58. The _____ is a major mountain range of western North America, extending from southern British Columbia through Washington and Oregon to Northern California. It includes both non-volcanic mountains, such as the North Cascades, and the notable volcanoes known as the High Cascades. The _____ is part of the Pacific Ring of Fire, the ring of volcanoes and associated mountains around the Pacific Ocean. All of the known historic eruptions in the contiguous United States have been from Cascade volcanoes.
   a. 1509 Istanbul earthquake
   b. 1703 Genroku earthquake
   c. 1700 Cascadia earthquake
   d. Cascade Range

59. The _____ is an oceanic tectonic plate beneath the Pacific Ocean off the west coast of Central America, named for Cocos Island, which rides upon it.
   a. 1700 Cascadia earthquake
   b. 1509 Istanbul earthquake
   c. 1703 Genroku earthquake
   d. Cocos plate

Chapter 2. Internal Structure of the Earth and Plate Tectonics

60. _____ is the name of a sedimentary carbonate rock and a mineral, both composed of calcium magnesium carbonate found in crystals. _____ rock is composed predominantly of the mineral _____. Limestone that is partially replaced by _____ is referred to as dolomitic limestone.
   a. 1509 Istanbul earthquake
   b. 1700 Cascadia earthquake
   c. 1703 Genroku earthquake
   d. Dolomite

61. The _____ are a mountain range in Asia, separating the Indian subcontinent from the Tibetan Plateau. By extension, it is also the name of the massive mountain system which includes the Himalaya proper, the Karakoram, the Hindu Kush, and a host of minor ranges extending from the Pamir Knot.
   a. 1700 Cascadia earthquake
   b. 1509 Istanbul earthquake
   c. 1703 Genroku earthquake
   d. Himalayan Mountains

62. A _____ is a chain of volcanic islands or mountains formed by plate tectonics as an oceanic tectonic plate subducts under another tectonic plate and produces magma.
   a. 1509 Istanbul earthquake
   b. 1703 Genroku earthquake
   c. Volcanic arc
   d. 1700 Cascadia earthquake

63. The _____ is the deepest known submarine trench, and the deepest location in the Earth's crust itself. It is located in the floor of the western North Pacific Ocean.
   a. 1703 Genroku earthquake
   b. Mariana Trench
   c. 1509 Istanbul earthquake
   d. 1700 Cascadia earthquake

64. _____ are naturally occurring substances that are considered valuable in their relatively unmodified or natural form. Its value rests in the amount of the material available and the demand for the certain material.
   a. 1703 Genroku earthquake
   b. 1700 Cascadia earthquake
   c. 1509 Istanbul earthquake
   d. Natural resources

65. The _____ is an oceanic trench in the eastern Pacific Ocean, about 160 kilometers off the coast of Peru and Chile.
   a. 1509 Istanbul earthquake
   b. 1700 Cascadia earthquake
   c. Peru-Chile trench
   d. 1703 Genroku earthquake

66. _____ is a 16-ton, manned deep-ocean research submersible owned by the United States Navy and operated by the Woods Hole Oceanographic Institution in Woods Hole, Massachusetts. The three-person vessel allows for two scientists and one pilot to dive for up to nine hours at 4500 metersor 15,000 feet.
   a. Alvin
   b. AL 333
   c. AL 129-1
   d. AASHTO Soil Classification System

67. A _____ is a place where, through continental collision, two continental plates have joined together. The Himilayas and the Alps mark these zones as do other very high mountain ranges.
   a. 1509 Istanbul earthquake
   b. 1703 Genroku earthquake
   c. Suture zone
   d. 1700 Cascadia earthquake

68. A _____ is a geological fault that is a special case of strike-slip faulting which terminates abruptly, at both ends, at a major transverse geological feature. Also known as a conservative plate boundary.

Chapter 2. Internal Structure of the Earth and Plate Tectonics

a. Transform fault
b. 1703 Genroku earthquake
c. 1509 Istanbul earthquake
d. 1700 Cascadia earthquake

69. In plate tectonics, a _____ is said to occur when tectonic plates slide and grind against each other along a transform fault. The relative motion of such plates is horizontal in either sinistral or dextral direction. Many transform boundaries are locked in tension before suddenly releasing, and causing earthquakes.
    a. 1703 Genroku earthquake
    b. 1509 Istanbul earthquake
    c. Transform boundary
    d. 1700 Cascadia earthquake

70. The _____ are a vast system of mountains in eastern North America.
    a. AL 333
    b. AASHTO Soil Classification System
    c. AL 129-1
    d. Appalachian Mountains

71. _____ is a cape on the coast of North Carolina. It is the point that protrudes the farthest to the southeast along the northeast-to-southwest line of the Atlantic coast of North America. Two major Atlantic currents collide just off _____, the southerly-flowing cold water Labrador Current and the northerly-flowing warm water Florida Current (Gulf Stream), creating turbulent waters and a large expanse of shallow sandbars extending up to 14 miles offshore.
    a. 1700 Cascadia earthquake
    b. 1703 Genroku earthquake
    c. 1509 Istanbul earthquake
    d. Cape Hatteras

72. Due to shore erosion in the Outer Bank of North Carolina a navagational lighthouse had to be moved leading to the _____.
    a. 1700 Cascadia earthquake
    b. 1703 Genroku earthquake
    c. 1509 Istanbul earthquake
    d. Cape Hatteras Lighthouse controversy

73. _____ is a term used in Geology to refer to the state of gravitational equilibrium between the Earth's lithosphere and asthenosphere such that the tectonic plates "float" at an elevation which depends on their thickness and density. It is invoked to explain how different topographic heights can exist at the Earth's surface.
    a. Engineering geology
    b. Environmental geology
    c. Ubehebe Crater
    d. Isostasy

74. A _____ is a dry region on the surface of the Earth that is leeward or behind of a mountain with respect to the prevailing wind direction.
    a. 1703 Genroku earthquake
    b. 1700 Cascadia earthquake
    c. 1509 Istanbul earthquake
    d. Rain shadow

75. The _____ (symbol Ci) is a unit of radioactivity, defined as

    1 Ci = 3.7×10^{10} decays per second or becquerels.

This is roughly the activity of 1 gramme of the radium isotope ^{226}Ra, a substance studied by the pioneers of radiology, Marie and Pierre _____. The _____ has since been replaced by an SI derived unit, the becquerel (Bq), which equates to one decay per second.

Chapter 2. Internal Structure of the Earth and Plate Tectonics   29

    a. Curie
    b. 1509 Istanbul earthquake
    c. 1703 Genroku earthquake
    d. 1700 Cascadia earthquake

76. The _____ is a term in physics and materials science and refers to a characteristic property of a ferromagnetic or piezoelectric material.
    a. 1509 Istanbul earthquake
    b. 1703 Genroku earthquake
    c. 1700 Cascadia earthquake
    d. Curie point

77. In physics, a _____ is a solenoidal vector field in the space surrounding moving electric charges and magnetic dipoles, such as those in electric currents and magnets.
    a. 1509 Istanbul earthquake
    b. 1703 Genroku earthquake
    c. 1700 Cascadia earthquake
    d. Magnetic field

78. _____ is approximately a magnetic dipole, with one pole near the north pole and the other near the geographic south pole.
    a. AL 129-1
    b. AL 333
    c. AASHTO Soil Classification System
    d. Earths magnetic field

79. _____ refers to the study of the record of the Earth's magnetic field preserved in various magnetic minerals through time. The study of _____ has demonstrated that the Earth's magnetic field varies substantially in both orientation and intensity through time.
    a. 1703 Genroku earthquake
    b. 1700 Cascadia earthquake
    c. 1509 Istanbul earthquake
    d. Paleomagnetism

80. In physics, there are two kinds of _____s . An electric _____ is a separation of positive and negative charge. The simplest example of this is a pair of electric charges of equal magnitude but opposite sign, separated by some, usually small, distance. By contrast, a magnetic _____ is a closed circulation of electric current. A simple example of this is a single loop of wire with some constant current flowing through it.
    a. Dipole
    b. 1703 Genroku earthquake
    c. 1509 Istanbul earthquake
    d. 1700 Cascadia earthquake

81. An _____ phenomenon is an observed event which deviates from what is expected according to existing rules or scientific theory.
    a. AASHTO Soil Classification System
    b. Anomalous
    c. AL 129-1
    d. AL 333

82. _____ are minute disruptions in the earths magnetic field due to either a greater or lesser difference in surrounding constant normal values.
    a. Magnetic anomalies
    b. 1509 Istanbul earthquake
    c. 1703 Genroku earthquake
    d. 1700 Cascadia earthquake

83. A _____ is a scientific instrument used to measure the strength and/or direction of the magnetic field in the vicinity of the instrument.
    a. 1703 Genroku earthquake
    b. Magnetometer
    c. 1509 Istanbul earthquake
    d. 1700 Cascadia earthquake

Chapter 2. Internal Structure of the Earth and Plate Tectonics

84. The _____ is the bottom of the ocean. At the bottom of the continental slope is the continental rise, which is caused by sediment cascading down the continental slope
   a. AL 333
   b. AASHTO Soil Classification System
   c. AL 129-1
   d. Ocean floor

85. _____ refer to marine animals from the class Anthozoa and exist as small sea anemone-like polyps, typically in colonies of many identical individuals. The group includes the important reef builders that are found in tropical oceans, which secrete calcium carbonate to form a hard skeleton.
   a. 1700 Cascadia earthquake
   b. 1509 Istanbul earthquake
   c. 1703 Genroku earthquake
   d. Coral

86. The _____ is composed of the Hawaiian Ridge, consisting of the islands of the Hawaiian chain northwest to Kure Atoll, and the Emperor Seamounts, a vast underwater mountain region of islands and intervening seamounts, atolls, shallows, banks and reefs along a line trending southeast to northwest beneath the northern Pacific Ocean.
   a. 1509 Istanbul earthquake
   b. 1700 Cascadia earthquake
   c. 1703 Genroku earthquake
   d. Hawaiian Emperor chain of volcanic islands

87. In geology, a _____ is a location on the Earth's surface that has experienced active volcanism for a long period of time.
   a. 1700 Cascadia earthquake
   b. 1703 Genroku earthquake
   c. Hotspot
   d. 1509 Istanbul earthquake

88. A _____ is an opening in a planet's surface or crust, which allows hot, molten rock, ash, and gases to escape from below the surface. Volcanic activity involving the extrusion of rock tends to form mountains or features like mountains over a period of time.

   _____es are generally found where tectonic plates are diverging or converging.

   a. 1703 Genroku earthquake
   b. 1509 Istanbul earthquake
   c. 1700 Cascadia earthquake
   d. Volcano

89. The _____ is the centerpiece of the Greater Yellowstone Ecosystem, the largest intact ecosystem in the Earth's northern temperate zone. Located mostly in the U.S. state of Wyoming, the park extends into Montana and Idaho. The park is known for its wildlife and geothermal features; Old Faithful Geyser is one of the most popular features in the park.
   a. Yellowstone National Park
   b. 1700 Cascadia earthquake
   c. 1509 Istanbul earthquake
   d. 1703 Genroku earthquake

90. An _____ is an oceanic reef formation, often having a characteristic ring-like shape surrounding a lagoon. _____s are formed when coral reef grows around a volcanic island that later subsides into the ocean.
   a. AL 333
   b. AL 129-1
   c. AASHTO Soil Classification System
   d. Atoll

91. A _____ is a mountain rizing from the ocean seafloor that does not reach to the water's surface, and thus is not an island. These are typically formed from extinct volcanoes, that rise abruptly and are usually found rizing from a seafloor of 1,000 - 4,000 meters depth. They are defined by oceanographers as independent features that rise to at least 1,000 meters above the seafloor.

a. 1700 Cascadia earthquake
b. 1509 Istanbul earthquake
c. 1703 Genroku earthquake
d. Seamount

92. The _____ is the name for one of the great mountain range systems of Europe, stretching from Austria and Slovenia in the east, through Italy, Switzerland, Liechtenstein and Germany to France in the west.
   a. AASHTO Soil Classification System
   b. Alps
   c. AL 129-1
   d. AL 333

93. _____s are the mineralized or otherwise preserved remains or traces of animals, plants, and other organisms. The totality of _____s, both discovered and undiscovered, and their placement in fossiliferous rock formations and sedimentary layers is known as the _____ record.
   a. 1700 Cascadia earthquake
   b. 1703 Genroku earthquake
   c. Fossil
   d. 1509 Istanbul earthquake

94. The southern supercontinent _____ included most of the landmasses in today's southern hemisphere, including Antarctica, South America, Africa, Madagascar, Australia-New Guinea, and New Zealand, as well as Arabia and the Indian subcontinent, which are in the Northern Hemisphere.
   a. 1703 Genroku earthquake
   b. Gondwana
   c. 1509 Istanbul earthquake
   d. 1700 Cascadia earthquake

95. _____ was a supercontinent that most recently existed as a part of the split of the Pangaean supercontinent in the late Mesozoic era. It included most of the landmasses which make up today's continents of the northern hemisphere, chiefly Laurentia, Baltica, Siberia, Kazakhstania, and the North China and East China Cratons.
   a. 1509 Istanbul earthquake
   b. 1700 Cascadia earthquake
   c. Laurasia
   d. 1703 Genroku earthquake

96. _____ is a seamount and undersea volcano in the Hawaiian archipelago, located roughly 30 km south of the southeast coast of the Island of Hawaiʻi. It is one of three active volcanoes thought to presently sit over the Hawaiian hotspot.
   a. Paleoceanography
   b. Lōʻihi
   c. Transatlantic telephone cable
   d. Western Hemisphere Warm Pool

97. _____ is a 2.4 square mile atoll located in the North Pacific Ocean at 28°13′N 177°22′WCoordinates: 28°13′N 177°22′W, about one-third of the way between Honolulu and Tokyo. It is less than 140 nautical miles east of the International Date Line, about 2,800 nautical miles west of San Francisco and 2,200 nautical miles east of Tokyo. It consists of a ring-shaped barrier reef and several sand islets.
   a. 1703 Genroku earthquake
   b. 1509 Istanbul earthquake
   c. Midway Island
   d. 1700 Cascadia earthquake

98. The _____ was a Mesozoic era ocean that existed between the continents of Gondwana and Laurasia before the opening of the Indian Ocean. What was once the _____ has become the Mediterranean Sea. Other remnants are the Black, Caspian and Aral Seas.
   a. 1509 Istanbul earthquake
   b. 1703 Genroku earthquake
   c. 1700 Cascadia earthquake
   d. Tethys Sea

99. _____ in its broadest sense includes everything that is used to determine or demonstrate the truth of an assertion. Giving or procuring _____ is the process of using those things that are either a) presumed to be true, or b) were themselves proven via _____, to demonstrate an assertion's truth. _____ is the currency by which one fulfills the burden of proof.
- a. AASHTO Soil Classification System
- b. AL 333
- c. AL 129-1
- d. Evidence

100. A _____ is an urban area with a high population and a particular administrative, legal, or historical status.

Large industrialized cities generally have advanced systems for sanitation, utilities, land usage, housing, and transportation and more. This close proximity greatly facilitates interaction between people and firms, benefiting both parties in the process.

- a. City
- b. 1703 Genroku earthquake
- c. 1509 Istanbul earthquake
- d. 1700 Cascadia earthquake

101. The _____ is the coastal sediment-filled plain located between the peninsular and transverse ranges in southern California in the United States containing the central part of the city of Los Angeles as well as its southern and southeastern suburbs (both in Los Angeles and Orange counties.) It is approximately 35 miles (56 km) long and 15 miles (24 km) wide, bounded on the north by the Santa Monica Mountains and Puente Hills, and on the east and south by the Santa Ana Mountains and San Joaquin Hills. The Palos Verdes Peninsula, formerly an island, marks the outer edge of the basin along the coast.
- a. 1509 Istanbul earthquake
- b. 1700 Cascadia earthquake
- c. 1703 Genroku earthquake
- d. Los Angeles Basin

102. The City of New York, most often called _____, is the most populous city in the United States, in a metropolitan area that ranks among the world's most-populous urban areas. It is a leading global city, exerting a powerful influence over worldwide commerce, finance, culture, and entertainment. The city is also an important center for international affairs, hosting the United Nations headquarters.
- a. New York City
- b. 1700 Cascadia earthquake
- c. 1509 Istanbul earthquake
- d. 1703 Genroku earthquake

103. _____ involves the study of the interaction of humans with the geologic environment including the biosphere, the lithosphere, the hydrosphere, and to some extent the atmosphere.
- a. Environmental geology
- b. Ubehebe Crater
- c. Isostasy
- d. Engineering geology

104. _____ is the science and study of the solid matter that constitute the Earth. Encompassing such things as rocks, soil, and gemstones, _____ studies the composition, structure, physical properties, history, and the processes that shape Earth's components.
- a. 1509 Istanbul earthquake
- b. Glacial motion
- c. Glaciology
- d. Geology

Chapter 3. Minerals and Rocks

1. _____ describes any of a group of minerals that can be fibrous, many of which are metamorphic and are hydrous magnesium silicates.
   a. AL 333
   b. Asbestos
   c. AASHTO Soil Classification System
   d. AL 129-1

2. _____ is an asbestiform sub-group within the serpentine group of minerals. There are three known species and they form the fibrous members of the this group and have been extensively mined as asbestos.
   a. 1509 Istanbul earthquake
   b. 1700 Cascadia earthquake
   c. 1703 Genroku earthquake
   d. Chrysotile

3. _____ is a form of riebeckite that is an asbestiform.
   a. Crocidolite
   b. 1703 Genroku earthquake
   c. 1700 Cascadia earthquake
   d. 1509 Istanbul earthquake

4. In chemistry and physics, the _____ is the number of protons found in the nucleus of an atom. It is traditionally represented by the symbol Z.
   a. AASHTO Soil Classification System
   b. Atomic number
   c. AL 333
   d. AL 129-1

5. An _____ generally comes from its latin name. It is an abbreviation or short representation of the name of a chemical element. Natural elements all have symbols of one or two letters; some man-made elements have temporary symbols of three letters.
   a. Atomic symbol
   b. AL 333
   c. AASHTO Soil Classification System
   d. AL 129-1

6. _____ are the fundamental building blocks of chemistry, and are conserved in chemical reactions.
   a. AASHTO Soil Classification System
   b. AL 333
   c. AL 129-1
   d. Atoms

7. The _____ is a fundamental subatomic particle that carries a negative electric charge.
   a. AL 333
   b. AL 129-1
   c. Electron
   d. AASHTO Soil Classification System

8. In the _____ analogy, the probability density of an electron, or wavefunction, is described as a small cloud moving around the atomic or molecular nucleus, with the thickness of the cloud proportional to the probability density.
   a. AASHTO Soil Classification System
   b. AL 129-1
   c. AL 333
   d. Electron cloud

9. An _____ is a type of atom that is defined by its atomic number; that is, by the number of protons in its nucleus.
   a. AASHTO Soil Classification System
   b. Element
   c. AL 333
   d. AL 129-1

10. A _____ is a naturally occurring substance formed through geological processes that has a characteristic chemical composition, a highly ordered atomic structure and specific physical properties. A rock, by comparison, is an aggregate of _____ s and need not have a specific chemical composition. _____ s range in composition from pure elements and simple salts to very complex silicates with thousands of known forms.

Chapter 3. Minerals and Rocks

a. 1700 Cascadia earthquake
b. 1703 Genroku earthquake
c. 1509 Istanbul earthquake
d. Mineral

11. In physics, the _____ is a subatomic particle with no net electric charge.
    a. Neutron
    b. 1703 Genroku earthquake
    c. 1509 Istanbul earthquake
    d. 1700 Cascadia earthquake

12. The _____ of the chemical elements is a tabular method of displaying the chemical elements, first devized in 1869 by the Russian chemist Dmitri Mendeleev.
    a. Periodic Table
    b. 1700 Cascadia earthquake
    c. 1509 Istanbul earthquake
    d. 1703 Genroku earthquake

13. In physics, the _____ is a subatomic particle with an electric charge of one positive fundamental unit a diameter of about 1.5×10^{-15} m, and a mass of 938.27231(28) MeV/c2 (1.6726×10^{-27} kg), 1.007 276 466 88(13) u or about 1836 times the mass of an electron.
    a. Proton
    b. 1700 Cascadia earthquake
    c. 1509 Istanbul earthquake
    d. 1703 Genroku earthquake

14. An _____ is a negetive ion.
    a. Anion
    b. AL 333
    c. AASHTO Soil Classification System
    d. AL 129-1

15. The _____ is the mass of an atom at rest, most often expressed in unified _____ units.[
    a. AL 333
    b. AL 129-1
    c. AASHTO Soil Classification System
    d. Atomic mass

16. _____: a _____ is an ion with a positive charge. It is the inverse anion.
    a. 1703 Genroku earthquake
    b. 1700 Cascadia earthquake
    c. 1509 Istanbul earthquake
    d. Cation

17. _____ are any of the several different forms of an element each having different atomic mass. _____ of an element have nuclei with the same number of protons but different numbers of neutrons.
    a. AL 333
    b. AASHTO Soil Classification System
    c. AL 129-1
    d. Isotopes

18. In analytical chemistry, a _____ is an element in a sample that has an average concentration of less than 100 parts per million atoms, or less than 100 micrograms per gram.

In biochemistry, a _____ is a chemical element that is needed in minute quantities for the proper growth, development, and physiology of the organism. In biochemistry, a _____ is also referred to as a micronutrient.

    a. 1509 Istanbul earthquake
    b. Trace element
    c. 1703 Genroku earthquake
    d. 1700 Cascadia earthquake

Chapter 3. Minerals and Rocks

19. The _____ A, also called atomic _____ or nucleon number, is the number of nucleons in an atomic nucleus. The _____ is unique for each isotope of an element and is written either after the element name or as a superscript to the left of an element's symbol. For example, carbon-12 has 6 protons and 6 neutrons.
    a. Mass number
    b. 1509 Istanbul earthquake
    c. 1700 Cascadia earthquake
    d. 1703 Genroku earthquake

20. A _____ substance is a material with a definite _____ composition. It is a concept that became firmly established in the late eighteenth century after work by the chemist Joseph Proust on the composition of some pure _____ compounds such as basic copper carbonate.
    a. 1509 Istanbul earthquake
    b. Chemical property
    c. Chemical
    d. 1700 Cascadia earthquake

21. _____ is the physical process responsible for the attractive interactions between atoms and molecules, and that which confers stability to diatomic and polyatomic chemical compounds.
    a. Chemical bonding
    b. 1700 Cascadia earthquake
    c. 1509 Istanbul earthquake
    d. 1703 Genroku earthquake

22. A _____ is a chemical substance of two or more different chemically bonded chemical elements, with a fixed ratio determining the composition. The ratio of each element is usually expressed by chemical formula.
    a. 1700 Cascadia earthquake
    b. Chemical compound
    c. 1509 Istanbul earthquake
    d. 1703 Genroku earthquake

23. A _____ bond is a form of chemical bonding that is characterized by the sharing of pairs of electrons between atoms, or between atoms and other _____ bonds. In short, attraction-to-repulsion stability that forms between atoms when they share electrons is known as _____ bonding.
    a. 1509 Istanbul earthquake
    b. 1700 Cascadia earthquake
    c. 1703 Genroku earthquake
    d. Covalent

24. _____ is a form of chemical bonding that is characterized by the sharing of pairs of electrons between atoms.
    a. Covalent bonding
    b. 1703 Genroku earthquake
    c. 1509 Istanbul earthquake
    d. 1700 Cascadia earthquake

25. _____ is the natural mineral form of lead sulfide. It is the most important lead ore mineral. It is one of the most abundant and widely distributed sulfide minerals. It crystallizes in the cubic crystal system often showing octahedral forms. It is often associated with the minerals sphalerite, calcite and fluorite.
    a. 1703 Genroku earthquake
    b. Galena
    c. 1700 Cascadia earthquake
    d. 1509 Istanbul earthquake

26. An _____ bond is a type of chemical bond that can often form between metal and non-metal ions or polyatomic ions such as ammonium through electrostatic attraction. In short, it is a bond formed by the attraction between two oppositely charged ions.
    a. AL 333
    b. AASHTO Soil Classification System
    c. AL 129-1
    d. Ionic

27. An _____ is a type of chemical bond based on electrostatic forces between two oppositely-charged ions. In this formation, a metal donates an electron, due to a low electronegativity to form a positive ion or cation.

Chapter 3. Minerals and Rocks

    a. AL 129-1   b. AL 333
    c. AASHTO Soil Classification System   d. Ionic bond

28. _____ is the bonding between atoms within metals. It involves the delocalized sharing of free electrons among a lattice of metal atoms. Thus, _____s may be compared to molten salts. Metallic bonding is the electrostatic attraction between the metal atoms or ions and the delocalized electrons, also called conduction electrons.
    a. 1700 Cascadia earthquake   b. 1509 Istanbul earthquake
    c. Metallic bond   d. 1703 Genroku earthquake

29. _____ is the bonding between atoms within metals. It involves the delocalized sharing of free electrons among a lattice of metal atoms. Thus, they may be compared to molten salts.
    a. Metallic bonding   b. 1703 Genroku earthquake
    c. 1509 Istanbul earthquake   d. 1700 Cascadia earthquake

30. In chemistry _____ is sometimes used as a synonym for non-covalent or intermolecular forces—forces that are weak compared to those appearing in covalent bonding.
    a. Van der Waals bonding   b. 1703 Genroku earthquake
    c. 1509 Istanbul earthquake   d. 1700 Cascadia earthquake

31. _____ is the mineral form of sodium chloride. _____ forms isometric crystals. It commonly occurs with other evaporite deposit minerals such as several of the sulfates, halides and borates. _____ occurs in vast lakes of sedimentary evaporite minerals that result from the drying up of enclosed beds, playas, and seas.
    a. 1700 Cascadia earthquake   b. 1509 Istanbul earthquake
    c. 1703 Genroku earthquake   d. Halite

32. The mineral _____ is iron disulfide, FeS2. It has isometric crystals that usually appear as cubes. Its metallic luster and pale-to-normal, brass-yellow hue have earned it a nickname due to many miners mistaking it for the real thing.
    a. 1700 Cascadia earthquake   b. 1703 Genroku earthquake
    c. 1509 Istanbul earthquake   d. Pyrite

33. _____ is the second most common mineral in the Earth's continental crust. It is made up of a lattice of silica tetrahedra. _____ belongs to the rhombohedral crystal system. In nature _____ crystals are often twinned, distorted, or so intergrown with adjacent crystals of _____ or other minerals as to only show part of this shape, or to lack obvious crystal faces altogether and appear massive.
    a. Quartz   b. 1703 Genroku earthquake
    c. 1509 Istanbul earthquake   d. 1700 Cascadia earthquake

34. _____ is a dietary mineral composed primarily of sodium chloride that is essential for animal life, but toxic to most land plants. _____ flavor is one of the basic tastes, an important preservative and a popular food seasoning.

_____ for human consumption is produced in different forms: unrefined _____ (such as sea _____), refined _____ (table _____), and iodized _____.

    a. 1700 Cascadia earthquake   b. 1509 Istanbul earthquake
    c. 1703 Genroku earthquake   d. Salt

Chapter 3. Minerals and Rocks

35. In geology and astronomy, the term _____ is used to denote types of rock that consist predominantly of _____ minerals. Such rocks include a wide range of igneous, metamorphic and sedimentary types. Most of the Earth's mantle and crust are made up of _____ rocks. The same is true of the Moon and the other rocky planets.
    a. 1509 Istanbul earthquake
    b. Silicate
    c. 1703 Genroku earthquake
    d. 1700 Cascadia earthquake

36. A _____ is a solid in which the constituent atoms, molecules, or ions are packed in a regularly ordered, repeating pattern extending in all three spatial dimensions. Most metals encountered in everyday life are polycrystals. _____s are often symmetrically intergrown to form _____ twins.
    a. 1509 Istanbul earthquake
    b. 1703 Genroku earthquake
    c. 1700 Cascadia earthquake
    d. Crystal

37. A _____ is a unique arrangement of atoms in a crystal. It is composed of a unit cell, a set of atoms arranged in a particular way, which is periodically repeated in three dimensions on a lattice. The spacing between unit cells in various directions is called its lattice parameters. The symmetry properties of the crystal are embodied in its space group.
    a. 1703 Genroku earthquake
    b. 1509 Istanbul earthquake
    c. 1700 Cascadia earthquake
    d. Crystal structure

38. _____ involves the change in the composition of rock, often leading to a 'break down' in its form.
    a. Chemical weathering
    b. 1703 Genroku earthquake
    c. 1509 Istanbul earthquake
    d. 1700 Cascadia earthquake

39. _____ is a theory of geology that has been developed to explain the observed evidence for large scale motions of the Earth's lithosphere. The theory encompassed and superseded the older theory of continental drift.
    a. 1703 Genroku earthquake
    b. 1700 Cascadia earthquake
    c. Plate tectonics
    d. 1509 Istanbul earthquake

40. _____ is the chemical element in the periodic table that has the symbol Na and atomic number 11. _____ is a soft, waxy, silvery reactive metal belonging to the alkali metals that is abundant in natural compounds (especially halite). It is highly reactive.
    a. Styrofoam
    b. Sulfur
    c. Sodium
    d. Seaborgium

41. _____ is the salt most responsible for the salinity of the ocean and of the extracellular fluid of many multicellular organisms. Sodium metal is produced commercially through the electrolysis of liquid _____. Sodium chloride is used in other chemical processes for the large-scale production of compounds containing sodium or chlorine.
    a. 1703 Genroku earthquake
    b. Sodium chloride
    c. 1509 Istanbul earthquake
    d. 1700 Cascadia earthquake

42. The _____ is a spatial arrangement of atoms which is tiled in three-dimensional space to describe the crystal. It is given by its lattice parameters, the length of the cell edges and the angles between them, while the positions of the atoms inside it are described by the set of atomic positions measured from a lattice point.
    a. AL 129-1
    b. AASHTO Soil Classification System
    c. AL 333
    d. Unit cell

Chapter 3. Minerals and Rocks

43. _____ is the process of breaking down rocks, soils and their minerals through direct contact with the atmosphere. _____ occurs without movement. Two main classifications of _____ processes exist. Mechanical or physical _____ involves the breakdown of rocks and soils through direct contact with atmospheric conditions. The second classification, chemical _____, involves the direct effect of atmospheric chemicals in the breakdown of rocks, soils and minerals.
   a. 1509 Istanbul earthquake
   b. 1703 Genroku earthquake
   c. 1700 Cascadia earthquake
   d. Weathering

44. _____ is a field of study within geology concerned generally with the structures within the crust of the Earth, or other planets, and particularly with the forces and movements that have operated in a region to create these structures.
   a. 1700 Cascadia earthquake
   b. 1703 Genroku earthquake
   c. 1509 Istanbul earthquake
   d. Tectonics

45. _____ is a common phyllosilicate mineral within the mica group. Primarily a solid-solution series between the iron-endmember annite, and the magnesium-endmember phlogopite; more aluminous endmembers include siderophyllite.
   a. 1509 Istanbul earthquake
   b. Biotite
   c. 1703 Genroku earthquake
   d. 1700 Cascadia earthquake

46. _____ is a carbonate mineral and the most stable polymorph of calcium carbonate ($CaCO_3$.) The other polymorphs are the minerals aragonite and vaterite. Aragonite will change to _____ at 470°C, and vaterite is even less stable.
   a. 1703 Genroku earthquake
   b. 1700 Cascadia earthquake
   c. 1509 Istanbul earthquake
   d. Calcite

47. _____ is a chemical element in the periodic table that has the symbol Cu and atomic number 29. It is a ductile metal with excellent electrical conductivity, and finds extensive use as a building material, as an electrical conductor, and as a component of various alloys.
   a. 1700 Cascadia earthquake
   b. 1509 Istanbul earthquake
   c. 1703 Genroku earthquake
   d. Copper

48. The _____ group of sheet silicate minerals includes several closely related materials having highly perfect basal cleavage. All are monoclinic with a tendency towards pseudo-hexagonal crystals and are similar in chemical composition. The highly perfect cleavage, which is the most prominent characteristic of _____, is explained by the hexagonal sheet-like arrangement of its atoms.
   a. Mica
   b. 1703 Genroku earthquake
   c. 1509 Istanbul earthquake
   d. 1700 Cascadia earthquake

49. _____ is a chemical element in the periodic table that has the symbol Au and atomic number 79. A soft, shiny, yellow, dense, malleable, ductile (trivalent and univalent) transition metal, _____ does not react with most chemicals but is attacked by chlorine, fluorine and aqua regia.
   a. 1703 Genroku earthquake
   b. 1509 Istanbul earthquake
   c. 1700 Cascadia earthquake
   d. Gold

50. In organic chemistry, a _____ is a salt of carbonic acid.

Chapter 3. Minerals and Rocks

a. Carbonate
b. 1703 Genroku earthquake
c. 1700 Cascadia earthquake
d. 1509 Istanbul earthquake

51. _____ are those minerals containing the carbonate ion: CO_3^{2-}.
   a. 1700 Cascadia earthquake
   b. 1703 Genroku earthquake
   c. 1509 Istanbul earthquake
   d. Carbonate minerals

52. _____ is a term used to describe a group of hydrous aluminium phyllosilicate minerals, that are typically less than 2 micrometres in diameter. _____ consists of a variety of phyllosilicate minerals rich in silicon and aluminium oxides and hydroxides which include variable amounts of structural water. _____s are generally formed by the chemical weathering of silicate-bearing rocks by carbonic acid but some are formed by hydrothermal activity.
   a. 1509 Istanbul earthquake
   b. 1700 Cascadia earthquake
   c. 1703 Genroku earthquake
   d. Clay

53. In geology, a _____ is the outermost layer of a planet, part of its lithosphere. They are generally composed of a less dense material than its deeper layers.Earths' is composed mainly of basalt and granite. It is cooler and more rigid than the deeper layers of the mantle and core.
   a. Crust
   b. 1509 Istanbul earthquake
   c. 1703 Genroku earthquake
   d. 1700 Cascadia earthquake

54. _____ is an ore consisting in a mixture of hydrated iron oxide-hydroxide of varying composition. It often contains a varying amount of oxide compared to hydroxide.
   a. 1509 Istanbul earthquake
   b. Limonite
   c. 1703 Genroku earthquake
   d. 1700 Cascadia earthquake

55. A _____ is the amount of force required to accelerate a body with a mass of one kilogram at a rate of one meter per second squared.
   a. Newton
   b. 1703 Genroku earthquake
   c. 1509 Istanbul earthquake
   d. 1700 Cascadia earthquake

56. An _____ is a chemical compound containing an oxygen atom and other elements. Most of the earth's crust consists of them. They result when elements are oxidized by air.
   a. AASHTO Soil Classification System
   b. AL 333
   c. AL 129-1
   d. Oxide

57. Two important classifications of weathering processes exist -- physical and chemical weathering. Mechanical or _____ involves the breakdown of rocks and soils through direct contact with atmospheric conditions, such as heat, water, ice and pressure. The second classification, chemical weathering, involves the direct effect of atmospheric chemicals or biologically produced chemicals (also known as biological weathering) in the breakdown of rocks, soils and minerals.
   a. 1509 Istanbul earthquake
   b. Physical weathering
   c. 1700 Cascadia earthquake
   d. 1703 Genroku earthquake

58. _____ is the oxide that is formed by open-air oxidation of iron.
   a. 1509 Istanbul earthquake
   b. 1703 Genroku earthquake
   c. Rust
   d. 1700 Cascadia earthquake

Chapter 3. Minerals and Rocks

59. _____ is the name of a group of rock-forming minerals which make up as much as sixty percent of the Earth's crust. _____s crystallize from magma in both intrusive and extrusive rocks, and they can also occur as compact minerals, as veins, and are also present in many types of metamorphic rock.
   a. 1509 Istanbul earthquake
   b. Feldspar
   c. 1703 Genroku earthquake
   d. 1700 Cascadia earthquake

60. A _____ is one which contains both magnesium and iron.
   a. 1700 Cascadia earthquake
   b. 1703 Genroku earthquake
   c. 1509 Istanbul earthquake
   d. Ferromagnesian mineral

61. The term _____ refers to several types of chemical compounds containing sulfur in its lowest oxidation number of −2.
   a. 1700 Cascadia earthquake
   b. 1509 Istanbul earthquake
   c. Sulfide
   d. 1703 Genroku earthquake

62. A _____ is a mineral containing sulfide as the major anion. Closely related and often included within the sulfide class are selenide and telluride minerals.
   a. 1509 Istanbul earthquake
   b. 1700 Cascadia earthquake
   c. 1703 Genroku earthquake
   d. Sulfide mineral

63. _____ is an important tectosilicate mineral, which forms igneous rock. _____ is named based on the Greek for "straight fracture," because its two cleavages are at right angles to each other. _____ crystallizes in the monoclinic crystal system. It has a hardness of 6, a specific gravity of 2.56-2.58, and a vitreous to pearly luster. It can be colored white, gray, yellow, pink, or red; rarely green.
   a. AL 333
   b. AL 129-1
   c. Orthoclase
   d. AASHTO Soil Classification System

64. _____ defines an important group of generally dark-colored rock-forming inosilicate minerals linked at the vertices and generally containing ions of iron and/or magnesium in their structures. _____s crystallize into two crystal systems, monoclinic and orthorhombic.
   a. AASHTO Soil Classification System
   b. AL 333
   c. AL 129-1
   d. Amphibole

65. _____ is a phyllosilicate mineral of aluminium and potassium. It has a highly perfect basal cleavage yielding remarkably thin laminae, which are often highly elastic. Sheets of _____ 5 metres by 3 metres have been found in Nellore, India.
   a. 1700 Cascadia earthquake
   b. 1703 Genroku earthquake
   c. 1509 Istanbul earthquake
   d. Muscovite

66. The mineral _____ is a magnesium iron silicate. It is one of the most common minerals on Earth, and has also been identified on the Moon, Mars, and comet Wild 2.
   a. AL 333
   b. AL 129-1
   c. Olivine
   d. AASHTO Soil Classification System

67. _____ is a very important series of tectosilicate minerals within the feldspar family. Rather than referring to a particular mineral with a specific chemical composition, it is a solid solution series.

Chapter 3. Minerals and Rocks 41

   a. Plagioclase
   b. 1509 Istanbul earthquake
   c. 1703 Genroku earthquake
   d. 1700 Cascadia earthquake

68. The _____ are a group of important rock-forming silicate minerals found in many igneous and metamorphic rocks. They share a common structure comprised of single chains of silica tetrahedra and they crystalise in the monoclinic and orthorhombic system.
   a. 1509 Istanbul earthquake
   b. 1700 Cascadia earthquake
   c. 1703 Genroku earthquake
   d. Pyroxenes

69. Cleavage, in mineralogy, is the tendency of crystalline materials to split along definite crystallographic structural planes. These planes of relative weakness are a result of the regular locations of atoms and ions in the crystal, which create smooth repeating surfaces that are visible both in the microscope and to the naked eye.

Cleavage forms parallel to crystallographic planes:

Biotite with _____.

- Basal or pinacoidal cleavage occurs parallel to the base of a crystal. This orientation is given by the {001} plane in the crystal lattice , and is the same as the {0001} plane in Bravais-Miller indices, which are often used for rhombohedral and hexagonal crystals. _____ is exhibited by the mica group and by graphite.

- Cubic cleavage occurs on the {001} planes, parallel to the faces of a cube for a crystal with cubic symmetry. This is the source of the cubic shape seen in crystals of ground table salt, the mineral halite.

   a. Basal cleavage
   b. 1700 Cascadia earthquake
   c. 1509 Istanbul earthquake
   d. 1703 Genroku earthquake

70. _____, in mineralogy, is the tendency of crystalline materials to split along definite planes, creating smooth surfaces.
   a. 1703 Genroku earthquake
   b. 1509 Istanbul earthquake
   c. 1700 Cascadia earthquake
   d. Cleavage

71. _____ is an aluminium ore. It consists largely of the Al minerals gibbsite, boehmite and diaspore, together with the iron oxides goethite and hematite, the clay mineral kaolinite and small amounts of anatase.
   a. 1700 Cascadia earthquake
   b. 1703 Genroku earthquake
   c. 1509 Istanbul earthquake
   d. Bauxite

72. _____ is a sedimentary rock composed largely of the mineral calcite. _____ often contains variable amounts of silica in the form of chert or flint, as well as varying amounts of clay, silt and sand as disseminations, nodules, or layers within the rock. The primary source of the calcite in _____ is most commonly marine organisms. These organisms secrete shells that settle out of the water column and are deposited on ocean floors as pelagic ooze or alternatively is conglomerated in a coral reef.
   a. 1509 Istanbul earthquake
   b. 1700 Cascadia earthquake
   c. 1703 Genroku earthquake
   d. Limestone

73. _____ is either magnetic magnetite or magnetic iron ore.

Chapter 3. Minerals and Rocks

    a. 1700 Cascadia earthquake
    b. 1703 Genroku earthquake
    c. 1509 Istanbul earthquake
    d. Lodestone

74. _____ is a ferrimagnetic mineral one of several iron oxides and a member of the spinel group. The chemical IUPAC name is iron oxide and the common chemical name ferrous-ferric oxide.
    a. 1703 Genroku earthquake
    b. 1509 Istanbul earthquake
    c. 1700 Cascadia earthquake
    d. Magnetite

75. _____ rocks form when molten rock, magma, cools and solidifies, with or without crystallization, either below the surface as intrusive, plutonic rocks or on the surface as extrusive, volcanic, rocks.
    a. AL 129-1
    b. AASHTO Soil Classification System
    c. Igneous
    d. AL 333

76. _____ forms when rock cools and solidifies either below the surface as intrusive rocks or on the surface as extrusive rocks. This magma can be derived from partial melts of pre-existing rocks in either the Earth's mantle or crust. Typically, the melting is caused by one or more of the following processes -- an increase in temperature, a decrease in pressure, or a change in composition.
    a. Igneous rock
    b. AL 333
    c. AASHTO Soil Classification System
    d. AL 129-1

77. _____ is the result of the transformation of a pre-existing rock type, the protolith, in a process called metamorphism, which means "change in form". It makes up a large part of the Earth's crust and are classified by texture and by chemical and mineral assemblage. It is also formed when rock is heated up by the intrusion of hot molten rock called magma from the Earth's interior.
    a. Metamorphic rock
    b. 1703 Genroku earthquake
    c. 1509 Istanbul earthquake
    d. 1700 Cascadia earthquake

78. In geology, _____ is a naturally occurring aggregate of minerals and/or mineraloids.

The Earth's outer solid layer, the lithosphere, is made of _____. In general _____s are of three types, namely, igneous, sedimentary, and metamorphic.

    a. Rock
    b. 1509 Istanbul earthquake
    c. 1703 Genroku earthquake
    d. 1700 Cascadia earthquake

79. The _____ is a geologic transform fault that runs a length of roughly 800 miles (1,300 km) through California in the United States. The fault's motion is right-lateral strike-slip (horizontal motion.) It forms the tectonic boundary between the Pacific Plate and the North American Plate.
    a. 1700 Cascadia earthquake
    b. 1509 Istanbul earthquake
    c. San Andreas fault
    d. 1703 Genroku earthquake

80. _____ rock is one of the three main rock groups. Rock formed from these covers 75% of the Earth's land area, and includes common types such as chalk, limestone, dolomite, sandstone, and shale.
    a. Clasts
    b. Sedimentary
    c. Sedimentary basin
    d. Sedimentary depositional environment

Chapter 3. Minerals and Rocks

81. _____ is one of the three main rock types (the others being igneous and metamorphic rock.) _____ is formed by deposition and consolidation of mineral and organic material and from precipitation of minerals from solution. The processes that form _____ occur at the surface of the Earth and within bodies of water.
- a. 1509 Istanbul earthquake
- b. 1700 Cascadia earthquake
- c. 1703 Genroku earthquake
- d. Sedimentary rock

82. _____s are planar rock fractures, which show evidence of relative movement. Large _____s within the Earth's crust are the result of shear motion and active _____ zones are the causal locations of most earthquakes. Earthquakes are caused by energy release during rapid slippage along _____s.
- a. 1703 Genroku earthquake
- b. 1509 Istanbul earthquake
- c. 1700 Cascadia earthquake
- d. Fault

83. The _____ is a fundamental concept in geology that describes the dynamic transitions through geologic time among the three main rock types: sedimentary, metamorphic, and igneous.
- a. 1509 Istanbul earthquake
- b. 1700 Cascadia earthquake
- c. 1703 Genroku earthquake
- d. Rock cycle

84. The principle or _____ states that sediments are deposited under the influence of gravity as nearly horizontal beds. Observations in a wide variety of sedimentary environments support this principle. If we find folded or faulted strata, we know that the layers were deformed by tectonic forces after the sediments were deposited. This principle can be combined with the principle of superposition.
- a. AL 333
- b. Original horizontality
- c. AASHTO Soil Classification System
- d. AL 129-1

85. A _____ is any disturbed state of an astronomical body's atmosphere, especially affecting its surface, and strongly implying severe weather. It may be marked by strong wind, thunder and lightning, heavy precipitation, such as ice, or wind transporting some substance through the atmosphere.
- a. 1509 Istanbul earthquake
- b. Storm
- c. 1703 Genroku earthquake
- d. 1700 Cascadia earthquake

86. The basic idea of this is that an object, event or entity can be spanned across multiple realities or universes. When combined, these multiple, unique, pan-dimensional segments of the object, consciousness or event, make up parts or constituents of its _____.
- a. 1703 Genroku earthquake
- b. 1700 Cascadia earthquake
- c. 1509 Istanbul earthquake
- d. Superposition

87. _____ are large emplacements of igneous intrusive rock that forms from cooled magma deep in the Earth's crust. They are almost always made mostly of felsic or intermediate rock-types, such as granite, quartz monzonite, or diorite.
- a. Batholiths
- b. 1509 Istanbul earthquake
- c. 1703 Genroku earthquake
- d. 1700 Cascadia earthquake

88. A _____ is an intrusion into a cross-cutting fissure, meaning a _____ cuts across other pre-existing layers or bodies of rock, this means that a _____ is always younger than the rocks that contain it. The thickness is usually much smaller than the other two dimensions. Thickness can vary from sub-centimeter scale to many meters in thickness and the lateral dimensions can extend over many kilometers.

a. 1703 Genroku earthquake
b. 1700 Cascadia earthquake
c. Dike
d. 1509 Istanbul earthquake

89. _____ refers to the mode of igneous volcanic rock formation in which hot magma from inside the Earth flows out onto the surface as lava or explodes violently into the atmosphere to fall back as pyroclastics or tuff.
a. AL 129-1
b. AL 333
c. AASHTO Soil Classification System
d. Extrusive

90. _____ are chemical substances that may or may not be present in a cell, depending on the cell type. _____ are stored nutrients, secretory products, and pigment granules. Examples of _____ are; glycogen granules in the liver and muscle cells; lipid droplets in fat cells; pigment granules in certain cells of skin and hair; water containing vacuoles; and crystals of various types.
a. AL 333
b. AL 129-1
c. Inclusions
d. AASHTO Soil Classification System

91. An _____ is a body of igneous rock that has crystallized from a molten magma below the surface of the Earth.
a. AL 333
b. AL 129-1
c. AASHTO Soil Classification System
d. Intrusion

92. _____ is molten rock located beneath the surface of the Earth, and which often collects in a _____ chamber. _____ is a complex high-temperature fluid substance. Most are silicate solutions. It is capable of intrusion into adjacent rocks or of extrusion onto the surface as lava or ejected explosively as tephra to form pyroclastic rock. Environments of _____ formation include subduction zones, continental rift zones, mid-oceanic ridges, and hotspots, some of which are interpreted as mantle plumes.
a. 1703 Genroku earthquake
b. 1700 Cascadia earthquake
c. 1509 Istanbul earthquake
d. Magma

93. A _____ is a relatively large and usually conspicuous crystal distinctly larger than the grains of the rock groundmass of a porphyritic igneous rock. They often have euhedral forms either due to early growth within a magma or by post-emplacement recrystallization.
a. 1703 Genroku earthquake
b. Phenocryst
c. 1509 Istanbul earthquake
d. 1700 Cascadia earthquake

94. A _____ in geology is an intrusive igneous rock body that crystallized from a magma below the surface of the Earth. _____s include batholiths, dikes, sills, laccoliths, lopoliths, and other igneous bodies. In practice, "_____" usually refers to a distinctive mass of igneous rock, typically kilometers in dimension, without a tabular shape like those of dikes and sills.
a. 1700 Cascadia earthquake
b. 1509 Istanbul earthquake
c. 1703 Genroku earthquake
d. Pluton

95. In geology, a _____ is a tabular pluton that has intruded between older layers of sedimentary rock, beds of volcanic lava or tuff, or even along the direction of foliation in metamorphic rock. The term _____ is synonymous with concordant intrusive sheet. This means that the _____ does not cut across preexisting rocks. Contrast this with dikes.
a. 1700 Cascadia earthquake
b. 1509 Istanbul earthquake
c. Sill
d. 1703 Genroku earthquake

Chapter 3. Minerals and Rocks

96. _____ is a common extrusive volcanic rock. It is usually gray to black and fine-grained due to rapid cooling of lava at the surface of a planet. It may be porphyritic containing larger crystals in a fine matrix, or vesicular, or frothy scoria.
    a. 1700 Cascadia earthquake
    b. 1509 Istanbul earthquake
    c. Basalt
    d. 1703 Genroku earthquake

97. A _____ is a rock consisting of individual stones that have become cemented together. _____s are sedimentary rocks consisting of rounded fragements and are thus differentiated from breccias, which consist of angular clasts. Both _____s and breccias are characterized by clasts larger than sand.
    a. 1703 Genroku earthquake
    b. 1509 Istanbul earthquake
    c. 1700 Cascadia earthquake
    d. Conglomerate

98. _____ is a common and widely distributed type of rock formed by high-grade regional metamorphic processes from preexisting formations that were originally either igneous or sedimentary rocks. Gneissic rocks are usually medium to coarse foliated and largely recrystallized but do not carry large quantities of micas, chlorite or other platy minerals.
    a. Gneiss
    b. 1703 Genroku earthquake
    c. 1509 Istanbul earthquake
    d. 1700 Cascadia earthquake

99. _____ is a common and widely occurring type of intrusive, felsic, igneous rock. _____s are usually medium to coarsely crystalline, occasionally with some individual crystals larger than the groundmass forming a rock known as porphyry. _____s can be pink to dark gray or even black, depending on their chemistry and mineralogy.
    a. 1703 Genroku earthquake
    b. 1509 Istanbul earthquake
    c. Granite
    d. 1700 Cascadia earthquake

100. _____ is a sedimentary rock composed mainly of sand-size mineral or rock grains. Most _____ is composed of quartz and/or feldspar because these are the most common minerals in the Earth's crust. Like sand, _____ may be any color, but the most common colors are tan, brown, yellow, red, gray and white.
    a. 1509 Istanbul earthquake
    b. Sandstone
    c. 1703 Genroku earthquake
    d. 1700 Cascadia earthquake

101. The _____ refers to a group of medium-grade metamorphic rocks, chiefly notable for the preponderance of lamellar minerals such as micas, chlorite, talc, hornblende, graphite, and others. Quartz often occurs in drawn-out grains to such an extent that a particular form called quartz _____ is produced.
    a. Yttrium
    b. Schist
    c. Xenon
    d. Thallium

102. In geology, a _____ is a depression with predominant extent in one direction. The terms U-shaped and V-shaped are descriptive terms of geography to characterize the form of _____s. Most _____s belong to one of these two main types or a mixture of them, at least with respect of the cross section of the slopes or hillsides.
    a. Valley
    b. 1509 Istanbul earthquake
    c. 1703 Genroku earthquake
    d. 1700 Cascadia earthquake

103. _____ is an umbrella term for the various processes by which magmas undergo bulk chemical change during the partial melting process, cooling, emplacement of eruption.

When a rock melts it melts to form a liquid, the liquid is known as a primary melt. Primary melts have not undergone any differentiation and represent the starting composition of a magma.

Chapter 3. Minerals and Rocks

a. AL 333
b. Igneous differentiation
c. AASHTO Soil Classification System
d. AL 129-1

104. _____ refers to accumulations of large blocks of volcanic material often found around vents. They are defined as rocks containing at least 75% bombs. They typically consist of blocks of various igneous rocks, often mixed with material of rudimentary origin and embedded in a finer-grained matrix.
a. AASHTO Soil Classification System
b. AL 333
c. AL 129-1
d. Agglomerate

105. _____ are clastic rocks composed solely or primarily of volcanic materials.
a. 1509 Istanbul earthquake
b. 1703 Genroku earthquake
c. 1700 Cascadia earthquake
d. Pyroclastics

106. _____ is air-fall material produced by a volcanic eruption regardless of composition or fragment size. It is typically rhyolitic in composition as most explosive volcanoes are the product of the more viscous felsic or high silica magmas.
a. 1700 Cascadia earthquake
b. 1509 Istanbul earthquake
c. Tephra
d. 1703 Genroku earthquake

107. A _____ is an opening in a planet's surface or crust, which allows hot, molten rock, ash, and gases to escape from below the surface. Volcanic activity involving the extrusion of rock tends to form mountains or features like mountains over a period of time.

_____es are generally found where tectonic plates are diverging or converging.

a. 1509 Istanbul earthquake
b. Volcano
c. 1703 Genroku earthquake
d. 1700 Cascadia earthquake

108. _____ are pyroclastic rocks formed by explosive eruption of lava and any rocks which are entrained within the eruptive column. This may include rocks plucked off the wall of the magma conduit, or physically picked up by the ensuing pyroclastic surge.
a. 1700 Cascadia earthquake
b. Volcanic breccia
c. 1703 Genroku earthquake
d. 1509 Istanbul earthquake

109. _____ is a rock composed of angular fragments of rocks or minerals in a matrix, that is a cementing material, that may be similar or different in composition to the fragments.
a. 1509 Istanbul earthquake
b. Breccia
c. 1703 Genroku earthquake
d. 1700 Cascadia earthquake

110. _____ is an absorbent aluminium phyllosilicate generally impure clay consisting mostly of montmorillonite.
a. Bentonite
b. 1700 Cascadia earthquake
c. 1509 Istanbul earthquake
d. 1703 Genroku earthquake

111. _____ is when long fractures form vertically in rock as it cools and contracts.

Chapter 3. Minerals and Rocks

a. 1700 Cascadia earthquake
b. Columnar jointing
c. 1703 Genroku earthquake
d. 1509 Istanbul earthquake

112. A _____ is a barrier across flowing water that obstructs, directs or slows down the flow, often creating a reservoir, lake or impoundment.
a. 1700 Cascadia earthquake
b. 1703 Genroku earthquake
c. 1509 Istanbul earthquake
d. Dam

113. The _____ was a federally built earthen dam on the Teton River in southeastern Idaho in the United States which when filling for the first time suffered a catastrophic failure on June 5, 1976. The collapse of the dam resulted in the deaths of 11 people and 13,000 head of cattle. The dam cost about USD $100 million to build, and the federal government paid over $300 million in claims related to the dam failure.
a. Teton Dam
b. 1700 Cascadia earthquake
c. 1509 Istanbul earthquake
d. 1703 Genroku earthquake

114. _____ is a type of rock consisting of consolidated volcanic ash ejected from vents during a volcanic eruption.
a. 1700 Cascadia earthquake
b. Tuff
c. 1703 Genroku earthquake
d. 1509 Istanbul earthquake

115. A _____ is a deep valley between cliffs often carved from the landscape by a river. Most were formed by a process of long-time erosion from a plateau level. The cliffs form because harder rock strata that are resistant to erosion and weathering remain exposed on the valley walls.
a. 1703 Genroku earthquake
b. 1509 Istanbul earthquake
c. 1700 Cascadia earthquake
d. Canyon

116. _____ is a geological term used to describe particles of rock derived from pre-existing rock through processes of weathering and erosion.
a. 1703 Genroku earthquake
b. 1700 Cascadia earthquake
c. 1509 Istanbul earthquake
d. Detrital

117. In geology and oceanography, _____ is any chemical, physical, or biological change undergone by a sediment after its initial deposition and during and after its lithification, exclusive of surface alteration, weathering and metamorphism. These changes happen at relatively low temperatures and pressures and result in changes to the rock's original mineralogy and texture
a. 1700 Cascadia earthquake
b. 1509 Istanbul earthquake
c. Diagenesis
d. 1703 Genroku earthquake

118. The _____ is a very colorful, steep-sided gorge, carved by the Colorado River in the U.S. state of Arizona. It is one of the first national parks in the United States.
a. Grand Canyon
b. 1509 Istanbul earthquake
c. 1703 Genroku earthquake
d. 1700 Cascadia earthquake

119. An _____ is the result from the sudden release of stored energy in the Earth's crust that creates seismic waves. At the Earth's surface, _____s may manifest themselves by a shaking or displacement of the ground. An _____ is caused by tectonic plates getting stuck and putting a strain on the ground. The strain becomes so great that rocks give way by breaking and sliding along fault planes.

a. AASHTO Soil Classification System
b. Earthquake
c. AL 333
d. AL 129-1

120. _____ are where one sedimetary deposit ends and another one begins. The rock is prone to breakage at these points because of the weakness between the layers.
   a. 1703 Genroku earthquake
   b. 1700 Cascadia earthquake
   c. 1509 Istanbul earthquake
   d. Bedding planes

121. A _____ should ideally be a distinctive rock that forms under certain conditions of sedimentation, reflecting a particular process or environment.
   a. Facies
   b. 1509 Istanbul earthquake
   c. 1703 Genroku earthquake
   d. 1700 Cascadia earthquake

122. _____ is a detrital sedimentary rock, specifically a type of containing at least 25% feldspar.
   a. Arkosic sandstone
   b. AASHTO Soil Classification System
   c. AL 333
   d. AL 129-1

123. _____ is a soft, white, porous sedimentary rock, a form of limestone composed of the mineral calcite. It forms under relatively deep marine conditions from the gradual accumulation of minute calcite plates shed from micro-organisms called coccolithophores. It is common to find flint nodules embedded in it.
   a. 1703 Genroku earthquake
   b. 1509 Istanbul earthquake
   c. 1700 Cascadia earthquake
   d. Chalk

124. _____ is a fine-grained silica-rich cryptocrystalline sedimentary rock that may contain small fossils. It varies greatly in color from white to black, but most often manifests as gray, brown, grayish brown and light green to rusty red; its color is an expression of trace elements present in the rock, and both red and green are most often related to traces of iron.
   a. 1700 Cascadia earthquake
   b. 1703 Genroku earthquake
   c. 1509 Istanbul earthquake
   d. Chert

125. _____ -- also known as TSS, diatomite, diahydro, kieselguhr, kieselgur or celite -- is a naturally occurring, soft, chalk-like sedimentary rock that is easily crumbled into a fine white to off-white powder. This powder has an abrasive feel, similar to pumice powder, and is very light, due to its high porosity. The typical chemical composition of _____ is 86% silica, 5% sodium, 3% magnesium and 2% iron.
   a. 1509 Istanbul earthquake
   b. Phosphorite
   c. Terrigenous
   d. Diatomaceous earth

126. _____ is a very soft mineral composed of calcium sulfate dihydrate, with the chemical formula $CaSO_4 \cdot 2H_2O$. _____ occurs in nature as flattened and often twinned crystals and transparent cleavable masses. It may also occur silky and fibrous. Finally it may also be granular or quite compact.
   a. 1700 Cascadia earthquake
   b. 1509 Istanbul earthquake
   c. 1703 Genroku earthquake
   d. Gypsum

127. _____ is a measure of the void spaces in a material, and is measured as a fraction, between 0–1, or as a percentage between 0–100%.

Chapter 3. Minerals and Rocks 49

    a. 1703 Genroku earthquake
    c. 1700 Cascadia earthquake
    b. 1509 Istanbul earthquake
    d. Porosity

128. _____ is a sedimentary rock which has a composition intermediate in grain size between the coarser sandstones and the finer mudstones and shales.
    a. 1509 Istanbul earthquake
    c. 1703 Genroku earthquake
    b. Siltstone
    d. 1700 Cascadia earthquake

129. _____ can be defined as the solid state recrystallisation of pre-existing rocks due to changes in heat and/or pressure and/or introduction of fluids. There will be mineralogical, chemical and crystallographic changes. _____ produced with increasing pressure and temperature conditions is known as prograde _____. Conversely, decreasing temperatures and pressure characterize retrograde _____.
    a. 1703 Genroku earthquake
    c. Metamorphism
    b. 1509 Istanbul earthquake
    d. 1700 Cascadia earthquake

130. In geology, a _____ zone is an area on Earth where two tectonic plates meet and move towards one another, with one sliding underneath the other and moving down into the mantle, at rates typically measured in centimeters per year. An oceanic plate ordinarily slides underneath a continental plate; this often creates an orogenic zone with many volcanoes and earthquakes.
    a. 1509 Istanbul earthquake
    c. 1700 Cascadia earthquake
    b. 1703 Genroku earthquake
    d. Subduction

131. A _____ is an area on Earth where two tectonic plates meet and move towards one another, with one sliding underneath the other and moving down into the mantle, at rates typically measured in centimeters per year. In a sense, _____s are the opposite of divergent boundaries, areas where material rises up from the mantle and plates are moving apart.
    a. 1703 Genroku earthquake
    c. 1700 Cascadia earthquake
    b. Subduction zone
    d. 1509 Istanbul earthquake

132. _____ occurs typically around intrusive igneous rocks as a result of the temperature increase caused by the intrusion of magma into cooler country rock. The area surrounding the intrusion (called aureoles) where the _____ effects are present is called the metamorphic aureole. Contact metamorphic rocks are usually known as hornfels.
    a. 1700 Cascadia earthquake
    c. 1703 Genroku earthquake
    b. 1509 Istanbul earthquake
    d. Contact metamorphism

133. _____ has penetrative planar fabric present within it. It is common to rocks affected by regional metamorphic compression typical of orogenic belts.
    a. Foliated metamorphic rock
    c. 1509 Istanbul earthquake
    b. 1703 Genroku earthquake
    d. 1700 Cascadia earthquake

134. _____ is a fine-grained, homogeneous, metamorphic rock derived from an original shale-type sedimentary rock composed of clay or volcanic ash through low grade regional metamorphism. The result is a foliated rock in which the foliation may not correspond to the original sedimentary layering.
    a. 1703 Genroku earthquake
    c. 1700 Cascadia earthquake
    b. 1509 Istanbul earthquake
    d. Slate

Chapter 3. Minerals and Rocks

135. _____ is a biological process by which an animal physically develops after birth or hatching, involving a conspicuous and relatively abrupt change in the animal's form or structure through cell growth and differentiation.
   a. 1703 Genroku earthquake
   b. 1700 Cascadia earthquake
   c. 1509 Istanbul earthquake
   d. Metamorphosis

136. _____ is associated with large-scale lithospheric extensional tectonics. They often have very large displacement 10s of km and juxtapose unmetamorphosed hanging walls against medium to high-grade metamorphic footwalls.
   a. Detachment faulting
   b. 1703 Genroku earthquake
   c. 1700 Cascadia earthquake
   d. 1509 Istanbul earthquake

137. A _____ is a long, narrow estuary with steep sides, made when a glacial valley is flooded by the sea. The seeds of a _____ are laid when a glacier cuts a U-shaped valley through abrasion of the surrounding bedrock by the rocks and sediment it carries. Many such valleys were formed during recent ice ages when the sea was at a much lower level than it is today. At the end of such a period, the climate warms up again and glaciers retreat.
   a. 1700 Cascadia earthquake
   b. Fjord
   c. 1509 Istanbul earthquake
   d. 1703 Genroku earthquake

138. _____ is a metamorphic rock resulting from the metamorphism of limestone, composed mostly of calcite. It is extensively used for sculpture, as a building material, and in many other applications. The word '_____' is colloquially used to refer to many other stones that are capable of taking a high polish.
   a. 1509 Istanbul earthquake
   b. 1700 Cascadia earthquake
   c. 1703 Genroku earthquake
   d. Marble

139. _____ is a hard, metamorphic rock which was originally sandstone. Sandstone is converted into _____ through heating and pressure usually related to tectonic compression within orogenic belts.
   a. 1509 Istanbul earthquake
   b. Quartzite
   c. 1703 Genroku earthquake
   d. 1700 Cascadia earthquake

140. In materials science, _____ is a change in the shape or size of an object due to an applied force. This can be a result of tensile (pulling) forces, compressive (pushing) forces, shear, bending or torsion (twisting.) _____ is often described as strain.
   a. 1700 Cascadia earthquake
   b. Deformation
   c. 1703 Genroku earthquake
   d. 1509 Istanbul earthquake

141. _____ have the mechanical property of being capable of sustaining large plastic deformations due to tensile stress without fracture in metals, such as being drawn into a wire. It is characterized by the material flowing under shear stress. It is contrasted with brittleness.
   a. 1700 Cascadia earthquake
   b. 1509 Istanbul earthquake
   c. 1703 Genroku earthquake
   d. Ductile materials

142. _____ is a general term that includes rocks and materials that are not by definition rocks but are commonly regarded as rocks.
   a. AASHTO Soil Classification System
   b. Earth materials
   c. AL 333
   d. AL 129-1

143. _____ is reversible. Once the forces are no longer applied, the object returns to its original shape.

Chapter 3. Minerals and Rocks

a. AASHTO Soil Classification System
b. AL 129-1
c. AL 333
d. Elastic deformation

144. The _____ was a concrete gravity-arch dam, designed to create a reservoir as part of the Los Angeles Aqueduct. The dam was located 40 miles northwest of Los Angeles, California, near the city of Santa Clarita. It was built between 1924 and 1926 under the supervision of William Mulholland, chief engineer and general manager of the Los Angeles Department of Water and Power.
   a. Sun Belt
   b. 1700 Cascadia earthquake
   c. 1509 Istanbul earthquake
   d. St. Francis Dam

145. _____ is the capacity of a material to withstand axially directed pushing forces.
   a. Compressive strength
   b. 1700 Cascadia earthquake
   c. 1703 Genroku earthquake
   d. 1509 Istanbul earthquake

146. _____ in engineering is a term used to describe the strength of a material or component against the type of yield or structural failure where the material or component fails in shear.

In structural and mechanical engineering the _____ of a component is important for designing the dimensions and materials to be used for the manufacture/construction of the component (e.g. beams, plates, or bolts) In a reinforced concrete beam, the main purpose of stirrups is to increase the _____.

For shear stress τ applies

$$\tau = \frac{\sigma_1 - \sigma_2}{2}.$$

where

σ_1 is major principal stress
σ_2 is minor principal stress

In general: ductile materials fail in shear (ex.

   a. Shear strength
   b. 1703 Genroku earthquake
   c. 1509 Istanbul earthquake
   d. 1700 Cascadia earthquake

147. _____ measures the force required to pull something such as rope, wire, or a structural beam to the point where it breaks.
   a. 1509 Istanbul earthquake
   b. 1700 Cascadia earthquake
   c. Tensile strength
   d. 1703 Genroku earthquake

148. The term _____ is used in geology when one or a stack of originally flat and planar surfaces, such as sedimentary strata, are bent or curved as a result of plastic, i.e. permanent, deformation.

Chapter 3. Minerals and Rocks

a. Fold
b. 1703 Genroku earthquake
c. 1509 Istanbul earthquake
d. 1700 Cascadia earthquake

149. A _____ is any local separation or discontinuous plane in a geologic formation, such as joints or faults into two or more pieces under the action of stress.
   a. 1509 Istanbul earthquake
   b. 1700 Cascadia earthquake
   c. 1703 Genroku earthquake
   d. Rock fracture

150. _____ is an unconformity where horizontally parallel strata of sedimentary rock are deposited on tilted and eroded layers that may be either vertical or at an angle to the overlying horizontal layers
   a. AL 333
   b. AASHTO Soil Classification System
   c. AL 129-1
   d. Angular unconformity

151. An _____ is a fold that is convex up or to the youngest beds. _____s are usually recognized by a sequence of rock layers that are progressively older toward the center of the fold because the uplifted core of the fold is preferentially eroded to a deeper stratigraphic level relative to the topographically lower flanks. If an _____ plunges, the surface strata will form Vs that point in the direction of the plunge.
   a. AASHTO Soil Classification System
   b. AL 333
   c. AL 129-1
   d. Anticline

152. The _____ are a vast system of mountains in eastern North America.
   a. AL 129-1
   b. AASHTO Soil Classification System
   c. AL 333
   d. Appalachian Mountains

153. In structural geology, a _____ is a downward-curving fold, with layers that dip toward the center of the structure. On a geologic map, _____s are recognized by a sequence of rock layers that grow progressively younger, followed by the youngest layer at the fold's center or hinge, and by a reverse sequence of the same rock layers on the opposite side of the hinge.
   a. 1700 Cascadia earthquake
   b. 1703 Genroku earthquake
   c. 1509 Istanbul earthquake
   d. Syncline

154. An _____ is a buried erosion surface separating two rock masses or strata of different ages, indicating that sediment deposition was not continuous. In general, the older layer was exposed to erosion for an interval of time before deposition of the younger, but the term is used to describe any break in the sedimentary geologic record.
   a. AASHTO Soil Classification System
   b. AL 333
   c. AL 129-1
   d. Unconformity

155. _____ is displacement of solids by the agents of ocean currents, wind, water, or ice by downward or down-slope movement in response to gravity or by living organisms.
   a. AASHTO Soil Classification System
   b. AL 129-1
   c. Erosion
   d. AL 333

156. A _____ is an unconformity between parallel layers of sedimentary rocks which represents a period of erosion or non-deposition.

Chapter 3. Minerals and Rocks

a. 1700 Cascadia earthquake
c. 1509 Istanbul earthquake

b. 1703 Genroku earthquake
d. Disconformity

157. _____ is one of the 20 Regions of Italy. It has an area of 25,399 km

_____ is surrounded on three sides by the Alps, including the Monviso, where the Po rises, and the Monte Rosa. It borders with France, Switzerland and the Italian regions of Lombardy, Liguria, Emilia-Romagna and Aosta Valley.

a. 1703 Genroku earthquake
c. 1700 Cascadia earthquake

b. 1509 Istanbul earthquake
d. Piedmont

158. A _____ is a spatial entity with common geologic attributes. A _____ may include a single dominant structural element such as a basin or a fold belt, or a number of contiguous related elements.

a. 1509 Istanbul earthquake
c. 1703 Genroku earthquake

b. Province
d. 1700 Cascadia earthquake

159. A _____ or geophysical hazards is a threat of an event that will have a negative effect on people or the environment. Many _____s are related, e.g. earthquakes can result in tsunamis, drought can lead directly to famine and disease. A concrete example of the division between hazard and disaster is that the 1906 San Francisco earthquake was a disaster, whereas earthquakes are a hazard.

a. 1703 Genroku earthquake
c. Natural hazard

b. 1509 Istanbul earthquake
d. 1700 Cascadia earthquake

Chapter 4. Introduction to Natural Hazards

1. _____ was first recognised after the Taal Volcano eruption of 1965, where a visiting volcanologist recognised the phenomenon as congruent to _____ in atomic explosions. The USGS defines _____ as turbulent, low-density cloud of rock debris and water and (or) steam that moves over the ground surface at high speed. _____s are generated by explosions.
   a. 1703 Genroku earthquake
   b. Base surge
   c. 1700 Cascadia earthquake
   d. 1509 Istanbul earthquake

2. A _____ is a storm system characterized by a low pressure center and numerous thunderstorms that produce strong winds and flooding rain. _____s feed on heat released when moist air rises, resulting in condensation of water vapour contained in the moist air. They are fueled by a different heat mechanism than other cyclonic windstorms such as nor'easters, European windstorms, and polar lows, leading to their classification as 'warm core' storm systems. Depending on its location and strength, a _____ is referred to by many other names, such as hurricane, typhoon, tropical storm, cyclonic storm, tropical depression, and simply cyclone.
   a. Persia
   b. Khmer Empire
   c. Kenya
   d. Tropical cyclone

3. In meteorology, _____ are an area of low atmospheric pressure characterized by inward spiraling winds that rotate counter clockwise in the northern hemisphere and clockwise in the southern hemisphere of the Earth.
   a. 1703 Genroku earthquake
   b. Cyclones
   c. 1700 Cascadia earthquake
   d. 1509 Istanbul earthquake

4. A _____ is an extended period of months or years when a region notes a deficiency in its water supply. Generally, this occurs when a region receives consistently below average precipitation.
   a. 1509 Istanbul earthquake
   b. 1703 Genroku earthquake
   c. Drought
   d. 1700 Cascadia earthquake

5. An _____ is the result from the sudden release of stored energy in the Earth's crust that creates seismic waves. At the Earth's surface, _____s may manifest themselves by a shaking or displacement of the ground. An _____ is caused by tectonic plates getting stuck and putting a strain on the ground. The strain becomes so great that rocks give way by breaking and sliding along fault planes.
   a. AASHTO Soil Classification System
   b. AL 129-1
   c. AL 333
   d. Earthquake

6. _____ (æ—¥æœ¬ Nihon or Nippon making it an archipelago. The largest islands are Honshū, Hokkaidō, Kyūshū and Shikoku, together accounting for 97% of _____'s land area. Most of the islands are mountainous, many volcanic; for example, _____'s highest peak, Mount Fuji, is a volcano.
   a. Kabul
   b. Kenya
   c. Java
   d. Japan

7. _____ (ç¥žæˆ¸å¸‚, Kōbe-shi For most of its history the area was never a single political entity, even during the Tokugawa Period, when the port was controlled directly by the Tokugawa Shogunate. _____ did not exist in its current form until its founding in 1889. Its name comes from 'kanbe' Hyōgo Port in the 19th century The Bund in _____ around 1890

Stone artifacts and tools found in western _____ demonstrate that the area was populated at least from the Jōmon period.

Chapter 4. Introduction to Natural Hazards

a. Korean War
b. Peninsula
c. Japan
d. Kobe

8. The _____ was an earthquake in Japan that measured 6.9 on the Richter magnitude scale and 7.2 on the Japanese seismic intensity scale. It occurred on January 17, 1995 at 5:46:46 a.m. in the southern part of Hyogo Prefecture and lasted for approximately 20 seconds.
   a. 1509 Istanbul earthquake
   b. 1703 Genroku earthquake
   c. Kobe earthquake
   d. 1700 Cascadia earthquake

9. _____ is an Andean stratovolcano in Caldas Department, Colombia. It is the northernmost and highest Colombian volcano with historical activity. Its 1985 eruption produced a lahar which completely buried Armero and caused an estimated 23,000 deaths.
   a. 1703 Genroku earthquake
   b. Nevado del Ruiz
   c. 1509 Istanbul earthquake
   d. 1700 Cascadia earthquake

10. A _____ is an opening in a planet's surface or crust, which allows hot, molten rock, ash, and gases to escape from below the surface. Volcanic activity involving the extrusion of rock tends to form mountains or features like mountains over a period of time.

    _____es are generally found where tectonic plates are diverging or converging.

    a. 1703 Genroku earthquake
    b. 1700 Cascadia earthquake
    c. Volcano
    d. 1509 Istanbul earthquake

11. _____ usually commence with phreatomagmatic eruptions which can be extremely noisy due the rising magma heating water in the ground. This is usually followed by the explosive throat clearing of the vent and the eruption column is dirty grey to black as old weathered rocks are blasted out of the vent. As the vent clears, further ash clouds become grey-white and creamy in colour, with convulations of the ash similar to those of plinian eruptions.
    a. 1700 Cascadia earthquake
    b. 1509 Istanbul earthquake
    c. 1703 Genroku earthquake
    d. Vulcanian eruptions

12. A _____ is the consequence of a natural hazard such as volcanic eruption, earthquake, landslide which becomes a physical event and interacts with human activities.
    a. 1509 Istanbul earthquake
    b. Natural disaster
    c. 1703 Genroku earthquake
    d. 1700 Cascadia earthquake

13. A _____ is flat or nearly flat land adjacent to a stream or river that experiences occasional or periodic flooding. It includes the floodway, which consists of the stream channel and adjacent areas that carry flood flows, and the flood fringe, which are areas covered by the flood, but which do not experience a strong current.
    a. 1703 Genroku earthquake
    b. 1700 Cascadia earthquake
    c. 1509 Istanbul earthquake
    d. Floodplain

14. The _____ form an archipelago of nineteen islands and atolls, numerous smaller islets, and undersea seamounts trending northwest by southeast in the North Pacific Ocean between latitudes 19° N and 29° N. The archipelago takes its name from the largest island in the group and extends some 1500 miles from the Island of Hawai'i in the south to northernmost Kure Atoll.

a. 1700 Cascadia earthquake
b. 1509 Istanbul earthquake
c. Hawaiian Islands
d. 1703 Genroku earthquake

15. A _____ is a geological phenomenon which includes a wide range of ground movement, such as rock falls, deep failure of slopes and shallow debris flows. Although gravity's action on an over-steepened slope is the primary reason for a _____, there are other contributing factors affecting the original slope stability.
a. 1700 Cascadia earthquake
b. 1703 Genroku earthquake
c. 1509 Istanbul earthquake
d. Landslide

16. The _____ is the second-longest named river in North America, with a length of 2320 miles from Lake Itasca to the Gulf of Mexico. It drains most of the area between the Rocky Mountains and the Appalachian Mountains, except for the areas drained by Hudson Bay via the Red River of the North, the Great Lakes and the Rio Grande.
a. 1700 Cascadia earthquake
b. Mississippi River
c. 1509 Istanbul earthquake
d. 1703 Genroku earthquake

17. In geology, engineering, and surveying, _____ is the motion of a surface as it shifts downward relative to a datum such as sea-level. The opposite of _____ is uplift, which results in an increase in elevation. In meteorology, _____ refers to the downward movement of air.
a. Subsidence
b. 1509 Istanbul earthquake
c. 1703 Genroku earthquake
d. 1700 Cascadia earthquake

18. A _____ is a barrier across flowing water that obstructs, directs or slows down the flow, often creating a reservoir, lake or impoundment.
a. 1509 Istanbul earthquake
b. 1700 Cascadia earthquake
c. 1703 Genroku earthquake
d. Dam

19. _____s are planar rock fractures, which show evidence of relative movement. Large _____s within the Earth's crust are the result of shear motion and active _____ zones are the causal locations of most earthquakes. Earthquakes are caused by energy release during rapid slippage along _____s.
a. 1703 Genroku earthquake
b. 1700 Cascadia earthquake
c. 1509 Istanbul earthquake
d. Fault

20. _____ is an unconsolidated tectonite (a rock formed by tectonic forces) with a very small grain size. _____ has no cohesion, it is normally an unconsolidated rock type, unless cementation took place at a later stage. _____ forms in the same way as fault breccia, the latter also having larger clasts.
a. 1509 Istanbul earthquake
b. 1700 Cascadia earthquake
c. 1703 Genroku earthquake
d. Fault gouge

21. The _____ is a geologic transform fault that runs a length of roughly 800 miles (1,300 km) through California in the United States. The fault's motion is right-lateral strike-slip (horizontal motion.) It forms the tectonic boundary between the Pacific Plate and the North American Plate.
a. 1509 Istanbul earthquake
b. 1703 Genroku earthquake
c. 1700 Cascadia earthquake
d. San Andreas fault

Chapter 4. Introduction to Natural Hazards 57

22. The _____ is defined as the part of the land adjoining or near the ocean. A coastline is properly a line on a map indicating the disposition of a _____, but the word is often used to refer to the _____ itself. The adjective coastal describes something as being on, near to, or associated with a _____.
   a. 1509 Istanbul earthquake
   b. 1700 Cascadia earthquake
   c. 1703 Genroku earthquake
   d. Coast

23. _____ is displacement of solids by the agents of ocean currents, wind, water, or ice by downward or down-slope movement in response to gravity or by living organisms.
   a. AL 333
   b. AASHTO Soil Classification System
   c. AL 129-1
   d. Erosion

24. _____ is a solid deposition of water vapor from saturated air. If solid surfaces in contact with the air are chilled below the deposition point, then spicules of ice grow out from the solid surface. _____ is often observed around cracks in wooden sidewalks due to the moist air escaping from the ground below. Other objects on which _____ develops are those with low specific heat and high thermal emissivity, such as blackened metals.
   a. 1703 Genroku earthquake
   b. 1700 Cascadia earthquake
   c. 1509 Istanbul earthquake
   d. Frost

25. _____ is an atmospheric discharge of electricity, which usually, but not always, occurs during rain storms, and frequently during volcanic eruptions or dust storms.
   a. 1509 Istanbul earthquake
   b. Lightning
   c. 1703 Genroku earthquake
   d. 1700 Cascadia earthquake

26. A _____ is a violently rotating column of air which is in contact with both a cumulonimbus cloud base and the surface of the earth. They come in many sizes, but are typically in the form of a visible condensation funnel, with the narrow end touching the earth. Often, a cloud of debris encircles the lower portion of the funnel.
   a. 1700 Cascadia earthquake
   b. 1703 Genroku earthquake
   c. 1509 Istanbul earthquake
   d. Tornado

27. _____ is the wearing away of land or the removal of beach or dune sediments by wave action, tidal currents, wave currents, or drainage. Waves, generated by storms or fast moving moter craft, cause _____, which may take the form of long-term losses of sediment and rocks, or merely in the temporary redistribution of coastal sediments; erosion in one location may result in accretion nearby.
   a. Beach erosion
   b. 1700 Cascadia earthquake
   c. 1509 Istanbul earthquake
   d. 1703 Genroku earthquake

28. A _____ is a landform where the mouth of a river flows into an ocean, sea, desert, estuary or lake. It builds up sediment outwards into the flat area which the river's flow encounters transported by the water and set down as the currents slow.
   a. Delta
   b. 1509 Istanbul earthquake
   c. 1700 Cascadia earthquake
   d. 1703 Genroku earthquake

29. A _____ is a body of water with a current, confined within a bed and banks. _____s are important as conduits in the water cycle, instruments in aquifer recharge, and corridors for fish and wildlife migration.

Chapter 4. Introduction to Natural Hazards

a. Stream
b. 1703 Genroku earthquake
c. 1509 Istanbul earthquake
d. 1700 Cascadia earthquake

30. _____ is the study of the past, particularly using written records. New technology, such as photography, and computer text files now sometimes complement traditional archival sources. _____ is a field of research producing a continuous narrative and a systematic analysis of past events of importance to the human race.
    a. 1700 Cascadia earthquake
    b. 1509 Istanbul earthquake
    c. Absolute time
    d. History

31. _____ is a national park located largely in Mariposa and Tuolumne Counties, California, United States. It is one of the largest and least fragmented habitat blocks in the Sierra Nevada, and the park supports a diversity of plants and animals. The park has an elevation range from 2,000 to 13,114 feet.
    a. 1703 Genroku earthquake
    b. Yosemite National Park
    c. 1509 Istanbul earthquake
    d. 1700 Cascadia earthquake

32. _____ is a general term that includes rocks and materials that are not by definition rocks but are commonly regarded as rocks.
    a. Earth materials
    b. AL 129-1
    c. AASHTO Soil Classification System
    d. AL 333

33. _____ is a common and widely occurring type of intrusive, felsic, igneous rock. _____s are usually medium to coarsely crystalline, occasionally with some individual crystals larger than the groundmass forming a rock known as porphyry. _____s can be pink to dark gray or even black, depending on their chemistry and mineralogy.
    a. Granite
    b. 1703 Genroku earthquake
    c. 1700 Cascadia earthquake
    d. 1509 Istanbul earthquake

34. Motto: Fluctuat nec mergitur The Eiffel Tower and the skyscrapers of Paris' suburban La Défense business district. _____ Time Zone CET Coordinates °52′0″N 2°19′59″E″>48°52′0″N 2°19′59″Eï»¿ / ï»¿48.86667, 2.33306 Administration Country France Region Île-de-France Department Paris Subdivisions 20 arrondissements Mayor Bertrand Delanoë
City Statistics Land area km) Urban Spread Urban Area 2,723 km The Paris unité urbaine extends well beyond the administrative city limits and has an estimated population of 9.93 million. The Paris aire urbaine has a population of nearly 12 million, and is one of the most populated metropolitan areas in Europe.

An important settlement for more than two millennia, Paris is today one of the world's leading business and cultural centres, and its influence in politics, education, entertainment, media, fashion, science and the arts all contribute to its status as one of the world's major global cities.

    a. 1509 Istanbul earthquake
    b. 1703 Genroku earthquake
    c. 1700 Cascadia earthquake
    d. Location

35. A _____ is a statement or claim that a particular event will occur in the future in more certain terms than a forecast. The etymology of this word is Latin (from præ- 'before' plus dicere 'to say'.) In regards to predicting the future Howard H. Stevenson Says, '_____ is at least two things: Important and hard.' Important, because we have to act, and hard because we have to realize the future we want, and what is the best way to get there.

Chapter 4. Introduction to Natural Hazards 59

    a. 1509 Istanbul earthquake
    c. 1700 Cascadia earthquake
    b. 1703 Genroku earthquake
    d. Prediction

36. In materials science, _____ is a change in the shape or size of an object due to an applied force. This can be a result of tensile (pulling) forces, compressive (pushing) forces, shear, bending or torsion (twisting.) _____ is often described as strain.
    a. 1509 Istanbul earthquake
    c. 1703 Genroku earthquake
    b. Deformation
    d. 1700 Cascadia earthquake

37. A _____ or geophysical hazards is a threat of an event that will have a negative effect on people or the environment. Many _____s are related, e.g. earthquakes can result in tsunamis, drought can lead directly to famine and disease. A concrete example of the division between hazard and disaster is that the 1906 San Francisco earthquake was a disaster, whereas earthquakes are a hazard.
    a. 1700 Cascadia earthquake
    c. Natural hazard
    b. 1509 Istanbul earthquake
    d. 1703 Genroku earthquake

38. A _____ is a body of water, not part of the ocean, that is larger and deeper than a pond.
    a. 1700 Cascadia earthquake
    c. 1509 Istanbul earthquake
    b. 1703 Genroku earthquake
    d. Lake

39. A _____ is any of a number of an extinct genus of proboscidean, often with long curved tusks and, in northern species, a covering of long hair. They lived from the Pliocene epoch from to around 4,000 years ago.
    a. Mammoth
    c. 1703 Genroku earthquake
    b. 1509 Istanbul earthquake
    d. 1700 Cascadia earthquake

40. _____ is an incorporated town in Mono County, California, United States. The population was 7,093 at the 2000 census. _____ resides on the edge of the Long Valley Caldera. The area around the town is geologically active, with hot springs and rhyolite domes that are less than 1000 years old.
    a. Mammoth Lakes
    c. 1509 Istanbul earthquake
    b. 1703 Genroku earthquake
    d. 1700 Cascadia earthquake

41. _____ is a concept that denotes the precise probability of specific eventualities. Technically, the notion of _____ is independent from the notion of value and, as such, eventualities may have both beneficial and adverse consequences. However, in general usage the convention is to focus only on potential negative impact to some characteristic of value that may arise from a future event.
    a. Risk
    c. 1703 Genroku earthquake
    b. 1509 Istanbul earthquake
    d. 1700 Cascadia earthquake

42. A _____ is a bipedal primate belonging to the mammalian species Homo sapiens in the family Hominidae. Compared to other living organisms on Earth, a _____ has a highly developed brain capable of abstract reasoning, language, and introspection.
    a. 1509 Istanbul earthquake
    c. 1703 Genroku earthquake
    b. 1700 Cascadia earthquake
    d. Human

43. _____ is a qualitative or quantitative evaluation of the environmental and health risk resulting from exposure to a chemical agent. It combines exposure assessment results with toxicity assessment results to estimate risk.

a. 1509 Istanbul earthquake
b. Risk assessment
c. 1700 Cascadia earthquake
d. 1703 Genroku earthquake

44. A _____ is an urban area with a high population and a particular administrative, legal, or historical status.

Large industrialized cities generally have advanced systems for sanitation, utilities, land usage, housing, and transportation and more. This close proximity greatly facilitates interaction between people and firms, benefiting both parties in the process.

a. City
b. 1700 Cascadia earthquake
c. 1509 Istanbul earthquake
d. 1703 Genroku earthquake

45. _____ is the term used for a branch of public policy which encompasses various disciplines which seek to order and regulate the use of land in an efficient and ethical way.
a. 1509 Istanbul earthquake
b. 1703 Genroku earthquake
c. 1700 Cascadia earthquake
d. Land use planning

46. A _____ is a section of a river of relatively steep gradient causing an increase in water flow and turbulence. A _____ is a hydrological feature between a run and a cascade. It is characterized by the river becoming shallower and having some rocks exposed above the flow surface.
a. 1509 Istanbul earthquake
b. 1703 Genroku earthquake
c. 1700 Cascadia earthquake
d. Rapid

47. In demographics and ecology, Population growth rate (PGR) is the fractional rate at which the number of individuals in a _____. Specifically, PGR ordinarily refers to the change in population over a unit time period, often expressed as a percentage of the number of individuals in the population at the beginning of that period. This can be written as the formula:

$$\text{Growth rate} = \frac{(\text{population at end of period} - \text{population at beginning of period})}{\text{population at beginning of period}}$$

(In the limit of a sufficiently small time period.)

a. 1700 Cascadia earthquake
b. Population increases
c. 1703 Genroku earthquake
d. 1509 Istanbul earthquake

48. The _____ is a scientific agency of the United States government. The scientists of the USGS study the landscape of the United States, its natural resources, and the natural hazards that threaten it.
a. Amblypoda
b. Andrija Mohorovičić
c. Ambulocetus
d. U.S. Geological Survey

49. _____, in law and economics, is a form of risk management primarily used to hedge against the risk of a contingent loss. _____ is defined as the equitable transfer of the risk of a loss, from one entity to another, in exchange for a premium, and can be thought of as a guaranteed small loss to prevent a large, possibly devastating loss. An insurer is a company selling the _____; an insured is the person or entity buying the _____.

Chapter 4. Introduction to Natural Hazards 61

   a. AL 129-1
   b. AASHTO Soil Classification System
   c. AL 333
   d. Insurance

50. _____ is the average and variations of weather over long periods of time. _____ zones can be defined using parameters such as temperature and rainfall.
   a. 1700 Cascadia earthquake
   b. 1509 Istanbul earthquake
   c. 1703 Genroku earthquake
   d. Climate

51. _____ is the increase in the average temperature of the Earth's near-surface air and oceans in recent decades and its projected continuation. An increase in global temperatures can in turn cause other changes, including sea level rise, and changes in the amount and pattern of precipitation resulting in floods and drought. There may also be changes in the frequency and intensity of extreme weather events.
   a. 1700 Cascadia earthquake
   b. 1703 Genroku earthquake
   c. 1509 Istanbul earthquake
   d. Global warming

52. _____ is any of a number of similar colors evoked by light consisting predominantly of the longest wavelengths of light discernible by the human eye, in the wavelength range of roughly 625-740 nm. Longer wavelengths than this are called infrared, or below _____ and cannot be seen by the naked human eye. _____ is used as one of the additive primary colors of light, complementary to cyan, in RGB color systems.
   a. 1509 Istanbul earthquake
   b. 1700 Cascadia earthquake
   c. 1703 Genroku earthquake
   d. Red

53. Mean _____ is the average height of the sea, with reference to a suitable reference surface.
   a. Sea level
   b. 1509 Istanbul earthquake
   c. 1703 Genroku earthquake
   d. 1700 Cascadia earthquake

54. _____ is the human modification of natural environment or wilderness into built environment such as fields, pastures, and settlements. The major effect of _____ on land cover since 1750 has been deforestation of temperate regions. More recent significant effects of _____ include urban sprawl, soil erosion, soil degradation, salinization, and desertification.
   a. 1703 Genroku earthquake
   b. 1700 Cascadia earthquake
   c. 1509 Istanbul earthquake
   d. Land use

55. The United Mexican States, commonly known as _____, is a federal constitutional republic in North America. It is bordered on the north by the United States; on the south and west by the North Pacific Ocean; on the southeast by Guatemala, Belize, and the Caribbean Sea; and on the east by the Gulf of _____. The United Mexican States are a federation comprising thirty-one states and a federal district, the capital _____ City, whose metropolitan area is one of the world's most populous.
   a. Andrija Mohorovičić
   b. Amblypoda
   c. Ambulocetus
   d. Mexico

56. _____ is the capital city of Mexico. It is the most important economic, industrial and cultural center in the country, and the most populous city with over 8,836,045 inhabitants in 2008. Greater _____ incorporates 59 adjacent municipalities of Mexico State and 1 municipality of the state of Hidalgo, according to the most recent definition agreed upon by the federal and state governments.

Chapter 4. Introduction to Natural Hazards

a. 1509 Istanbul earthquake
b. 1703 Genroku earthquake
c. 1700 Cascadia earthquake
d. Mexico City

57. In biology a _____ is the collection of inter-breeding organisms of a particular species; in sociology, a collection of human beings. A _____ shares a particular characteristic of interest, most often that of living in a given geographic area. In taxonomy _____ is a low-level taxonomic rank.
 a. Population
 b. 1509 Istanbul earthquake
 c. 1700 Cascadia earthquake
 d. Metapopulation

58. _____ is a measurement of population per unit area or unit volume. It is frequently applied to living organisms, humans in particular.
 a. Population decline
 b. Population momentum
 c. Population density
 d. Neo-Malthusianism

59. _____ is the change in population over time, and can be quantified as the change in the number of individuals in a population per unit time. The term _____ can technically refer to any species, but almost always refers to humans, and it is often used informally for the more specific demographic term _____ rate, and is often used to refer specifically to the growth of the population of the world.
 a. 1700 Cascadia earthquake
 b. 1509 Istanbul earthquake
 c. 1703 Genroku earthquake
 d. Population growth

60. _____ is a layer of gases surrounding the planet Earth and retained by the Earth's gravity, protecting life on Earth by absorbing ultraviolet solar radiation and reducing temperature extremes between day and night.
 a. AASHTO Soil Classification System
 b. AL 129-1
 c. AL 333
 d. Earths atmosphere

61. The _____ of a material is defined as its mass per unit volume:

$$\rho = \frac{m}{V}$$

Different materials usually have different densities, so _____ is an important concept regarding buoyancy, metal purity and packaging.

In some cases _____ is expressed as the dimensionless quantities specific gravity or relative _____, in which case it is expressed in multiples of the _____ of some other standard material, usually water or air.

In a well-known story, Archimedes was given the task of determining whether King Hiero's goldsmith was embezzling gold during the manufacture of a wreath dedicated to the gods and replacing it with another, cheaper alloy.

 a. 1509 Istanbul earthquake
 b. Density
 c. Particle density
 d. 1700 Cascadia earthquake

Chapter 4. Introduction to Natural Hazards

62. _____ is the degradation of land in arid, semi arid and dry sub-humid areas resulting from various climatic variations, but primarily human activities. Current _____ is taking place much faster worldwide than historically and usually arises from the demands of increased populations that settle on the land in order to grow crops and graze animals.
   a. 1703 Genroku earthquake
   b. 1700 Cascadia earthquake
   c. 1509 Istanbul earthquake
   d. Desertification

63. _____ is the conversion of forested areas to non-forest land use such as arable land, pasture, urban use, logged area or wasteland. _____ results from removal of trees without sufficient reforestation and results in declines in: habitat and biodiversity, wood for fuel and industrial use and decline in quality of life.
   a. 1703 Genroku earthquake
   b. 1700 Cascadia earthquake
   c. 1509 Istanbul earthquake
   d. Deforestation

64. In the _____ phase of emergency management, emergency managers develop plans of action for when the disaster strikes.
   a. 1703 Genroku earthquake
   b. 1509 Istanbul earthquake
   c. Disaster preparedness
   d. 1700 Cascadia earthquake

65. _____ is the process in which trees are cut down usually as part of a timber harvest. _____ can also remove wood for forest management goals. _____ is controversial due to its environmental and aesthetic impacts.
   a. 1509 Istanbul earthquake
   b. Logging
   c. 1703 Genroku earthquake
   d. 1700 Cascadia earthquake

66. The _____ is the longest river in Asia and the third longest in the world, after the Nile in Africa, and the Amazon in South America. The river is about 6,380 km long and flows from its source in Qinghai Province, eastwards into the East China Sea at Shanghai. It has traditionally been considered a dividing line between North and South China.
   a. 1700 Cascadia earthquake
   b. 1509 Istanbul earthquake
   c. Yangtze River
   d. 1703 Genroku earthquake

Chapter 5. Earthquakes and Related Phenomena

1. The _____ is the point on the Earth's surface that is directly above the point where an earthquake or other underground explosion originates or focus. It is directly above the hypocenter the actual location of the energy released inside the earth and usually suffers the maximum destruction.
   a. AL 129-1
   b. AL 333
   c. AASHTO Soil Classification System
   d. Epicenter

2. An _____ is the result from the sudden release of stored energy in the Earth's crust that creates seismic waves. At the Earth's surface, _____s may manifest themselves by a shaking or displacement of the ground. An _____ is caused by tectonic plates getting stuck and putting a strain on the ground. The strain becomes so great that rocks give way by breaking and sliding along fault planes.
   a. Earthquake
   b. AL 129-1
   c. AASHTO Soil Classification System
   d. AL 333

3. The _____ is a nonnegative scalar measure of a wave's magnitude of oscillation, that is, the magnitude of the maximum disturbance in the medium during one wave cycle. When _____ of sound wave changes, a listener would hear a change in pitch.
   a. AL 333
   b. Amplitude
   c. AL 129-1
   d. AASHTO Soil Classification System

4. _____ was introduced in 1979 by Tom Hanks and Hiroo Kanamori as a successor to the Richter scale and is used by seismologists to compare the energy released by earthquakes.
   a. Moment magnitude
   b. 1509 Istanbul earthquake
   c. 1703 Genroku earthquake
   d. 1700 Cascadia earthquake

5. The _____ scale, or more correctly local magnitude ML scale, assigns a single number to quantify the amount of seismic energy released by an earthquake. It is a base-10 logarithmic scale obtained by calculating the logarithm of the combined horizontal amplitude of the largest displacement from zero on a seismometer output
   a. 1700 Cascadia earthquake
   b. 1703 Genroku earthquake
   c. Richter magnitude
   d. 1509 Istanbul earthquake

6. A _____ is a graph output by a seismograph. It is a record of the ground motion at a measuring station. The energy measured in a _____ may result from an earthquake or from some other source, such as an explosion.
   a. 1703 Genroku earthquake
   b. 1700 Cascadia earthquake
   c. Seismogram
   d. 1509 Istanbul earthquake

7. A _____ is used by seismologists to measure and record the size and force of seismic waves.
   a. 1703 Genroku earthquake
   b. 1700 Cascadia earthquake
   c. 1509 Istanbul earthquake
   d. Seismograph

8. _____ is the scientific study of earthquakes and the propagation of elastic waves through the Earth.
   a. 1700 Cascadia earthquake
   b. 1509 Istanbul earthquake
   c. 1703 Genroku earthquake
   d. Seismology

9. _____ (æ—¥æœ¬ Nihon or Nippon making it an archipelago. The largest islands are HonshÅ«, HokkaidÅ, KyÅ«shÅ« and Shikoku, together accounting for 97% of _____'s land area. Most of the islands are mountainous, many volcanic; for example, _____'s highest peak, Mount Fuji, is a volcano.

Chapter 5. Earthquakes and Related Phenomena

    a. Kabul
    b. Java
    c. Kenya
    d. Japan

10. _____ (ç¥žæˆ¸å¸, KÅ be-shi For most of its history the area was never a single political entity, even during the Tokugawa Period, when the port was controlled directly by the Tokugawa Shogunate. _____ did not exist in its current form until its founding in 1889. Its name comes from 'kanbe' HyÅ go Port in the 19th century The Bund in _____ around 1890

Stone artifacts and tools found in western _____ demonstrate that the area was populated at least from the JÅ mon period.

    a. Peninsula
    b. Japan
    c. Kobe
    d. Korean War

11. The _____ was an earthquake in Japan that measured 6.9 on the Richter magnitude scale and 7.2 on the Japanese seismic intensity scale. It occurred on January 17, 1995 at 5:46:46 a.m. in the southern part of Hyogo Prefecture and lasted for approximately 20 seconds.
    a. 1509 Istanbul earthquake
    b. Kobe earthquake
    c. 1703 Genroku earthquake
    d. 1700 Cascadia earthquake

12. A _____ or geophysical hazards is a threat of an event that will have a negative effect on people or the environment. Many _____s are related, e.g. earthquakes can result in tsunamis, drought can lead directly to famine and disease. A concrete example of the division between hazard and disaster is that the 1906 San Francisco earthquake was a disaster, whereas earthquakes are a hazard.
    a. 1700 Cascadia earthquake
    b. 1703 Genroku earthquake
    c. 1509 Istanbul earthquake
    d. Natural hazard

13. The _____ is a scale used for measuring the intensity of an earthquake. The scale quantifies the effects of an earthquake on the Earth's surface, humans, objects of nature, and man-made structures on a scale of 1 through 12, with 1 denoting a weak earthquake and 12 one that causes almost complete destruction.
    a. Mercalli intensity scale
    b. 1703 Genroku earthquake
    c. 1509 Istanbul earthquake
    d. 1700 Cascadia earthquake

14. _____ is a Northern California mountain with elevation 3,786 feet and located at approximately 37.114° N, 121.846 W in the Santa Cruz Mountains. The peak is located on private property, about 11 miles west of Morgan Hill and within the boundaries of Santa Clara County.
    a. Loma Prieta
    b. 1700 Cascadia earthquake
    c. 1509 Istanbul earthquake
    d. 1703 Genroku earthquake

15. The _____ was a major earthquake affecting the greater San Francisco Bay Area of California. It occurred on Tuesday October 17, 1989 at 5:04 p.m. and measured 6.9 on the Moment magnitude scale. It lasted approximately 15 seconds and its epicenter was at located in Forest of Nisene Marks State Park, in the Santa Cruz Mountains.
    a. 1509 Istanbul earthquake
    b. 1703 Genroku earthquake
    c. Loma Prieta earthquake
    d. 1700 Cascadia earthquake

16. _____ is a theory of geology that has been developed to explain the observed evidence for large scale motions of the Earth's lithosphere. The theory encompassed and superseded the older theory of continental drift.
   a. 1700 Cascadia earthquake
   b. Plate tectonics
   c. 1509 Istanbul earthquake
   d. 1703 Genroku earthquake

17. The _____ is a geologic transform fault that runs a length of roughly 800 miles (1,300 km) through California in the United States. The fault's motion is right-lateral strike-slip (horizontal motion.) It forms the tectonic boundary between the Pacific Plate and the North American Plate.
   a. 1703 Genroku earthquake
   b. San Andreas fault
   c. 1509 Istanbul earthquake
   d. 1700 Cascadia earthquake

18. _____ is the largest city by population in the U.S state of Washington and the Northwestern United States. The encompassing _____-Tacoma-Bellevue metropolitan statistical area is the 15th largest in the United States, and the largest in the Pacific Northwest. _____ is part of the 13th largest combined statistical area in the us.
   a. 1700 Cascadia earthquake
   b. Seattle
   c. 1509 Istanbul earthquake
   d. 1703 Genroku earthquake

19. _____s are planar rock fractures, which show evidence of relative movement. Large _____s within the Earth's crust are the result of shear motion and active _____ zones are the causal locations of most earthquakes. Earthquakes are caused by energy release during rapid slippage along _____s.
   a. 1700 Cascadia earthquake
   b. 1509 Istanbul earthquake
   c. Fault
   d. 1703 Genroku earthquake

20. An _____ is an earthquake that occurs at the boundary between two tectonic plates. If one plate is trying to move past the other, they will be locked until sufficient stress builds up to cause the plates to slip relative to each other. The slipping process creates an earthquake with land deformations and resulting seismic waves which travel through the Earth and along the Earth's surface.
   a. Oceanic crust
   b. AASHTO Soil Classification System
   c. AL 129-1
   d. Interplate earthquake

21. _____ is the capital and largest city of Spain. It is the third-most populous municipality in the European Union after London and Berlin, and the fourth-most populous urban area in the European Union after Paris, London, and the Ruhr Area.

The city is located on the river Manzanares both in the centre of the country and Community of _____; this community is bordered by the autonomous communities of Castile and León and Castile-La Mancha.

   a. Madrid
   b. 1700 Cascadia earthquake
   c. 1703 Genroku earthquake
   d. 1509 Istanbul earthquake

22. The _____ is the second-longest named river in North America, with a length of 2320 miles from Lake Itasca to the Gulf of Mexico. It drains most of the area between the Rocky Mountains and the Appalachian Mountains, except for the areas drained by Hudson Bay via the Red River of the North, the Great Lakes and the Rio Grande.
   a. 1700 Cascadia earthquake
   b. Mississippi River
   c. 1509 Istanbul earthquake
   d. 1703 Genroku earthquake

Chapter 5. Earthquakes and Related Phenomena

23. The _____ is a major seismic zone in the Southern United States and Midwestern United States. The _____ system was responsible for the 1812 New Madrid Earthquake and has the potential to produce damaging earthquakes on an average of every 300 to 500 years.
    a. New Madrid fault
    b. 1700 Cascadia earthquake
    c. 1509 Istanbul earthquake
    d. 1703 Genroku earthquake

24. Seismology is the scientific study of earthquakes and the propagation of elastic waves through the Earth. The field also includes studies of earthquake effects, such as tsunamis as well as diverse _____ sources such as volcanic, tectonic, oceanic, atmospheric, and artificial processes (such as explosions.) A related field that uses geology to infer information regarding past earthquakes is paleoseismology.
    a. 1509 Istanbul earthquake
    b. Seismic
    c. 1703 Genroku earthquake
    d. 1700 Cascadia earthquake

25. A _____ travels through the Earth, most often as the result of a tectonic earthquake, sometimes from an explosion. They are also continually excited by the pounding of ocean waves and the wind.
    a. 1509 Istanbul earthquake
    b. 1703 Genroku earthquake
    c. 1700 Cascadia earthquake
    d. Seismic wave

26. A _____ is a disturbance that propagates through space or spacetime, transferring energy and momentum and sometimes angular momentum.
    a. 1703 Genroku earthquake
    b. 1509 Istanbul earthquake
    c. 1700 Cascadia earthquake
    d. Wave

27. An _____ is a fault which has had displacement or seismic activity during the geologically recent period. In the United States, an _____ is generally defined as a fault which displaced earth materials during the Holocene Epoch. An _____ is the most common source of earthquakes and tectonic movements.
    a. AL 333
    b. Active fault
    c. AL 129-1
    d. AASHTO Soil Classification System

28. An _____ is a fold that is convex up or to the youngest beds. _____s are usually recognized by a sequence of rock layers that are progressively older toward the center of the fold because the uplifted core of the fold is preferentially eroded to a deeper stratigraphic level relative to the topographically lower flanks. If an _____ plunges, the surface strata will form Vs that point in the direction of the plunge.
    a. Anticline
    b. AL 129-1
    c. AL 333
    d. AASHTO Soil Classification System

29. A _____ fault occurs when two rocks move apart vertically, parallel to the fault plane dip.
    a. Dip-slip
    b. 1703 Genroku earthquake
    c. 1509 Istanbul earthquake
    d. 1700 Cascadia earthquake

30. _____ can refer to: a period of time; a distinctive historical period or era, a unit of the geologic time scale, less than a period and greater than an age, or a phase in the development of the universe with distinctive properties.
    a. AL 333
    b. Epoch
    c. AL 129-1
    d. AASHTO Soil Classification System

31. The _____ is part of the Neogene and Quaternary periods. Human civilization dates entirely within the _____. The _____ was preceded by the Younger Dryas cold period, the final part of the Pleistocene epoch. The _____ starts late in the retreat of the Pleistocene glaciers. It can be considered an interglacial in the current ice age.
   a. 1700 Cascadia earthquake
   b. 1509 Istanbul earthquake
   c. 1703 Genroku earthquake
   d. Holocene

32. Dip-slip faults can be again classified into the types 'reverse' and 'normal'. A _____ occurs when the crust is extended. Alternatively such a fault can be called an extensional fault.
   a. 1509 Istanbul earthquake
   b. 1700 Cascadia earthquake
   c. 1703 Genroku earthquake
   d. Normal fault

33. The _____ on the geologic timescale had been intended to cover the world's recent period of repeated glaciations. The _____ follows the Pliocene and is followed by the Holocene. The _____ is the third epoch of the Neogene period or 6th epoch of the Cenozoic era. The end of the _____ corresponds with the end of the Paleolithic age used in archaeology. The _____ is divided into the Early _____, Middle _____ and Late _____, and numerous faunal stages.
   a. 1703 Genroku earthquake
   b. 1700 Cascadia earthquake
   c. 1509 Istanbul earthquake
   d. Pleistocene

34. A _____ is a planar rock fracture, which show evidence of relative movement. Large ones within the Earth's crust are the result of shear motion and active fault zones are the causal locations of most earthquakes. Earthquakes are caused by energy release during rapid slippage along a fault.
   a. 1703 Genroku earthquake
   b. 1700 Cascadia earthquake
   c. 1509 Istanbul earthquake
   d. Geologic fault

35. In structural geology, a _____ is a downward-curving fold, with layers that dip toward the center of the structure. On a geologic map, _____s are recognized by a sequence of rock layers that grow progressively younger, followed by the youngest layer at the fold's center or hinge, and by a reverse sequence of the same rock layers on the opposite side of the hinge.
   a. 1700 Cascadia earthquake
   b. 1509 Istanbul earthquake
   c. 1703 Genroku earthquake
   d. Syncline

36. A _____ fault is a particular type of fault, or break in the fabric of the Earth's crust with resulting movement of each side against the other, in which a lower stratigraphic position is pushed up and over another. This is the result of compressional forces.
   a. 1509 Istanbul earthquake
   b. 1703 Genroku earthquake
   c. Thrust
   d. 1700 Cascadia earthquake

37. A _____ is a particular type of fault, or break in the fabric of the Earth's crust with resulting movement of each side against the other, in which a lower stratigraphic position is pushed up and over another. This is the result of compressional forces.
   a. 1509 Istanbul earthquake
   b. Thrust fault
   c. 1703 Genroku earthquake
   d. 1700 Cascadia earthquake

38. _____, is the slow downward progression of rock and soil down a low grade slope; it can also refer to slow deformation of such materials as a result of prolonged pressure and stress.

Chapter 5. Earthquakes and Related Phenomena 69

    a. 1703 Genroku earthquake
    b. Creep
    c. 1509 Istanbul earthquake
    d. 1700 Cascadia earthquake

39. _____ is a field of study within geology concerned generally with the structures within the crust of the Earth, or other planets, and particularly with the forces and movements that have operated in a region to create these structures.
    a. 1509 Istanbul earthquake
    b. 1700 Cascadia earthquake
    c. 1703 Genroku earthquake
    d. Tectonics

40. _____ are waves that have vibrations along or parallel to their direction of travel. They include waves in which the motion of the medium is in the same direction as the motion of the wave.
    a. 1700 Cascadia earthquake
    b. 1509 Istanbul earthquake
    c. 1703 Genroku earthquake
    d. Compressional waves

41. The _____ is one of the two main types of elastic body waves, so named because they move through the body of an object, unlike surface waves. It moves as a shear or transverse wave, so motion is perpendicular to the direction of wave propagation: S-shaped, like waves in a rope, as opposed to waves moving through a slinky, the P-wave.
    a. 1703 Genroku earthquake
    b. 1700 Cascadia earthquake
    c. 1509 Istanbul earthquake
    d. S waves

42. A type of seismic wave is one of the two main types of elastic body waves, so named because they move through the body of an object, unlike surface waves. The _____ moves as a shear or transverse wave, so motion is perpendicular to the direction of wave propagation. The wave moves through elastic mediums, and the main restoring force comes from shear effects.
    a. 1703 Genroku earthquake
    b. 1700 Cascadia earthquake
    c. 1509 Istanbul earthquake
    d. S-wave

43. In physics, _____ can refer to a mechanical wave that propagates along the interface between differing media, usually two fluids with different densities. A _____ can also be an electromagnetic wave guided by a refractive index gradient.
    a. 1703 Genroku earthquake
    b. 1700 Cascadia earthquake
    c. Surface wave
    d. 1509 Istanbul earthquake

44. _____ is the measurement of the number of occurrences of a repeated event per unit of time. It is also defined as the rate of change of phase of a sinusoidal waveform.
    a. 1509 Istanbul earthquake
    b. 1700 Cascadia earthquake
    c. Frequency
    d. 1703 Genroku earthquake

45. Motto: Fluctuat nec mergitur The Eiffel Tower and the skyscrapers of Paris' suburban La Défense business district. _____ Time Zone CET Coordinates °52'0"N 2°19'59"E">48°52'0"N 2°19'59"Eï»¿ / ï»¿48.86667, 2.33306 Administration Country France Region Île-de-France Department Paris Subdivisions 20 arrondissements Mayor Bertrand Delanoë
City Statistics Land area km) Urban Spread Urban Area 2,723 km The Paris unité urbaine extends well beyond the administrative city limits and has an estimated population of 9.93 million. The Paris aire urbaine has a population of nearly 12 million, and is one of the most populated metropolitan areas in Europe.

An important settlement for more than two millennia, Paris is today one of the world's leading business and cultural centres, and its influence in politics, education, entertainment, media, fashion, science and the arts all contribute to its status as one of the world's major global cities.

　a. 1703 Genroku earthquake
　b. 1700 Cascadia earthquake
　c. 1509 Istanbul earthquake
　d. Location

46. _____ is the reduction in amplitude and intensity of a signal.
　a. AL 333
　b. AASHTO Soil Classification System
　c. Attenuation
　d. AL 129-1

47. A _____ is an urban area with a high population and a particular administrative, legal, or historical status.

Large industrialized cities generally have advanced systems for sanitation, utilities, land usage, housing, and transportation and more. This close proximity greatly facilitates interaction between people and firms, benefiting both parties in the process.

　a. 1703 Genroku earthquake
　b. 1700 Cascadia earthquake
　c. City
　d. 1509 Istanbul earthquake

48. A _____ is a geological phenomenon which includes a wide range of ground movement, such as rock falls, deep failure of slopes and shallow debris flows. Although gravity's action on an over-steepened slope is the primary reason for a _____, there are other contributing factors affecting the original slope stability.

　a. 1509 Istanbul earthquake
　b. Landslide
　c. 1703 Genroku earthquake
　d. 1700 Cascadia earthquake

49. The United Mexican States , commonly known as _____ , is a federal constitutional republic in North America. It is bordered on the north by the United States; on the south and west by the North Pacific Ocean; on the southeast by Guatemala, Belize, and the Caribbean Sea; and on the east by the Gulf of _____. The United Mexican States are a federation comprising thirty-one states and a federal district, the capital _____ City, whose metropolitan area is one of the world's most populous.

　a. Andrija Mohorovičić
　b. Mexico
　c. Ambulocetus
　d. Amblypoda

50. _____ is the capital city of Mexico. It is the most important economic, industrial and cultural center in the country, and the most populous city with over 8,836,045 inhabitants in 2008. Greater _____ incorporates 59 adjacent municipalities of Mexico State and 1 municipality of the state of Hidalgo, according to the most recent definition agreed upon by the federal and state governments.

　a. 1700 Cascadia earthquake
　b. Mexico City
　c. 1703 Genroku earthquake
　d. 1509 Istanbul earthquake

51. _____ is a layer of gases surrounding the planet Earth and retained by the Earth's gravity, protecting life on Earth by absorbing ultraviolet solar radiation and reducing temperature extremes between day and night.

Chapter 5. Earthquakes and Related Phenomena

a. AASHTO Soil Classification System
b. AL 129-1
c. AL 333
d. Earths atmosphere

52. Peak _____ is a measure of earthquake acceleration. Unlike the Richter magnitude scale, it is not a measure of the total size of the earthquake, but rather how hard the earth shakes in a given geographic area.
   a. 1700 Cascadia earthquake
   b. 1509 Istanbul earthquake
   c. 1703 Genroku earthquake
   d. Ground acceleration

53. _____ is a transcontinental country extending over much of northern Eurasia. It is a semi-presidential republic comprising 83 federal subjects. _____ shares land borders with the following countries: Norway, Finland, Estonia, Latvia, Lithuania, Poland, Belarus, Ukraine, Georgia, Azerbaijan, Kazakhstan, China, Mongolia and North Korea.
   a. 1703 Genroku earthquake
   b. 1509 Istanbul earthquake
   c. Russia
   d. 1700 Cascadia earthquake

54. _____ is a large elongated island in the North Pacific, lying between 45°50' and 54°24' N.
   a. 1509 Istanbul earthquake
   b. 1703 Genroku earthquake
   c. 1700 Cascadia earthquake
   d. Sakhalin

55. An _____ is an earthquake that occurs after a previous earthquake. An _____ is in the same region of the main shock but is always of smaller magnitude. It occurs with a pattern that follows Omori's law. Omori's law, or more correctly the modified Omori's law, is an empirical relation for the temporal decay of _____ rates.
   a. Aftershock
   b. AASHTO Soil Classification System
   c. AL 333
   d. AL 129-1

56. _____ are earthquakes in the same region of the central shock but of smaller magnitude and which occur with a pattern that follows Omori's law.
   a. AL 129-1
   b. Aftershocks
   c. AL 333
   d. AASHTO Soil Classification System

57. In geology, the _____ theory was the first theory to satisfactorily explain earthquakes. The theory is that earthquake are the result of the _____ of previously stored elastic strain energy in the rocks on either side of the fault. In an interseismic period the earth's plates move relative to each other except at most plate boundaries where they are locked.
   a. AL 129-1
   b. AASHTO Soil Classification System
   c. AL 333
   d. Elastic rebound

58. A _____ is a smaller earthquake preceding a much larger earthquake. Many scientists hope to use them to predict upcoming earthquakes.
   a. 1703 Genroku earthquake
   b. Foreshock
   c. 1509 Istanbul earthquake
   d. 1700 Cascadia earthquake

59. _____ is a concept for disposing of High Level Radioactive Waste from Nuclear reactors. The system seeks to place the waste as much as five kilometers beneath the surface of the Earth and relies primarily on the immense natural geological barrier to do most of the work of confining the waste safely and permanently so that it will never pose a threat to the environment.

a. 1509 Istanbul earthquake
b. 1703 Genroku earthquake
c. 1700 Cascadia earthquake
d. Deep waste disposal

60. A _____ is a bipedal primate belonging to the mammalian species Homo sapiens in the family Hominidae. Compared to other living organisms on Earth, a _____ has a highly developed brain capable of abstract reasoning, language, and introspection.
   a. 1703 Genroku earthquake
   b. 1700 Cascadia earthquake
   c. 1509 Istanbul earthquake
   d. Human

61. _____ is the human modification of natural environment or wilderness into built environment such as fields, pastures, and settlements. The major effect of _____ on land cover since 1750 has been deforestation of temperate regions. More recent significant effects of _____ include urban sprawl, soil erosion, soil degradation, salinization, and desertification.
   a. 1703 Genroku earthquake
   b. 1700 Cascadia earthquake
   c. Land use
   d. 1509 Istanbul earthquake

62. A _____ occurs as a result of the rapid release of energy from an uncontrolled nuclear reaction. The driving reaction may be nuclear fission, nuclear fusion or a multistage cascading combination of the two.
   a. Nuclear explosion
   b. 1700 Cascadia earthquake
   c. 1509 Istanbul earthquake
   d. 1703 Genroku earthquake

63. _____ are a class of astronomical objects. The term is generally used to indicate a diverse group of small celestial bodies that drift in the solar system in orbit around the Sun.
   a. Asteroids
   b. AL 333
   c. AL 129-1
   d. AASHTO Soil Classification System

64. The _____ is defined as the part of the land adjoining or near the ocean. A coastline is properly a line on a map indicating the disposition of a _____, but the word is often used to refer to the _____ itself. The adjective coastal describes something as being on, near to, or associated with a _____.
   a. 1509 Istanbul earthquake
   b. 1700 Cascadia earthquake
   c. 1703 Genroku earthquake
   d. Coast

65. _____ is the wearing away of land or the removal of beach or dune sediments by wave action, tidal currents, wave currents, or drainage. Waves, generated by storms or fast moving moter craft, cause _____, which may take the form of long-term losses of sediment and rocks, or merely in the temporary redistribution of coastal sediments; erosion in one location may result in accretion nearby.
   a. 1509 Istanbul earthquake
   b. 1700 Cascadia earthquake
   c. 1703 Genroku earthquake
   d. Beach erosion

66. _____ is displacement of solids by the agents of ocean currents, wind, water, or ice by downward or down-slope movement in response to gravity or by living organisms.
   a. Erosion
   b. AL 333
   c. AASHTO Soil Classification System
   d. AL 129-1

67. An _____ is a sudden increase in volume and release of energy in an extreme manner, usually with the generation of high temperatures and the release of gases. An _____ creates a shock wave.

Chapter 5. Earthquakes and Related Phenomena

_____s do not commonly occur in nature.

   a. AL 129-1
   c. Chemical hazard
   b. AASHTO Soil Classification System
   d. Explosion

68. _____ is unwanted or undesired material.
   a. 1509 Istanbul earthquake
   c. Waste
   b. 1700 Cascadia earthquake
   d. 1703 Genroku earthquake

69. _____ is when a mass of water in a reservoir alters the pressure in the rock below, which can trigger earthquakes.
   a. 1700 Cascadia earthquake
   c. 1703 Genroku earthquake
   b. 1509 Istanbul earthquake
   d. Reservoir induced seismicity

70. The _____ was a United States chemical weapons manufacturing center located in the Denver Metropolitan Area in Commerce City, Colorado. The site was operated by the United States Army throughout the later 20th century and was controversial among local residents until its closure.
   a. Rocky Mountain Arsenal
   c. 1703 Genroku earthquake
   b. 1509 Istanbul earthquake
   d. 1700 Cascadia earthquake

71. _____ is a class of diseases in which a group of cells display the traits of uncontrolled growth growth and division beyond the normal limits, invasion intrusion on and destruction of adjacent tissues, and sometimes metastasis spread to other locations in the body via lymph or blood. These three malignant properties of _____s differentiate them from benign tumors, which are self-limited, do not invade or metastasize. Most _____s form a tumor but some, like leukemia, do not.
   a. 1700 Cascadia earthquake
   c. Cancer
   b. 1703 Genroku earthquake
   d. 1509 Istanbul earthquake

72. A _____ or medical condition is an abnormal condition of an organism that impairs bodily functions and can be deadly. It is also defined as a way of the body harming itself in an abnormal way, associated with specific symptoms and signs.

In human beings,'_____' is often used more broadly to refer to any condition that causes extreme pain, dysfunction, distress, social problems, and/or death to the person afflicted, or similar problems for those in contact with the person.

   a. 1700 Cascadia earthquake
   c. Disease
   b. Black lung disease
   d. 1509 Istanbul earthquake

73. A _____ is the topographic expression of faulting due to the displacement of the land surface by movement along the fault. It can be caused by differential erosion along an old inactive fault with hard & weak rock, or by an active geologic fault. In many cases, bluffs form from the upthrown block and can be very steep.
   a. 1703 Genroku earthquake
   c. 1700 Cascadia earthquake
   b. Fault scarp
   d. 1509 Istanbul earthquake

Chapter 5. Earthquakes and Related Phenomena

74. An _____ is a transition zone between different physiogeographic provinces that involves an elevation differential, often involving high cliffs. Most commonly, an _____, is a transition from one series of sedimentary rocks to another series of a different age and composition. In such cases, the _____ usually represents the line of erosional loss of the newer rock over the older.
   a. AL 129-1
   b. Escarpment
   c. AL 333
   d. AASHTO Soil Classification System

75. _____ describes the behavior of soils that, when loaded, suddenly suffer a transition from a solid state to a liquefied state, or having the consistency of a heavy liquid. Liquefaction is more likely to occur in loose to moderate saturated granular soils with poor drainage, such as silty sands or sands and gravels capped or containing seams of impermeable sediments . During loading, usually cyclic undrained loading, e.g. earthquake loading, loose sands tend to decrease in volume, which produces an increase in their porewater pressures and consequently a decrease in shear strength, i.e. reduction in effective stress.
   a. 1700 Cascadia earthquake
   b. 1703 Genroku earthquake
   c. Soil liquefaction
   d. 1509 Istanbul earthquake

76. _____ I salβİžaË^ðÌžoÌžÉ¾]) is a country in Central America. The area was originally called by the Pipil 'Cuzhcatl', in Spanish 'Cuzcatlan', which in Nahuatl means 'the land of precious things.'

After the Spanish conquest, the land was baptized by Spanish conquistadors as 'Provincia De Nuestro Señor Jesucristo _____ Del Mundo', now abbreviated as 'República de _____'.

The country borders the Pacific Ocean between Guatemala and Honduras.

   a. AL 129-1
   b. AL 333
   c. AASHTO Soil Classification System
   d. El Salvador

77. _____ can be a change from a gas to a liquid through condensation, usually by cooling, or a change from a solid to a liquid through melting, usually by heating or by grinding and blending with another liquid to induce dissolution.
   a. 1700 Cascadia earthquake
   b. 1703 Genroku earthquake
   c. 1509 Istanbul earthquake
   d. Liquefaction

78. _____ is a city on the northeast coast of Brazil and the capital of the Northeastern Brazilian state of Bahia. _____ is also known as Brazil's capital of happiness due to its easygoing population and countless popular outdoor parties, including its street carnival. The first colonial capital of Brazil, the city is one of the oldest in the country and in the New World; for a long time, it was also known as Bahia, and appears under that name on many maps and books from before the mid-20th century.
   a. Ambulocetus
   b. Salvador
   c. Amblypoda
   d. Andrija MohoroviÄ iÄ‡

79. In geology, engineering, and surveying, _____ is the motion of a surface as it shifts downward relative to a datum such as sea-level. The opposite of _____ is uplift, which results in an increase in elevation. In meteorology, _____ refers to the downward movement of air.
   a. 1703 Genroku earthquake
   b. 1700 Cascadia earthquake
   c. 1509 Istanbul earthquake
   d. Subsidence

Chapter 5. Earthquakes and Related Phenomena

80. A _____ is a series of waves created when a body of water, such as an ocean, is rapidly displaced on a massive scale. Earthquakes, mass movements above or below water, volcanic eruptions and other underwater explosions, landslides, large meteorite impacts and testing with nuclear weapons at sea all have the potential to generate a _____. The effects of a _____ can range from unnoticeable to devastating.
   a. 1703 Genroku earthquake
   b. Tsunami
   c. 1509 Istanbul earthquake
   d. 1700 Cascadia earthquake

81. In materials science, _____ is a change in the shape or size of an object due to an applied force. This can be a result of tensile (pulling) forces, compressive (pushing) forces, shear, bending or torsion (twisting.) _____ is often described as strain.
   a. 1703 Genroku earthquake
   b. 1700 Cascadia earthquake
   c. 1509 Istanbul earthquake
   d. Deformation

82. _____ is a general term that includes rocks and materials that are not by definition rocks but are commonly regarded as rocks.
   a. AASHTO Soil Classification System
   b. Earth materials
   c. AL 333
   d. AL 129-1

83. An _____ is a prediction that an earthquake of a specific magnitude will occur in a particular place at a particular time (or ranges thereof.) Despite considerable research efforts by seismologists, scientifically reproducible predictions cannot yet be made to a specific hour, day seismic hazard assessment maps can estimate the probability that an earthquake of a given size will affect a given location over a certain number of years.

Once a earthquake has already begun, early warning devices can provide a few seconds' warning before major shaking arrives at a given location.

   a. AL 129-1
   b. AL 333
   c. AASHTO Soil Classification System
   d. Earthquake prediction

84. A _____ is a statement or claim that a particular event will occur in the future in more certain terms than a forecast. The etymology of this word is Latin (from præ- 'before' plus dicere 'to say'.) In regards to predicting the future Howard H. Stevenson Says, '_____ is at least two things: Important and hard.' Important, because we have to act, and hard because we have to realize the future we want, and what is the best way to get there.
   a. Prediction
   b. 1703 Genroku earthquake
   c. 1509 Istanbul earthquake
   d. 1700 Cascadia earthquake

85. _____ is a concept that denotes the precise probability of specific eventualities. Technically, the notion of _____ is independent from the notion of value and, as such, eventualities may have both beneficial and adverse consequences. However, in general usage the convention is to focus only on potential negative impact to some characteristic of value that may arise from a future event.
   a. 1509 Istanbul earthquake
   b. 1703 Genroku earthquake
   c. 1700 Cascadia earthquake
   d. Risk

86. When building a house, regional _____ maps are used to find the best place to locate for earthquake shaking. Although greatly confused with its sister, seismic risk, _____ is the study of expected earthquake ground motions at any point on the earth.

Chapter 5. Earthquakes and Related Phenomena

   a. 1703 Genroku earthquake
   c. 1700 Cascadia earthquake
   b. 1509 Istanbul earthquake
   d. Seismic hazard

87. A _____ is a visual representation of an area--a symbolic depiction highlighting relationships between elements of that space such as objects, regions, and themes.

Many _____s are static two-dimensional, geometrically accurate representations of three-dimensional space, while others are dynamic or interactive, even three-dimensional. Although most commonly used to depict geography, _____s may represent any space, real or imagined, without regard to context or scale; e.g. Brain mapping, DNA mapping, and extraterrestrial mapping.

   a. 1509 Istanbul earthquake
   c. Cartography
   b. Map
   d. 1700 Cascadia earthquake

88. The 1975 _____ measuring 7.3 on the Richter Scale occurred at 19:36 CST on February 4, 1975 in Haicheng, Liaoning, China, a city that at the time had approximately 1 million residents.

Seismologists sent out warnings about this earthquake a day. Because of this correct prediction, many lives were saved.

   a. 1703 Genroku earthquake
   c. Haicheng earthquake
   b. 1509 Istanbul earthquake
   d. 1700 Cascadia earthquake

89. A _____ is a very low intensity earthquake which is usually three or less on the Richter scale. They are at times caused by large masses stomping their feet, the first such recorded instance being the Earthquake Game in 1988. They do not usually hurt anyone.
   a. 1700 Cascadia earthquake
   c. 1509 Istanbul earthquake
   b. 1703 Genroku earthquake
   d. Microearthquake

90. _____ refers to a major group of organisms. In general they are multicellular, responsive to their environment, and feed by consuming other organisms or parts of them. Their body plan becomes fixed as they develop, usually early on in their development as embryos, although some undergo a process of metamorphosis later on.
   a. AL 129-1
   c. AL 333
   b. AASHTO Soil Classification System
   d. Animal

91. _____ is located on Honshû island on the coast of the Sea of Japan. _____ stretches about 240 km along the Sea of Japan from southwest to north east, with a coastal plain between the mountains and the sea. It also includes Sado Island.
   a. Green River
   c. Craters of the Moon
   b. Niigata
   d. High Plains

92. _____ is a chemical element in the periodic table that has the symbol Rn and atomic number 86. A radioactive noble gas that is formed by the decay of radium, _____ is one of the heaviest gases and is considered to be a health hazard.

Chapter 5. Earthquakes and Related Phenomena

a. Radon
b. Tantalum
c. Selenium
d. Ytterbium

93. The general effects of _____ to the human body are due to its radioactivity and consequent risk of radiation-induced cancer.
   a. 1703 Genroku earthquake
   b. 1509 Istanbul earthquake
   c. Radon emissions
   d. 1700 Cascadia earthquake

94. A _____ is a segment of an active geologic fault or subduction zone that has not slipped in an unusually long time; they are often considered susceptible to future strong earthquakes
   a. Seismic gap
   b. 1509 Istanbul earthquake
   c. 1700 Cascadia earthquake
   d. 1703 Genroku earthquake

95. An _____ phenomenon is an observed event which deviates from what is expected according to existing rules or scientific theory.
   a. AL 333
   b. Anomalous
   c. AASHTO Soil Classification System
   d. AL 129-1

96. _____ is a fossil fuel formed in swamp ecosystems where plant remains were saved by water and mud from oxidization and biodegradation. It is a sedimentary rock, but the harder forms, such as anthracite _____, can be regarded as metamorphic rocks because of later exposure to elevated temperature and pressure. It is composed primarily of carbon along with assorted other elements, including sulfur.
   a. 1703 Genroku earthquake
   b. 1509 Istanbul earthquake
   c. Coal
   d. 1700 Cascadia earthquake

97. _____ is commonly practiced where a coal seam outcrops a hilly terrain. It removes the overburden above the coal seam and then creates a bench arounf the hill.
   a. Contour strip mining
   b. 1509 Istanbul earthquake
   c. 1700 Cascadia earthquake
   d. 1703 Genroku earthquake

98. _____ is vibration transmitted through a solid, liquid composed of frequencies within the range of hearing and of a level sufficiently strong to be heard. Human ear

For humans, hearing is limited to frequencies between about 20 Hz and 20,000 Hz (20 kHz), with the upper limit generally decreasing with age. Other species have a different range of hearing.

   a. 1509 Istanbul earthquake
   b. Sound
   c. 1703 Genroku earthquake
   d. 1700 Cascadia earthquake

99. _____ is the extraction of valuable minerals or other geological materials from the earth, usually from an ore body, vein, or seam. Any material that cannot be grown from agricultural processes, or created artificially in a laboratory or factory, is usually extracted from the earth by this method.
   a. 1703 Genroku earthquake
   b. 1509 Istanbul earthquake
   c. 1700 Cascadia earthquake
   d. Mining

Chapter 5. Earthquakes and Related Phenomena

100. The general effects of _____ to the human body are due to its radioactivity and consequent risk of radiation-induced cancer.
   a. 1703 Genroku earthquake
   b. 1509 Istanbul earthquake
   c. 1700 Cascadia earthquake
   d. Radon gas emissions

101. _____ is the highest mountain in the U.S. state of Idaho. It is located in the central section of the Lost River Range and within the Challis National Forest. The peak is named for William Edgar Borah, a U.S. Senator from Idaho serving from 1907 to 1940.
   a. Borah Peak
   b. 1509 Istanbul earthquake
   c. 1703 Genroku earthquake
   d. 1700 Cascadia earthquake

102. The _____ is a major active right lateral-moving geologic fault in northern Anatolia which runs along the tectonic boundary between the Eurasian Plate and the Anatolian Plate. The fault extends westward from a junction with the East Anatolian Fault at the Karliova Triple Junction in eastern Turkey, across northern Turkey and into the Aegean Sea. It runs about 20 km south of Istanbul.
   a. 1509 Istanbul earthquake
   b. North Anatolian fault
   c. 1703 Genroku earthquake
   d. 1700 Cascadia earthquake

103. A _____ is either of two species of large birds in the genus Meleagris native to North America.
   a. Turkey
   b. 1509 Istanbul earthquake
   c. 1703 Genroku earthquake
   d. 1700 Cascadia earthquake

104. The _____ is a scientific agency of the United States government. The scientists of the USGS study the landscape of the United States, its natural resources, and the natural hazards that threaten it.
   a. U.S. Geological Survey
   b. Amblypoda
   c. Andrija Mohorovičić
   d. Ambulocetus

105. _____
   a. Armenia
   b. Andrija Mohorovičić
   c. Amblypoda
   d. Ambulocetus

106. The _____ was a tremor with a moment magnitude of 7.2 that took place on December 7, 1988 at 11:41 local time in the Spitak region of Armenia, then part of the Soviet Union.
   a. Armenia earthquake
   b. AASHTO Soil Classification System
   c. AL 333
   d. AL 129-1

107. _____, in law and economics, is a form of risk management primarily used to hedge against the risk of a contingent loss. _____ is defined as the equitable transfer of the risk of a loss, from one entity to another, in exchange for a premium, and can be thought of as a guaranteed small loss to prevent a large, possibly devastating loss. An insurer is a company selling the _____; an insured is the person or entity buying the _____.
   a. AASHTO Soil Classification System
   b. Insurance
   c. AL 333
   d. AL 129-1

108. _____ is the term used for a branch of public policy which encompasses various disciplines which seek to order and regulate the use of land in an efficient and ethical way.

Chapter 5. Earthquakes and Related Phenomena

a. 1700 Cascadia earthquake
b. 1509 Istanbul earthquake
c. 1703 Genroku earthquake
d. Land use planning

109. _____ is the identification of areas that have potentially hazardous earthquake effects.
   a. 1509 Istanbul earthquake
   b. 1700 Cascadia earthquake
   c. 1703 Genroku earthquake
   d. Microzonation

110. _____ is the third or vertical dimension of land surface. When _____ is described underwater, the term bathymetry is used.
   a. 1509 Istanbul earthquake
   b. 1703 Genroku earthquake
   c. Terrain
   d. 1700 Cascadia earthquake

111. A _____ is an extended period of months or years when a region notes a deficiency in its water supply. Generally, this occurs when a region receives consistently below average precipitation.
   a. 1509 Istanbul earthquake
   b. 1703 Genroku earthquake
   c. 1700 Cascadia earthquake
   d. Drought

112. A _____ is a storm system characterized by a low pressure center and numerous thunderstorms that produce strong winds and flooding rain. _____s feed on heat released when moist air rises, resulting in condensation of water vapour contained in the moist air. They are fueled by a different heat mechanism than other cyclonic windstorms such as nor'easters, European windstorms, and polar lows, leading to their classification as 'warm core' storm systems. Depending on its location and strength, a _____ is referred to by many other names, such as hurricane, typhoon, tropical storm, cyclonic storm, tropical depression, and simply cyclone.
   a. Khmer Empire
   b. Persia
   c. Kenya
   d. Tropical cyclone

113. A _____ is an opening in a planet's surface or crust, which allows hot, molten rock, ash, and gases to escape from below the surface. Volcanic activity involving the extrusion of rock tends to form mountains or features like mountains over a period of time.

   _____es are generally found where tectonic plates are diverging or converging.

   a. 1700 Cascadia earthquake
   b. 1703 Genroku earthquake
   c. 1509 Istanbul earthquake
   d. Volcano

114. _____ usually commence with phreatomagmatic eruptions which can be extremely noisy due the rising magma heating water in the ground. This is usually followed by the explosive throat clearing of the vent and the eruption column is dirty grey to black as old weathered rocks are blasted out of the vent. As the vent clears, further ash clouds become grey-white and creamy in colour, with convulations of the ash similar to those of plinian eruptions.
   a. Vulcanian eruptions
   b. 1700 Cascadia earthquake
   c. 1509 Istanbul earthquake
   d. 1703 Genroku earthquake

115. A _____ is any system of biological or technical nature deployed by an individual or group to inform of a future danger. Its purpose is to enable the deployer of the _____ to prepare for the danger and act accordingly to mitigate against or avoid it.

a. 1509 Istanbul earthquake
b. Warning system
c. 1703 Genroku earthquake
d. 1700 Cascadia earthquake

116. The _____ , headquartered at the University of Southern California, was founded in 1991 with a mission to:

- gather new information about earthquakes in Southern California;
- integrate this information into a comprehensive and predictive understanding of earthquake phenomena; and
- communicate this understanding to end-users in the earthquake engineering profession and the general public in order to increase earthquake awareness, reduce economic losses, and save lives.

An outstanding community of over 600 scientists from 16 Core Institutions, 40 Participating Institutions, and elsewhere participate in _____ Southern California Earthquake Center also partners with a large number of other research and education/outreach organizations in many disciplines. Funding for _____ activities is provided by the National Science Foundation and the United States Geological Survey.

To support this community, _____ engages in information technology research that will revolutionize our methods of doing collaborative research and distributing research products on-line.

a. 1509 Istanbul earthquake
b. 1703 Genroku earthquake
c. Southern California Earthquake Center
d. 1700 Cascadia earthquake

Chapter 6. Volcanic Activity

1. _____ is molten rock located beneath the surface of the Earth, and which often collects in a _____ chamber. _____ is a complex high-temperature fluid substance. Most are silicate solutions. It is capable of intrusion into adjacent rocks or of extrusion onto the surface as lava or ejected explosively as tephra to form pyroclastic rock. Environments of _____ formation include subduction zones, continental rift zones, mid-oceanic ridges, and hotspots, some of which are interpreted as mantle plumes.
    a. 1700 Cascadia earthquake
    b. 1509 Istanbul earthquake
    c. Magma
    d. 1703 Genroku earthquake

2. The _____ is a geologic transform fault that runs a length of roughly 800 miles (1,300 km) through California in the United States. The fault's motion is right-lateral strike-slip (horizontal motion.) It forms the tectonic boundary between the Pacific Plate and the North American Plate.
    a. San Andreas fault
    b. 1509 Istanbul earthquake
    c. 1703 Genroku earthquake
    d. 1700 Cascadia earthquake

3. A _____ is an opening in a planet's surface or crust, which allows hot, molten rock, ash, and gases to escape from below the surface. Volcanic activity involving the extrusion of rock tends to form mountains or features like mountains over a period of time.

    _____es are generally found where tectonic plates are diverging or converging.

    a. 1700 Cascadia earthquake
    b. 1703 Genroku earthquake
    c. 1509 Istanbul earthquake
    d. Volcano

4. _____ usually commence with phreatomagmatic eruptions which can be extremely noisy due the rising magma heating water in the ground. This is usually followed by the explosive throat clearing of the vent and the eruption column is dirty grey to black as old weathered rocks are blasted out of the vent. As the vent clears, further ash clouds become grey-white and creamy in colour, with convulations of the ash similar to those of plinian eruptions.
    a. 1700 Cascadia earthquake
    b. 1703 Genroku earthquake
    c. 1509 Istanbul earthquake
    d. Vulcanian eruptions

5. _____s are planar rock fractures, which show evidence of relative movement. Large _____s within the Earth's crust are the result of shear motion and active _____ zones are the causal locations of most earthquakes. Earthquakes are caused by energy release during rapid slippage along _____s.
    a. 1703 Genroku earthquake
    b. 1700 Cascadia earthquake
    c. 1509 Istanbul earthquake
    d. Fault

6. _____ is the measurement of the number of occurrences of a repeated event per unit of time. It is also defined as the rate of change of phase of a sinusoidal waveform.
    a. 1700 Cascadia earthquake
    b. Frequency
    c. 1703 Genroku earthquake
    d. 1509 Istanbul earthquake

7. Motto: Fluctuat nec mergitur The Eiffel Tower and the skyscrapers of Paris' suburban La Défense business district. _____ Time Zone CET Coordinates °52'0"N 2°19'59"E">48°52'0"N 2°19'59"Eï»¿ / ï»¿48.86667, 2.33306 Administration Country France Region Île-de-France Department Paris Subdivisions 20 arrondissements Mayor Bertrand Delanoë
City Statistics Land area km) Urban Spread Urban Area 2,723 km The Paris unité urbaine extends well beyond the administrative city limits and has an estimated population of 9.93 million. The Paris aire urbaine has a population of nearly 12 million, and is one of the most populated metropolitan areas in Europe.

An important settlement for more than two millennia, Paris is today one of the world's leading business and cultural centres, and its influence in politics, education, entertainment, media, fashion, science and the arts all contribute to its status as one of the world's major global cities.

    a. 1509 Istanbul earthquake
    b. 1703 Genroku earthquake
    c. Location
    d. 1700 Cascadia earthquake

8. A _____ or geophysical hazards is a threat of an event that will have a negative effect on people or the environment. Many _____s are related, e.g. earthquakes can result in tsunamis, drought can lead directly to famine and disease. A concrete example of the division between hazard and disaster is that the 1906 San Francisco earthquake was a disaster, whereas earthquakes are a hazard.
    a. 1703 Genroku earthquake
    b. 1509 Istanbul earthquake
    c. Natural hazard
    d. 1700 Cascadia earthquake

9. _____ is a theory of geology that has been developed to explain the observed evidence for large scale motions of the Earth's lithosphere. The theory encompassed and superseded the older theory of continental drift.
    a. 1509 Istanbul earthquake
    b. 1700 Cascadia earthquake
    c. 1703 Genroku earthquake
    d. Plate tectonics

10. _____ is a field of study within geology concerned generally with the structures within the crust of the Earth, or other planets, and particularly with the forces and movements that have operated in a region to create these structures.
    a. 1703 Genroku earthquake
    b. 1509 Istanbul earthquake
    c. 1700 Cascadia earthquake
    d. Tectonics

11. A popular way of classifying magmatic volcanoes goes by their frequency of eruption, or _____, with those that erupt regularly called active, those that have erupted in historical times but are now quiet called dormant, and those that have not erupted in historical times called extinct.
    a. Volcanic activity
    b. 1700 Cascadia earthquake
    c. 1509 Istanbul earthquake
    d. 1703 Genroku earthquake

12. _____ is molten rock expelled by a volcano during an eruption. When first extruded from a volcanic vent, it is a liquid at temperatures from 700 °C to 1,200 °C.
    a. Lava
    b. 1700 Cascadia earthquake
    c. 1509 Istanbul earthquake
    d. 1703 Genroku earthquake

13. The _____ is an oceanic tectonic plate beneath the Pacific Ocean.
    a. 1509 Istanbul earthquake
    b. 1700 Cascadia earthquake
    c. 1703 Genroku earthquake
    d. Pacific plate

14. A _____ is generally a large area of exposed Precambrian crystalline igneous and high-grade metamorphic rocks that form tectonically stable areas.
    a. Shield
    b. 1700 Cascadia earthquake
    c. 1703 Genroku earthquake
    d. 1509 Istanbul earthquake

Chapter 6. Volcanic Activity

15. A _____ is a large volcano with shallowly-sloping sides. A _____ is formed by lava flows of low viscosity — lava that flows easily. Consequently, a volcanic mountain having a broad profile is built up over time by flow after flow of relatively fluid basaltic lava issuing from vents or fissures on the surface of the volcano.
   a. Shield volcano
   b. 1509 Istanbul earthquake
   c. 1703 Genroku earthquake
   d. 1700 Cascadia earthquake

16. _____ is a measure of the resistance of a fluid to deform under shear stress. It is commonly perceived as "thickness", or resistance to flow. _____ describes a fluid's internal resistance to flow and may be thought of as a measure of fluid friction.
   a. Viscosity
   b. 1509 Istanbul earthquake
   c. 1703 Genroku earthquake
   d. 1700 Cascadia earthquake

17. _____ is a common extrusive volcanic rock. It is usually gray to black and fine-grained due to rapid cooling of lava at the surface of a planet. It may be porphyritic containing larger crystals in a fine matrix, or vesicular, or frothy scoria.
   a. 1703 Genroku earthquake
   b. 1700 Cascadia earthquake
   c. 1509 Istanbul earthquake
   d. Basalt

18. _____ in meteorology are large scale patterns in the atmospheric pressure field that are nearly stationary, effectively "blocking" or redirecting migratory cyclones. These _____ can remain in place for several days or even weeks, causing the areas affected by them to have the same kind of weather for an extended period of time.
   a. 1509 Istanbul earthquake
   b. 1703 Genroku earthquake
   c. 1700 Cascadia earthquake
   d. Blocks

19. A _____ is a fragment of cooled pyroclastic material, lava or magma.
   a. 1700 Cascadia earthquake
   b. 1703 Genroku earthquake
   c. Cinder
   d. 1509 Istanbul earthquake

20. _____ are steep, conical hills of volcanic fragments that accumulate around and downwind from a volcanic vent. The rock fragments, often called cinders are glassy and contain numerous gas bubbles "frozen" into place as magma exploded into the air and then cooled quickly.
   a. 1509 Istanbul earthquake
   b. 1700 Cascadia earthquake
   c. 1703 Genroku earthquake
   d. Cinder cones

21. A _____, is a tall, conical volcano composed of many layers of hardened lava, tephra, and volcanic ash. These volcanoes are characterized by a steep profile and periodic, explosive eruptions. The lava that flows from them is viscous, and cools and hardens before spreading very far.
   a. 1509 Istanbul earthquake
   b. 1700 Cascadia earthquake
   c. 1703 Genroku earthquake
   d. Stratovolcano

22. _____ are clastic rocks composed solely or primarily of volcanic materials.
   a. Pyroclastics
   b. 1700 Cascadia earthquake
   c. 1509 Istanbul earthquake
   d. 1703 Genroku earthquake

23. In geology, _____ is a naturally occurring aggregate of minerals and/or mineraloids.

The Earth's outer solid layer, the lithosphere, is made of _____. In general _____s are of three types, namely, igneous, sedimentary, and metamorphic.

   a. 1700 Cascadia earthquake
   b. Rock
   c. 1703 Genroku earthquake
   d. 1509 Istanbul earthquake

24. _____ is air-fall material produced by a volcanic eruption regardless of composition or fragment size. It is typically rhyolitic in composition as most explosive volcanoes are the product of the more viscous felsic or high silica magmas.
   a. 1703 Genroku earthquake
   b. 1700 Cascadia earthquake
   c. 1509 Istanbul earthquake
   d. Tephra

25. _____ is a fossil fuel formed in swamp ecosystems where plant remains were saved by water and mud from oxidization and biodegradation. It is a sedimentary rock, but the harder forms, such as anthracite _____, can be regarded as metamorphic rocks because of later exposure to elevated temperature and pressure. It is composed primarily of carbon along with assorted other elements, including sulfur.
   a. 1700 Cascadia earthquake
   b. 1703 Genroku earthquake
   c. 1509 Istanbul earthquake
   d. Coal

26. In geology, a _____ is a deformational feature consisting of symmetrically-dipping anticlines; their general outline on a geologic map is circular or oval.
   a. 1509 Istanbul earthquake
   b. 1703 Genroku earthquake
   c. Dome
   d. 1700 Cascadia earthquake

27. _____ is an igneous, volcanic rock, of intermediate composition, with aphanitic to porphyritic texture. The mineral assemblage is typically dominated by plagioclase plus pyroxene and/or hornblende. Magnetite, zircon, apatite, ilmenite, biotite, and garnet are common accessory minerals.
   a. AL 129-1
   b. AASHTO Soil Classification System
   c. AL 333
   d. Andesite

28. The _____ is an engineering property of granular materials. The _____ is the maximum angle of a stable slope determined by friction, cohesion and the shapes of the particles.
   a. AL 333
   b. AL 129-1
   c. AASHTO Soil Classification System
   d. Angle of repose

29. _____ are volcanic features formed by the collapse of land following a volcanic eruption. They are often confused with volcanic craters.
   a. 1700 Cascadia earthquake
   b. Calderas
   c. 1703 Genroku earthquake
   d. 1509 Istanbul earthquake

30. _____ is an active volcano in the Hawaiian Islands, one of five shield volcanoes that together form the Island of Hawai'i. In Hawaiian, the word _____ means "spewing" or "much spreading", in reference to the mountain's frequent outpouring of lava. It is presently the most active volcano and one of the most visited active volcanoes on the planet.
   a. 1703 Genroku earthquake
   b. 1509 Istanbul earthquake
   c. Kilauea
   d. 1700 Cascadia earthquake

Chapter 6. Volcanic Activity

31. _____ is a census-designated place (CDP) in KauaÊ»i County, HawaiÊ»i, United States. The population was 2,092 at the 2000 census.

_____ is located at 22°12'40"N 159°24'35"WÃ¯Â»Â¿ / Ã¯Â»Â¿22.21111°N 159.40972°WÃ¯Â»Â¿ / 22.21111; -159.40972 (22.211103, -159.409609.)
   - a. 1700 Cascadia earthquake
   - b. 1703 Genroku earthquake
   - c. KÄ«lauea
   - d. 1509 Istanbul earthquake

32. In geology, a _____ is a place where the Earth's crust and lithosphere are being pulled apart.
   - a. 1700 Cascadia earthquake
   - b. 1509 Istanbul earthquake
   - c. 1703 Genroku earthquake
   - d. Rift

33. A _____ is a feature of some volcanoes in which a linear series of fissures in the volcanic edifice allows lava to be erupted from the volcano's flank instead of from its summit.
   - a. 1509 Istanbul earthquake
   - b. 1700 Cascadia earthquake
   - c. 1703 Genroku earthquake
   - d. Rift zone

34. A stratovolcano, sometimes called a composite volcano, is a tall, conical volcano with many layers (strata) of hardened lava, tephra, and volcanic ash. _____ are characterized by a steep profile and periodic, explosive eruptions. The lava that flows from _____ tends to be viscous; it cools and hardens before spreading far.
   - a. 1509 Istanbul earthquake
   - b. 1700 Cascadia earthquake
   - c. 1703 Genroku earthquake
   - d. Stratovolcanoes

35. _____ is a volcano in the Mexican state of Michoacán, close to a lava-covered village of the same name. It appears on many versions of the Seven Natural Wonders of the World.
   - a. 1509 Istanbul earthquake
   - b. 1700 Cascadia earthquake
   - c. 1703 Genroku earthquake
   - d. Paricutin

36. _____ is an igneous, volcanic rock, of felsic composition. It may have any texture from aphanitic to porphyritic. The mineral assemblage is usually quartz, alkali feldspar and plagioclase. Biotite and pyroxene are common accessory minerals.
   - a. 1700 Cascadia earthquake
   - b. 1509 Istanbul earthquake
   - c. 1703 Genroku earthquake
   - d. Rhyolite

37. In geology, a _____ is a location on the Earth's surface that has experienced active volcanism for a long period of time.
   - a. 1700 Cascadia earthquake
   - b. 1509 Istanbul earthquake
   - c. Hotspot
   - d. 1703 Genroku earthquake

38. The _____ is a major mountain range of western North America, extending from southern British Columbia through Washington and Oregon to Northern California. It includes both non-volcanic mountains, such as the North Cascades, and the notable volcanoes known as the High Cascades. The _____ is part of the Pacific Ring of Fire, the ring of volcanoes and associated mountains around the Pacific Ocean. All of the known historic eruptions in the contiguous United States have been from Cascade volcanoes.

Chapter 6. Volcanic Activity

   a. 1509 Istanbul earthquake
   b. 1700 Cascadia earthquake
   c. 1703 Genroku earthquake
   d. Cascade Range

39. The _____ is a subduction zone, a type of convergent plate boundary that stretches from northern Vancouver Island to northern California.

The zone separates the Juan de Fuca, Explorer, Gorda and the North American Plates. Here, the oceanic crust of the Pacific Ocean sinks beneath the continent at a rate of 40 mm/yr.

   a. Cascadia subduction zone
   b. 1703 Genroku earthquake
   c. 1509 Istanbul earthquake
   d. 1700 Cascadia earthquake

40. In geology, a _____ zone is an area on Earth where two tectonic plates meet and move towards one another, with one sliding underneath the other and moving down into the mantle, at rates typically measured in centimeters per year. An oceanic plate ordinarily slides underneath a continental plate; this often creates an orogenic zone with many volcanoes and earthquakes.

   a. 1509 Istanbul earthquake
   b. 1703 Genroku earthquake
   c. 1700 Cascadia earthquake
   d. Subduction

41. A _____ is an area on Earth where two tectonic plates meet and move towards one another, with one sliding underneath the other and moving down into the mantle, at rates typically measured in centimeters per year. In a sense, _____s are the opposite of divergent boundaries, areas where material rises up from the mantle and plates are moving apart.

   a. Subduction zone
   b. 1700 Cascadia earthquake
   c. 1703 Genroku earthquake
   d. 1509 Istanbul earthquake

42. _____ is an igneous rock of volcanic origin. They often have a vesicular texture, which is the result voids left by volatiles escaping from the molten lava. Pumice is a rock, which is an example of explosive volcanic eruption. It is so vesicular that it floats in water.

   a. 1703 Genroku earthquake
   b. 1700 Cascadia earthquake
   c. Volcanic rock
   d. 1509 Istanbul earthquake

43. The _____ lies across parts of the U.S. states of Washington, Oregon, and Idaho. During late Miocene and early Pliocene times, one of the largest flood basalts ever to appear on the earth's surface engulfed about 63,000 square miles of the Pacific Northwest, forming a large igneous province.

   a. Columbia Plateau
   b. 1703 Genroku earthquake
   c. 1509 Istanbul earthquake
   d. 1700 Cascadia earthquake

44. A _____ is an approximately circular depression in the surface of a planet, moon or other solid body in the Solar System, formed by the hyper-velocity impact of a smaller body with the surface. Impact _____s typically have raised rims, and they range from small, simple, bowl-shaped depressions to large, complex, multi-ringed, impact basins.

   a. 1509 Istanbul earthquake
   b. 1703 Genroku earthquake
   c. Crater
   d. 1700 Cascadia earthquake

Chapter 6. Volcanic Activity

45. A _____ is the result of a giant volcanic eruption or series of eruptions that coats large stretches of land or the ocean floor with basalt lava. _____s have erupted at random intervals throughout history and are clear evidence that the Earth undergoes periods of enhanced activity rather than being in a uniform steady state.
   a. 1703 Genroku earthquake
   b. 1700 Cascadia earthquake
   c. 1509 Istanbul earthquake
   d. Flood basalt

46. A _____ is a spring that is produced by the emergence of geothermally-heated groundwater from the earth's crust. They are all over the earth, on every continent and even under the oceans and seas.
   a. 1700 Cascadia earthquake
   b. 1509 Istanbul earthquake
   c. 1703 Genroku earthquake
   d. Hot spring

47. A _____ is an area of highland, usually consisting of relatively flat rural area.
   a. 1509 Istanbul earthquake
   b. 1703 Genroku earthquake
   c. 1700 Cascadia earthquake
   d. Plateau

48. _____ is a geographical term that is used in various ways among the different branches of geography. In general, a _____ is a medium-scale area of land, Earth or water, smaller than the whole areas of interest, and larger than a specific site or location. A _____ can be seen as a collection of smaller units or as one part of a larger whole.
   a. 1700 Cascadia earthquake
   b. 1509 Istanbul earthquake
   c. Champs-Élysées
   d. Region

49. A _____ is a type of hot spring that erupts periodically, ejecting a column of hot water and steam into the air.
   a. 1509 Istanbul earthquake
   b. 1700 Cascadia earthquake
   c. Geyser
   d. 1703 Genroku earthquake

50. _____ is located in Yellowstone National Park, Wyoming, United States. It was named in 1870 during the Washburn-Langford-Doane Expedition and was the first one in the park to receive a name. An eruption can shoot 3,700–8,400 gallons of boiling water to a height of 106–184 feet lasting from 1.5–5 minutes.
   a. Old Faithful Geyser
   b. AL 333
   c. AASHTO Soil Classification System
   d. AL 129-1

51. A _____ column is a column of rizing air in the lower altitudes of the Earth's atmosphere. _____s are created by the uneven heating of the Earth's surface from solar radiation, and are an example of convection. The Sun warms the ground, which in turn warms the air directly above it.
   a. 1700 Cascadia earthquake
   b. 1703 Genroku earthquake
   c. 1509 Istanbul earthquake
   d. Thermal

52. In geology, a _____ is a depression with predominant extent in one direction. The terms U-shaped and V-shaped are descriptive terms of geography to characterize the form of _____s. Most _____s belong to one of these two main types or a mixture of them, at least with respect of the cross section of the slopes or hillsides.
   a. 1703 Genroku earthquake
   b. 1509 Istanbul earthquake
   c. 1700 Cascadia earthquake
   d. Valley

53. The _____ is the centerpiece of the Greater Yellowstone Ecosystem, the largest intact ecosystem in the Earth's northern temperate zone. Located mostly in the U.S. state of Wyoming, the park extends into Montana and Idaho. The park is known for its wildlife and geothermal features; Old Faithful Geyser is one of the most popular features in the park.

Chapter 6. Volcanic Activity

a. 1703 Genroku earthquake
c. 1700 Cascadia earthquake
b. 1509 Istanbul earthquake
d. Yellowstone National Park

54. The _____ is a scientific agency of the United States government. The scientists of the USGS study the landscape of the United States, its natural resources, and the natural hazards that threaten it.
a. Andrija Mohorovičić
c. Amblypoda
b. Ambulocetus
d. U.S. Geological Survey

55. The _____ of an edge is $c_f(u,v) = c(u,v) - f(u,v)$. This defines a residual network denoted $G_f(V, \overline{E}_f)$, giving the amount of available capacity. See that there can be an edge from u to v in the residual network, even though there is no edge from u to v in the original network.
a. 1700 Cascadia earthquake
c. 1509 Istanbul earthquake
b. 1703 Genroku earthquake
d. Residual capacity

56. _____ in general can refer to a cooling of the Earth. More specifically, it refers to a conjecture during the 1970s of imminent cooling of the Earth's surface and atmosphere along with a posited commencement of glaciation.
a. 1703 Genroku earthquake
c. Global cooling
b. 1700 Cascadia earthquake
d. 1509 Istanbul earthquake

57. _____ are very large slides of snow or rock down a mountainside, caused when a buildup of snow is released down a slope, and is one of the major dangers faced in the mountains.
a. AL 333
c. Avalanches
b. AL 129-1
d. AASHTO Soil Classification System

58. _____, officially the Republic of _____, is an island country in Northern Europe, located in the North Atlantic Ocean between mainland Europe and Greenland. It has a population of about 320,000 and a total area of 103,000 km Its capital and largest city is Reykjavík.

Located on the Mid-Atlantic Ridge, _____ is volcanically and geologically active on a large scale; this defines the landscape.

a. Ireland
c. Iron Curtain
b. Independence
d. Iceland

59. A _____ is a geological phenomenon which includes a wide range of ground movement, such as rock falls, deep failure of slopes and shallow debris flows. Although gravity's action on an over-steepened slope is the primary reason for a _____, there are other contributing factors affecting the original slope stability.
a. Landslide
c. 1509 Istanbul earthquake
b. 1703 Genroku earthquake
d. 1700 Cascadia earthquake

60. _____ is a common and devastating result of some volcanic eruptions. The flows are fast-moving fluidized bodies of hot gas, ash and rock which can travel away from the vent at up to 700 km/h. The gas is usually at a temperature of up to 1000 degrees Celsius. The flows normally hug the ground and travel downhill under gravity, their speed depending upon the gradient of the slope and the size of the flow.

a. 1509 Istanbul earthquake
b. 1703 Genroku earthquake
c. Nuee ardente
d. 1700 Cascadia earthquake

61. An _____ is traditionally considered any chemical compound that, when dissolved in water, gives a solution with a hydrogen ion activity greater than in pure water, i.e. a pH less than 7.0. That approximates the modern definition of Johannes Nicolaus Brønsted and Martin Lowry, who independently defined an _____ as a compound which donates a hydrogen ion to another compound. Common examples include acetic _____ and sulfuric _____. Acid/base systems are different from redox reactions in that there is no change in oxidation state.
   a. AASHTO Soil Classification System
   b. AL 333
   c. Acid
   d. AL 129-1

62. The term _____ is commonly used to mean the deposition of acidic components in rain, snow, dew, or dry particles. _____ occurs when sulfur dioxide and nitrogen oxides are emitted into the atmosphere, undergo chemical transformations and are absorbed by water droplets in clouds. The droplets then fall to earth as rain, snow, mist, dry dust, hail, or sleet. This increases the acidity of the soil, and affects the chemical balance of lakes and streams.
   a. AL 333
   b. Acid precipitation
   c. AASHTO Soil Classification System
   d. AL 129-1

63. _____

African Economic Community map

Although it has abundant natural resources, _____ remains the world's poorest and most underdeveloped continent, due largely to the effects of: tropical diseases, the slave trade, corrupt governments, failed central planning, the international trade regime and geopolitics; as well as widespread human rights violations, the negative effects of colonialism, despotism, illiteracy, superstition, tribal and military conflict. According to the United Nations' Human Development Report in 2003, the bottom 25 ranked nations were all African nations.

Widespread poverty, illiteracy, malnutrition and inadequate water supply and sanitation, as well as poor health, affect a large majority of the people who reside in the African continent.

   a. AASHTO Soil Classification System
   b. AL 129-1
   c. Africa
   d. AL 333

64. The Republic of _____ is a unitary republic of central and western Africa. It is bordered by Nigeria to the west; Chad to the northeast; the Central African Republic to the east; and Equatorial Guinea, Gabon, and the Republic of the Congo to the south. _____'s coastline lies on the Bight of Bonny, part of the Gulf of Guinea and the Atlantic Ocean.
   a. Zambia
   b. Cameroon
   c. Guinea-Bissau
   d. Guinea

65. _____ is a chemical element in the periodic table that has the symbol C and atomic number 6. An abundant nonmetallic, tetravalent element, _____ has several allotropic forms.
   a. 1509 Istanbul earthquake
   b. 1703 Genroku earthquake
   c. Carbon
   d. 1700 Cascadia earthquake

Chapter 6. Volcanic Activity

66. _____ is a chemical compound, normally in a gaseous state, and is composed of one carbon and two oxygen atoms. It is often referred to by its formula CO2. It is present in the Earth's atmosphere at a concentration of approximately .000383 by volume and is an important greenhouse gas due to its ability to absorb many infrared wavelengths of sunlight, and due to the length of time it stays in the atmosphere.
   a. Carbon dioxide
   b. 1700 Cascadia earthquake
   c. 1703 Genroku earthquake
   d. 1509 Istanbul earthquake

67. A _____ is a body of water, not part of the ocean, that is larger and deeper than a pond.
   a. 1509 Istanbul earthquake
   b. Lake
   c. 1703 Genroku earthquake
   d. 1700 Cascadia earthquake

68. _____ is an active volcano and is the highest peak in the Aleutian Range on the Alaska Peninsula in Alaska. It is located in the Chigmit Mountains southwest of Anchorage, Alaska.
   a. 1509 Istanbul earthquake
   b. 1703 Genroku earthquake
   c. 1700 Cascadia earthquake
   d. Mount Redoubt

69. _____ is the chemical element in the periodic table that has the symbol S and atomic number 16. It is an abundant, tasteless, odorless, multivalent non-metal. _____, in its native form, is a yellow crystaline solid. In nature, it can be found as the pure element or as sulfide and sulfate minerals.
   a. Thulium
   b. Zinc
   c. Vinyl
   d. Sulfur

70. _____ is a chemical compound with the formula SO2. This important gas is the main product from the combustion of sulfur compounds and is of significant environmental concern. Sulphur dioxide is produced by volcanoes and in various industrial processes.
   a. 1700 Cascadia earthquake
   b. Sulfur dioxide
   c. 1509 Istanbul earthquake
   d. 1703 Genroku earthquake

71. _____ is most commonly a noun, adjective, or adverb indicating direction or geography.

    _____ is one of the four cardinal directions or compass points. It is the opposite of east and is perpendicular to north and south.

   a. 1700 Cascadia earthquake
   b. 1509 Istanbul earthquake
   c. 1703 Genroku earthquake
   d. West

72. _____ is a layer of gases surrounding the planet Earth and retained by the Earth's gravity, protecting life on Earth by absorbing ultraviolet solar radiation and reducing temperature extremes between day and night.
   a. AL 333
   b. AL 129-1
   c. AASHTO Soil Classification System
   d. Earths atmosphere

73. _____ is a chemical, physical, or biological agent that modifies the natural characteristics of the atmosphere. The atmosphere is a complex, dynamic natural gaseous system that is essential to support life on planet Earth. Stratospheric ozone depletion due to _____ has long been recognized as a threat to human health as well as to the Earth's ecosystems. Worldwide _____ is responsible for large numbers of deaths and cases of respiratory disease.

Chapter 6. Volcanic Activity

a. AASHTO Soil Classification System
b. AL 129-1
c. Air pollution
d. AL 333

74. _____ is the geological process whereby material is added to a landform. This is the process by which wind and water create a sediment deposit, through the laying down of granular material that has been eroded and transported from another geographical location.
   a. 1700 Cascadia earthquake
   b. 1509 Istanbul earthquake
   c. 1703 Genroku earthquake
   d. Deposition

75. _____ is vibration transmitted through a solid, liquid composed of frequencies within the range of hearing and of a level sufficiently strong to be heard. Human ear

For humans, hearing is limited to frequencies between about 20 Hz and 20,000 Hz (20 kHz), with the upper limit generally decreasing with age. Other species have a different range of hearing.

   a. Sound
   b. 1509 Istanbul earthquake
   c. 1703 Genroku earthquake
   d. 1700 Cascadia earthquake

76. _____ is the introduction of substances or energy into the environment, resulting in deleterious effects of such a nature as to endanger human health, harm living resources and ecosystems, and impair or interfere with amenities and other legitimate uses of the environment.
   a. 1703 Genroku earthquake
   b. 1700 Cascadia earthquake
   c. 1509 Istanbul earthquake
   d. Pollution

77. _____ often refers to mudslides, mudflows, jökulhlaups, or debris avalanches. They consist primarily of geological material mixed with water. They may be generated when hillside colluvium or landslide material becomes rapidly saturated with water and flows into a channel.
   a. 1703 Genroku earthquake
   b. 1700 Cascadia earthquake
   c. 1509 Istanbul earthquake
   d. Debris flow

78. _____ is an Andean stratovolcano in Caldas Department, Colombia. It is the northernmost and highest Colombian volcano with historical activity. Its 1985 eruption produced a lahar which completely buried Armero and caused an estimated 23,000 deaths.
   a. Nevado del Ruiz
   b. 1509 Istanbul earthquake
   c. 1703 Genroku earthquake
   d. 1700 Cascadia earthquake

79. A _____ is the most rapid up to 80 km/h and fluid type of downhill mass wasting.
   a. 1703 Genroku earthquake
   b. 1509 Istanbul earthquake
   c. 1700 Cascadia earthquake
   d. Mudflow

80. The _____ is a fundamental subatomic particle that carries a negative electric charge.
   a. AL 129-1
   b. AASHTO Soil Classification System
   c. AL 333
   d. Electron

81. A _____ is a type of mudflow composed of pyroclastic material and water that flows down from a volcano, typically along a river valley.

Chapter 6. Volcanic Activity

a. Lahar
b. 1700 Cascadia earthquake
c. 1703 Genroku earthquake
d. 1509 Istanbul earthquake

82. _____ is an informal term used mostly by popular media and popular scientific societies to describe a very large tsunami wave beyond the typical size reached by most tsunamis.
a. 1700 Cascadia earthquake
b. 1509 Istanbul earthquake
c. 1703 Genroku earthquake
d. Megatsunami

83. _____s, alternatively referred to as _____ matter (PM) or fine particles, are tiny particles of solid or liquid suspended in a gas or liquid. In contrast, aerosol refers to particles and the gas together. Sources of _____ matter can be man made or natural.
a. 1703 Genroku earthquake
b. 1700 Cascadia earthquake
c. 1509 Istanbul earthquake
d. Particulate

84. _____ are tiny particles of solid or liquid suspended in a gas. They range in size from less than 10 nanometres to more than 100 micrometres in diameter.
a. Particulates
b. 1509 Istanbul earthquake
c. 1703 Genroku earthquake
d. 1700 Cascadia earthquake

85. The _____, is an island country located in Southeast Asia with Manila as its capital city. The _____ comprises 7,107 islands in the western Pacific Ocean, sharing maritime borders with Indonesia, Malaysia, Palau, the Republic of China, and Vietnam. The _____ is the world's 12th most populous country with a population of 90 million people.
a. 1700 Cascadia earthquake
b. Philippines
c. Philippine Islands
d. 1509 Istanbul earthquake

86. _____ is the substance of which physical objects are composed. _____ can be solid, liquid, plasma or gas. It constitutes the observable universe.
a. 1509 Istanbul earthquake
b. 1700 Cascadia earthquake
c. 1703 Genroku earthquake
d. Matter

87. _____ is the science and study of the solid matter that constitute the Earth. Encompassing such things as rocks, soil, and gemstones, _____ studies the composition, structure, physical properties, history, and the processes that shape Earth's components.
a. Glacial motion
b. Glaciology
c. 1509 Istanbul earthquake
d. Geology

88. Seismology is the scientific study of earthquakes and the propagation of elastic waves through the Earth. The field also includes studies of earthquake effects, such as tsunamis as well as diverse _____ sources such as volcanic, tectonic, oceanic, atmospheric, and artificial processes (such as explosions.) A related field that uses geology to infer information regarding past earthquakes is paleoseismology.
a. 1700 Cascadia earthquake
b. 1509 Istanbul earthquake
c. 1703 Genroku earthquake
d. Seismic

89. _____ is the average and variations of weather over long periods of time. _____ zones can be defined using parameters such as temperature and rainfall.

Chapter 6. Volcanic Activity

a. 1509 Istanbul earthquake
b. 1703 Genroku earthquake
c. 1700 Cascadia earthquake
d. Climate

90. _____ refers to the variation in the Earth's global climate or in regional climates over time. It describes changes in the variability or average state of the atmosphere over time scales ranging from decades to millions of years. These changes can be caused by processes internal to the Earth, external forces or, more recently, human activities.
    a. 1703 Genroku earthquake
    b. 1700 Cascadia earthquake
    c. 1509 Istanbul earthquake
    d. Climate change

91. _____ is the study of the past, particularly using written records. New technology, such as photography, and computer text files now sometimes complement traditional archival sources. _____ is a field of research producing a continuous narrative and a systematic analysis of past events of importance to the human race.
    a. Absolute time
    b. 1509 Istanbul earthquake
    c. 1700 Cascadia earthquake
    d. History

92. In computer science, _____ computing (RTC) is the study of hardware and software systems that are subject to a '_____ constraint'--i.e., operational deadlines from event to system response. By contrast, a non-_____ system is one for which there is no deadline, even if fast response or high performance is desired or preferred. The needs of _____ software are often addressed in the context of _____ operating systems, and synchronous programming languages, which provide frameworks on which to build _____ application software.
    a. 1509 Istanbul earthquake
    b. Real-time
    c. 1703 Genroku earthquake
    d. 1700 Cascadia earthquake

93. The _____ is currently the only fully functional Global Navigation Satellite System. Utilizing a constellation of at least 24 medium Earth orbit satellites that transmit precise microwave signals, the system enables a GPS receiver to determine its location, speed and direction.
    a. Global Positioning System
    b. 1703 Genroku earthquake
    c. 1700 Cascadia earthquake
    d. 1509 Istanbul earthquake

Chapter 7. Rivers and Flooding

1. A _____ is a natural or artificial slope or wall, usually earthen and often parallels the course of a river.
   a. 1703 Genroku earthquake
   b. 1509 Istanbul earthquake
   c. 1700 Cascadia earthquake
   d. Levee

2. _____ is the natural or artificial removal of surface and sub-surface water from a given area. Many agricultural soils need _____ to improve production or to manage water supplies.
   a. 1509 Istanbul earthquake
   b. 1703 Genroku earthquake
   c. 1700 Cascadia earthquake
   d. Drainage

3. A _____ is flat or nearly flat land adjacent to a stream or river that experiences occasional or periodic flooding. It includes the floodway, which consists of the stream channel and adjacent areas that carry flood flows, and the flood fringe, which are areas covered by the flood, but which do not experience a strong current.
   a. 1509 Istanbul earthquake
   b. 1703 Genroku earthquake
   c. Floodplain
   d. 1700 Cascadia earthquake

4. The _____ is the second-longest named river in North America, with a length of 2320 miles from Lake Itasca to the Gulf of Mexico. It drains most of the area between the Rocky Mountains and the Appalachian Mountains, except for the areas drained by Hudson Bay via the Red River of the North, the Great Lakes and the Rio Grande.
   a. 1703 Genroku earthquake
   b. 1700 Cascadia earthquake
   c. 1509 Istanbul earthquake
   d. Mississippi River

5. An _____ plain is a relatively flat and gently sloping landform found at the base of a range of hills or mountains, formed by the deposition of _____ soil over a long period of time by one or more rivers coming from the mountains.
   a. AL 129-1
   b. AL 333
   c. AASHTO Soil Classification System
   d. Alluvial

6. _____ or sediments are deposited by a river or other running water. _____ is typically made up of a variety of materials, including fine particles of silt and clay and larger particles of sand and gravel.
   a. AL 333
   b. AL 129-1
   c. AASHTO Soil Classification System
   d. Alluvial soil

7. A _____ is a body of water with a current, confined within a bed and banks. _____s are important as conduits in the water cycle, instruments in aquifer recharge, and corridors for fish and wildlife migration.
   a. 1700 Cascadia earthquake
   b. 1509 Istanbul earthquake
   c. 1703 Genroku earthquake
   d. Stream

8. _____ is a national park located largely in Mariposa and Tuolumne Counties, California, United States. It is one of the largest and least fragmented habitat blocks in the Sierra Nevada, and the park supports a diversity of plants and animals. The park has an elevation range from 2,000 to 13,114 feet.
   a. Yosemite National Park
   b. 1509 Istanbul earthquake
   c. 1703 Genroku earthquake
   d. 1700 Cascadia earthquake

9. The _____ of a river or stream is the lowest point to which it can flow, often referred to as the 'mouth' of the river. For large rivers, sea level is usually the _____, but a large river or lake is likewise the _____ for tributary streams.
   a. 1509 Istanbul earthquake
   b. 1703 Genroku earthquake
   c. Base level
   d. 1700 Cascadia earthquake

Chapter 7. Rivers and Flooding 95

10. The Earth's water is always in movement, and the _____, describes the continuous movement of water on, above, and below the surface of the Earth. Since the _____ is truly a "cycle," there is no beginning or end. Water can change states among liquid, vapor, and ice at various places in the _____, with these processes happening in the blink of an eye and over millions of years. Although the balance of water on Earth remains fairly constant over time, individual water molecules can come and go in a hurry.
   a. 1703 Genroku earthquake
   b. Hydrologic cycle
   c. 1509 Istanbul earthquake
   d. 1700 Cascadia earthquake

11. _____ is the study of the movement, distribution, and quality of water throughout the Earth, and thus addresses both the hydrologic cycle and water resources.
   a. 1703 Genroku earthquake
   b. Hydrology
   c. 1509 Istanbul earthquake
   d. 1700 Cascadia earthquake

12. _____ is used to describe the steepness, incline, gradient, or grade of a straight line. A higher _____ value indicates a steeper incline. The _____ is defined as the ratio of the 'rise' divided by the 'run' between two points on a line, or in other words, the ratio of the altitude change to the horizontal distance between any two points on the line.
   a. 1509 Istanbul earthquake
   b. 1700 Cascadia earthquake
   c. 1703 Genroku earthquake
   d. Slope

13. An alluvial fan is a fan-shaped deposit formed where a fast flowing stream flattens, slows, and spreads typically at the exit of a canyon onto a flatter plain. A convergence of neighboring _____ into a single apron of deposits against a slope is called a bajada, or compound alluvial fan.
   a. Alluvial fans
   b. AASHTO Soil Classification System
   c. AL 333
   d. AL 129-1

14. _____ is a term to describe the larger particles, relative to the suspended load, that are carried along the bottom of a stream.
   a. 1700 Cascadia earthquake
   b. 1509 Istanbul earthquake
   c. 1703 Genroku earthquake
   d. Bed load

15. _____ is a cape on the coast of North Carolina. It is the point that protrudes the farthest to the southeast along the northeast-to-southwest line of the Atlantic coast of North America. Two major Atlantic currents collide just off _____, the southerly-flowing cold water Labrador Current and the northerly-flowing warm water Florida Current (Gulf Stream), creating turbulent waters and a large expanse of shallow sandbars extending up to 14 miles offshore.
   a. 1700 Cascadia earthquake
   b. 1509 Istanbul earthquake
   c. 1703 Genroku earthquake
   d. Cape Hatteras

16. Due to shore erosion in the Outer Bank of North Carolina a navagational lighthouse had to be moved leading to the _____.
   a. 1700 Cascadia earthquake
   b. 1703 Genroku earthquake
   c. 1509 Istanbul earthquake
   d. Cape Hatteras Lighthouse controversy

17. In electromagnetic theory, the _____ is derived from two of Maxwell's equations. It states that the divergence of the current density is equal to the negative rate of change of the charge density.

a. Continuity equation
b. 1703 Genroku earthquake
c. 1700 Cascadia earthquake
d. 1509 Istanbul earthquake

18. A _____ is a landform where the mouth of a river flows into an ocean, sea, desert, estuary or lake. It builds up sediment outwards into the flat area which the river's flow encounters transported by the water and set down as the currents slow.
   a. Delta
   b. 1509 Istanbul earthquake
   c. 1703 Genroku earthquake
   d. 1700 Cascadia earthquake

19. _____ is the geological process whereby material is added to a landform. This is the process by which wind and water create a sediment deposit, through the laying down of granular material that has been eroded and transported from another geographical location.
   a. 1509 Istanbul earthquake
   b. 1700 Cascadia earthquake
   c. 1703 Genroku earthquake
   d. Deposition

20. The ways in which sediments are transported by streams, or the stream load is comprised of three types: Bed Loads, _____, Suspended Loads.
   a. Dissolved loads
   b. 1703 Genroku earthquake
   c. 1509 Istanbul earthquake
   d. 1700 Cascadia earthquake

21. A _____ is a stream that branches off and flows away from a main stream channel. They are a common feature of river deltas. The phenomenon is known as river bifurcation.
   a. 1509 Istanbul earthquake
   b. 1703 Genroku earthquake
   c. 1700 Cascadia earthquake
   d. Distributary

22. A _____ or geophysical hazards is a threat of an event that will have a negative effect on people or the environment. Many _____s are related, e.g. earthquakes can result in tsunamis, drought can lead directly to famine and disease. A concrete example of the division between hazard and disaster is that the 1906 San Francisco earthquake was a disaster, whereas earthquakes are a hazard.
   a. Natural hazard
   b. 1509 Istanbul earthquake
   c. 1700 Cascadia earthquake
   d. 1703 Genroku earthquake

23. _____ is any particulate matter that can be transported by fluid flow and which eventually is deposited as a layer of solid particles on the bed or bottom of a body of water or other liquid.
   a. 1700 Cascadia earthquake
   b. 1509 Istanbul earthquake
   c. 1703 Genroku earthquake
   d. Sediment

24. _____ rock is one of the three main rock groups. Rock formed from these covers 75% of the Earth's land area, and includes common types such as chalk, limestone, dolomite, sandstone, and shale.
   a. Clasts
   b. Sedimentary depositional environment
   c. Sedimentary basin
   d. Sedimentary

25. _____ is the term for the fine particles that are light enough to be carried in a stream without touching the stream bed. These particles are generally of the sand, silt and clay size, although they can be larger, especially in cases of high discharge, such as during floods. This is in contrast to bed load which is carried along the bottom of the stream.

a. 1509 Istanbul earthquake
b. 1700 Cascadia earthquake
c. 1703 Genroku earthquake
d. Suspended load

26. In physics, _____ is defined as the rate of change of displacement or the rate of displacement. Simply put, it is distance per units of time.
   a. Supercritical fluid
   b. Tension
   c. Synthetic aperture radar
   d. Velocity

27. A _____ is an approximately circular depression in the surface of a planet, moon or other solid body in the Solar System, formed by the hyper-velocity impact of a smaller body with the surface. Impact _____s typically have raised rims, and they range from small, simple, bowl-shaped depressions to large, complex, multi-ringed, impact basins.
   a. 1703 Genroku earthquake
   b. 1700 Cascadia earthquake
   c. Crater
   d. 1509 Istanbul earthquake

28. _____ is displacement of solids by the agents of ocean currents, wind, water, or ice by downward or down-slope movement in response to gravity or by living organisms.
   a. AL 129-1
   b. AASHTO Soil Classification System
   c. AL 333
   d. Erosion

29. The _____ is a river in Ventura County, California. The river forms at the confluence of Matilija Creek and North Fork Matilija Creek, 15 miles upstream from the Pacific Ocean. San Antonio Creek joins the river halfway to the ocean and Coyote Creek does the same a couple of miles downstream.
   a. 1700 Cascadia earthquake
   b. 1509 Istanbul earthquake
   c. 1703 Genroku earthquake
   d. Ventura River

30. _____ (December 16, 1863, Madrid - September 26, 1952, Rome), was a philosopher, essayist, poet, and novelist.

A lifelong Spanish citizen, Santayana was raised and educated in the United States, wrote in English and is generally considered an American man of letters, although, of his nearly 89 years, he spent only 39 in the U.S. He is perhaps best known as an aphorist, and for the oft-misquoted remark, 'Those who cannot remember the past, are condemned to repeat it,' (hence, 'Santayana's Aphorism on Repetitive Consequences') from Reason in Common Sense, the first volume of his The Life of Reason.

Born Jorge Agustín Nicolás Ruíz de Santayana y Borrás, he spent his early childhood in Ávila, Spain.

   a. Garrett James Hardin
   b. Luna Bergere Leopold
   c. Hambali
   d. George Santayana

31. A _____ occurs when two reversible processes occur at the same rate.
   a. Dynamic equilibrium
   b. 1509 Istanbul earthquake
   c. 1703 Genroku earthquake
   d. 1700 Cascadia earthquake

32. _____ is the condition of a system in which competing influences are balanced.

a. AL 129-1
b. Equilibrium
c. AASHTO Soil Classification System
d. AL 333

33. A _____ is a bipedal primate belonging to the mammalian species Homo sapiens in the family Hominidae. Compared to other living organisms on Earth, a _____ has a highly developed brain capable of abstract reasoning, language, and introspection.
   a. 1703 Genroku earthquake
   b. 1509 Istanbul earthquake
   c. 1700 Cascadia earthquake
   d. Human

34. _____ is the degradation of land in arid, semi arid and dry sub-humid areas resulting from various climatic variations, but primarily human activities. Current _____ is taking place much faster worldwide than historically and usually arises from the demands of increased populations that settle on the land in order to grow crops and graze animals.
   a. 1509 Istanbul earthquake
   b. 1703 Genroku earthquake
   c. 1700 Cascadia earthquake
   d. Desertification

35. A _____ is a storm system characterized by a low pressure center and numerous thunderstorms that produce strong winds and flooding rain. _____s feed on heat released when moist air rises, resulting in condensation of water vapour contained in the moist air. They are fueled by a different heat mechanism than other cyclonic windstorms such as nor'easters, European windstorms, and polar lows, leading to their classification as 'warm core' storm systems. Depending on its location and strength, a _____ is referred to by many other names, such as hurricane, typhoon, tropical storm, cyclonic storm, tropical depression, and simply cyclone.
   a. Khmer Empire
   b. Kenya
   c. Persia
   d. Tropical cyclone

36. In meteorology, _____ are an area of low atmospheric pressure characterized by inward spiraling winds that rotate counter clockwise in the northern hemisphere and clockwise in the southern hemisphere of the Earth.
   a. Cyclones
   b. 1509 Istanbul earthquake
   c. 1703 Genroku earthquake
   d. 1700 Cascadia earthquake

37. The Tropics, seated in the equatorial regions of the world, are limited in latitude by the Tropic of Cancer in the northern hemisphere at approximately 23°26' N latitude, and the Tropic of Capricorn in the southern hemisphere at 23°26' S latitude. The Tropics are also referred to as the _____ zone and the torrid zone. A noontime scene from the Philippines on a day when the Sun is almost directly overhead.

The Tropics includes all the areas on the Earth where the sun reaches a point directly overhead at least once during the solar year.

   a. 1703 Genroku earthquake
   b. 1700 Cascadia earthquake
   c. 1509 Istanbul earthquake
   d. Tropical

38. _____ are networks of small channels that are ever-changing and interlacing. They make up one large river or stream.
   a. Braided channels
   b. 1509 Istanbul earthquake
   c. 1700 Cascadia earthquake
   d. 1703 Genroku earthquake

Chapter 7. Rivers and Flooding

39. A _____ is a bend in a river. A stream or river flowing through a wide valley or flat plain will tend to form a meandering stream course as it alternatively erodes and deposits sediments along its course. The result is a snaking pattern.
   a. 1703 Genroku earthquake
   b. Meander
   c. 1509 Istanbul earthquake
   d. 1700 Cascadia earthquake

40. A _____ is a depositional feature of streams. _____s are found in abundance in mature or meandering streams, they are located on the inside of a stream bend, known as a meander.
   a. 1703 Genroku earthquake
   b. 1509 Istanbul earthquake
   c. Point bar
   d. 1700 Cascadia earthquake

41. The _____ (1968) is a book written by Paul R. Ehrlich. A best-selling work, it predicted disaster for humanity due to overpopulation and the 'population explosion'. The book predicted that 'in the 1970s and 1980s hundreds of millions of people will starve to death', that nothing can be done to avoid mass famine greater than any in the history, and radical action is needed to limit the overpopulation.
   a. Population bomb
   b. Andrija Mohorovićić
   c. Amblypoda
   d. Ambulocetus

42. The _____ environment consists of all navigable rivers of interest.
   a. 1703 Genroku earthquake
   b. 1700 Cascadia earthquake
   c. 1509 Istanbul earthquake
   d. Riverine

43. A _____ is a rapid flooding of geomorphic low-lying areas, rivers and streams, caused by the intense rainfall associated with a thunderstorm, or multiple training thunderstorms.
   a. Flash flood
   b. 1509 Istanbul earthquake
   c. 1703 Genroku earthquake
   d. 1700 Cascadia earthquake

44. _____ is the point at which the surface of a river, creek, or other body of water has risen to a sufficient level to cause damage or affects use of man-made structures. When a body of water rises to this level, it is considered a flood event.

Definition

_____ means a manmade feature is underwater.

   a. Flood stage
   b. 1509 Istanbul earthquake
   c. 1703 Genroku earthquake
   d. 1700 Cascadia earthquake

45. A _____ is a geological phenomenon which includes a wide range of ground movement, such as rock falls, deep failure of slopes and shallow debris flows. Although gravity's action on an over-steepened slope is the primary reason for a _____, there are other contributing factors affecting the original slope stability.
   a. 1700 Cascadia earthquake
   b. 1509 Istanbul earthquake
   c. 1703 Genroku earthquake
   d. Landslide

46. The term _____ describes the type of alluvial geological deposit or sediment that is deposited on the flood plain of a river. Because it occurs outside the main channel, away from faster flow, the deposit tends to be fine-grained.

a. AASHTO Soil Classification System
b. AL 333
c. AL 129-1
d. Overbank

47. The _____ is a scientific agency of the United States government. The scientists of the USGS study the landscape of the United States, its natural resources, and the natural hazards that threaten it.
   a. Ambulocetus
   b. Andrija Mohorovičić
   c. Amblypoda
   d. U.S. Geological Survey

48. _____ is any of a number of similar colors evoked by light consisting predominantly of the longest wavelengths of light discernible by the human eye, in the wavelength range of roughly 625-740 nm. Longer wavelengths than this are called infrared, or below _____ and cannot be seen by the naked human eye. _____ is used as one of the additive primary colors of light, complementary to cyan, in RGB color systems.
   a. 1509 Istanbul earthquake
   b. Red
   c. 1703 Genroku earthquake
   d. 1700 Cascadia earthquake

49. _____ refers to directed, regular, or systematic movement of a group of objects, organisms, or people.
   a. 1703 Genroku earthquake
   b. 1700 Cascadia earthquake
   c. 1509 Istanbul earthquake
   d. Migration

50. _____ is the measurement of the number of occurrences of a repeated event per unit of time. It is also defined as the rate of change of phase of a sinusoidal waveform.
   a. 1700 Cascadia earthquake
   b. 1703 Genroku earthquake
   c. 1509 Istanbul earthquake
   d. Frequency

51. A _____ is any disturbed state of an astronomical body's atmosphere, especially affecting its surface, and strongly implying severe weather. It may be marked by strong wind, thunder and lightning, heavy precipitation, such as ice, or wind transporting some substance through the atmosphere.
   a. 1700 Cascadia earthquake
   b. 1703 Genroku earthquake
   c. 1509 Istanbul earthquake
   d. Storm

52. A _____ is designed to drain excess rain and ground water from paved streets, parking lots, sidewalks, and roofs. They are present on most motorways, freeways and other busy roads, as well as towns in areas which experience heavy rainfall, flooding and coastal towns which experience regular storms.
   a. Storm drain
   b. 1509 Istanbul earthquake
   c. 1703 Genroku earthquake
   d. 1700 Cascadia earthquake

53. _____ is the increase in the population of cities in proportion to the region's rural population. _____ is studied in terms of its effects on the ecology and economy of a region.
   a. AASHTO Soil Classification System
   b. AL 129-1
   c. AL 333
   d. Urbanization

54. A _____ is an artificial conduit or system of conduits used to carry and remove sewage and to provide drainage.
   a. 1703 Genroku earthquake
   b. 1509 Istanbul earthquake
   c. Sewer
   d. 1700 Cascadia earthquake

Chapter 7. Rivers and Flooding

55. There are two distinct views on the meaning of _____. One view is that _____ is part of the fundamental structure of the universe, a dimension in which events occur in sequence, and _____ itself is something that can be measured. A contrasting view is that _____ is part of the fundamental intellectual structure in which _____, rather than being an objective thing to be measured, is part of the mental measuring system.
   a. 1703 Genroku earthquake
   b. 1509 Istanbul earthquake
   c. Time
   d. 1700 Cascadia earthquake

56. _____ refers to a member of any human group whose adult males grow to less than 150 cm in average height or less than 155 cm. A member of a slightly taller group is termed pygmoid. The best known _____ are the Aka, Efe and Mbuti of central Africa.
   a. 1700 Cascadia earthquake
   b. 1509 Istanbul earthquake
   c. 1703 Genroku earthquake
   d. Pygmies

57. A _____ is a man-made barrier designed to temporarily contain the waters of a river or other waterway which may rise to unusual levels during seasonal or extreme weather events. Flood walls are mainly used on locations where space is scarce, such as cities or where building levees or dikes would interfere with other interests, such as existing buildings, historical architecture or commercial exploitation of embankments.
   a. 1700 Cascadia earthquake
   b. 1509 Istanbul earthquake
   c. 1703 Genroku earthquake
   d. Floodwall

58. _____ secures a definite available depth for navigation; and the discharge of the river generally is amply sufficient for maintaining the impounded waterlevel, as well as providing the necessary water for locking.
   a. 1703 Genroku earthquake
   b. 1509 Istanbul earthquake
   c. 1700 Cascadia earthquake
   d. Channelization

59. _____ ecology is the study of renewing a degraded, damaged, or destroyed ecosystem through active human intervention. It specifically refers to the scientific study that has evolved as recently as the 1980's.
   a. 1509 Istanbul earthquake
   b. 1703 Genroku earthquake
   c. Restoration
   d. 1700 Cascadia earthquake

60. _____ is rock or other material used to armor shorelines or stream banks against water erosion
   a. 1703 Genroku earthquake
   b. 1700 Cascadia earthquake
   c. 1509 Istanbul earthquake
   d. Riprap

61. The _____ is a river in south-central Florida, USA.
   a. Kissimmee River
   b. 1703 Genroku earthquake
   c. 1700 Cascadia earthquake
   d. 1509 Istanbul earthquake

62. _____ is a quantity expressing the two-dimensional size of a defined part of a surface, typically a region bounded by a closed curve. The term surface _____ refers to the total _____ of the exposed surface of a 3-dimensional solid, such as the sum of the _____s of the exposed sides of a polyhedron. _____ is an important invariant in the differential geometry of surfaces.
   a. AL 333
   b. Area
   c. AASHTO Soil Classification System
   d. AL 129-1

63. _____ denotes the specific insurance coverage against property loss from flooding.

a. 1509 Istanbul earthquake
b. 1703 Genroku earthquake
c. Flood Insurance
d. 1700 Cascadia earthquake

64. _____, in law and economics, is a form of risk management primarily used to hedge against the risk of a contingent loss. _____ is defined as the equitable transfer of the risk of a loss, from one entity to another, in exchange for a premium, and can be thought of as a guaranteed small loss to prevent a large, possibly devastating loss. An insurer is a company selling the _____; an insured is the person or entity buying the _____.
   a. AL 129-1
   b. AL 333
   c. AASHTO Soil Classification System
   d. Insurance

65. _____ is the largest city in the state of California and the American West as well as second largest in the United States. Often abbreviated as L.A. and nicknamed The City of Angels, _____ is rated an alpha world city, has an estimated population of 3.8 million and spans over 498.3 square miles (1,290.6 km who hail from all over the globe and speak 224 different languages. _____ is the seat of _____ County, the most populated and one of the most diverse counties in the United States.
   a. 1700 Cascadia earthquake
   b. Los Angeles
   c. Coachella Valley
   d. 1509 Istanbul earthquake

66. The _____ enables property owners in participating communities to purchase insurance protection from the government against losses from flooding.
   a. Amblypoda
   b. National Flood Insurance Program
   c. Andrija Mohorovičić
   d. Ambulocetus

67. The _____ is an agency of the United States Department of Homeland Security. It's purpose is to coordinate the response to a disaster which has occurred in the United States and which overwhelms the resouces of local ands state authorities.
   a. Federal Emergency Management Agency
   b. Ambulocetus
   c. Andrija Mohorovičić
   d. Amblypoda

68. A _____ is an extended period of months or years when a region notes a deficiency in its water supply. Generally, this occurs when a region receives consistently below average precipitation.
   a. 1700 Cascadia earthquake
   b. Drought
   c. 1703 Genroku earthquake
   d. 1509 Istanbul earthquake

69. An _____ is the result from the sudden release of stored energy in the Earth's crust that creates seismic waves. At the Earth's surface, _____s may manifest themselves by a shaking or displacement of the ground. An _____ is caused by tectonic plates getting stuck and putting a strain on the ground. The strain becomes so great that rocks give way by breaking and sliding along fault planes.
   a. AL 129-1
   b. Earthquake
   c. AASHTO Soil Classification System
   d. AL 333

70. A _____ is an opening in a planet's surface or crust, which allows hot, molten rock, ash, and gases to escape from below the surface. Volcanic activity involving the extrusion of rock tends to form mountains or features like mountains over a period of time.

_____es are generally found where tectonic plates are diverging or converging.

a. 1700 Cascadia earthquake
c. 1509 Istanbul earthquake
b. Volcano
d. 1703 Genroku earthquake

71. _____ usually commence with phreatomagmatic eruptions which can be extremely noisy due the rising magma heating water in the ground. This is usually followed by the explosive throat clearing of the vent and the eruption column is dirty grey to black as old weathered rocks are blasted out of the vent. As the vent clears, further ash clouds become grey-white and creamy in colour, with convulations of the ash similar to those of plinian eruptions.

a. 1703 Genroku earthquake
c. 1509 Istanbul earthquake
b. 1700 Cascadia earthquake
d. Vulcanian eruptions

72. _____ is a term used in urban planning for a system of land-use regulation in various parts of the world, including North America, the United Kingdom, and Australia.

a. 1700 Cascadia earthquake
c. 1509 Istanbul earthquake
b. 1703 Genroku earthquake
d. Zoning

73. The _____ is a non-departmental public body of the Department for Environment, Food and Rural Affairs and an Assembly Sponsored Public Body of the National Assembly for Wales.

The Agency's purpose is to protect the environment from threats such as flood and pollution and to enhance the environment taken as a whole. The _____'s remit covers the whole of England and Wales; about 15 million hectares of land, 22,000 miles (35,000 km) of river and 3,100 miles (5,000 km) of coastline seawards to the three mile limit which includes 2 million hectares of coastal waters.

a. AL 129-1
c. AASHTO Soil Classification System
b. AL 333
d. Environment Agency

Chapter 8. Slope Processes, Landslides, and Subsidence

1. The _____ region is the largest area of natural vegetation remaining on the Palos Verdes Peninsula. Though once slated for development (and in fact the projected route of Crenshaw Boulevard through the area still shows on many maps), the area is geologically unstable and is unsuitable for building.

The geographical location and geological history of the peninsula make the remaining habitat extremely valuable for ecological and other scientific reasons.

   a. 1703 Genroku earthquake
   b. 1700 Cascadia earthquake
   c. 1509 Istanbul earthquake
   d. Portuguese Bend

2. A _____ is a geological phenomenon which includes a wide range of ground movement, such as rock falls, deep failure of slopes and shallow debris flows. Although gravity's action on an over-steepened slope is the primary reason for a _____, there are other contributing factors affecting the original slope stability.
   a. 1700 Cascadia earthquake
   b. 1509 Istanbul earthquake
   c. 1703 Genroku earthquake
   d. Landslide

3. _____ is the geomorphic process by which soil, regolith, and rock move downslope under the force of gravity. Types of _____ include creep, slides, flows, topples, and falls, each with their own characteristic features, and take place over timescales from seconds to years. _____ occurs on both terrestrial and submarine slopes, and has been observed on Earth, Mars, and Venus.
   a. 1700 Cascadia earthquake
   b. 1509 Istanbul earthquake
   c. 1703 Genroku earthquake
   d. Mass wasting

4. _____ is used to describe the steepness, incline, gradient, or grade of a straight line. A higher _____ value indicates a steeper incline. The _____ is defined as the ratio of the 'rise' divided by the 'run' between two points on a line, or in other words, the ratio of the altitude change to the horizontal distance between any two points on the line.
   a. 1509 Istanbul earthquake
   b. 1703 Genroku earthquake
   c. Slope
   d. 1700 Cascadia earthquake

5. In geology, engineering, and surveying, _____ is the motion of a surface as it shifts downward relative to a datum such as sea-level. The opposite of _____ is uplift, which results in an increase in elevation. In meteorology, _____ refers to the downward movement of air.
   a. 1703 Genroku earthquake
   b. 1700 Cascadia earthquake
   c. Subsidence
   d. 1509 Istanbul earthquake

6. _____ is a term given to broken rock that appears at the bottom of crags, mountain cliffs or valley shoulders, forming a _____ slope. The maximum inclination of such deposits corresponds to the angle of repose of the mean debris size.
   a. 1509 Istanbul earthquake
   b. Scree
   c. 1703 Genroku earthquake
   d. 1700 Cascadia earthquake

7. _____ is a national park located largely in Mariposa and Tuolumne Counties, California, United States. It is one of the largest and least fragmented habitat blocks in the Sierra Nevada, and the park supports a diversity of plants and animals. The park has an elevation range from 2,000 to 13,114 feet.
   a. Yosemite National Park
   b. 1703 Genroku earthquake
   c. 1509 Istanbul earthquake
   d. 1700 Cascadia earthquake

Chapter 8. Slope Processes, Landslides, and Subsidence

8. _____ is a fossil fuel formed in swamp ecosystems where plant remains were saved by water and mud from oxidization and biodegradation. It is a sedimentary rock, but the harder forms, such as anthracite _____, can be regarded as metamorphic rocks because of later exposure to elevated temperature and pressure. It is composed primarily of carbon along with assorted other elements, including sulfur.

   a. Coal
   b. 1703 Genroku earthquake
   c. 1509 Istanbul earthquake
   d. 1700 Cascadia earthquake

9. _____ is commonly practiced where a coal seam outcrops a hilly terrain. It removes the overburden above the coal seam and then creates a bench arounf the hill.

   a. Contour strip mining
   b. 1700 Cascadia earthquake
   c. 1703 Genroku earthquake
   d. 1509 Istanbul earthquake

10. _____ is the extraction of valuable minerals or other geological materials from the earth, usually from an ore body, vein, or seam. Any material that cannot be grown from agricultural processes, or created artificially in a laboratory or factory, is usually extracted from the earth by this method.

   a. 1700 Cascadia earthquake
   b. 1509 Istanbul earthquake
   c. 1703 Genroku earthquake
   d. Mining

11. _____ is a form of mass wasting event that occurs when loosely consolidated materials or rock layers move a short distance down a slope. When the movement occurs in soil, there is often a distinctive rotational movement to the mass, that cuts vertically through bedding planes.

   a. 1700 Cascadia earthquake
   b. 1509 Istanbul earthquake
   c. 1703 Genroku earthquake
   d. Slump

12. _____ in meteorology are large scale patterns in the atmospheric pressure field that are nearly stationary, effectively "blocking" or redirecting migratory cyclones. These _____ can remain in place for several days or even weeks, causing the areas affected by them to have the same kind of weather for an extended period of time.

   a. 1509 Istanbul earthquake
   b. 1703 Genroku earthquake
   c. Blocks
   d. 1700 Cascadia earthquake

13. In geology, _____ is a naturally occurring aggregate of minerals and/or mineraloids.

The Earth's outer solid layer, the lithosphere, is made of _____. In general _____s are of three types, namely, igneous, sedimentary, and metamorphic.

   a. 1700 Cascadia earthquake
   b. 1509 Istanbul earthquake
   c. 1703 Genroku earthquake
   d. Rock

14. _____ are downslope, viscous flows of saturated, fine-grained materials, that move at any speed from slow to fast. Typically, they can move at speeds from .17 to 20 km/h. Though these are a lot like mudflows, overall they are slower moving and are covered with solid material carried along by flow from within.

   a. Earthflows
   b. AL 129-1
   c. AASHTO Soil Classification System
   d. AL 333

15. A _____ is the most rapid up to 80 km/h and fluid type of downhill mass wasting.

a. Mudflow
b. 1703 Genroku earthquake
c. 1509 Istanbul earthquake
d. 1700 Cascadia earthquake

16. _____ is the name for loose bodies of sediment that have been deposited or built up at the bottom of a low grade slope or against a barrier on that slope, transported by gravity. The deposits that collect at the foot of a steep slope or cliff are also known by the same name.
   a. 1509 Istanbul earthquake
   b. 1700 Cascadia earthquake
   c. Colluvium
   d. 1703 Genroku earthquake

17. _____, is the slow downward progression of rock and soil down a low grade slope; it can also refer to slow deformation of such materials as a result of prolonged pressure and stress.
   a. 1703 Genroku earthquake
   b. 1700 Cascadia earthquake
   c. Creep
   d. 1509 Istanbul earthquake

18. _____ is a general term that includes rocks and materials that are not by definition rocks but are commonly regarded as rocks.
   a. AL 129-1
   b. AASHTO Soil Classification System
   c. AL 333
   d. Earth materials

19. _____ refers to quantities of rock falling freely from a cliff face.
   a. 1703 Genroku earthquake
   b. 1509 Istanbul earthquake
   c. Rockfall
   d. 1700 Cascadia earthquake

20. The field of _____ encompasses the analysis of static and dynamic stability of slopes of earth and rock-fill dams, slopes of other types of embankments, excavated slopes, and natural slopes in soil and soft rock.
   a. 1509 Istanbul earthquake
   b. 1700 Cascadia earthquake
   c. 1703 Genroku earthquake
   d. Slope stability

21. In materials science, _____ is a change in the shape or size of an object due to an applied force. This can be a result of tensile (pulling) forces, compressive (pushing) forces, shear, bending or torsion (twisting.) _____ is often described as strain.
   a. Deformation
   b. 1700 Cascadia earthquake
   c. 1509 Istanbul earthquake
   d. 1703 Genroku earthquake

22. _____ are very large slides of snow or rock down a mountainside, caused when a buildup of snow is released down a slope, and is one of the major dangers faced in the mountains.
   a. AL 129-1
   b. AL 333
   c. AASHTO Soil Classification System
   d. Avalanches

23. _____ often refers to mudslides, mudflows, jökulhlaups, or debris avalanches. They consist primarily of geological material mixed with water. They may be generated when hillside colluvium or landslide material becomes rapidly saturated with water and flows into a channel.
   a. 1700 Cascadia earthquake
   b. 1509 Istanbul earthquake
   c. 1703 Genroku earthquake
   d. Debris flow

Chapter 8. Slope Processes, Landslides, and Subsidence

24. The _____ of an edge is $c_f(u, v) = c(u, v) - f(u, v)$. This defines a residual network denoted $G_f(V, E_f)$, giving the amount of available capacity. See that there can be an edge from u to v in the residual network, even though there is no edge from u to v in the original network.
    a. 1509 Istanbul earthquake
    b. 1700 Cascadia earthquake
    c. 1703 Genroku earthquake
    d. Residual capacity

25. _____ is any particulate matter that can be transported by fluid flow and which eventually is deposited as a layer of solid particles on the bed or bottom of a body of water or other liquid.
    a. 1700 Cascadia earthquake
    b. Sediment
    c. 1509 Istanbul earthquake
    d. 1703 Genroku earthquake

26. _____ is the study of Earth's surface features or those of other planets, moons, and asteroids
    a. 1703 Genroku earthquake
    b. 1700 Cascadia earthquake
    c. 1509 Istanbul earthquake
    d. Topography

27. _____ is the average and variations of weather over long periods of time. _____ zones can be defined using parameters such as temperature and rainfall.
    a. 1509 Istanbul earthquake
    b. 1703 Genroku earthquake
    c. 1700 Cascadia earthquake
    d. Climate

28. _____ is a cape on the coast of North Carolina. It is the point that protrudes the farthest to the southeast along the northeast-to-southwest line of the Atlantic coast of North America. Two major Atlantic currents collide just off _____, the southerly-flowing cold water Labrador Current and the northerly-flowing warm water Florida Current (Gulf Stream), creating turbulent waters and a large expanse of shallow sandbars extending up to 14 miles offshore.
    a. 1509 Istanbul earthquake
    b. Cape Hatteras
    c. 1700 Cascadia earthquake
    d. 1703 Genroku earthquake

29. Due to shore erosion in the Outer Bank of North Carolina a navagational lighthouse had to be moved leading to the _____.
    a. 1509 Istanbul earthquake
    b. 1700 Cascadia earthquake
    c. 1703 Genroku earthquake
    d. Cape Hatteras Lighthouse controversy

30. The common name _____ refers to Carpobrotus edulis, a creeping, mat-forming succulent species, and member of the Stone Plant family Aizoaceae, one of about 30 species in the genus Carpobrotus.
    a. AL 129-1
    b. AL 333
    c. Ice plant
    d. AASHTO Soil Classification System

31. _____ is a general term for the plant life of a region; it refers to the ground cover provided by plants, and is, by far, the most abundant biotic element of the biosphere. Primeval redwood forests, coastal mangrove stands, sphagnum bogs, desert soil crusts, roadside weed patches, wheat fields, cultivated gardens and lawns; are all encompassed by the term _____.
    a. 1703 Genroku earthquake
    b. 1700 Cascadia earthquake
    c. 1509 Istanbul earthquake
    d. Vegetation

108 *Chapter 8. Slope Processes, Landslides, and Subsidence*

32. An interbasin _____ is a hydrological project undertaken to divert water from one drainage basin into another. This is usually to boost water levels for hydroelectricity, or to supply drinking water nearby.

- Campbell-Heber Diversion
- Coquitlam-Buntzen Diversion
- Kemano Diversion
- Vernon Irrigation District Diversion

- Churchill Diversion-Southern Indian Lake

- Saint John Water Supply

- Bay d'Espoir Diversions
- Deer Lake Diversion
- Smallwood Reservoir-Julian Diversion
- Smallwood Reservoir-Kanairiktok Diversion
- Smallwood Reservoir-Naskaupi Diversion

- Wellington Lake Hydro Project Diversion (with Saskatchewan)

- Ingram Diversion
- Jordan Diversion
- Wreck Cove Diversions

- Long Lake Diversion
- Ogoki Diversion
- Opasatika Diversion
- Root River Diversion

- Barrière Diversion
- Boyd-Sakami Diversion
- Lac de la Frégate Diversion
- Laforge Diversion
- Manouane Diversion
- Mégiscane Diversion
- Sault aux Cochons Diversion

- Cypress Lake Diversion (with Alberta)
- Pasquia Land Resettlement Diversion (with Manitoba)
- Swift Current Diversion

a. Water diversion
b. 1509 Istanbul earthquake
c. 1700 Cascadia earthquake
d. 1703 Genroku earthquake

Chapter 8. Slope Processes, Landslides, and Subsidence

33. An _____ is traditionally considered any chemical compound that, when dissolved in water, gives a solution with a hydrogen ion activity greater than in pure water, i.e. a pH less than 7.0. That approximates the modern definition of Johannes Nicolaus Brønsted and Martin Lowry, who independently defined an _____ as a compound which donates a hydrogen ion to another compound. Common examples include acetic _____ and sulfuric _____. Acid/base systems are different from redox reactions in that there is no change in oxidation state.
    a. AASHTO Soil Classification System
    b. AL 333
    c. AL 129-1
    d. Acid

34. _____ is the production of food, feed, fiber, fuel and other goods by the systematic raizing of plants and animals.
    a. AL 129-1
    b. AASHTO Soil Classification System
    c. Agriculture
    d. AL 333

35. The _____ is a major mountain range of western North America, extending from southern British Columbia through Washington and Oregon to Northern California. It includes both non-volcanic mountains, such as the North Cascades, and the notable volcanoes known as the High Cascades. The _____ is part of the Pacific Ring of Fire, the ring of volcanoes and associated mountains around the Pacific Ocean. All of the known historic eruptions in the contiguous United States have been from Cascade volcanoes.
    a. 1703 Genroku earthquake
    b. 1509 Istanbul earthquake
    c. Cascade Range
    d. 1700 Cascadia earthquake

36. _____ is a term used to describe a group of hydrous aluminium phyllosilicate minerals, that are typically less than 2 micrometres in diameter. _____ consists of a variety of phyllosilicate minerals rich in silicon and aluminium oxides and hydroxides which include variable amounts of structural water. _____s are generally formed by the chemical weathering of silicate-bearing rocks by carbonic acid but some are formed by hydrothermal activity.
    a. 1509 Istanbul earthquake
    b. 1700 Cascadia earthquake
    c. 1703 Genroku earthquake
    d. Clay

37. A _____ is a barrier across flowing water that obstructs, directs or slows down the flow, often creating a reservoir, lake or impoundment.
    a. 1700 Cascadia earthquake
    b. 1509 Istanbul earthquake
    c. 1703 Genroku earthquake
    d. Dam

38. A _____ is a bipedal primate belonging to the mammalian species Homo sapiens in the family Hominidae. Compared to other living organisms on Earth, a _____ has a highly developed brain capable of abstract reasoning, language, and introspection.
    a. 1703 Genroku earthquake
    b. Human
    c. 1509 Istanbul earthquake
    d. 1700 Cascadia earthquake

39. _____ is the human modification of natural environment or wilderness into built environment such as fields, pastures, and settlements. The major effect of _____ on land cover since 1750 has been deforestation of temperate regions. More recent significant effects of _____ include urban sprawl, soil erosion, soil degradation, salinization, and desertification.
    a. Land use
    b. 1700 Cascadia earthquake
    c. 1509 Istanbul earthquake
    d. 1703 Genroku earthquake

Chapter 8. Slope Processes, Landslides, and Subsidence

40. _____ can be a change from a gas to a liquid through condensation, usually by cooling, or a change from a solid to a liquid through melting, usually by heating or by grinding and blending with another liquid to induce dissolution.
   a. 1703 Genroku earthquake
   b. 1700 Cascadia earthquake
   c. 1509 Istanbul earthquake
   d. Liquefaction

41. _____ is the process in which trees are cut down usually as part of a timber harvest. _____ can also remove wood for forest management goals. _____ is controversial due to its environmental and aesthetic impacts.
   a. 1700 Cascadia earthquake
   b. 1703 Genroku earthquake
   c. 1509 Istanbul earthquake
   d. Logging

42. _____ is a unique form of highly sensitive marine clay, with the tendency to change from a relatively stiff condition to a liquid mass when it is disturbed.

Undisturbed _____ resembles a water-saturated gel. When a mass of _____ undergoes sufficient stress, however, it instantly turns into a flowing ooze, a process known as liquefaction.

   a. 1509 Istanbul earthquake
   b. 1700 Cascadia earthquake
   c. Quick clay
   d. 1703 Genroku earthquake

43. There are two distinct views on the meaning of _____. One view is that _____ is part of the fundamental structure of the universe, a dimension in which events occur in sequence, and _____ itself is something that can be measured. A contrasting view is that _____ is part of the fundamental intellectual structure in which _____, rather than being an objective thing to be measured, is part of the mental measuring system.
   a. 1509 Istanbul earthquake
   b. 1700 Cascadia earthquake
   c. Time
   d. 1703 Genroku earthquake

44. The _____ is defined as the part of the land adjoining or near the ocean. A coastline is properly a line on a map indicating the disposition of a _____, but the word is often used to refer to the _____ itself. The adjective coastal describes something as being on, near to, or associated with a _____.
   a. 1703 Genroku earthquake
   b. 1700 Cascadia earthquake
   c. 1509 Istanbul earthquake
   d. Coast

45. _____ is the wearing away of land or the removal of beach or dune sediments by wave action, tidal currents, wave currents, or drainage. Waves, generated by storms or fast moving moter craft, cause _____, which may take the form of long-term losses of sediment and rocks, or merely in the temporary redistribution of coastal sediments; erosion in one location may result in accretion nearby.
   a. 1509 Istanbul earthquake
   b. Beach erosion
   c. 1703 Genroku earthquake
   d. 1700 Cascadia earthquake

46. _____ is displacement of solids by the agents of ocean currents, wind, water, or ice by downward or down-slope movement in response to gravity or by living organisms.
   a. Erosion
   b. AL 129-1
   c. AASHTO Soil Classification System
   d. AL 333

Chapter 8. Slope Processes, Landslides, and Subsidence

47. In agriculture, _____ is the process of gathering mature crops from the fields. Reaping is the _____ of grain crops. The harvest marks the end of the growing season, or the growing cycle for a particular crop. _____ in general usage includes an immediate post-harvest handling, all of the actions taken immediately after removing the crop—cooling, sorting, cleaning, packing—up to the point of further on-farm processing, or shipping to the wholesale or consumer market.
   a. 1509 Istanbul earthquake
   b. 1700 Cascadia earthquake
   c. 1703 Genroku earthquake
   d. Harvesting

48. _____ , is the second largest city of Brazil, behind São Paulo, and the third largest city in the continent, behind São Paulo and Buenos Aires. The city is capital of the state of _____. It was the capital of Brazil for almost two centuries, from 1763 to 1822 while it was a Portuguese colony and from 1822 to 1960 as an independent nation.
   a. Ambulocetus
   b. Andrija MohoroviÄ iÄ‡
   c. Amblypoda
   d. Rio de Janeiro

49. _____ is the increase in the population of cities in proportion to the region's rural population. _____ is studied in terms of its effects on the ecology and economy of a region.
   a. AL 129-1
   b. Urbanization
   c. AASHTO Soil Classification System
   d. AL 333

50. _____ is the largest city in the state of California and the American West as well as second largest in the United States. Often abbreviated as L.A. and nicknamed The City of Angels, _____ is rated an alpha world city, has an estimated population of 3.8 million and spans over 498.3 square miles (1,290.6 km who hail from all over the globe and speak 224 different languages. _____ is the seat of _____ County, the most populated and one of the most diverse counties in the United States.
   a. Coachella Valley
   b. 1509 Istanbul earthquake
   c. 1700 Cascadia earthquake
   d. Los Angeles

51. _____ is the natural or artificial removal of surface and sub-surface water from a given area. Many agricultural soils need _____ to improve production or to manage water supplies.
   a. Drainage
   b. 1700 Cascadia earthquake
   c. 1509 Istanbul earthquake
   d. 1703 Genroku earthquake

52. A _____ is a natural depression or hole in the surface topography caused by the removal of soil or bedrock, often both, by water. They may vary in size from less than a meter to several hundred meters both in diameter and depth, and vary in form from soil-lined bowls to bedrock-edged chasms.
   a. 1703 Genroku earthquake
   b. 1509 Istanbul earthquake
   c. 1700 Cascadia earthquake
   d. Sinkhole

53. In geology, a _____ is a depression with predominant extent in one direction. The terms U-shaped and V-shaped are descriptive terms of geography to characterize the form of _____s. Most _____s belong to one of these two main types or a mixture of them, at least with respect of the cross section of the slopes or hillsides.
   a. 1703 Genroku earthquake
   b. 1509 Istanbul earthquake
   c. Valley
   d. 1700 Cascadia earthquake

54. _____ is one of the four seasons of temperate zones. Almost all English-language calendars, going by astronomy, state that _____ begins on the _____ solstice, and ends on the spring equinox. Calculated more by the weather, it begins and ends earlier and is the season with the shortest days and the lowest temperatures.

Chapter 8. Slope Processes, Landslides, and Subsidence

a. 1700 Cascadia earthquake
b. 1703 Genroku earthquake
c. 1509 Istanbul earthquake
d. Winter

55. _____ is an alpine ski resort in _____, Colorado in the Rocky Mountains. Located just off U.S. Highway 40, the resort is about an hour and a half's drive from Denver, Colorado.
a. 1703 Genroku earthquake
b. Winter Park
c. 1509 Istanbul earthquake
d. 1700 Cascadia earthquake

56. In geology, a _____ is a deformational feature consisting of symmetrically-dipping anticlines; their general outline on a geologic map is circular or oval.
a. Dome
b. 1703 Genroku earthquake
c. 1509 Istanbul earthquake
d. 1700 Cascadia earthquake

57. A _____ is a body of water, not part of the ocean, that is larger and deeper than a pond.
a. 1509 Istanbul earthquake
b. Lake
c. 1703 Genroku earthquake
d. 1700 Cascadia earthquake

58. _____ is a dietary mineral composed primarily of sodium chloride that is essential for animal life, but toxic to most land plants. _____ flavor is one of the basic tastes, an important preservative and a popular food seasoning.

_____ for human consumption is produced in different forms: unrefined _____ (such as sea _____), refined _____ (table _____), and iodized _____.

a. 1703 Genroku earthquake
b. 1700 Cascadia earthquake
c. 1509 Istanbul earthquake
d. Salt

59. A _____ is formed when a thick bed of evaporite minerals found at depth intrudes vertically into surrounding rock strata, forming a diapir.
a. 1703 Genroku earthquake
b. 1509 Istanbul earthquake
c. 1700 Cascadia earthquake
d. Salt Dome

60. The _____ is the surface where the water pressure is equal to atmospheric pressure. A large amount of water within a body of sand or rock below the _____ is called an aquifer, and the ability of rocks to store such groundwater is dependent on their porosity and permeability.
a. Water table
b. 1509 Istanbul earthquake
c. 1703 Genroku earthquake
d. 1700 Cascadia earthquake

61. _____ is a naturally occurring liquid found in formations in the Earth consisting of a complex mixture of hydrocarbons of various lengths.
a. 1509 Istanbul earthquake
b. 1703 Genroku earthquake
c. 1700 Cascadia earthquake
d. Petroleum

62. The _____ is an emergency petroleum store maintained by the United States Department of Energy. It is the largest emergency supply in the world with the current capacity to hold up to 1 billion barrels of crude oil. The second largest emergency supply of petroleum is Japan's with a 2003 reported capacity of 579 million barrels.

a. Strategic Petroleum Reserve b. Ambulocetus
c. Amblypoda d. Andrija Mohorovi Ä iÄ‡

63. A _____ is an extended period of months or years when a region notes a deficiency in its water supply. Generally, this occurs when a region receives consistently below average precipitation.
   a. 1700 Cascadia earthquake b. 1509 Istanbul earthquake
   c. 1703 Genroku earthquake d. Drought

64. An _____ is the result from the sudden release of stored energy in the Earth's crust that creates seismic waves. At the Earth's surface, _____s may manifest themselves by a shaking or displacement of the ground. An _____ is caused by tectonic plates getting stuck and putting a strain on the ground. The strain becomes so great that rocks give way by breaking and sliding along fault planes.
   a. AASHTO Soil Classification System b. Earthquake
   c. AL 333 d. AL 129-1

65. A _____ is a storm system characterized by a low pressure center and numerous thunderstorms that produce strong winds and flooding rain. _____s feed on heat released when moist air rises, resulting in condensation of water vapour contained in the moist air. They are fueled by a different heat mechanism than other cyclonic windstorms such as nor'easters, European windstorms, and polar lows, leading to their classification as 'warm core' storm systems. Depending on its location and strength, a _____ is referred to by many other names, such as hurricane, typhoon, tropical storm, cyclonic storm, tropical depression, and simply cyclone.
   a. Persia b. Kenya
   c. Khmer Empire d. Tropical cyclone

66. A _____ is an opening in a planet's surface or crust, which allows hot, molten rock, ash, and gases to escape from below the surface. Volcanic activity involving the extrusion of rock tends to form mountains or features like mountains over a period of time.

_____es are generally found where tectonic plates are diverging or converging.

   a. 1509 Istanbul earthquake b. 1700 Cascadia earthquake
   c. 1703 Genroku earthquake d. Volcano

67. _____ usually commence with phreatomagmatic eruptions which can be extremely noisy due the rising magma heating water in the ground. This is usually followed by the explosive throat clearing of the vent and the eruption column is dirty grey to black as old weathered rocks are blasted out of the vent. As the vent clears, further ash clouds become grey-white and creamy in colour, with convulations of the ash similar to those of plinian eruptions.
   a. 1509 Istanbul earthquake b. 1700 Cascadia earthquake
   c. Vulcanian eruptions d. 1703 Genroku earthquake

68. A _____ or geophysical hazards is a threat of an event that will have a negative effect on people or the environment. Many _____s are related, e.g. earthquakes can result in tsunamis, drought can lead directly to famine and disease. A concrete example of the division between hazard and disaster is that the 1906 San Francisco earthquake was a disaster, whereas earthquakes are a hazard.

a. 1703 Genroku earthquake
c. 1509 Istanbul earthquake
b. 1700 Cascadia earthquake
d. Natural hazard

Chapter 9. Coastal Processes

1. The _____ are a 100-mile long string of narrow barrier islands off the coast of North Carolina on the East Coast of the United States. They cover approximately the northern half of North Carolina's coastline, separating the Albemarle Sound and Pamlico Sound from the Atlantic Ocean.
   a. AL 129-1
   b. AASHTO Soil Classification System
   c. AL 333
   d. Outer Banks

2. _____ is a cape on the coast of North Carolina. It is the point that protrudes the farthest to the southeast along the northeast-to-southwest line of the Atlantic coast of North America. Two major Atlantic currents collide just off _____, the southerly-flowing cold water Labrador Current and the northerly-flowing warm water Florida Current (Gulf Stream), creating turbulent waters and a large expanse of shallow sandbars extending up to 14 miles offshore.
   a. Cape Hatteras
   b. 1703 Genroku earthquake
   c. 1509 Istanbul earthquake
   d. 1700 Cascadia earthquake

3. Due to shore erosion in the Outer Bank of North Carolina a navagational lighthouse had to be moved leading to the _____.
   a. 1700 Cascadia earthquake
   b. 1509 Istanbul earthquake
   c. Cape Hatteras Lighthouse controversy
   d. 1703 Genroku earthquake

4. The _____ is defined as the part of the land adjoining or near the ocean. A coastline is properly a line on a map indicating the disposition of a _____, but the word is often used to refer to the _____ itself. The adjective coastal describes something as being on, near to, or associated with a _____.
   a. 1700 Cascadia earthquake
   b. 1703 Genroku earthquake
   c. 1509 Istanbul earthquake
   d. Coast

5. Ocean _____ are any more or less continuous, directed movement of ocean water that flows in one of the Earth's oceans. They are rivers of hot or cold water within the ocean. They are generated from the forces acting upon the water like the earth's rotation, the wind, the temperature and salinity differences and the gravitation of the moon.
   a. 1509 Istanbul earthquake
   b. 1700 Cascadia earthquake
   c. 1703 Genroku earthquake
   d. Currents

6. In physics, _____ is a scalar physical quantity that describes the amount of work that can be performed by a force. _____ is an attribute of objects and systems that is subject to a conservation law. Several different forms of _____ exist to explain all known natural phenomena.
   a. AASHTO Soil Classification System
   b. AL 129-1
   c. AL 333
   d. Energy

7. _____ is a term for the length of water over which a given wind has blown. It is used in geography and meteorology and is usually associated with coastal erosion. It plays a large part in longshore drift as well.
   a. 1700 Cascadia earthquake
   b. 1703 Genroku earthquake
   c. 1509 Istanbul earthquake
   d. Fetch

8. _____ is the increase in the average temperature of the Earth's near-surface air and oceans in recent decades and its projected continuation. An increase in global temperatures can in turn cause other changes, including sea level rise, and changes in the amount and pattern of precipitation resulting in floods and drought. There may also be changes in the frequency and intensity of extreme weather events.

Chapter 9. Coastal Processes

   a. 1703 Genroku earthquake
   c. 1509 Istanbul earthquake
   b. Global warming
   d. 1700 Cascadia earthquake

9. A _____ is a storm system characterized by a low pressure center and numerous thunderstorms that produce strong winds and flooding rain. _____s feed on heat released when moist air rises, resulting in condensation of water vapour contained in the moist air. They are fueled by a different heat mechanism than other cyclonic windstorms such as nor'easters, European windstorms, and polar lows, leading to their classification as 'warm core' storm systems. Depending on its location and strength, a _____ is referred to by many other names, such as hurricane, typhoon, tropical storm, cyclonic storm, tropical depression, and simply cyclone.
   a. Tropical cyclone
   c. Persia
   b. Kenya
   d. Khmer Empire

10. A _____ is a strong flow of water returning seaward from the shore. Colloquially a _____ is known simply as a rip, or undertow. Although _____s would exist even without the tides, tides can make an existing rip much more dangerous.
   a. 1509 Istanbul earthquake
   c. Rip current
   b. 1700 Cascadia earthquake
   d. 1703 Genroku earthquake

11. The _____ is a scale classifying most Western Hemisphere tropical cyclones that exceed the intensities of "tropical depressions" and "tropical storms", and thereby become hurricanes. The categories into which the scale divides hurricanes are distinguished by the intensities of their respective sustained winds. The classifications are intended primarily for use in measuring the potential damage and flooding a hurricane will cause upon landfall
   a. 1700 Cascadia earthquake
   c. 1509 Istanbul earthquake
   b. Saffir-Simpson Hurricane Scale
   d. 1703 Genroku earthquake

12. Seismology is the scientific study of earthquakes and the propagation of elastic waves through the Earth. The field also includes studies of earthquake effects, such as tsunamis as well as diverse _____ sources such as volcanic, tectonic, oceanic, atmospheric, and artificial processes (such as explosions.) A related field that uses geology to infer information regarding past earthquakes is paleoseismology.
   a. Seismic
   c. 1703 Genroku earthquake
   b. 1509 Istanbul earthquake
   d. 1700 Cascadia earthquake

13. A _____ is any disturbed state of an astronomical body's atmosphere, especially affecting its surface, and strongly implying severe weather. It may be marked by strong wind, thunder and lightning, heavy precipitation, such as ice, or wind transporting some substance through the atmosphere.
   a. 1509 Istanbul earthquake
   c. 1703 Genroku earthquake
   b. 1700 Cascadia earthquake
   d. Storm

14. The Tropics, seated in the equatorial regions of the world, are limited in latitude by the Tropic of Cancer in the northern hemisphere at approximately 23°26' N latitude, and the Tropic of Capricorn in the southern hemisphere at 23°26' S latitude. The Tropics are also referred to as the _____ zone and the torrid zone. A noontime scene from the Philippines on a day when the Sun is almost directly overhead.

The Tropics includes all the areas on the Earth where the sun reaches a point directly overhead at least once during the solar year.

a. Tropical
b. 1509 Istanbul earthquake
c. 1700 Cascadia earthquake
d. 1703 Genroku earthquake

15. A _____ is a series of waves created when a body of water, such as an ocean, is rapidly displaced on a massive scale. Earthquakes, mass movements above or below water, volcanic eruptions and other underwater explosions, landslides, large meteorite impacts and testing with nuclear weapons at sea all have the potential to generate a _____. The effects of a _____ can range from unnoticeable to devastating.
 a. Tsunami
 b. 1509 Istanbul earthquake
 c. 1703 Genroku earthquake
 d. 1700 Cascadia earthquake

16. A _____ is a disturbance that propagates through space or spacetime, transferring energy and momentum and sometimes angular momentum.
 a. 1509 Istanbul earthquake
 b. 1703 Genroku earthquake
 c. 1700 Cascadia earthquake
 d. Wave

17. In fluid dynamics, the _____ of a surface wave denotes the difference between the elevations of a crest and a neighbouring trough. _____ is a term used by mariners, as well as in coastal, ocean engineering and naval engineering.

At sea, the term significant _____ is used as a means to introduce a well-defined and standardized statistic to denote the characteristic height of the random waves in a sea state.

 a. 1700 Cascadia earthquake
 b. Wave height
 c. 1509 Istanbul earthquake
 d. 1703 Genroku earthquake

18. In physics, _____ is the distance between repeating units of a propagating wave of a given frequency. It is commonly designated by the Greek letter lambda. Examples of wave-like phenomonena are light, water waves, and sound waves. _____ of a sine wave.In a wave, a property varies with the position.
 a. 1703 Genroku earthquake
 b. Wavelength
 c. 1509 Istanbul earthquake
 d. 1700 Cascadia earthquake

19. _____ is the flow of air. More generally, it is the flow of the gases which compose an atmosphere; since _____ is not only an Earth based phenomenon.
 a. 1700 Cascadia earthquake
 b. 1509 Istanbul earthquake
 c. 1703 Genroku earthquake
 d. Wind

20. _____ is the wearing away of land or the removal of beach or dune sediments by wave action, tidal currents, wave currents, or drainage. Waves, generated by storms or fast moving moter craft, cause _____, which may take the form of long-term losses of sediment and rocks, or merely in the temporary redistribution of coastal sediments; erosion in one location may result in accretion nearby.
 a. 1700 Cascadia earthquake
 b. 1703 Genroku earthquake
 c. 1509 Istanbul earthquake
 d. Beach erosion

21. In meteorology, _____ are an area of low atmospheric pressure characterized by inward spiraling winds that rotate counter clockwise in the northern hemisphere and clockwise in the southern hemisphere of the Earth.

Chapter 9. Coastal Processes

a. 1509 Istanbul earthquake
b. 1703 Genroku earthquake
c. Cyclones
d. 1700 Cascadia earthquake

22. _____ is displacement of solids by the agents of ocean currents, wind, water, or ice by downward or down-slope movement in response to gravity or by living organisms.
a. AL 333
b. AL 129-1
c. Erosion
d. AASHTO Soil Classification System

23. _____ is a chemical element in the periodic table that has the symbol Rn and atomic number 86. A radioactive noble gas that is formed by the decay of radium, _____ is one of the heaviest gases and is considered to be a health hazard.
a. Ytterbium
b. Tantalum
c. Selenium
d. Radon

24. A _____, in the context of an ocean, is a formation of long wavelength ocean surface waves on the sea. They are far more stable in their directions and frequency than normal oceanic waves since they are formed by tropical storms and by stable wind systems.
a. 1700 Cascadia earthquake
b. 1703 Genroku earthquake
c. Swell
d. 1509 Istanbul earthquake

25. _____ is the change in direction of a wave due to a change in its speed. This is most commonly seen when a wave passes from one medium to another.
a. 1700 Cascadia earthquake
b. 1703 Genroku earthquake
c. 1509 Istanbul earthquake
d. Refraction

26. _____s are a family of carbon allotropes, molecules composed entirely of carbon, in the form of a hollow sphere, ellipsoid, tube, or plane. Spherical _____s are also called buckyballs, and cylindrical ones are called carbon nanotubes or buckytubes. Graphene is an example of a planar _____ sheet.
a. 1509 Istanbul earthquake
b. Fullerene
c. 1703 Genroku earthquake
d. 1700 Cascadia earthquake

27. In coastal systems, a _____ is a raised ridge of pebbles or sand found at high tide or storm tide marks on a beach.
a. 1700 Cascadia earthquake
b. 1703 Genroku earthquake
c. 1509 Istanbul earthquake
d. Berm

28. _____ are level spaces, shelves or raised barriers separating two areas.
a. Berms
b. 1700 Cascadia earthquake
c. 1703 Genroku earthquake
d. 1509 Istanbul earthquake

29. A _____ is a hill of sand built by eolian processes. _____s are subject to different forms and sizes based on their interaction with the wind. Most kinds of _____ are longer on the windward side where the sand is pushed up the _____, and a shorter in the lee of the wind. The trough between _____s is called a slack. A "_____ field" is an area covered by extensive sand _____s. Large _____ fields are known as ergs.

Chapter 9. Coastal Processes

a. 1700 Cascadia earthquake
b. 1509 Istanbul earthquake
c. Dune
d. 1703 Genroku earthquake

30. The _____ is defined as the area between the high water and low water marks, or the portion of the lake that is less than 15 feet in depth.
   a. Lysocline
   b. Water mass
   c. Littoral
   d. Chemical oceanography

31. A _____ or sandbar is a somewhat linear landform within or extending into a body of water, typically composed of sand, silt or small pebbles. A bar is characteristically long and narrow and develops where a stream or ocean current promote deposition of granular material, resulting in localized shallowing of the water. Bars can appear in the sea, in a lake, or in a river.

The term bar can apply to landform features spanning a considerable range in size, from a length of a few meters in a small stream to marine depositions stretching for hundreds of kilometres along a coastline, often called barrier islands.

   a. 1703 Genroku earthquake
   b. 1509 Istanbul earthquake
   c. Shoal
   d. 1700 Cascadia earthquake

32. Longshore drift, sometimes known as shore drift, _____, LSD (not common as it is more typically used in reference to a drug) or littoral drift is a geological process by which sediments such as sand or other materials, move along a beach shore. It uses the process of swash to push the material up the beach and backwash down the beach; until it reaches a groyne or another obstacle.

Where waves approach the coastline at an angle, when they break their swash pushes beach material up the beach at the same angle.

   a. 1509 Istanbul earthquake
   b. 1700 Cascadia earthquake
   c. 1703 Genroku earthquake
   d. Longshore current

33. _____ is a geological process by which sediments such as sand or other materials, move along a beach shore.
   a. 1700 Cascadia earthquake
   b. 1703 Genroku earthquake
   c. 1509 Istanbul earthquake
   d. Longshore drift

34. _____ comprises a beach, an estate and a harbor. It lies 4 miles east of North Berwick, East Lothian, Scotland.
   a. 1700 Cascadia earthquake
   b. 1703 Genroku earthquake
   c. 1509 Istanbul earthquake
   d. Seacliff

35. With _____ the crest undergoes deformation and destabilizes, resulting in it spilling over the front of the wave. This wave tends to create a frothy appearance. It occurs most often on gentle beaches.
   a. 1700 Cascadia earthquake
   b. 1509 Istanbul earthquake
   c. 1703 Genroku earthquake
   d. Spilling breakers

36. As ocean surface waves come closer to shore they break, forming the foamy, bubbly surface we call surf. The region of breaking waves defines the _____.

Chapter 9. Coastal Processes

a. 1700 Cascadia earthquake
b. Surf zone
c. 1703 Genroku earthquake
d. 1509 Istanbul earthquake

37. _____ (uprush and backwash), in geography, is the water that washes up on shore after an incoming wave has broken. This action will cause sand and other light particles to be transported up the beach. The direction of the _____ varies with the prevailing wind, whereas the backwash is always perpendicular to the coastline.
a. 1703 Genroku earthquake
b. 1700 Cascadia earthquake
c. 1509 Istanbul earthquake
d. Swash

38. In geology, a _____ generally refers to a linear structural depression that extends laterally over a distance, while being less steep than a trench. It can be a narrow basin or a geologic rift. In meteorolology a _____ is an elongated region of relatively low atmospheric pressure, often associated with fronts.
a. Riparian zone
b. Shelf break
c. Wilson cycle
d. Trough

39. An _____ is an assessment of the likely influence a project may have on the environment. The purpose of the assessment is to ensure that decision-makers consider _____s before deciding whether to proceed with new projects.
a. Environmental impact
b. AL 129-1
c. AL 333
d. AASHTO Soil Classification System

40. A _____ is a macro-scale storm whose winds come from the northeast, especially in the coastal areas of the Northeastern United States and Atlantic Canada. More specifically, it describes a low pressure area whose center of rotation is just off the coast and whose leading winds in the left forward quadrant rotate onto land from the northeast.
a. Nor'easter
b. 1703 Genroku earthquake
c. 1509 Istanbul earthquake
d. 1700 Cascadia earthquake

41. A _____ is the interface between the land and water. It is continually changing because of the dynamic interaction between the oceans and the land.
a. 1700 Cascadia earthquake
b. 1509 Istanbul earthquake
c. 1703 Genroku earthquake
d. Coastal zone

42. A _____ is a barrier across flowing water that obstructs, directs or slows down the flow, often creating a reservoir, lake or impoundment.
a. 1703 Genroku earthquake
b. 1700 Cascadia earthquake
c. 1509 Istanbul earthquake
d. Dam

43. _____ refers to a member of any human group whose adult males grow to less than 150 cm in average height or less than 155 cm. A member of a slightly taller group is termed pygmoid. The best known _____ are the Aka, Efe and Mbuti of central Africa.
a. 1703 Genroku earthquake
b. 1700 Cascadia earthquake
c. 1509 Istanbul earthquake
d. Pygmies

44. _____ is the increase in the population of cities in proportion to the region's rural population. _____ is studied in terms of its effects on the ecology and economy of a region.

Chapter 9. Coastal Processes

a. AASHTO Soil Classification System
b. AL 129-1
c. AL 333
d. Urbanization

45. A _____ is a geological phenomenon which includes a wide range of ground movement, such as rock falls, deep failure of slopes and shallow debris flows. Although gravity's action on an over-steepened slope is the primary reason for a _____, there are other contributing factors affecting the original slope stability.
   a. 1509 Istanbul earthquake
   b. 1703 Genroku earthquake
   c. 1700 Cascadia earthquake
   d. Landslide

46. Consumption of a _____ requires resources and contributes to air and water pollution. In the industrialized world the development of a _____ has become essential for agriculture, transportation, waste collection, information technology, communications that have become prerequisites of a developed society.
   a. AASHTO Soil Classification System
   b. AL 129-1
   c. AL 333
   d. Energy resource

47. A _____ is a structure constructed on coasts as part of coastal defense or to protect an anchorage from the effects of weather and longshore drift.
   a. 1703 Genroku earthquake
   b. 1509 Istanbul earthquake
   c. Breakwater
   d. 1700 Cascadia earthquake

48. _____ is an excavation activity or operation usually carried out at least partly underwater, in shallow seas or fresh water areas with the purpose of gathering up bottom sediments and disposing of them at a different location.

This technique is often used to keep waterways navigable. It is also used as a way to replenish sand on some public beaches, where too much sand has been lost because of coastal erosion.

   a. 1700 Cascadia earthquake
   b. 1509 Istanbul earthquake
   c. 1703 Genroku earthquake
   d. Dredging

49. A _____ is a rigid hydraulic structure built out from the shore or from the bank and interrupts the flow of water and sediment. _____s serve a multitude of functions.
   a. Groyne
   b. 1703 Genroku earthquake
   c. 1509 Istanbul earthquake
   d. 1700 Cascadia earthquake

50. The term _____ signifyies something thrown out, is applied to a variety of structures employed in river, dock, and maritime works which are generally carried out in pairs from river banks, or in continuation of river channels at their outlets into deep water; or out into docks, and outside their entrances; or for forming basins along the sea-coast for ports in tideless seas.
   a. 1509 Istanbul earthquake
   b. 1700 Cascadia earthquake
   c. 1703 Genroku earthquake
   d. Jetty

51. A _____ is a deposition landform found off coasts. A spit is a type of bar or beach that develops where a re-entrant occurs, such as at a cove, bay, ria, or river mouth.
   a. 1703 Genroku earthquake
   b. 1700 Cascadia earthquake
   c. Sand spit
   d. 1509 Istanbul earthquake

Chapter 9. Coastal Processes

52. _____ are a form of hard coastal defense constructed on the inland part of a coast to reduce the effects of strong waves and to defend the coast around a town or harbor from erosion. The walls can be sloping, vertical or curved to reflect wave power.
   a. 1700 Cascadia earthquake
   b. 1703 Genroku earthquake
   c. Seawalls
   d. 1509 Istanbul earthquake

53. A _____ is a deposition landform found off coasts. A _____ is a type of bar or beach that develops where a re-entrant occurs, such as at a cove, bay, ria, or river mouth. A _____ is formed by the movement of sediment along a shore by a process known as longshore drift. Where the direction of the shore turns inland the longshore current spreads out or dissipates. No longer able to carry the full load, much of the sediment is dropped. This causes a bar to build out from the shore, eventually becoming a _____.
   a. 1509 Istanbul earthquake
   b. Spit
   c. 1703 Genroku earthquake
   d. 1700 Cascadia earthquake

54. The _____ is a federal agency made up of some 34,600 civilian and 650 military men and women. The Corps' mission is to provide engineering services to the United States. The _____. The _____ is organized geographically into eight permanent divisions, one provisional division, and one provisional district. They are defined by watershed boundaries for civil works projects, and by political boundaries for military projects.
   a. Ambulocetus
   b. Andrija Mohorovičić
   c. U.S. Army Corps of Engineers
   d. Amblypoda

55. A _____ is an urban area with a high population and a particular administrative, legal, or historical status.

Large industrialized cities generally have advanced systems for sanitation, utilities, land usage, housing, and transportation and more. This close proximity greatly facilitates interaction between people and firms, benefiting both parties in the process.

   a. 1509 Istanbul earthquake
   b. 1700 Cascadia earthquake
   c. 1703 Genroku earthquake
   d. City

56. _____ is a city in Cape May County, New Jersey, United States.
   a. AL 333
   b. AASHTO Soil Classification System
   c. AL 129-1
   d. Ocean City

57. The outer barrier refers to the string of _____s that divide the lagoons south of Long Island from the Atlantic Ocean.

These islands include Long Beach _____, Jones Beach Island, Fire Island and West Hampton Dunes. The outer barrier extends seventy-five miles 120 km along the south shore of Long Island, New York, from Rockaway Beach on the NYC/Nassau County border from Long Beach _____s western edge, to Suffolk County's east end of Shinnecock Bay.

   a. 1703 Genroku earthquake
   b. 1700 Cascadia earthquake
   c. 1509 Istanbul earthquake
   d. Barrier island

Chapter 9. Coastal Processes

58. A _____ is a bipedal primate belonging to the mammalian species Homo sapiens in the family Hominidae. Compared to other living organisms on Earth, a _____ has a highly developed brain capable of abstract reasoning, language, and introspection.
   a. 1703 Genroku earthquake
   b. 1700 Cascadia earthquake
   c. 1509 Istanbul earthquake
   d. Human

59. _____ is the human modification of natural environment or wilderness into built environment such as fields, pastures, and settlements. The major effect of _____ on land cover since 1750 has been deforestation of temperate regions. More recent significant effects of _____ include urban sprawl, soil erosion, soil degradation, salinization, and desertification.
   a. 1700 Cascadia earthquake
   b. 1509 Istanbul earthquake
   c. 1703 Genroku earthquake
   d. Land use

60. _____ is a barrier island, comprising the southern portion of Maryland's Atlantic coast and part of Virginia's Eastern Shore.
   a. AASHTO Soil Classification System
   b. AL 129-1
   c. AL 333
   d. Assateague Island

61. The Laurentian _____ are a group of five large lakes in North America on or near the Canada-United States border. They are the largest group of fresh water lakes on Earth.
   a. 1509 Istanbul earthquake
   b. 1700 Cascadia earthquake
   c. 1703 Genroku earthquake
   d. Great Lakes

62. The _____ region of the United States comprises the coasts of states which border the Gulf of Mexico. The states of Texas, Louisiana, Mississippi, Alabama, and Florida are known as the Gulf States. All Gulf States are located in the Southern region of the United States.
   a. 1509 Istanbul earthquake
   b. 1703 Genroku earthquake
   c. Gulf Coast
   d. 1700 Cascadia earthquake

63. A _____ is a body of water, not part of the ocean, that is larger and deeper than a pond.
   a. Lake
   b. 1700 Cascadia earthquake
   c. 1509 Istanbul earthquake
   d. 1703 Genroku earthquake

64. _____ is any product of the condensation of atmospheric water vapor that is deposited on the earth's surface. It occurs when the atmosphere becomes saturated with water vapour and the water condenses and falls out of solution. Air becomes saturated via two processes, cooling and adding moisture.
   a. 1703 Genroku earthquake
   b. Precipitation
   c. 1509 Istanbul earthquake
   d. 1700 Cascadia earthquake

65. The _____ is the second-largest of the world's oceanic divisions; with a total area of about 106.4 million square kilometres (41.1 million square miles.) It covers approximately one-fifth of the Earth's surface. The _____ occupies an elongated, S-shaped basin extending longitudinally between the Americas to the west, and Eurasia and Africa to the east.
   a. AL 333
   b. AL 129-1
   c. AASHTO Soil Classification System
   d. Atlantic Ocean

Chapter 9. Coastal Processes

66. The _____ is a bay that forms the northeastern part of the Indian Ocean. It resembles a triangle in shape, and is bordered on the east by Malay Peninsula, and on the west by India.
    a. Bay of Bengal
    b. Strait of Messina
    c. Sea of Okhotsk
    d. 1509 Istanbul earthquake

67. The _____ is a region of mostly calm weather found at the center of strong tropical cyclones. The _____ of a storm is usually circular and typically 30–65 km in diameter. The _____ is possibly the most recognizable feature of tropical cyclones.
    a. AL 333
    b. AL 129-1
    c. AASHTO Soil Classification System
    d. Eye

68. A _____, or a low for short, is a region where the atmospheric pressure is lowest with relation to the surrounding area.
    a. Low pressure cell
    b. 1509 Istanbul earthquake
    c. 1703 Genroku earthquake
    d. 1700 Cascadia earthquake

69. _____ is a layer of gases surrounding the planet Earth and retained by the Earth's gravity, protecting life on Earth by absorbing ultraviolet solar radiation and reducing temperature extremes between day and night.
    a. AL 129-1
    b. AASHTO Soil Classification System
    c. AL 333
    d. Earths atmosphere

70. _____ can refer to atmospheric pressure, the pressure of air environmentally or pressure of air in a system.
    a. AL 129-1
    b. AASHTO Soil Classification System
    c. AL 333
    d. Air pressure

71. A _____ is an offshore rise of water associated with a low pressure weather system, typically a tropical cyclone. _____ is caused primarily by high winds pushing on the ocean's surface, causing the water to pile up higher than the ordinary sea level.
    a. 1509 Istanbul earthquake
    b. 1703 Genroku earthquake
    c. 1700 Cascadia earthquake
    d. Storm surge

72. _____ (symbol: p or sometimes P) is the force per unit area applied to an object in a direction perpendicular to the surface. Gauge _____ is the _____ relative to the local atmospheric or ambient _____.

    _____ is an effect which occurs when a force is applied on a surface.

    a. 1700 Cascadia earthquake
    b. 1703 Genroku earthquake
    c. 1509 Istanbul earthquake
    d. Pressure

73. A _____ is the consequence of a natural hazard such as volcanic eruption, earthquake, landslide which becomes a physical event and interacts with human activities.
    a. 1703 Genroku earthquake
    b. 1700 Cascadia earthquake
    c. 1509 Istanbul earthquake
    d. Natural disaster

74. The _____ is an agency of the United States Department of Homeland Security. It's purpose is to coordinate the response to a disaster which has occurred in the United States and which overwhelms the resouces of local ands state authorities.
   a. Andrija Mohorovićić
   b. Ambulocetus
   c. Amblypoda
   d. Federal Emergency Management Agency

75. The _____ of the USA is the working arm of the United States National Academy of Sciences and the United States National Academy of Engineering, carrying out most of the studies done in their names.
   a. Amblypoda
   b. National Research Council
   c. Andrija Mohorovićić
   d. Ambulocetus

Chapter 10. Impact of Extraterrestrial Objects

1. The _____ was a massive explosion that occurred near the Podkamennaya above the Earth's surface.
   - a. 1703 Genroku earthquake
   - b. 1509 Istanbul earthquake
   - c. 1700 Cascadia earthquake
   - d. Tunguska event

2. A _____ is a term from compressible fluid dynamics. It is normally understood to be the pressure and flow resulting from the deposition of a large amount of energy in a small very localised volume. The flow field can be approximated as a lead shock wave, followed by a 'self-similar' subsonic flow field.
   - a. 1509 Istanbul earthquake
   - b. 1700 Cascadia earthquake
   - c. Blast wave
   - d. 1703 Genroku earthquake

3. A _____ is an approximately circular depression in the surface of a planet, moon or other solid body in the Solar System, formed by the hyper-velocity impact of a smaller body with the surface. Impact _____s typically have raised rims, and they range from small, simple, bowl-shaped depressions to large, complex, multi-ringed, impact basins.
   - a. 1509 Istanbul earthquake
   - b. 1703 Genroku earthquake
   - c. 1700 Cascadia earthquake
   - d. Crater

4. A _____ is a large sand to boulder-sized particle of debris in the Solar system. Its visible path when it enters the Earth's atmosphere is commonly called a shooting star or falling star.
   - a. 1700 Cascadia earthquake
   - b. 1703 Genroku earthquake
   - c. 1509 Istanbul earthquake
   - d. Meteoroid

5. A _____ is a type of propagating disturbance. They are characterized by an abrupt, nearly discontinuous, change in the characteristics of the medium. Across a shock there is always an extremely rapid rise in pressure, temperature and density of the flow
   - a. 1509 Istanbul earthquake
   - b. 1700 Cascadia earthquake
   - c. 1703 Genroku earthquake
   - d. Shock wave

6. _____ , is the name given to the vast region constituting almost all of Northern Asia and for the most part currently serving as the massive central and eastern portion of the Russian Federation, having served in the same capacity previously for the U.S.S.R. from its beginning, and the Russian Empire beginning in the 16th century. Geographically, it includes a large part of the Eurasian Steppe and extends eastward from the Ural Mountains to the watershed between Pacific and Arctic drainage basins, and southward from the Arctic Ocean to the hills of north-central Kazakhstan and the national borders of both Mongolia and China. It makes up about 77% of Russia's territory, but only 30% of Russia's population.
   - a. Andrija Mohorovičić
   - b. Siberia
   - c. Amblypoda
   - d. Ambulocetus

7. In geology, a _____ is a depression with predominant extent in one direction. The terms U-shaped and V-shaped are descriptive terms of geography to characterize the form of _____s. Most _____s belong to one of these two main types or a mixture of them, at least with respect of the cross section of the slopes or hillsides.
   - a. 1509 Istanbul earthquake
   - b. 1700 Cascadia earthquake
   - c. Valley
   - d. 1703 Genroku earthquake

8. _____ are a class of astronomical objects. The term is generally used to indicate a diverse group of small celestial bodies that drift in the solar system in orbit around the Sun.
   - a. AASHTO Soil Classification System
   - b. AL 129-1
   - c. AL 333
   - d. Asteroids

Chapter 10. Impact of Extraterrestrial Objects

9. An _____ is a sudden increase in volume and release of energy in an extreme manner, usually with the generation of high temperatures and the release of gases. An _____ creates a shock wave.

   _____s do not commonly occur in nature.

   a. Chemical hazard
   b. AASHTO Soil Classification System
   c. AL 129-1
   d. Explosion

10. A _____ is a disturbance that propagates through space or spacetime, transferring energy and momentum and sometimes angular momentum.
    a. 1700 Cascadia earthquake
    b. 1509 Istanbul earthquake
    c. Wave
    d. 1703 Genroku earthquake

11. The _____ is the region of the Solar System located roughly between the planets Mars and Jupiter where 98.5% of asteroid orbits can be found. This region is termed the main belt when contrasted with other concentrations of minor planets.
    a. AL 129-1
    b. Asteroid belt
    c. AASHTO Soil Classification System
    d. AL 333

12. _____ are small bodies in the solar system that orbit the Sun and occasionally exhibit a coma or atmosphere and/or a tail — both primarily from the effects of solar radiation upon its nucleus, which itself is a minor body composed of rock, dust, and ice.
    a. 1700 Cascadia earthquake
    b. Comets
    c. 1509 Istanbul earthquake
    d. 1703 Genroku earthquake

13. Comet _____ was probably the most widely observed comet of the twentieth century, and one of the brightest seen for many decades. It was visible to the naked eye for a record 18 months, twice as long as the previous record holder, the Great Comet of 1811.
    a. 1703 Genroku earthquake
    b. Hale-Bopp
    c. 1509 Istanbul earthquake
    d. 1700 Cascadia earthquake

14. _____ is the fifth planet from the Sun and the largest planet within the solar system. It is two and a half times as massive as all of the other planets in our solar system combined. _____, along with Saturn, Uranus and Neptune, is classified as a gas giant.
    a. 1509 Istanbul earthquake
    b. 1700 Cascadia earthquake
    c. 1703 Genroku earthquake
    d. Jupiter

15. _____ the fourth planet from the Sun in the Solar System. The planet is named after _____, the Roman god of war. It is also referred to as the "Red Planet" because of its reddish appearance as seen from Earth.
    a. 1509 Istanbul earthquake
    b. 1703 Genroku earthquake
    c. Mars
    d. 1700 Cascadia earthquake

16. A _____ is a natural object originating in outer space that survives an impact with the Earth's surface without being destroyed. While in space it is called a meteoroid. When it enters the atmosphere, air resistance causes the body to heat up and emit light, thus forming a fireball.

a. Meteorite
b. 1703 Genroku earthquake
c. 1509 Istanbul earthquake
d. 1700 Cascadia earthquake

17. _____, some of which are known as 'meteor storms', or 'meteor outbursts' are celestial events in which a number of meteors are observed to radiate from one point in the sky. These meteors are caused by streams of cosmic debris called meteoroids entering Earth's atmosphere at extremely high speed on parallel trajectories. Most are smaller than a grain of sand, so almost all meteoroids disintegrate and never hit the earth's surface.
   a. Meteor showers
   b. 1703 Genroku earthquake
   c. 1509 Istanbul earthquake
   d. 1700 Cascadia earthquake

18. _____ is the eighth and farthest known planet from the Sun in the Solar System. It is the fourth largest planet by diameter, and the third largest by mass.
   a. 1703 Genroku earthquake
   b. Neptune
   c. 1509 Istanbul earthquake
   d. 1700 Cascadia earthquake

19. The _____ is a postulated spherical cloud of comets situated about 50 to 50,000 AU from the Sun. This is approximately 1000 times the distance from the Sun to Pluto or nearly a light year. The outer extent of the _____ places the boundary of our Solar System at nearly a quarter of the distance to Proxima Centauri, the nearest star to the Sun.
   a. AASHTO Soil Classification System
   b. AL 129-1
   c. AL 333
   d. Oort Cloud

20. _____ is a theory of geology that has been developed to explain the observed evidence for large scale motions of the Earth's lithosphere. The theory encompassed and superseded the older theory of continental drift.
   a. 1700 Cascadia earthquake
   b. 1703 Genroku earthquake
   c. 1509 Istanbul earthquake
   d. Plate tectonics

21. The _____ is Earth's only natural satellite. It makes a complete orbit around the Earth every 27.3 days, and the periodic variations in the geometry of the Earth–_____–Sun system are responsible for the lunar phases that repeat every 29.5 days.
   a. 1703 Genroku earthquake
   b. Moon
   c. 1509 Istanbul earthquake
   d. 1700 Cascadia earthquake

22. A _____ is a massive, luminous ball of plasma. _____s group together to form galaxies, and they dominate the visible universe. The nearest _____ to Earth is the Sun, which is the source of most of the energy on Earth, including daylight. Other _____s are visible in the night sky, when they are not outshone by the Sun. A _____ shines because nuclear fusion in its core releases energy which traverses the _____'s interior and then radiates into outer space.
   a. 1703 Genroku earthquake
   b. 1509 Istanbul earthquake
   c. 1700 Cascadia earthquake
   d. Star

23. _____ is a field of study within geology concerned generally with the structures within the crust of the Earth, or other planets, and particularly with the forces and movements that have operated in a region to create these structures.
   a. 1509 Istanbul earthquake
   b. Tectonics
   c. 1703 Genroku earthquake
   d. 1700 Cascadia earthquake

Chapter 10. Impact of Extraterrestrial Objects

24. _____ is a chemical element with the symbol Fe and atomic number 26. _____ is a lustrous, silvery soft metal. _____ and nickel are notable for being the final elements produced by stellar nucleosynthesis, and thus are the heaviest elements which do not require a supernova or similarly cataclysmic event for formation.
   a. AASHTO Soil Classification System
   b. Iron
   c. AL 333
   d. AL 129-1

25. The _____ consists of the Sun and the other celestial objects gravitationally bound to it: the eight planets, their 165 known moons, three currently identified dwarf planets and their four known moons, and billions of small bodies.
   a. Solar system
   b. 1509 Istanbul earthquake
   c. 1700 Cascadia earthquake
   d. 1703 Genroku earthquake

26. The State of _____ is a state located in the southwestern region of the United States. The capital and largest city is Phoenix. The second largest city is Tucson, followed by the four Phoenix-area conurbation cities of Mesa, Glendale, Chandler, and Scottsdale.
   a. AASHTO Soil Classification System
   b. Kaibab Plateau
   c. AL 129-1
   d. Arizona

27. An _____ is a generally symmetrical apron of ejecta that surrounds a crater; it is layered thickly at the crater's rim and thin to discontinuous at the blanket's outer edge
   a. AL 129-1
   b. AL 333
   c. AASHTO Soil Classification System
   d. Ejecta blanket

28. _____ can be defined as the solid state recrystallisation of pre-existing rocks due to changes in heat and/or pressure and/or introduction of fluids. There will be mineralogical, chemical and crystallographic changes. _____ produced with increasing pressure and temperature conditions is known as prograde _____. Conversely, decreasing temperatures and pressure characterize retrograde _____.
   a. Metamorphism
   b. 1700 Cascadia earthquake
   c. 1703 Genroku earthquake
   d. 1509 Istanbul earthquake

29. A _____ is a naturally occurring substance formed through geological processes that has a characteristic chemical composition, a highly ordered atomic structure and specific physical properties. A rock, by comparison, is an aggregate of _____s and need not have a specific chemical composition. _____s range in composition from pure elements and simple salts to very complex silicates with thousands of known forms.
   a. 1509 Istanbul earthquake
   b. 1700 Cascadia earthquake
   c. 1703 Genroku earthquake
   d. Mineral

30. _____ is a metallic chemical element in the periodic table that has the symbol Ni and atomic number 28. _____ is a silvery white metal that takes on a high polish. It belongs to the iron group, and is hard, malleable, and ductile. It occurs combined with sulfur in millerite, with arsenic in the mineral niccolite, and with arsenic and sulfur in _____ glance.
   a. Nickel
   b. 1509 Istanbul earthquake
   c. 1703 Genroku earthquake
   d. 1700 Cascadia earthquake

31. The mineral _____ is a magnesium iron silicate. It is one of the most common minerals on Earth, and has also been identified on the Moon, Mars, and comet Wild 2.

a. AASHTO Soil Classification System   b. Olivine
c. AL 333   d. AL 129-1

32. The _____ are a group of important rock-forming silicate minerals found in many igneous and metamorphic rocks. They share a common structure comprised of single chains of silica tetrahedra and they crystalise in the monoclinic and orthorhombic system.
   a. 1703 Genroku earthquake   b. Pyroxenes
   c. 1509 Istanbul earthquake   d. 1700 Cascadia earthquake

33. In geology and astronomy, the term _____ is used to denote types of rock that consist predominantly of _____ minerals. Such rocks include a wide range of igneous, metamorphic and sedimentary types. Most of the Earth's mantle and crust are made up of _____ rocks. The same is true of the Moon and the other rocky planets.
   a. 1700 Cascadia earthquake   b. 1703 Genroku earthquake
   c. Silicate   d. 1509 Istanbul earthquake

34. The _____ of an object is the extra energy which it possesses due to its motion. It is defined as the work needed to accelerate a body of a given mass from rest to its current velocity. Term or phrase NOT in the knowledge-core.
   a. Kinetic energy   b. 1703 Genroku earthquake
   c. 1509 Istanbul earthquake   d. 1700 Cascadia earthquake

35. _____ is the second most common mineral in the Earth's continental crust. It is made up of a lattice of silica tetrahedra. _____ belongs to the rhombohedral crystal system. In nature _____ crystals are often twinned, distorted, or so intergrown with adjacent crystals of _____ or other minerals as to only show part of this shape, or to lack obvious crystal faces altogether and appear massive.
   a. 1700 Cascadia earthquake   b. 1509 Istanbul earthquake
   c. 1703 Genroku earthquake   d. Quartz

36. In geology, _____ is a naturally occurring aggregate of minerals and/or mineraloids.

The Earth's outer solid layer, the lithosphere, is made of _____. In general _____s are of three types, namely, igneous, sedimentary, and metamorphic.

   a. 1509 Istanbul earthquake   b. 1700 Cascadia earthquake
   c. Rock   d. 1703 Genroku earthquake

37. A _____ is an opening in a planet's surface or crust, which allows hot, molten rock, ash, and gases to escape from below the surface. Volcanic activity involving the extrusion of rock tends to form mountains or features like mountains over a period of time.

_____es are generally found where tectonic plates are diverging or converging.

   a. 1509 Istanbul earthquake   b. 1700 Cascadia earthquake
   c. 1703 Genroku earthquake   d. Volcano

Chapter 10. Impact of Extraterrestrial Objects

38. A popular way of classifying magmatic volcanoes goes by their frequency of eruption, or _____, with those that erupt regularly called active, those that have erupted in historical times but are now quiet called dormant, and those that have not erupted in historical times called extinct.
    a. 1700 Cascadia earthquake
    b. Volcanic activity
    c. 1703 Genroku earthquake
    d. 1509 Istanbul earthquake

39. In physics, _____ is a scalar physical quantity that describes the amount of work that can be performed by a force. _____ is an attribute of objects and systems that is subject to a conservation law. Several different forms of _____ exist to explain all known natural phenomena.
    a. AASHTO Soil Classification System
    b. AL 129-1
    c. AL 333
    d. Energy

40. _____ is a rock composed of angular fragments of rocks or minerals in a matrix, that is a cementing material, that may be similar or different in composition to the fragments.
    a. 1700 Cascadia earthquake
    b. 1703 Genroku earthquake
    c. 1509 Istanbul earthquake
    d. Breccia

41. _____ is displacement of solids by the agents of ocean currents, wind, water, or ice by downward or down-slope movement in response to gravity or by living organisms.
    a. Erosion
    b. AASHTO Soil Classification System
    c. AL 333
    d. AL 129-1

42. _____ 9 (SL9, formally designated D/1993 F2) was a comet that collided with Jupiter in 1994, providing the first direct observation of an extraterrestrial collision of solar system objects. This generated a large amount of coverage in the popular media, and SL9 was closely observed by astronomers worldwide. The collision provided new information about Jupiter and highlighted its role in reducing space debris in the inner solar system.
    a. 1509 Istanbul earthquake
    b. 1700 Cascadia earthquake
    c. Tallinn
    d. Comet Shoemaker-Levy

43. _____ is the science and study of the solid matter that constitute the Earth. Encompassing such things as rocks, soil, and gemstones, _____ studies the composition, structure, physical properties, history, and the processes that shape Earth's components.
    a. Glacial motion
    b. Glaciology
    c. 1509 Istanbul earthquake
    d. Geology

44. The _____ is used by geologists and other scientists to describe the timing and relationships between events that have occurred during the history of Earth.
    a. 1700 Cascadia earthquake
    b. 1703 Genroku earthquake
    c. 1509 Istanbul earthquake
    d. Geological time scale

45. _____ is a sharp decrease in the number of species in a relatively short period of time. It has sometimes accelerated the evolution of life on earth. Global warming is one of the causes of _____.
    a. 1703 Genroku earthquake
    b. Mass extinction
    c. 1509 Istanbul earthquake
    d. 1700 Cascadia earthquake

46. The _____ is the portion of Earth between the land surface and the phreatic zone or zone of saturation.

a. 1700 Cascadia earthquake
b. 1509 Istanbul earthquake
c. 1703 Genroku earthquake
d. Vadose zone

47. In biology and ecology, _____ is the cessation of existence of a species or group of taxa, reducing biodiversity. The moment of _____ is generally considered to be the death of the last individual of that species.
   a. AL 333
   b. AASHTO Soil Classification System
   c. AL 129-1
   d. Extinction

48. There are two distinct views on the meaning of _____. One view is that _____ is part of the fundamental structure of the universe, a dimension in which events occur in sequence, and _____ itself is something that can be measured. A contrasting view is that _____ is part of the fundamental intellectual structure in which _____, rather than being an objective thing to be measured, is part of the mental measuring system.
   a. Time
   b. 1509 Istanbul earthquake
   c. 1700 Cascadia earthquake
   d. 1703 Genroku earthquake

49. The _____ is a geologic period of the Paleozoic era. During the _____ the first fish evolved legs and started to walk on land as tetrapods and the first insects and spiders also started to colonize terrestrial habitats. The first seed-bearing plants spread across dry land, forming huge forests. In the oceans, Primitive sharks became more numerous. The first ammonite mollusks appeared, and trilobites as well as great coral reefs were still common.
   a. 1700 Cascadia earthquake
   b. 1703 Genroku earthquake
   c. 1509 Istanbul earthquake
   d. Devonian

50. The _____ is the second of the six periods of the Paleozoic era. It follows the Cambrian period and is followed by the Silurian period. The _____ started at a major extinction called the Cambrian-_____ extinction and lasted for about 44.6 million years. It ended with another major extinction event that wiped out 60% of marine genera.
   a. AL 129-1
   b. AASHTO Soil Classification System
   c. AL 333
   d. Ordovician

51. The _____ is the last period of the Palaeozoic Era. As the _____ opened, the Earth was still in the grip of an ice age, so the polar regions were covered with deep layers of ice. During the _____, all the Earth's major land masses except portions of East Asia were collected into a single supercontinent known as Pangaea. The _____ ended with the most extensive extinction event recorded in paleontology: the _____-Triassic extinction event.
   a. 1509 Istanbul earthquake
   b. 1700 Cascadia earthquake
   c. Permian
   d. 1703 Genroku earthquake

52. _____ is an ancient impact crater buried underneath the Yucatán Peninsula, with its center located approximately underneath the town of Chicxulub. Investigations suggest that this impact structure is dated from the late Cretaceous Period. Thus the meteorite associated with the crater is implicated in causing the extinction of the dinosaurs.
   a. 1509 Istanbul earthquake
   b. Chicxulub crater
   c. 1703 Genroku earthquake
   d. 1700 Cascadia earthquake

53. _____ is a term used to describe a group of hydrous aluminium phyllosilicate minerals, that are typically less than 2 micrometres in diameter. _____ consists of a variety of phyllosilicate minerals rich in silicon and aluminium oxides and hydroxides which include variable amounts of structural water. _____s are generally formed by the chemical weathering of silicate-bearing rocks by carbonic acid but some are formed by hydrothermal activity.

Chapter 10. Impact of Extraterrestrial Objects 133

    a. 1700 Cascadia earthquake
    b. 1509 Istanbul earthquake
    c. 1703 Genroku earthquake
    d. Clay

54. The _____ is the longest geological period and constitutes nearly half of the Mesozoic. The end of the Cretaceous defines the boundary between the Mesozoic and Cenozoic eras. The Cretaceous as a separate period was first defined using strata in the Paris Basin and named for the extensive beds of chalk.
    a. Cretaceous period
    b. 1509 Istanbul earthquake
    c. 1703 Genroku earthquake
    d. 1700 Cascadia earthquake

55. _____ were vertebrate animals that dominated terrestrial ecosystems for over 160 million years, first appearing approximately 230 million years ago. At the end of the Cretaceous Period, approximately 65 million years ago, a catastrophic extinction event ended _____' dominance on land.
    a. Dinosaurs
    b. 1509 Istanbul earthquake
    c. 1703 Genroku earthquake
    d. 1700 Cascadia earthquake

56. The _____ is a major division of the geologic timescale and the second epoch of the Palaeogene period in the Cenozoic era. It spans the time from the end of the Paleocene epoch to the beginning of the Oligocene epoch. The start of this period is marked by the emergence of the first modern mammals.
    a. Eocene period
    b. AL 333
    c. AASHTO Soil Classification System
    d. AL 129-1

57. _____ can refer to: a period of time; a distinctive historical period or era, a unit of the geologic time scale, less than a period and greater than an age, or a phase in the development of the universe with distinctive properties.
    a. Epoch
    b. AL 333
    c. AASHTO Soil Classification System
    d. AL 129-1

58. _____ is a chemical element in the periodic table that has the symbol Ir and atomic number 77. A dense, very hard, brittle, silvery-white transition metal of the platinum family, _____ is used in high strength alloys that can withstand high temperatures and occurs in natural alloys with platinum or osmium.
    a. AL 333
    b. AL 129-1
    c. AASHTO Soil Classification System
    d. Iridium

59. The _____ was the catastrophic mass extinction of extant animal species in a comparatively short period of time. The event occurred approximately 65.5 million years ago.
    a. 1700 Cascadia earthquake
    b. 1509 Istanbul earthquake
    c. 1703 Genroku earthquake
    d. Cretaceous-Tertiary event

60. A _____ is a piece of land that is nearly surrounded by water but connected to mainland via an isthmus.

134 *Chapter 10. Impact of Extraterrestrial Objects*

A _____ can also be a headland, cape, island promontory, bill, point, or spit.

A beach on the Mornington _____

- Beecraft _____, New South Wales
- Bellarine _____, Victoria
- Cape York _____, Queensland
- Cobourg _____, Northern Territory
- Cronulla sand dunes, Kurnell _____
- Dampier _____, Western Australia
- Eyre _____, South Australia
- Fleurieu _____, South Australia
- Freycinet _____, Tasmania
- Inskip _____, Queensland.
- Jervis Bay Territory
- Mornington _____, Victoria
- Redcliffe, Queensland
- Stockton, New South Wales
- Tasman _____, Tasmania
- Tasmania itself was one a _____ connected to Australia during the great Ice Ages
- Wilsons Promontory, Victoria
- Woy Woy, New South Wales
- Yorke _____, South Australia
- Younghusband _____, South Australia

Looking north over the Kurnell _____.

- Aupouri _____, North Island
- Banks _____, South Island
- Bluff _____, South Island
- Bream Head, North Island
- Cape Brett, North Island
- Cape Campbell, South Island
- Cape Foulwind, South Island
- Cape Kidnappers, North Island
- Cape Turnagain, North Island
- Coromandel _____, North Island
- Farewell Spit, South Island
- Kaikoura _____, South Island
- Karikari _____, North Island
- Mahia _____, North Island
- Miramar _____, North Island
- Mount Maunganui, North Island
- North Auckland _____, North Island
- Otago _____, South Island
- Tiwai Point, South Island

- Gazelle _____, New Britain
- Huon _____

- Europe is composed of many _____s, such as the Iberian _____, Scandinavian, etc.

The Balkans is a _____ including the Republic of Macedonia, Greece ,Bosnia and Herzegovina, Bulgaria, Croatia, Serbia, Albania, and Montenegro.

   a. Kinmen
   b. Peninsula
   c. Japan
   d. Human beings

61. The _____ on the geologic timescale had been intended to cover the world's recent period of repeated glaciations. The _____ follows the Pliocene and is followed by the Holocene. The _____ is the third epoch of the Neogene period or 6th epoch of the Cenozoic era. The end of the _____ corresponds with the end of the Paleolithic age used in archaeology. The _____ is divided into the Early _____, Middle _____ and Late _____, and numerous faunal stages.

   a. 1703 Genroku earthquake
   b. Pleistocene
   c. 1700 Cascadia earthquake
   d. 1509 Istanbul earthquake

62. The _____ covers roughly the time span between the demise of the non-avian dinosaurs and beginning of the most recent Ice Age. Each epoch of the _____ was marked by striking developments in mammalian life. The earliest recognizable hominoid relatives of humans appeared. Tectonic activity continued as Gondwana finally split completely apart.

   a. 1703 Genroku earthquake
   b. Tertiary
   c. 1509 Istanbul earthquake
   d. 1700 Cascadia earthquake

63. The _____ separates the Caribbean Sea from the Gulf of Mexico. The peninsula lies east of the Isthmus of Tehuantepec, a northwestern geographic partition separating the region of Central America from the rest of North America.

   a. Yucatan Peninsula
   b. 1700 Cascadia earthquake
   c. 1703 Genroku earthquake
   d. 1509 Istanbul earthquake

64. A _____ is a natural depression or hole in the surface topography caused by the removal of soil or bedrock, often both, by water. They may vary in size from less than a meter to several hundred meters both in diameter and depth, and vary in form from soil-lined bowls to bedrock-edged chasms.

   a. 1700 Cascadia earthquake
   b. 1703 Genroku earthquake
   c. 1509 Istanbul earthquake
   d. Sinkhole

65. _____ are in the Yucatan Peninsula a type of freshwater filled limestone sinkhole.

   a. 1509 Istanbul earthquake
   b. 1700 Cascadia earthquake
   c. 1703 Genroku earthquake
   d. Cenotes

66. _____s are the mineralized or otherwise preserved remains or traces of animals, plants, and other organisms. The totality of _____s, both discovered and undiscovered, and their placement in fossiliferous rock formations and sedimentary layers is known as the _____ record.

   a. Fossil
   b. 1703 Genroku earthquake
   c. 1509 Istanbul earthquake
   d. 1700 Cascadia earthquake

67. The _____ is the ninth largest body of water in the world. It is an ocean basin largely surrounded by the North American continent and the island of Cuba. It is bounded on the northeast, north and northwest by the Gulf Coast of the United States, on the southwest and south by Mexico, and on the southeast by Cuba.

Chapter 10. Impact of Extraterrestrial Objects

  a. 1509 Istanbul earthquake
  b. Gulf of Mexico
  c. 1703 Genroku earthquake
  d. 1700 Cascadia earthquake

68. _____ is a sedimentary rock composed largely of the mineral calcite. _____ often contains variable amounts of silica in the form of chert or flint, as well as varying amounts of clay, silt and sand as disseminations, nodules, or layers within the rock. The primary source of the calcite in _____ is most commonly marine organisms. These organisms secrete shells that settle out of the water column and are deposited on ocean floors as pelagic ooze or alternatively is conglomerated in a coral reef.
  a. 1700 Cascadia earthquake
  b. 1703 Genroku earthquake
  c. 1509 Istanbul earthquake
  d. Limestone

69. The United Mexican States, commonly known as _____, is a federal constitutional republic in North America. It is bordered on the north by the United States; on the south and west by the North Pacific Ocean; on the southeast by Guatemala, Belize, and the Caribbean Sea; and on the east by the Gulf of _____. The United Mexican States are a federation comprising thirty-one states and a federal district, the capital _____ City, whose metropolitan area is one of the world's most populous.
  a. Ambulocetus
  b. Amblypoda
  c. Andrija Mohorovičić
  d. Mexico

70. _____ is any particulate matter that can be transported by fluid flow and which eventually is deposited as a layer of solid particles on the bed or bottom of a body of water or other liquid.
  a. 1700 Cascadia earthquake
  b. Sediment
  c. 1509 Istanbul earthquake
  d. 1703 Genroku earthquake

71. _____ is the result of the transformation of a pre-existing rock type, the protolith, in a process called metamorphism, which means "change in form". It makes up a large part of the Earth's crust and are classified by texture and by chemical and mineral assemblage. It is also formed when rock is heated up by the intrusion of hot molten rock called magma from the Earth's interior.
  a. Metamorphic rock
  b. 1700 Cascadia earthquake
  c. 1703 Genroku earthquake
  d. 1509 Istanbul earthquake

72. _____ or impact metamorphism describes the effects of shock-wave related deformation and heating during impact events. The formation of similar features during explosive volcanism is generally discounted due to the lack of metamorphic effects unequivocally associated with explosions and the difficulty in reaching sufficient pressures during such an event.

Planar fractures are parallel sets of multiple planar cracks or cleavages in quartz grains; they develop at the lowest pressures characteristic of shock waves (~5-8 GPa) and a common feature of quartz grains found associated with impact structures.

  a. Shock metamorphism
  b. 1703 Genroku earthquake
  c. 1509 Istanbul earthquake
  d. 1700 Cascadia earthquake

Chapter 10. Impact of Extraterrestrial Objects 137

73. An _____ is traditionally considered any chemical compound that, when dissolved in water, gives a solution with a hydrogen ion activity greater than in pure water, i.e. a pH less than 7.0. That approximates the modern definition of Johannes Nicolaus Brønsted and Martin Lowry, who independently defined an _____ as a compound which donates a hydrogen ion to another compound. Common examples include acetic _____ and sulfuric _____. Acid/base systems are different from redox reactions in that there is no change in oxidation state.
   a. AL 333
   b. AL 129-1
   c. AASHTO Soil Classification System
   d. Acid

74. The term _____ is commonly used to mean the deposition of acidic components in rain, snow, dew, or dry particles. _____ occurs when sulfur dioxide and nitrogen oxides are emitted into the atmosphere, undergo chemical transformations and are absorbed by water droplets in clouds. The droplets then fall to earth as rain, snow, mist, dry dust, hail, or sleet. This increases the acidity of the soil, and affects the chemical balance of lakes and streams.
   a. AASHTO Soil Classification System
   b. AL 129-1
   c. Acid precipitation
   d. AL 333

75. A _____ is a distinctive mushroom-shaped cloud of smoke, flame, or debris resulting from a very large explosion. They are most commonly associated with nuclear explosions, but any sufficiently large blast will produce the same sort of effect.
   a. 1700 Cascadia earthquake
   b. Mushroom cloud
   c. 1509 Istanbul earthquake
   d. 1703 Genroku earthquake

76. _____ is a chemical element which has the symbol N and atomic number 7 in the periodic table. Elemental _____ is a colorless, odorless, tasteless and mostly inert diatomic gas at standard conditions, constituting 78.08% percent of Earth's atmosphere.
   a. 1700 Cascadia earthquake
   b. 1703 Genroku earthquake
   c. 1509 Istanbul earthquake
   d. Nitrogen

77. _____ is a metabolic pathway that converts carbon dioxide into organic compounds, especially sugars, using the energy from sunlight. _____ occurs in plants, algae, and many species of Bacteria, but not in Archaea. Photosynthetic organisms are called photoautotrophs, but not all organisms that use light as a source of energy carry out _____, since photoheterotrophs use organic compounds, rather than carbon dioxide, as a source of carbon.
   a. Photosynthesis
   b. 1509 Istanbul earthquake
   c. Light-independent reactions
   d. Carbon fixation

78. Seismology is the scientific study of earthquakes and the propagation of elastic waves through the Earth. The field also includes studies of earthquake effects, such as tsunamis as well as diverse _____ sources such as volcanic, tectonic, oceanic, atmospheric, and artificial processes (such as explosions.) A related field that uses geology to infer information regarding past earthquakes is paleoseismology.
   a. 1509 Istanbul earthquake
   b. Seismic
   c. 1703 Genroku earthquake
   d. 1700 Cascadia earthquake

79. _____ is a project at the University of Arizona that specializes in the study of minor planets, including various types of asteroids and comets.
   a. 1703 Genroku earthquake
   b. 1509 Istanbul earthquake
   c. Spacewatch
   d. 1700 Cascadia earthquake

Chapter 10. Impact of Extraterrestrial Objects

80. _____ is a strong mineral acid. It is soluble in water at all concentrations. _____ has many applications, and is one of the top products of the chemical industry. Principal uses include ore processing, fertilizer manufacturing, oil refining, wastewater processing, and chemical synthesis.

   a. 1509 Istanbul earthquake
   b. 1703 Genroku earthquake
   c. Sulfuric acid
   d. 1700 Cascadia earthquake

81. A _____ is a series of waves created when a body of water, such as an ocean, is rapidly displaced on a massive scale. Earthquakes, mass movements above or below water, volcanic eruptions and other underwater explosions, landslides, large meteorite impacts and testing with nuclear weapons at sea all have the potential to generate a _____. The effects of a _____ can range from unnoticeable to devastating.

   a. 1700 Cascadia earthquake
   b. 1509 Istanbul earthquake
   c. 1703 Genroku earthquake
   d. Tsunami

82. An _____ is a layer of gases that may surround a material body of sufficient mass, by the gravity of the body, and are retained for a longer duration if gravity is high and the _____'s temperature is low. Some planets consist mainly of various gases, and therefore have very deep _____s

The term stellar _____ describes the outer region of a star, and typically includes the portion starting from the opaque photosphere outwards.

   a. AL 129-1
   b. AASHTO Soil Classification System
   c. AL 333
   d. Atmosphere

83. _____ is a concept that denotes the precise probability of specific eventualities. Technically, the notion of _____ is independent from the notion of value and, as such, eventualities may have both beneficial and adverse consequences. However, in general usage the convention is to focus only on potential negative impact to some characteristic of value that may arise from a future event.

   a. 1700 Cascadia earthquake
   b. 1509 Istanbul earthquake
   c. 1703 Genroku earthquake
   d. Risk

84. _____ is a program run by NASA and Jet Propulsion Laboratory to discover near-Earth objects. The _____ system began observations in December 1995.

The original principal investigator was Eleanor F. Helin, with co-investigators Steven H. Pravdo and David L. Rabinowitz.

   a. 1703 Genroku earthquake
   b. 1700 Cascadia earthquake
   c. 1509 Istanbul earthquake
   d. Near Earth Asteroid Tracking

85. A _____ occurs as a result of the rapid release of energy from an uncontrolled nuclear reaction. The driving reaction may be nuclear fission, nuclear fusion or a multistage cascading combination of the two.

   a. 1509 Istanbul earthquake
   b. 1703 Genroku earthquake
   c. 1700 Cascadia earthquake
   d. Nuclear explosion

Chapter 10. Impact of Extraterrestrial Objects

86. A _____ is a Solar System object whose orbit brings it into close proximity with the Earth. All NEOs have a perihelion distance < 1.3 AU . They include a few thousand near-Earth asteroids (NEAs), near-Earth comets, a number of solar-orbiting spacecraft, and meteoroids large enough to be tracked in space before striking the Earth.
   a. 1509 Istanbul earthquake
   b. 1703 Genroku earthquake
   c. 1700 Cascadia earthquake
   d. Near-Earth object

87. Consumption of a _____ requires resources and contributes to air and water pollution. In the industrialized world the development of a _____ has become essential for agriculture, transportation, waste collection, information technology, communications that have become prerequisites of a developed society.
   a. AL 333
   b. AASHTO Soil Classification System
   c. Energy resource
   d. AL 129-1

88. _____ are hydrocarbons, primarily coal and petroleum, formed from the fossilized remains of dead plants and animals by exposure to heat and pressure in the Earth's crust over hundreds of millions of years. The burning of _____ by humans is the largest source of emissions of carbon dioxide, which is one of the greenhouse gases that enhances radiative forcing and contributes to global warming.
   a. 1509 Istanbul earthquake
   b. 1703 Genroku earthquake
   c. 1700 Cascadia earthquake
   d. Fossil fuels

89. _____ is water located beneath the ground surface in soil pore spaces and in the fractures of geologic formations. _____ is recharged from, and eventually flows to, the surface naturally; natural discharge often occurs at springs and seeps, streams and can often form oases or wetlands.
   a. 1509 Istanbul earthquake
   b. 1700 Cascadia earthquake
   c. 1703 Genroku earthquake
   d. Groundwater

90. _____ are sources of water that are useful or potentially useful to humans. It is important because it is needed for life to exist. Many uses of water include agricultural, industrial, household, recreational and environmental activities.
   a. 1509 Istanbul earthquake
   b. 1700 Cascadia earthquake
   c. 1703 Genroku earthquake
   d. Water resources

Chapter 11. Water Resources

1. _____ is an island located in southeastern New York, USA, just east of Manhattan. Stretching northeast into the Atlantic Ocean, _____ contains four counties, two of which are boroughs of New York City, and two of which are mainly suburban. Numerous bridges and tunnels through Queens and Brooklyn connect _____ to the three other boroughs of New York City.
    a. 1700 Cascadia earthquake
    b. 1509 Istanbul earthquake
    c. Long Island
    d. 1703 Genroku earthquake

2. _____ are sources of water that are useful or potentially useful to humans. It is important because it is needed for life to exist. Many uses of water include agricultural, industrial, household, recreational and environmental activities.
    a. 1703 Genroku earthquake
    b. 1700 Cascadia earthquake
    c. Water resources
    d. 1509 Istanbul earthquake

3. _____ is water located beneath the ground surface in soil pore spaces and in the fractures of geologic formations. _____ is recharged from, and eventually flows to, the surface naturally; natural discharge often occurs at springs and seeps, streams and can often form oases or wetlands.
    a. 1700 Cascadia earthquake
    b. 1703 Genroku earthquake
    c. 1509 Istanbul earthquake
    d. Groundwater

4. A _____, is a site for the disposal of waste materials by burial and is the oldest form of waste treatment.
    a. 1700 Cascadia earthquake
    b. 1703 Genroku earthquake
    c. 1509 Istanbul earthquake
    d. Landfill

5. _____ is the capital, largest city, and commercial centre of the Commonwealth of the Bahamas. The city has a population of 210,832, nearly 70 percent of the entire population of the Bahamas. Lynden Pindling International Airport, the major airport for the Bahamas, is located about 10 miles west of _____ city centre, and has daily flights to major cities in the United Kingdom, United States, Canada and the Caribbean.
    a. 1509 Istanbul earthquake
    b. 1703 Genroku earthquake
    c. Nassau
    d. 1700 Cascadia earthquake

6. A _____ is a salt of nitric acid with an ion composed of one nitrogen and three oxygen atoms. In freshwater or estuarine systems close to land, _____ can reach high levels that can potentially cause the death of fish. Water quality may also be affected through ground water resources that have a high number of septic systems in a watershed.
    a. Nitrate
    b. 1700 Cascadia earthquake
    c. 1509 Istanbul earthquake
    d. 1703 Genroku earthquake

7. _____ is a natural process that occurs in virtually all coastal aquifers. It consists in salt water flowing inland in freshwater aquifers. This behavior is caused by the fact that sea water has a higher density than freshwater.
    a. Saltwater intrusion
    b. 1700 Cascadia earthquake
    c. 1703 Genroku earthquake
    d. 1509 Istanbul earthquake

8. _____ is a method of controlled disposal of refuse on land. _____ involves natural fermentation brought by microorganisms. It is often employed to reclaim otherwise useless land.
    a. 1703 Genroku earthquake
    b. 1509 Istanbul earthquake
    c. 1700 Cascadia earthquake
    d. Sanitary landfill

9. _____ is the increase in the population of cities in proportion to the region's rural population. _____ is studied in terms of its effects on the ecology and economy of a region.

Chapter 11. Water Resources

a. AASHTO Soil Classification System
b. Urbanization
c. AL 333
d. AL 129-1

10. _____ is a large set of adverse effects upon water bodies such as lakes, rivers, oceans, and groundwater caused by human activities. Although natural phenomena such as volcanoes, algae blooms, storms, and earthquakes also cause major changes in water quality and the ecological status of water, these are not deemed to be pollution. _____ has many causes and characteristics.
  a. 1700 Cascadia earthquake
  b. Water pollution
  c. 1509 Istanbul earthquake
  d. 1703 Genroku earthquake

11. An _____ is a body of igneous rock that has crystallized from a molten magma below the surface of the Earth.
  a. AASHTO Soil Classification System
  b. AL 333
  c. AL 129-1
  d. Intrusion

12. _____ is the introduction of substances or energy into the environment, resulting in deleterious effects of such a nature as to endanger human health, harm living resources and ecosystems, and impair or interfere with amenities and other legitimate uses of the environment.
  a. 1700 Cascadia earthquake
  b. Pollution
  c. 1703 Genroku earthquake
  d. 1509 Istanbul earthquake

13. The Earth's water is always in movement, and the _____, describes the continuous movement of water on, above, and below the surface of the Earth. Since the _____ is truly a "cycle," there is no beginning or end. Water can change states among liquid, vapor, and ice at various places in the _____, with these processes happening in the blink of an eye and over millions of years. Although the balance of water on Earth remains fairly constant over time, individual water molecules can come and go in a hurry.
  a. 1700 Cascadia earthquake
  b. 1509 Istanbul earthquake
  c. 1703 Genroku earthquake
  d. Hydrologic cycle

14. _____ is a cape on the coast of North Carolina. It is the point that protrudes the farthest to the southeast along the northeast-to-southwest line of the Atlantic coast of North America. Two major Atlantic currents collide just off _____, the southerly-flowing cold water Labrador Current and the northerly-flowing warm water Florida Current (Gulf Stream), creating turbulent waters and a large expanse of shallow sandbars extending up to 14 miles offshore.
  a. 1700 Cascadia earthquake
  b. 1703 Genroku earthquake
  c. Cape Hatteras
  d. 1509 Istanbul earthquake

15. Due to shore erosion in the Outer Bank of North Carolina a navagational lighthouse had to be moved leading to the _____.
  a. 1703 Genroku earthquake
  b. 1509 Istanbul earthquake
  c. 1700 Cascadia earthquake
  d. Cape Hatteras Lighthouse controversy

16. _____ is the natural or artificial removal of surface and sub-surface water from a given area. Many agricultural soils need _____ to improve production or to manage water supplies.
  a. 1509 Istanbul earthquake
  b. 1703 Genroku earthquake
  c. Drainage
  d. 1700 Cascadia earthquake

Chapter 11. Water Resources

17. A _____, is the separation between neighboring drainage basins. In hilly country, it lies along topographical peaks and ridges, but in flat country or on a high plateau, especially where the ground is marshy, it may be invisible - just a more or less notional line on the ground on either side of which falling raindrops will start a journey to different rivers, and even to different sides of a country or continent.
    a. 1509 Istanbul earthquake
    b. 1703 Genroku earthquake
    c. Drainage divide
    d. 1700 Cascadia earthquake

18. _____ is any particulate matter that can be transported by fluid flow and which eventually is deposited as a layer of solid particles on the bed or bottom of a body of water or other liquid.
    a. Sediment
    b. 1703 Genroku earthquake
    c. 1509 Istanbul earthquake
    d. 1700 Cascadia earthquake

19. _____ is a term used to describe the flow of water, from rain, snowmelt, or other sources, over the land surface, and is a major component of the water cycle.
    a. Surface runoff
    b. 1703 Genroku earthquake
    c. 1700 Cascadia earthquake
    d. 1509 Istanbul earthquake

20. Water collecting on the ground or in a stream, river, lake, or wetland is called _____; as opposed to groundwater. _____ is naturally replenished by precipitation and naturally lost through discharge to the oceans, evaporation, and sub-surface seepage into the groundwater. _____ is the largest source of fresh water.
    a. 1700 Cascadia earthquake
    b. 1703 Genroku earthquake
    c. 1509 Istanbul earthquake
    d. Surface water

21. The _____ is the second-longest named river in North America, with a length of 2320 miles from Lake Itasca to the Gulf of Mexico. It drains most of the area between the Rocky Mountains and the Appalachian Mountains, except for the areas drained by Hudson Bay via the Red River of the North, the Great Lakes and the Rio Grande.
    a. 1509 Istanbul earthquake
    b. 1703 Genroku earthquake
    c. 1700 Cascadia earthquake
    d. Mississippi River

22. _____ is the production of food, feed, fiber, fuel and other goods by the systematic raizing of plants and animals.
    a. AL 129-1
    b. AASHTO Soil Classification System
    c. Agriculture
    d. AL 333

23. _____ is the average and variations of weather over long periods of time. _____ zones can be defined using parameters such as temperature and rainfall.
    a. 1700 Cascadia earthquake
    b. 1509 Istanbul earthquake
    c. Climate
    d. 1703 Genroku earthquake

24. _____ is the total length of all the streams and rivers in a drainage basin divided by the total area of the drainage basin.
    a. 1700 Cascadia earthquake
    b. 1703 Genroku earthquake
    c. 1509 Istanbul earthquake
    d. Drainage density

25. _____ is feeding on growing herbage, attached algae, or phytoplankton.

Chapter 11. Water Resources

a. 1703 Genroku earthquake　　　　　　　b. 1700 Cascadia earthquake
c. 1509 Istanbul earthquake　　　　　　　d. Grazing

26.　A _____ is a bipedal primate belonging to the mammalian species Homo sapiens in the family Hominidae. Compared to other living organisms on Earth, a _____ has a highly developed brain capable of abstract reasoning, language, and introspection.
a. 1700 Cascadia earthquake　　　　　　　b. 1703 Genroku earthquake
c. Human　　　　　　　　　　　　　　　　d. 1509 Istanbul earthquake

27.　_____ is the third or vertical dimension of land surface. When _____ is described underwater, the term bathymetry is used.
a. 1700 Cascadia earthquake　　　　　　　b. 1509 Istanbul earthquake
c. 1703 Genroku earthquake　　　　　　　d. Terrain

28.　In geology, _____ is a naturally occurring aggregate of minerals and/or mineraloids.

The Earth's outer solid layer, the lithosphere, is made of _____. In general _____s are of three types, namely, igneous, sedimentary, and metamorphic.

a. 1509 Istanbul earthquake　　　　　　　b. 1703 Genroku earthquake
c. 1700 Cascadia earthquake　　　　　　　d. Rock

29.　_____ is a general term for the plant life of a region; it refers to the ground cover provided by plants, and is, by far, the most abundant biotic element of the biosphere. Primeval redwood forests, coastal mangrove stands, sphagnum bogs, desert soil crusts, roadside weed patches, wheat fields, cultivated gardens and lawns; are all encompassed by the term _____.

a. 1703 Genroku earthquake　　　　　　　b. 1700 Cascadia earthquake
c. 1509 Istanbul earthquake　　　　　　　d. Vegetation

30.　An _____ is traditionally considered any chemical compound that, when dissolved in water, gives a solution with a hydrogen ion activity greater than in pure water, i.e. a pH less than 7.0. That approximates the modern definition of Johannes Nicolaus Brønsted and Martin Lowry, who independently defined an _____ as a compound which donates a hydrogen ion to another compound. Common examples include acetic _____ and sulfuric _____. Acid/base systems are different from redox reactions in that there is no change in oxidation state.
a. AL 333　　　　　　　　　　　　　　　b. AASHTO Soil Classification System
c. Acid　　　　　　　　　　　　　　　　d. AL 129-1

31.　The _____ of a material is defined as its mass per unit volume:

$$\rho = \frac{m}{V}$$

Different materials usually have different densities, so _____ is an important concept regarding buoyancy, metal purity and packaging.

Chapter 11. Water Resources

In some cases _____ is expressed as the dimensionless quantities specific gravity or relative _____, in which case it is expressed in multiples of the _____ of some other standard material, usually water or air.

In a well-known story, Archimedes was given the task of determining whether King Hiero's goldsmith was embezzling gold during the manufacture of a wreath dedicated to the gods and replacing it with another, cheaper alloy.

   a. Density
   b. 1509 Istanbul earthquake
   c. 1700 Cascadia earthquake
   d. Particle density

32. _____ is the degradation of land in arid, semi arid and dry sub-humid areas resulting from various climatic variations, but primarily human activities. Current _____ is taking place much faster worldwide than historically and usually arises from the demands of increased populations that settle on the land in order to grow crops and graze animals.
   a. 1703 Genroku earthquake
   b. 1700 Cascadia earthquake
   c. Desertification
   d. 1509 Istanbul earthquake

33. _____ refers to a member of any human group whose adult males grow to less than 150 cm in average height or less than 155 cm. A member of a slightly taller group is termed pygmoid. The best known _____ are the Aka, Efe and Mbuti of central Africa.
   a. Pygmies
   b. 1703 Genroku earthquake
   c. 1509 Istanbul earthquake
   d. 1700 Cascadia earthquake

34. _____ is the artificial application of water to the soil usually for assisting in growing crops. In crop production it is mainly used to replace missing rainfall in periods of drought, but also to protect plants against frost.
   a. AL 129-1
   b. AASHTO Soil Classification System
   c. AL 333
   d. Irrigation

35. A _____ is a body of water with a current, confined within a bed and banks. _____s are important as conduits in the water cycle, instruments in aquifer recharge, and corridors for fish and wildlife migration.
   a. 1700 Cascadia earthquake
   b. 1703 Genroku earthquake
   c. 1509 Istanbul earthquake
   d. Stream

36. _____ refers to an area of land of low topographic relief that historically supported grasses and herbs, with few trees, and having generally a mesic climate.
   a. 1509 Istanbul earthquake
   b. 1700 Cascadia earthquake
   c. 1703 Genroku earthquake
   d. Prairie

37. The _____ is the portion of Earth between the land surface and the phreatic zone or zone of saturation.
   a. Vadose Zone
   b. 1703 Genroku earthquake
   c. 1509 Istanbul earthquake
   d. 1700 Cascadia earthquake

38. The _____ is the surface where the water pressure is equal to atmospheric pressure. A large amount of water within a body of sand or rock below the _____ is called an aquifer, and the ability of rocks to store such groundwater is dependent on their porosity and permeability.

a. 1703 Genroku earthquake
c. 1700 Cascadia earthquake
b. 1509 Istanbul earthquake
d. Water table

39. An _____ is an underground layer of water-bearing permeable rock or unconsolidated materials from which groundwater can be usefully extracted using a water well.
   a. AL 129-1
   b. Aquifer
   c. AASHTO Soil Classification System
   d. AL 333

40. An _____ occurs in recharging aquifers, this happens because the water table at its recharge zone is at a higher elevation than the head of the well.
   a. AASHTO Soil Classification System
   b. Artesian well
   c. AL 333
   d. AL 129-1

41. A _____ has the water table above their upper boundary and is typically found below unconfined aquifers. It has very low storativity values, which means that the aquifer is storing water using the mechanisms of aquifer matrix expansion and the compressibility of water, which typically are both quite small quantities.
   a. 1509 Istanbul earthquake
   b. 1703 Genroku earthquake
   c. 1700 Cascadia earthquake
   d. Confined aquifer

42. A _____ is a storm system characterized by a low pressure center and numerous thunderstorms that produce strong winds and flooding rain. _____s feed on heat released when moist air rises, resulting in condensation of water vapour contained in the moist air. They are fueled by a different heat mechanism than other cyclonic windstorms such as nor'easters, European windstorms, and polar lows, leading to their classification as 'warm core' storm systems. Depending on its location and strength, a _____ is referred to by many other names, such as hurricane, typhoon, tropical storm, cyclonic storm, tropical depression, and simply cyclone.
   a. Persia
   b. Tropical cyclone
   c. Khmer Empire
   d. Kenya

43. _____ is the volumetric flow rate of groundwater through an aquifer.

Total _____, as reported through a specified area, is similarly expressed as:

$$Q = \frac{dh}{dl} K A$$

where

   Q is the total _____ ([L³T⁻¹]; m³/s), and
   A is the area which the groundwater is flowing through ([L²]; m²)

For example, this can be used to determine the flow rate of water flowing along a plane with known geometry.

- Groundwater flow equation
- Groundwater energy balance
- Submarine _____
- Discharge (hydrology) - for rivers
- volumetric flow rate
- flux (transport definition)
- Darcy's Law

a. 1509 Istanbul earthquake
b. 1700 Cascadia earthquake
c. 1703 Genroku earthquake
d. Groundwater discharge

44. _____ or deep drainage or deep percolation is a hydrologic process where water moves downward from surface water to groundwater. This process usually occurs in the vadose zone below plant roots and is often expressed as a flux to the water table surface. Recharge occurs both naturally (through the water cycle) and anthropologically (i.e., 'artificial _____'), where rainwater and or reclaimed water is routed to the subsurface.

a. 1700 Cascadia earthquake
b. 1509 Istanbul earthquake
c. 1703 Genroku earthquake
d. Groundwater recharge

45. _____ or piezometric head is a specific measurement of water pressure above a geodetic datum. It is usually measured as a water surface elevation, expressed in units of length, at the entrance (or bottom) of a piezometer. In an aquifer, it can be calculated from the depth to water in a piezometric well (a specialized water well), and given information of the piezometer's elevation and screen depth.

a. 1509 Istanbul earthquake
b. 1703 Genroku earthquake
c. 1700 Cascadia earthquake
d. Hydraulic head

46. In vector calculus, the _____ of a scalar field is a vector field which points in the direction of the greatest rate of increase of the scalar field, and whose magnitude is the greatest rate of change.

A generalization of the _____ for functions on a Euclidean space which have values in another Euclidean space is the Jacobian. A further generalization for a function from one Banach space to another is the Fréchet derivative.

a. Gradient
b. 1703 Genroku earthquake
c. 1509 Istanbul earthquake
d. 1700 Cascadia earthquake

47. An _____ is a zone within the earth that restricts the flow of groundwater from one aquifer to another.
a. AL 129-1
b. AL 333
c. AASHTO Soil Classification System
d. Aquitard/aquiclude

48. _____, symbolically represented as K, is a property of vascular plants, soil or rock, that describes the ease with which water can move through pore spaces or fractures

Chapter 11. Water Resources

a. 1703 Genroku earthquake
b. Hydraulic conductivity
c. 1509 Istanbul earthquake
d. 1700 Cascadia earthquake

49. _____ is a measure of the void spaces in a material, and is measured as a fraction, between 0–1, or as a percentage between 0–100%.
   a. 1509 Istanbul earthquake
   b. 1700 Cascadia earthquake
   c. 1703 Genroku earthquake
   d. Porosity

50. _____ is the extraction of valuable minerals or other geological materials from the earth, usually from an ore body, vein, or seam. Any material that cannot be grown from agricultural processes, or created artificially in a laboratory or factory, is usually extracted from the earth by this method.
   a. 1700 Cascadia earthquake
   b. 1509 Istanbul earthquake
   c. Mining
   d. 1703 Genroku earthquake

51. _____ flow beneath the water table and gain water froman outflow, groundwater or the water table which creates an increased flow.
   a. AASHTO Soil Classification System
   b. AL 333
   c. Effluent streams
   d. AL 129-1

52. The _____ is a vast yet shallow underground water table aquifer located beneath the Great Plains in the United States.
   a. AL 333
   b. AASHTO Soil Classification System
   c. AL 129-1
   d. Ogallala aquifer

53. A _____ is a natural underground void large enough for a human to enter. Some people suggest that the term '_____' should only apply to cavities that have some part which does not receive daylight; however, in popular usage, the term includes smaller spaces like a sea _____, rock shelters, and grottos.
   a. 1509 Istanbul earthquake
   b. 1700 Cascadia earthquake
   c. 1703 Genroku earthquake
   d. Cave

54. The Woodville _____ is a 450 square mile karst area that runs from Tallahassee, Florida, USA to the Gulf of Mexico and includes numerous first magnitude springs, including Wakulla Springs, and the Leon Sinks Cave System, the longest underwater cave in the United States extending some 18 miles and ranks #90 among the top 100 deepest caves in the world. Also of interest are the Leon Sinks.
   a. 1509 Istanbul earthquake
   b. 1700 Cascadia earthquake
   c. 1703 Genroku earthquake
   d. Karst plain

55. _____ is a three-dimensional landscape shaped by the dissolution of a soluble layer or layers of bedrock, usually carbonate rock such as limestone or dolomite. These landscapes display distinctive surface features and underground drainages, and in some examples there may be little or no surface drainage.
   a. 1509 Istanbul earthquake
   b. 1703 Genroku earthquake
   c. Karst topography
   d. 1700 Cascadia earthquake

Chapter 11. Water Resources

56. _____ is a sedimentary rock composed largely of the mineral calcite. _____ often contains variable amounts of silica in the form of chert or flint, as well as varying amounts of clay, silt and sand as disseminations, nodules, or layers within the rock. The primary source of the calcite in _____ is most commonly marine organisms. These organisms secrete shells that settle out of the water column and are deposited on ocean floors as pelagic ooze or alternatively is conglomerated in a coral reef.
- a. 1509 Istanbul earthquake
- b. 1700 Cascadia earthquake
- c. 1703 Genroku earthquake
- d. Limestone

57. A _____ is any of a number of an extinct genus of proboscidean, often with long curved tusks and, in northern species, a covering of long hair. They lived from the Pliocene epoch from to around 4,000 years ago.
- a. 1509 Istanbul earthquake
- b. 1703 Genroku earthquake
- c. 1700 Cascadia earthquake
- d. Mammoth

58. _____ is a U.S. National Park in central Kentucky, encompassing portions of _____, the most elongated cave system known in the world. The park was established as a national park on July 1, 1941. It became a World Heritage Site on October 27, 1981, and an international Biosphere Reserve on September 26, 1990. The park's 52,830 acres are located in Edmonson County, Kentucky, with small areas extending eastward into Hart County and Barren County.
- a. 1703 Genroku earthquake
- b. 1700 Cascadia earthquake
- c. 1509 Istanbul earthquake
- d. Mammoth Cave

59. The United Mexican States , commonly known as _____ , is a federal constitutional republic in North America. It is bordered on the north by the United States; on the south and west by the North Pacific Ocean; on the southeast by Guatemala, Belize, and the Caribbean Sea; and on the east by the Gulf of _____. The United Mexican States are a federation comprising thirty-one states and a federal district, the capital _____ City, whose metropolitan area is one of the world's most populous.
- a. Amblypoda
- b. Ambulocetus
- c. Andrija Mohorovičić
- d. Mexico

60. A _____ is a natural depression or hole in the surface topography caused by the removal of soil or bedrock, often both, by water. They may vary in size from less than a meter to several hundred meters both in diameter and depth, and vary in form from soil-lined bowls to bedrock-edged chasms.
- a. Sinkhole
- b. 1509 Istanbul earthquake
- c. 1703 Genroku earthquake
- d. 1700 Cascadia earthquake

61. _____ is the process of breaking down rocks, soils and their minerals through direct contact with the atmosphere. _____ occurs without movement. Two main classifications of _____ processes exist. Mechanical or physical _____ involves the breakdown of rocks and soils through direct contact with atmospheric conditions. The second classification, chemical _____, involves the direct effect of atmospheric chemicals in the breakdown of rocks, soils and minerals.
- a. 1700 Cascadia earthquake
- b. 1509 Istanbul earthquake
- c. 1703 Genroku earthquake
- d. Weathering

62. _____ is the study of Earth's surface features or those of other planets, moons, and asteroids
- a. 1509 Istanbul earthquake
- b. 1703 Genroku earthquake
- c. Topography
- d. 1700 Cascadia earthquake

Chapter 11. Water Resources

63. _____ refers to composed sheetlike deposits of calcite formed where water flows down the walls or along the floors of a cave. They are typically found in "solution", or limestone caves, where they are the most common speleothem. However, they may form in any type of cave where water enters that has picked up dissolved minerals.
   a. 1700 Cascadia earthquake
   b. 1703 Genroku earthquake
   c. 1509 Istanbul earthquake
   d. Flowstone

64. A _____ is a type of speleothem that hangs from the ceiling or wall of limestone caves. _____s are formed by the deposition of calcium carbonate and other minerals, which is precipitated from mineralized water solutions. The corresponding formation on the floor underneath a _____ is known as a stalagmite.
   a. 1703 Genroku earthquake
   b. Stalactite
   c. 1509 Istanbul earthquake
   d. 1700 Cascadia earthquake

65. A _____ is a type of speleothem that rises from the floor of a limestone cave due to the dripping of mineralized solutions and the deposition of calcium carbonate. The corresponding formation on the ceiling of a cave is known as a stalactite. If these formations grow together, meeting in the middle, the result is known as a column.
   a. Stalagmite
   b. 1703 Genroku earthquake
   c. 1509 Istanbul earthquake
   d. 1700 Cascadia earthquake

66. _____ refers to any of several processes that remove excess salt and other minerals from water in order to obtain fresh water suitable for animal consumption or irrigation, and if almost all of the salt is removed, for human consumption.
   a. 1509 Istanbul earthquake
   b. 1703 Genroku earthquake
   c. 1700 Cascadia earthquake
   d. Desalination

67. _____ refers to a water body or system that is not located in a streambed or does not receive significant natural flows.
   a. AASHTO Soil Classification System
   b. AL 129-1
   c. AL 333
   d. Offstream water

68. Water of sufficient quality to serve as drinking water is termed _____ whether it is used as such or not.
   a. 1509 Istanbul earthquake
   b. 1703 Genroku earthquake
   c. Potable water
   d. 1700 Cascadia earthquake

69. _____ is a state located in the South Central United States nicknamed the Lone Star State. Austin is the state capital. _____--the second largest U.S. state in both area and population--spans 268,820 square miles (696,200 km Due to its long history as a center of the American cattle industry, _____ is associated throughout much of the world with the image of the cowboy.
   a. Texas
   b. Comal Springs
   c. 1700 Cascadia earthquake
   d. 1509 Istanbul earthquake

70. _____ are the largest concentration of naturally occurring freshwater springs in Texas. They are located in the city of New Braunfels and are the result of water percolating through the Edwards Aquifer formation.
   a. 1700 Cascadia earthquake
   b. 1509 Istanbul earthquake
   c. Comal Springs
   d. 1703 Genroku earthquake

71. _____ is the second largest natural cluster of springs in Texas. The springs are located in the city of San Marcos, Texas, about 30 miles northeast of San Antonio.

a. 1509 Istanbul earthquake
b. 1703 Genroku earthquake
c. San Marcos Springs
d. 1700 Cascadia earthquake

72. The _____ is an American environmental organization founded on May 28, 1892 in San Francisco, California by the well-known preservationist John Muir, who became its first president. It has hundreds of thousands of members in chapters located throughout the United States.
   a. Amblypoda
   b. Sierra Club
   c. Ambulocetus
   d. Andrija Mohorovičić

73. The _____ are a genus of small freshwater fish. Most are native to North America. Many can produce Schreckstoff substances that serve to warn nearby fish in case of an attack.
   a. Etheostoma
   b. AL 333
   c. AASHTO Soil Classification System
   d. AL 129-1

74. A _____ is an urban area with a high population and a particular administrative, legal, or historical status.

Large industrialized cities generally have advanced systems for sanitation, utilities, land usage, housing, and transportation and more. This close proximity greatly facilitates interaction between people and firms, benefiting both parties in the process.

   a. 1700 Cascadia earthquake
   b. 1703 Genroku earthquake
   c. City
   d. 1509 Istanbul earthquake

75. The City of New York, most often called _____, is the most populous city in the United States, in a metropolitan area that ranks among the world's most-populous urban areas. It is a leading global city, exerting a powerful influence over worldwide commerce, finance, culture, and entertainment. The city is also an important center for international affairs, hosting the United Nations headquarters.
   a. New York City
   b. 1703 Genroku earthquake
   c. 1700 Cascadia earthquake
   d. 1509 Istanbul earthquake

76. _____ is a large coastal Southern California city located in the southwestern corner of the continental United States. In 2007, the city's population was estimated to be 1,266,731. It is the second largest city in California and the eighth largest city in the United States, by population.
   a. 1509 Istanbul earthquake
   b. 1700 Cascadia earthquake
   c. San Diego
   d. Coachella Valley

77. In geology, a _____ is a depression with predominant extent in one direction. The terms U-shaped and V-shaped are descriptive terms of geography to characterize the form of _____s. Most _____s belong to one of these two main types or a mixture of them, at least with respect of the cross section of the slopes or hillsides.
   a. 1703 Genroku earthquake
   b. 1700 Cascadia earthquake
   c. 1509 Istanbul earthquake
   d. Valley

78. _____ is a layer of gases surrounding the planet Earth and retained by the Earth's gravity, protecting life on Earth by absorbing ultraviolet solar radiation and reducing temperature extremes between day and night.

Chapter 11. Water Resources

a. AL 129-1
b. AL 333
c. AASHTO Soil Classification System
d. Earths atmosphere

79. _____ is the process of self-provision or provision by third parties of water of various qualities to different users.
    a. Water supply
    b. 1509 Istanbul earthquake
    c. 1700 Cascadia earthquake
    d. 1703 Genroku earthquake

80. The _____ is a diverse scientific, social, and political movement for addressing the concerns of environmentalism. The _____ is represented by a range of organizations, from the large to grassroots. Due to its large membership, varying and strong beliefs, and occasionally speculative nature, the _____ is not always united in its goals.
    a. Ambulocetus
    b. Amblypoda
    c. Andrija Mohorović iÄ‡
    d. Environmental movement

81. In physics, the _____ states that the total amount of energy in an isolated system remains constant, although it may change forms, e.g. friction turns kinetic energy into thermal energy. In thermodynamics, the first law of thermodynamics is a statement of the _____ for thermodynamic systems, and is the more encompassing version of the _____.
    a. 1509 Istanbul earthquake
    b. 1700 Cascadia earthquake
    c. 1703 Genroku earthquake
    d. Conservation of energy

82. _____ contains low concentrations of dissolved salts and other total dissolved solids. It is an important renewable resource, necessary for the survival of most terrestrial organisms, and required by humans for drinking and agriculture, among many other uses.
    a. 1700 Cascadia earthquake
    b. 1703 Genroku earthquake
    c. 1509 Istanbul earthquake
    d. Fresh water

83. _____ is any water that has been adversely affected in quality by anthropogenic influence.
    a. 1700 Cascadia earthquake
    b. 1703 Genroku earthquake
    c. 1509 Istanbul earthquake
    d. Wastewater

84. In physics, _____ is a scalar physical quantity that describes the amount of work that can be performed by a force. _____ is an attribute of objects and systems that is subject to a conservation law. Several different forms of _____ exist to explain all known natural phenomena.
    a. AL 333
    b. AL 129-1
    c. AASHTO Soil Classification System
    d. Energy

85. An _____ is the manufacturing of a good or service within a category.
    a. AL 129-1
    b. AASHTO Soil Classification System
    c. AL 333
    d. Industry

86. The principal body of law currently in effect is based on the Federal Water Pollution Control Amendments of 1972, which significantly expanded and strengthened earlier legislation. Major amendments were enacted in the Clean Water Act of 1977 enacted by the 95th United States Congress and the _____ of 1987 enacted by the 100th United States Congress.

The Act governs discharges to waters of the United States. Older statutory language used the term 'navigable waters,' but this term was expanded in the 1972 law:

The term 'navigable waters' means the waters of the United States, including the territorial seas.

a. Fish and Wildlife Coordination Act
b. Flotsam
c. Jetsam
d. Water Quality Act

87. _____ (October 8, 1915 in Albuquerque, New Mexico - February 23, 2006 in Berkeley, California) was a leading U.S. geomorphologist, and son of Aldo Leopold.

A famous U.S. hydrologist, he suggested that a new philosophy of water management is needed, one based on geologic, geographic, and climatic factors as well as traditional economic, social, and political factors. He argued that the management of water resources cannot be successful as long as it is naïvely perceived from an economic and political standpoint, as it is in the status quo.

a. Luna Bergere Leopold
b. Roald Amundsen
c. Garrett James Hardin
d. George Santayana

88. The State of _____ is a state located in the southwestern region of the United States. The capital and largest city is Phoenix. The second largest city is Tucson, followed by the four Phoenix-area conurbation cities of Mesa, Glendale, Chandler, and Scottsdale.

a. AASHTO Soil Classification System
b. Kaibab Plateau
c. Arizona
d. AL 129-1

89. The _____ is a river in the southwestern United States and northwestern Mexico, approximately 1,450 mi long, draining a part of the arid regions on the western slope of the Rocky Mountains. The natural course of the river flows into the Gulf of California, but the heavy use of the river as an irrigation source for the Imperial Valley has desiccated the lower course of the river in Mexico such that it no longer consistently reaches the sea.

a. 1703 Genroku earthquake
b. 1700 Cascadia earthquake
c. 1509 Istanbul earthquake
d. Colorado River

90. The _____ is a scientific agency of the United States government. The scientists of the USGS study the landscape of the United States, its natural resources, and the natural hazards that threaten it.

a. U.S. Geological Survey
b. Ambulocetus
c. Andrija Mohorovičić
d. Amblypoda

91. _____ is the flow of air. More generally, it is the flow of the gases which compose an atmosphere; since _____ is not only an Earth based phenomenon.

a. 1700 Cascadia earthquake
b. 1703 Genroku earthquake
c. 1509 Istanbul earthquake
d. Wind

92. The _____ is a mountain range of the Rocky Mountains in western Wyoming in the United States.

a. 1703 Genroku earthquake
b. 1700 Cascadia earthquake
c. 1509 Istanbul earthquake
d. Wind River Range

93. A _____ is a deep valley between cliffs often carved from the landscape by a river. Most were formed by a process of long-time erosion from a plateau level. The cliffs form because harder rock strata that are resistant to erosion and weathering remain exposed on the valley walls.
   a. 1700 Cascadia earthquake
   b. 1509 Istanbul earthquake
   c. Canyon
   d. 1703 Genroku earthquake

94. A _____ is a barrier across flowing water that obstructs, directs or slows down the flow, often creating a reservoir, lake or impoundment.
   a. 1700 Cascadia earthquake
   b. 1509 Istanbul earthquake
   c. 1703 Genroku earthquake
   d. Dam

95. _____ is a dam on the Colorado River at Page, Arizona, operated by the United States Bureau of Reclamation. The purpose of the dam is to provide water storage for the arid southwestern United States, and to generate electricity for the region's growing population.
   a. 1700 Cascadia earthquake
   b. 1509 Istanbul earthquake
   c. 1703 Genroku earthquake
   d. Glen Canyon Dam

96. The _____ is a very colorful, steep-sided gorge, carved by the Colorado River in the U.S. state of Arizona. It is one of the first national parks in the United States.
   a. 1509 Istanbul earthquake
   b. 1703 Genroku earthquake
   c. Grand Canyon
   d. 1700 Cascadia earthquake

97. _____ is the saltiness or dissolved salt content of a body of water. In oceanography, it has been traditional to express halinity not as percent, but as parts per thousand, which is approximately grams of salt per liter of solution.
   a. 1700 Cascadia earthquake
   b. 1703 Genroku earthquake
   c. Salinity
   d. 1509 Istanbul earthquake

98. A _____ or sandbar is a somewhat linear landform within or extending into a body of water, typically composed of sand, silt or small pebbles. A bar is characteristically long and narrow and develops where a stream or ocean current promote deposition of granular material, resulting in localized shallowing of the water. Bars can appear in the sea, in a lake, or in a river.

The term bar can apply to landform features spanning a considerable range in size, from a length of a few meters in a small stream to marine depositions stretching for hundreds of kilometres along a coastline, often called barrier islands.

   a. 1509 Istanbul earthquake
   b. 1703 Genroku earthquake
   c. Shoal
   d. 1700 Cascadia earthquake

99. A _____ is a wetland type that accumulates acidic peat, a deposit of dead plant material. Moisture is provided entirely by precipitation, and for this reason _____ waters are acidic and termed ombrotrophic, which accounts for their low plant nutrient status

a. Bog
b. 1703 Genroku earthquake
c. 1509 Istanbul earthquake
d. 1700 Cascadia earthquake

100. The _____ is defined as the part of the land adjoining or near the ocean. A coastline is properly a line on a map indicating the disposition of a _____, but the word is often used to refer to the _____ itself. The adjective coastal describes something as being on, near to, or associated with a _____.
 a. Coast
 b. 1509 Istanbul earthquake
 c. 1703 Genroku earthquake
 d. 1700 Cascadia earthquake

101. In meteorology, _____ are an area of low atmospheric pressure characterized by inward spiraling winds that rotate counter clockwise in the northern hemisphere and clockwise in the southern hemisphere of the Earth.
 a. 1509 Istanbul earthquake
 b. 1703 Genroku earthquake
 c. 1700 Cascadia earthquake
 d. Cyclones

102. An _____ is a natural unit consisting of all plants, animals and micro organisms in an area functioning together with all the non living physical factors of the environment.
 a. AL 129-1
 b. Ecosystem
 c. AASHTO Soil Classification System
 d. AL 333

103. An _____ is an assessment of the likely influence a project may have on the environment. The purpose of the assessment is to ensure that decision-makers consider _____s before deciding whether to proceed with new projects.
 a. AL 129-1
 b. AASHTO Soil Classification System
 c. Environmental impact
 d. AL 333

104. _____ is the study of the movement, distribution, and quality of water throughout the Earth, and thus addresses both the hydrologic cycle and water resources.
 a. 1509 Istanbul earthquake
 b. 1700 Cascadia earthquake
 c. 1703 Genroku earthquake
 d. Hydrology

105. In geography, a _____ is a type of wetland which is subject to almost continuous inundation. Typically it features grasses, rushes, reeds, typhas, sedges, and other herbaceous plants in a context of shallow water. It is different from a swamp, which has a greater proportion of open water surface, and is generally deeper than a it.
 a. 1700 Cascadia earthquake
 b. 1509 Istanbul earthquake
 c. Marsh
 d. 1703 Genroku earthquake

106. Most often, a _____ refers to an artificial lake, used to store water for various uses. _____s are created first by building a sturdy dam, usually out of cement, earth, rock, or a mixture. Once the dam is completed, a stream is allowed to flow behind it and eventually fill it to capacity.
 a. 1703 Genroku earthquake
 b. 1700 Cascadia earthquake
 c. 1509 Istanbul earthquake
 d. Reservoir

107. _____ is a dietary mineral composed primarily of sodium chloride that is essential for animal life, but toxic to most land plants. _____ flavor is one of the basic tastes, an important preservative and a popular food seasoning.

_____ for human consumption is produced in different forms: unrefined _____ (such as sea _____), refined _____ (table _____), and iodized _____.

Chapter 11. Water Resources

a. 1509 Istanbul earthquake
c. 1703 Genroku earthquake
b. Salt
d. 1700 Cascadia earthquake

108. A _____ is a type of marsh that is a transitional intertidal between land and salty or brackish water (e.g.: sloughs, bays, estuaries.) It is dominated by halophytic (salt tolerant) herbaceous plants. Historically, they have sometimes been treated as 'wastelands', along with other wetlands.
a. 1509 Istanbul earthquake
c. Salt marsh
b. 1700 Cascadia earthquake
d. 1703 Genroku earthquake

109. A _____ is a wetland that features temporary or permanent inundation of large areas of land by shallow bodies of water, generally with a substantial number of hummocks, or dry-land protrusions, and covered by aquatic vegetation, or vegetation that tolerates periodical inundation.
a. 1703 Genroku earthquake
c. 1700 Cascadia earthquake
b. 1509 Istanbul earthquake
d. Swamp

110. _____ are temporary pools of water. They are devoid of fish, and thus allow the safe development of natal amphibian and insect species.
a. Vernal pools
c. 1703 Genroku earthquake
b. 1509 Istanbul earthquake
d. 1700 Cascadia earthquake

111. In physical geography, a _____ is an environment "at the interface between truly terrestrial ecosystems and aquatic systems making them inherently different from each other yet highly dependent on both". In essence, they are ecotones.
a. Wetland
c. 1509 Istanbul earthquake
b. 1703 Genroku earthquake
d. 1700 Cascadia earthquake

112. A _____ is an approximately circular depression in the surface of a planet, moon or other solid body in the Solar System, formed by the hyper-velocity impact of a smaller body with the surface. Impact _____s typically have raised rims, and they range from small, simple, bowl-shaped depressions to large, complex, multi-ringed, impact basins.
a. 1700 Cascadia earthquake
c. 1509 Istanbul earthquake
b. 1703 Genroku earthquake
d. Crater

113. The _____ (1968) is a book written by Paul R. Ehrlich. A best-selling work, it predicted disaster for humanity due to overpopulation and the 'population explosion'. The book predicted that 'in the 1970s and 1980s hundreds of millions of people will starve to death', that nothing can be done to avoid mass famine greater than any in the history, and radical action is needed to limit the overpopulation.
a. Andrija Mohorovičić
c. Ambulocetus
b. Amblypoda
d. Population bomb

114. A _____ is a type of disruption in the surface of a roadway where a portion of the road material has broken away, leaving a hole.
a. 1703 Genroku earthquake
c. 1700 Cascadia earthquake
b. 1509 Istanbul earthquake
d. Pothole

Chapter 12. Water Pollution

1. The _____ is the primary federal law in the United States governing water pollution. It established the symbolic goals of eliminating releases to water of toxic amounts of toxic substances, eliminating additional water pollution by 1985, and ensuring that surface waters would meet standards necessary for human sports and recreation by 1983.
   a. 1509 Istanbul earthquake
   b. 1703 Genroku earthquake
   c. Clean Water Act
   d. 1700 Cascadia earthquake

2. _____ is the introduction of substances or energy into the environment, resulting in deleterious effects of such a nature as to endanger human health, harm living resources and ecosystems, and impair or interfere with amenities and other legitimate uses of the environment.
   a. Pollution
   b. 1703 Genroku earthquake
   c. 1700 Cascadia earthquake
   d. 1509 Istanbul earthquake

3. _____ is a large set of adverse effects upon water bodies such as lakes, rivers, oceans, and groundwater caused by human activities. Although natural phenomena such as volcanoes, algae blooms, storms, and earthquakes also cause major changes in water quality and the ecological status of water, these are not deemed to be pollution. _____ has many causes and characteristics.
   a. Water pollution
   b. 1700 Cascadia earthquake
   c. 1703 Genroku earthquake
   d. 1509 Istanbul earthquake

4. Pollution is the introduction of contaminants into an environment that causes instability, disorder, harm or discomfort to the physical systems or living organisms. Pollution can take the form of chemical substances, or energy, such as noise, heat, or light energy. _____, the elements of pollution, can be foreign substances or energies, or naturally occurring; when naturally occurring, they are considered contaminants when they exceed natural levels.
   a. 1509 Istanbul earthquake
   b. 1703 Genroku earthquake
   c. 1700 Cascadia earthquake
   d. Pollutants

5. An _____ organism is an organism that has an oxygen based metabolism
   a. AASHTO Soil Classification System
   b. AL 333
   c. AL 129-1
   d. Aerobic

6. An _____ is an organism that has an oxygen based metabolism. Aerobes, in a process known as cellular respiration, use oxygen to oxidize substrates in order to obtain energy.
   a. AASHTO Soil Classification System
   b. AL 129-1
   c. Aerobic bacteria
   d. AL 333

7. The _____ are a large group of unicellular microorganisms. Typically a few micrometres in length, _____ have a wide range of shapes, ranging from spheres to rods and spirals. _____ are ubiquitous in every habitat on Earth, growing in soil, acidic hot springs, radioactive waste, water, and deep in the Earth's crust, as well as in organic matter and the live bodies of plants and animals.
   a. Hurricane Iniki
   b. Metabolism
   c. Cambodia
   d. Bacteria

8. _____ is a chemical procedure for determining how fast biological organisms use up oxygen in a body of water.
   a. 1700 Cascadia earthquake
   b. Biochemical oxygen demand
   c. 1703 Genroku earthquake
   d. 1509 Istanbul earthquake

Chapter 12. Water Pollution

9. _____ is a class of diseases in which a group of cells display the traits of uncontrolled growth growth and division beyond the normal limits, invasion intrusion on and destruction of adjacent tissues, and sometimes metastasis spread to other locations in the body via lymph or blood. These three malignant properties of _____s differentiate them from benign tumors, which are self-limited, do not invade or metastasize. Most _____s form a tumor but some, like leukemia, do not.
   a. 1703 Genroku earthquake
   b. 1509 Istanbul earthquake
   c. 1700 Cascadia earthquake
   d. Cancer

10. _____ bacteria are a commonly-used bacterial indicator of sanitary quality of foods and water.
    a. 1509 Istanbul earthquake
    b. 1700 Cascadia earthquake
    c. 1703 Genroku earthquake
    d. Coliform

11. _____ are the commonly-used bacterial indicator of sanitary quality of foods and water. They are defined as rod-shaped Gram-negative non-spore forming organisms that ferment lactose with the production of acid and gas when incubated at 35-37°C. Coliforms are abundant in the feces of warm-blooded animals, but can also be found in the aquatic environment, in soil and on vegetation.
    a. 1703 Genroku earthquake
    b. Coliform bacteria
    c. 1700 Cascadia earthquake
    d. 1509 Istanbul earthquake

12. A _____ or medical condition is an abnormal condition of an organism that impairs bodily functions and can be deadly. It is also defined as a way of the body harming itself in an abnormal way, associated with specific symptoms and signs.

    In human beings,'_____' is often used more broadly to refer to any condition that causes extreme pain, dysfunction, distress, social problems, and/or death to the person afflicted, or similar problems for those in contact with the person.

    a. Disease
    b. Black lung disease
    c. 1700 Cascadia earthquake
    d. 1509 Istanbul earthquake

13. _____ is one of the main species of bacteria living in the lower intestines of mammals, known as gut flora. When located in the large intestine, it actually assists with waste processing, vitamin K production, and food absorption.
    a. Escherichia coli
    b. AL 333
    c. AASHTO Soil Classification System
    d. AL 129-1

14. _____ is a facultatively-anaerobic, rod-shaped, gram-negative, non-sporulating bacteria. They are capable of growth in the presence of bile salts or similar surface agents, oxidase negative, and produce acid and gas from lactose within 48 hours at 44 ± 0.5°C.
    a. 1509 Istanbul earthquake
    b. 1700 Cascadia earthquake
    c. 1703 Genroku earthquake
    d. Fecal coliform bacteria

15. _____ is a province located in the central part of Canada, the largest by population and second largest, after Quebec, in total area. _____ is bordered by the provinces of Manitoba to the west and Quebec to the east, and the U.S. states of Minnesota, Michigan, Ohio, Pennsylvania, and New York to the south. Most of _____'s borders with the United States are natural, starting at the Lake of the Woods and continuing through four of the Great Lakes: Superior, Huron, Erie, and _____, then along the Saint Lawrence River near Cornwall.

a. Ambulocetus
b. Andrija Mohorovičić
c. Ontario
d. Amblypoda

16. _____ farming is a form of agriculture that excludes the use of synthetic fertilizers and pesticides, plant growth regulators, livestock feed additives, and genetically modified organisms.
   a. AL 333
   b. Organic
   c. AL 129-1
   d. AASHTO Soil Classification System

17. _____ is matter that has come from a recently living organism; is capable of decay, or the product of decay; or is composed of organic compounds. The definition of _____ varies upon the subject it is being used for.
   a. AL 333
   b. AL 129-1
   c. AASHTO Soil Classification System
   d. Organic matter

18. _____ refers to food waste and dead plant and animal tissue that consumes oxygen dissolved in water during its degragation and depleting oxygen required for survival of marine animals ans marine plants.
   a. Oxygen-demanding waste
   b. AL 333
   c. AASHTO Soil Classification System
   d. AL 129-1

19. A _____ is a biological agent that causes disease or illness to its host.
   a. 1703 Genroku earthquake
   b. 1509 Istanbul earthquake
   c. Pathogen
   d. 1700 Cascadia earthquake

20. _____ is the substance of which physical objects are composed. _____ can be solid, liquid, plasma or gas. It constitutes the observable universe.
   a. 1703 Genroku earthquake
   b. 1509 Istanbul earthquake
   c. Matter
   d. 1700 Cascadia earthquake

21. In biology and ecology, an _____ is a living complex adaptive system of organs that influence each other in such a way that they function in some way as a stable whole.
   a. AL 129-1
   b. AL 333
   c. AASHTO Soil Classification System
   d. Organism

22. _____ is a chemical element in the periodic table. It has the symbol O and atomic number 8. _____ is the second most common element on Earth, composing around 46% of the mass of Earth's crust and 28% of the mass of Earth as a whole, and is the third most common element in the universe.
   a. AL 129-1
   b. AASHTO Soil Classification System
   c. AL 333
   d. Oxygen

23. _____ is unwanted or undesired material.
   a. 1703 Genroku earthquake
   b. 1509 Istanbul earthquake
   c. 1700 Cascadia earthquake
   d. Waste

24. _____ is the contamination of water. The _____ include a wide spectrum of chemicals, pathogens, and physical chemistry or sensory changes. Many of the chemical substances are toxic. Most are eventually carried by the rivers into the oceans.

Chapter 12. Water Pollution

a. 1509 Istanbul earthquake
c. Water Pollutant
b. 1700 Cascadia earthquake
d. 1703 Genroku earthquake

25. _____ diseases are pathogenic microorganisms which are directly transmitted when contaminated drinking water is consumed.
   a. 1509 Istanbul earthquake
   c. 1703 Genroku earthquake
   b. 1700 Cascadia earthquake
   d. Waterborne

26. _____ encompass several groups of relatively simple living aquatic organisms that capture light energy through photosynthesis, using it to convert inorganic substances into organic matter.
   a. AASHTO Soil Classification System
   c. AL 333
   b. AL 129-1
   d. Algae

27. An _____ is a relatively rapid increase in the population of algae in an aquatic system. _____ smay occur in freshwater as well as marine environments.
   a. AL 129-1
   c. AL 333
   b. AASHTO Soil Classification System
   d. Algal bloom

28. _____ is a parasitic disease affecting the intestines of mammals. It is a disease spread through the fecal-oral route; the main symptom is self-limiting diarrhea in people with intact immune system.
   a. 1509 Istanbul earthquake
   c. 1700 Cascadia earthquake
   b. 1703 Genroku earthquake
   d. Cryptosporidiosis

29. _____ is the process that speeds up natural eutrophication because of human activity. Due to clearing of land and building of towns and cities, run - off water is accelerated and more nutrients such as phosphates and nitrate are supplied to the lakes and ponds
   a. 1703 Genroku earthquake
   c. 1509 Istanbul earthquake
   b. 1700 Cascadia earthquake
   d. Cultural eutrophication

30. _____ refers to an increase in the primary productivity of any ecosystem. _____ is caused by the increase of chemical nutrients, typically compounds containing nitrogen or phosphorus. It may occur on land or in water.
   a. AL 129-1
   c. AL 333
   b. AASHTO Soil Classification System
   d. Eutrophication

31. Seaweed is a loose colloquial term encompassing macroscopic, multicellular, benthic _____. The term includes some members of the red, brown and green algae. Seaweeds can also be classified by use (as food, medicine, fertilizer, industrial, etc.).
   a. 1700 Cascadia earthquake
   c. 1509 Istanbul earthquake
   b. 1703 Genroku earthquake
   d. Marine algae

32. _____ is a chemical element which has the symbol N and atomic number 7 in the periodic table. Elemental _____ is a colorless, odorless, tasteless and mostly inert diatomic gas at standard conditions, constituting 78.08% percent of Earth's atmosphere.
   a. Nitrogen
   c. 1703 Genroku earthquake
   b. 1509 Istanbul earthquake
   d. 1700 Cascadia earthquake

Chapter 12. Water Pollution

33. A _____ is a substance used in an organism's metabolism which must be taken in from the environment. Non-autotrophic organisms typically acquire _____s by the ingestion of foods. Methods for _____ intake vary, with animals and protists having an internal digestive system, while plants digest _____s externally and then ingested. The effects of _____s are dose-dependent.
   a. 1509 Istanbul earthquake
   b. 1703 Genroku earthquake
   c. 1700 Cascadia earthquake
   d. Nutrient

34. _____ is the chemical element in the periodic table that has the symbol P and atomic number 15. A multivalent nonmetal of the nitrogen group, _____ is commonly found in inorganic phosphate rocks.
   a. 1509 Istanbul earthquake
   b. Phosphorus
   c. 1703 Genroku earthquake
   d. 1700 Cascadia earthquake

35. _____ are a class of astronomical objects. The term is generally used to indicate a diverse group of small celestial bodies that drift in the solar system in orbit around the Sun.
   a. Asteroids
   b. AASHTO Soil Classification System
   c. AL 333
   d. AL 129-1

36. An _____ is a layer of gases that may surround a material body of sufficient mass, by the gravity of the body, and are retained for a longer duration if gravity is high and the _____'s temperature is low. Some planets consist mainly of various gases, and therefore have very deep _____s

The term stellar _____ describes the outer region of a star, and typically includes the portion starting from the opaque photosphere outwards.

   a. AASHTO Soil Classification System
   b. AL 129-1
   c. AL 333
   d. Atmosphere

37. _____ is the natural capability of giving life. As a measure, '_____ Rate' is the number of children born per couple, person or population. This is different from fecundity, which is defined as the potential for reproduction (influenced by gamete production, fertilisation and carrying a pregnancy to term.)
   a. 1703 Genroku earthquake
   b. 1700 Cascadia earthquake
   c. Fertility
   d. 1509 Istanbul earthquake

38. The _____ is the ninth largest body of water in the world. It is an ocean basin largely surrounded by the North American continent and the island of Cuba. It is bounded on the northeast, north and northwest by the Gulf Coast of the United States, on the southwest and south by Mexico, and on the southeast by Cuba.
   a. Gulf of Mexico
   b. 1509 Istanbul earthquake
   c. 1700 Cascadia earthquake
   d. 1703 Genroku earthquake

39. The United Mexican States, commonly known as _____, is a federal constitutional republic in North America. It is bordered on the north by the United States; on the south and west by the North Pacific Ocean; on the southeast by Guatemala, Belize, and the Caribbean Sea; and on the east by the Gulf of _____. The United Mexican States are a federation comprising thirty-one states and a federal district, the capital _____ City, whose metropolitan area is one of the world's most populous.

Chapter 12. Water Pollution

a. Andrija Mohorović ić
b. Mexico
c. Ambulocetus
d. Amblypoda

40. A _____ substance is a material with a definite _____ composition. It is a concept that became firmly established in the late eighteenth century after work by the chemist Joseph Proust on the composition of some pure _____ compounds such as basic copper carbonate.
a. 1700 Cascadia earthquake
b. Chemical property
c. 1509 Istanbul earthquake
d. Chemical

41. _____ was the original name of an oil tanker owned by the former Exxon Corporation. It gained widespread infamy after the March 24, 1989 oil spill in which the tanker, captained by Joseph Hazelwood, hit Prince William Sound's Bligh Reef and spilled an estimated 11 million gallons of crude oil.
a. AL 333
b. AASHTO Soil Classification System
c. Exxon Valdez
d. AL 129-1

42. The _____ was one of the largest manmade environmental disasters ever to occur at sea, seriously affecting plants and wildlife. Its remote location made government and industry response efforts difficult, and severely taxed existing plans for response.
a. AASHTO Soil Classification System
b. AL 129-1
c. AL 333
d. Exxon Valdez oil spill

43. _____ are dangerous compounds that cause contamination and are dangerous to human health and the environement.
a. 1700 Cascadia earthquake
b. 1509 Istanbul earthquake
c. 1703 Genroku earthquake
d. Hazardous chemicals

44. The _____ is the second-longest named river in North America, with a length of 2320 miles from Lake Itasca to the Gulf of Mexico. It drains most of the area between the Rocky Mountains and the Appalachian Mountains, except for the areas drained by Hudson Bay via the Red River of the North, the Great Lakes and the Rio Grande.
a. 1700 Cascadia earthquake
b. 1703 Genroku earthquake
c. 1509 Istanbul earthquake
d. Mississippi River

45. An _____ is the unintentional release of liquid petroleum hydrocarbon into the environment as a result of human activity.
a. Oil spill
b. AASHTO Soil Classification System
c. AL 129-1
d. AL 333

46. _____ is a sound of the Gulf of Alaska on the south coast of the U.S. state of Alaska. It is located on the east side of the Kenai Peninsula. Its largest port is Valdez, at the southern terminus of the Trans-Alaska Pipeline System.

In 1989, the oil tanker Exxon Valdez ran aground on Bligh Reef after leaving Valdez, causing a large oil spill, which resulted in massive damage to the environment, including the killing of around 250,000 seabirds, nearly 3,000 sea otters, 300 harbour seals, 250 bald eagles and up to 22 killer whales.

Chapter 12. Water Pollution

a. 1703 Genroku earthquake
b. 1700 Cascadia earthquake
c. 1509 Istanbul earthquake
d. Prince William Sound

47. Some of the _____ can be found in nature. It is an naturally occuring toxin found in certain plants and some wild mushrooms and berries. It refers to any chemical or mixture that may be harmful to the environment and to human health if inhaled, swalled, or absorbed through the skin.
    a. 1703 Genroku earthquake
    b. 1509 Istanbul earthquake
    c. Toxic substance
    d. 1700 Cascadia earthquake

48. _____ is a layer of gases surrounding the planet Earth and retained by the Earth's gravity, protecting life on Earth by absorbing ultraviolet solar radiation and reducing temperature extremes between day and night.
    a. AL 129-1
    b. Earths atmosphere
    c. AL 333
    d. AASHTO Soil Classification System

49. The term _____ refers to water and can be either a noun or an adjective. Dictionary definitions do not specify what kind of water, although in both general use and in the sciences, the implication is often that of fresh water.
    a. AL 333
    b. AASHTO Soil Classification System
    c. Aquatic
    d. AL 129-1

50. An _____ is an ecosystem located in a body of water. Communities of organisms that are dependent on each other and on their environment live in an _____. The two main types are marine ecosystems and freshwater ecosystems.
    a. AASHTO Soil Classification System
    b. AL 333
    c. AL 129-1
    d. Aquatic ecosystem

51. _____, is the increase in concentration of a substance, such as the pesticide DDT, that occurs in a food chain as a consequence of:

- Food chain energetics
- Low (or nonexistent) rate of excretion/degradation of the substance.

Although sometimes used interchangeably with 'bioaccumulation,' an important distinction is drawn between the two, and with bioconcentration.

- Bioaccumulation occurs within a trophic level, and is the increase in concentration of a substance in an individuals' tissues due to uptake from food and sediments in an aquatic milieu.
- Bioconcentration is defined as occurring when uptake from the water is greater than excretion (Landrum and Fisher, 1999)

Thus bioconcentration and bioaccumulation occur within an organism, and _____ occurs across trophic (food chain) levels.

Lipid soluble (lipophilic) substances cannot be excreted in urine, a water-based medium, and so accumulate in fatty tissues of an organism if the organism lacks enzymes to degrade them. When eaten by another organism, fats are absorbed in the gut, carrying the substance, which then accumulates in the fats of the predator. Since at each level of the food chain there is a lot of energy loss, a predator must consume many prey, including all of their lipophilic substances.

    a. 1700 Cascadia earthquake
    b. 1509 Istanbul earthquake
    c. 1703 Genroku earthquake
    d. Biomagnification

52. A _____ describes one of a number of pieces of legislation relating to the reduction of smog and air pollution in general. The use of governments to enforce clean air standards has contributed to an improvement in human health and longer life spans.
    a. 1509 Istanbul earthquake
    b. 1703 Genroku earthquake
    c. 1700 Cascadia earthquake
    d. Clean Air Act

53. The _____ is an agency of the federal government of the United States charged with protecting human health and with safeguarding the natural environment: air, water, and land.
    a. Ambulocetus
    b. Environmental Protection Agency
    c. Andrija Mohorovičić
    d. Amblypoda

54. _____ is a chemical element in the periodic table that has the symbol Hg and atomic number 80. A heavy, silvery, transition metal, _____ is one of five elements that are liquid at or near standard room temperature (the others are the metals caesium, francium, and gallium, and the nonmetal bromine).
    a. 1509 Istanbul earthquake
    b. Mercury
    c. 1703 Genroku earthquake
    d. 1700 Cascadia earthquake

55. _____ is an organometallic. It is a bioaccumulative environmental toxicant.
    a. Methylmercury
    b. 1509 Istanbul earthquake
    c. 1703 Genroku earthquake
    d. 1700 Cascadia earthquake

56. _____ are organic chemical compounds that have high enough vapour pressures under normal conditions to significantly vaporize and enter the atmosphere.
    a. 1703 Genroku earthquake
    b. 1509 Istanbul earthquake
    c. 1700 Cascadia earthquake
    d. Volatile organic compounds

57. A _____ is a chemical substance of two or more different chemically bonded chemical elements, with a fixed ratio determining the composition. The ratio of each element is usually expressed by chemical formula.
    a. 1509 Istanbul earthquake
    b. 1700 Cascadia earthquake
    c. 1703 Genroku earthquake
    d. Chemical compound

58. An _____ is a natural unit consisting of all plants, animals and micro organisms in an area functioning together with all the non living physical factors of the environment.
    a. AL 333
    b. AASHTO Soil Classification System
    c. AL 129-1
    d. Ecosystem

Chapter 12. Water Pollution

59. An _____ is any member of a large class of chemical compounds whose molecules contain carbon.
    a. AL 129-1
    b. AL 333
    c. AASHTO Soil Classification System
    d. Organic compound

60. _____ is a chemical, physical, or biological agent that modifies the natural characteristics of the atmosphere. The atmosphere is a complex, dynamic natural gaseous system that is essential to support life on planet Earth. Stratospheric ozone depletion due to _____ has long been recognized as a threat to human health as well as to the Earth's ecosystems. Worldwide _____ is responsible for large numbers of deaths and cases of respiratory disease.
    a. Air pollution
    b. AASHTO Soil Classification System
    c. AL 129-1
    d. AL 333

61. _____ are waste types containing radioactive chemical elements that do not have a practical purpose. It is sometimes the product of a nuclear process, such as nuclear fission. However, other industries not directly connected to the nuclear industry can produce large quantities of _____.
    a. 1700 Cascadia earthquake
    b. 1509 Istanbul earthquake
    c. 1703 Genroku earthquake
    d. Radioactive waste

62. A _____ column is a column of rizing air in the lower altitudes of the Earth's atmosphere. _____s are created by the uneven heating of the Earth's surface from solar radiation, and are an example of convection. The Sun warms the ground, which in turn warms the air directly above it.
    a. 1703 Genroku earthquake
    b. 1700 Cascadia earthquake
    c. 1509 Istanbul earthquake
    d. Thermal

63. _____ is a temperature change in natural water bodies caused by human influence. The main cause of _____ is the use of water as a coolant, especially in power plants. Water used as a coolant is returned to the natural environment at a higher temperature.
    a. 1509 Istanbul earthquake
    b. 1700 Cascadia earthquake
    c. 1703 Genroku earthquake
    d. Thermal pollution

64. _____ is any particulate matter that can be transported by fluid flow and which eventually is deposited as a layer of solid particles on the bed or bottom of a body of water or other liquid.
    a. 1700 Cascadia earthquake
    b. 1509 Istanbul earthquake
    c. 1703 Genroku earthquake
    d. Sediment

65. _____ comes from many unidentifiable sources with no specific solution to rectify the proble, making it difficult to regulate. An example would be urban runoff of items like oil, fertilizers, and lawn chemicals. As rainfall or snowmelt moves over and through the ground, it picks up and carries away natural and human-made pollutants.
    a. 1703 Genroku earthquake
    b. 1700 Cascadia earthquake
    c. 1509 Istanbul earthquake
    d. Nonpoint sources

66. A _____ is an approximately circular depression in the surface of a planet, moon or other solid body in the Solar System, formed by the hyper-velocity impact of a smaller body with the surface. Impact _____s typically have raised rims, and they range from small, simple, bowl-shaped depressions to large, complex, multi-ringed, impact basins.
    a. Crater
    b. 1703 Genroku earthquake
    c. 1509 Istanbul earthquake
    d. 1700 Cascadia earthquake

Chapter 12. Water Pollution

67. An _____ is traditionally considered any chemical compound that, when dissolved in water, gives a solution with a hydrogen ion activity greater than in pure water, i.e. a pH less than 7.0. That approximates the modern definition of Johannes Nicolaus Brønsted and Martin Lowry, who independently defined an _____ as a compound which donates a hydrogen ion to another compound. Common examples include acetic _____ and sulfuric _____. Acid/base systems are different from redox reactions in that there is no change in oxidation state.
   a. AL 333
   b. AASHTO Soil Classification System
   c. AL 129-1
   d. Acid

68. _____ refers to the outflow of acidic water from abandoned metal mines. However, other areas where the earth has been disturbed may also contribute _____ to the environment
   a. AL 333
   b. AASHTO Soil Classification System
   c. AL 129-1
   d. Acid mine drainage

69. _____ is the natural or artificial removal of surface and sub-surface water from a given area. Many agricultural soils need _____ to improve production or to manage water supplies.
   a. 1703 Genroku earthquake
   b. 1509 Istanbul earthquake
   c. 1700 Cascadia earthquake
   d. Drainage

70. _____ is the extraction of valuable minerals or other geological materials from the earth, usually from an ore body, vein, or seam. Any material that cannot be grown from agricultural processes, or created artificially in a laboratory or factory, is usually extracted from the earth by this method.
   a. 1509 Istanbul earthquake
   b. 1700 Cascadia earthquake
   c. Mining
   d. 1703 Genroku earthquake

71. _____ is a strong mineral acid. It is soluble in water at all concentrations. _____ has many applications, and is one of the top products of the chemical industry. Principal uses include ore processing, fertilizer manufacturing, oil refining, wastewater processing, and chemical synthesis.
   a. 1509 Istanbul earthquake
   b. 1700 Cascadia earthquake
   c. Sulfuric acid
   d. 1703 Genroku earthquake

72. _____ are the materials left over after the process of separating the valuable fraction from the worthless fraction of an ore. _____ represent external costs of mining. As mining techniques and the price of minerals improve, it is not unusual for _____ to be reprocessed using new methods, or more thoroughly with old methods, to recover additional minerals.
   a. 1509 Istanbul earthquake
   b. 1703 Genroku earthquake
   c. Tailings
   d. 1700 Cascadia earthquake

73. The _____ is located in Northeast Ohio in the United States. Outside of Ohio, the river is most famous for being "the river that caught on fire"—which has actually happened more than once—helping to spur the environmental movement.
   a. 1700 Cascadia earthquake
   b. 1509 Istanbul earthquake
   c. Cuyahoga River
   d. 1703 Genroku earthquake

74. An _____ is an underground layer of water-bearing permeable rock or unconsolidated materials from which groundwater can be usefully extracted using a water well.

Chapter 12. Water Pollution

    a. AL 129-1
    b. AL 333
    c. AASHTO Soil Classification System
    d. Aquifer

75. _____ is water located beneath the ground surface in soil pore spaces and in the fractures of geologic formations. _____ is recharged from, and eventually flows to, the surface naturally; natural discharge often occurs at springs and seeps, streams and can often form oases or wetlands.
    a. 1700 Cascadia earthquake
    b. 1703 Genroku earthquake
    c. 1509 Istanbul earthquake
    d. Groundwater

76. The _____ is a scientific agency of the United States government. The scientists of the USGS study the landscape of the United States, its natural resources, and the natural hazards that threaten it.
    a. Andrija Mohorovičić
    b. Ambulocetus
    c. U.S. Geological Survey
    d. Amblypoda

77. _____ is the physical, chemical and biological characteristics of water, characterized through the methods of hydrometry.
    a. 1509 Istanbul earthquake
    b. 1703 Genroku earthquake
    c. 1700 Cascadia earthquake
    d. Water quality

78. The _____ is a river on the Atlantic coast of the United States. The Delaware was explored by Adriaen Block as part of the New Netherlands Colony, and was named the South River to mark the southernmost reach of that colony.
    a. 1700 Cascadia earthquake
    b. 1703 Genroku earthquake
    c. 1509 Istanbul earthquake
    d. Delaware River

79. The _____ is the surface where the water pressure is equal to atmospheric pressure. A large amount of water within a body of sand or rock below the _____ is called an aquifer, and the ability of rocks to store such groundwater is dependent on their porosity and permeability.
    a. 1509 Istanbul earthquake
    b. 1703 Genroku earthquake
    c. 1700 Cascadia earthquake
    d. Water table

80. _____ is a natural process that occurs in virtually all coastal aquifers. It consists in salt water flowing inland in freshwater aquifers. This behavior is caused by the fact that sea water has a higher density than freshwater.
    a. 1703 Genroku earthquake
    b. Saltwater intrusion
    c. 1700 Cascadia earthquake
    d. 1509 Istanbul earthquake

81. An _____ is a body of igneous rock that has crystallized from a molten magma below the surface of the Earth.
    a. Intrusion
    b. AL 129-1
    c. AASHTO Soil Classification System
    d. AL 333

82. _____ can be defined as any process that uses microorganisms, fungi, green plants or their enzymes to return the natural environment altered by contaminants to its original condition. _____ may be employed to attack specific soil contaminants, such as degradation of chlorinated hydrocarbons by bacteria. An example of a more general approach is the cleanup of oil spills by the addition of nitrate and/or sulfate fertilisers to facilitate the decomposition of crude oil by indigenous or exogenous bacteria.

a. 1700 Cascadia earthquake
b. 1703 Genroku earthquake
c. 1509 Istanbul earthquake
d. Bioremediation

83. _____ is water that is intended to be ingested by humans. Water of sufficient quality to serve as _____ is termed potable water whether it is used as such or not.
    a. 1700 Cascadia earthquake
    b. 1509 Istanbul earthquake
    c. 1703 Genroku earthquake
    d. Drinking Water

84. The _____ is a United States federal law passed by the U.S. Congress on December 16, 1974. It is the main federal law that ensures safe drinking water for Americans.
    a. 1509 Istanbul earthquake
    b. 1700 Cascadia earthquake
    c. 1703 Genroku earthquake
    d. Safe Drinking Water Act

85. _____ is the gas phase component of a another state of matter which does not completely fill its container. It is distinguished from the pure gas phase by the presence of the same substance in another state of matter. Hence when a liquid has completely evaporated, it is said that the system has been completely transformed to the gas phase.
    a. 1509 Istanbul earthquake
    b. 1700 Cascadia earthquake
    c. 1703 Genroku earthquake
    d. Vapor

86. _____ is a layman's term used to describe newborns with cyanotic conditions, such as • Cyanotic heart defects • Tetralogy of Fallot • Dextro-Transposition of the great arteries • Hypoplastic left heart syndrome • Methemoglobinemia • Respiratory distress syndrome
    a. 1703 Genroku earthquake
    b. Blue baby
    c. 1509 Istanbul earthquake
    d. 1700 Cascadia earthquake

87. A _____ is a salt of nitric acid with an ion composed of one nitrogen and three oxygen atoms. In freshwater or estuarine systems close to land, _____ can reach high levels that can potentially cause the death of fish. Water quality may also be affected through ground water resources that have a high number of septic systems in a watershed.
    a. 1700 Cascadia earthquake
    b. Nitrate
    c. 1703 Genroku earthquake
    d. 1509 Istanbul earthquake

88. The _____ is a diverse scientific, social, and political movement for addressing the concerns of environmentalism. The _____ is represented by a range of organizations, from the large to grassroots. Due to its large membership, varying and strong beliefs, and occasionally speculative nature, the _____ is not always united in its goals.
    a. Amblypoda
    b. Andrija Mohorovičić
    c. Ambulocetus
    d. Environmental movement

89. A _____ is a geological phenomenon which includes a wide range of ground movement, such as rock falls, deep failure of slopes and shallow debris flows. Although gravity's action on an over-steepened slope is the primary reason for a _____, there are other contributing factors affecting the original slope stability.
    a. 1509 Istanbul earthquake
    b. 1703 Genroku earthquake
    c. 1700 Cascadia earthquake
    d. Landslide

90. A _____, the key component of a septic system, is a small scale sewage treatment system common in areas with no connection to main sewerage pipes provided by private corporations or local governments.

Chapter 12. Water Pollution

a. 1700 Cascadia earthquake
b. 1509 Istanbul earthquake
c. 1703 Genroku earthquake
d. Septic tank

91. _____ is a set of management strategies for prevention of soil being eroded from the earth's surface or becoming chemically altered by overuse, salinization, acidification, or other chemical soil contamination.
   a. 1700 Cascadia earthquake
   b. 1509 Istanbul earthquake
   c. 1703 Genroku earthquake
   d. Soil Conservation

92. The _____ is an agency of the United States Department of Agriculture that provides technical assistance to private land owners and managers. Its mission is to improve, protect, and conserve natural resources on private lands through a cooperative partnership with local and state agencies.
   a. Andrija Mohorovičić
   b. Amblypoda
   c. Ambulocetus
   d. Soil Conservation Service

93. _____ is any water that has been adversely affected in quality by anthropogenic influence.
   a. 1703 Genroku earthquake
   b. Wastewater
   c. 1509 Istanbul earthquake
   d. 1700 Cascadia earthquake

94. _____ is the term used for a branch of public policy which encompasses various disciplines which seek to order and regulate the use of land in an efficient and ethical way.
   a. 1509 Istanbul earthquake
   b. 1700 Cascadia earthquake
   c. 1703 Genroku earthquake
   d. Land use planning

95. _____ is a small scale sewage treatment system common in areas with no connection to main sewerage pipes provided by private corporations or local governments
   a. 1703 Genroku earthquake
   b. 1700 Cascadia earthquake
   c. 1509 Istanbul earthquake
   d. Septic system

96. _____ removes the materials that can be easily collected from the raw wastewater and disposed of.
   a. 1509 Istanbul earthquake
   b. 1700 Cascadia earthquake
   c. Primary treatment
   d. 1703 Genroku earthquake

97. _____ is the residual semi-solid material left from industrial, water treatment, or wastewater treatment processes.
   a. Sludge
   b. 1509 Istanbul earthquake
   c. 1700 Cascadia earthquake
   d. 1703 Genroku earthquake

98. _____ are a major group of living things including familiar organisms such as trees, flowers, herbs, bushes, grasses, vines, ferns, and mosses.
   a. 1700 Cascadia earthquake
   b. 1703 Genroku earthquake
   c. 1509 Istanbul earthquake
   d. Plants

99. _____ is a process dealing with the treatment of sewage and industrial wastewaters. Atmospheric air or pure oxygen is bubbled through primary treated sewage combined with organisms to develop a biological floc which reduces the organic content of the sewage. The combination of raw sewage and biological mass is commonly known as Mixed Liquor.

a. AL 129-1
b. AASHTO Soil Classification System
c. AL 333
d. Activated sludge

100. _____, sometimes called recycled water, is former wastewater (sewage) that has been treated to remove solids and certain impurities, and then allowed to recharge the aquifer rather than being discharged to surface water. This recharging is often done by using the treated wastewater for irrigation. In most locations, it is only intended to be used for nonpotable uses, such as irrigation, dust control, and fire suppression, and there is controversy about possible health and environmental effects for those uses.
   a. 1509 Istanbul earthquake
   b. 1700 Cascadia earthquake
   c. 1703 Genroku earthquake
   d. Reclaimed water

101. _____ is designed to substantially degrade the biological content of the sewage such as are derived from human waste, food waste, soaps and detergent. The majority of municipal and industrial plants treat the settled sewage liquor using aerobic biological processes. For this to be effective, the biota require both oxygen and a substrate on which to live.
   a. 1509 Istanbul earthquake
   b. 1703 Genroku earthquake
   c. 1700 Cascadia earthquake
   d. Secondary treatment

102. An interbasin _____ is a hydrological project undertaken to divert water from one drainage basin into another. This is usually to boost water levels for hydroelectricity, or to supply drinking water nearby.

- Campbell-Heber Diversion
- Coquitlam-Buntzen Diversion
- Kemano Diversion
- Vernon Irrigation District Diversion

- Churchill Diversion-Southern Indian Lake

- Saint John Water Supply

- Bay d'Espoir Diversions
- Deer Lake Diversion
- Smallwood Reservoir-Julian Diversion
- Smallwood Reservoir-Kanairiktok Diversion
- Smallwood Reservoir-Naskaupi Diversion

- Wellington Lake Hydro Project Diversion (with Saskatchewan)

- Ingram Diversion
- Jordan Diversion
- Wreck Cove Diversions

- Long Lake Diversion
- Ogoki Diversion
- Opasatika Diversion
- Root River Diversion

- Barrière Diversion
- Boyd-Sakami Diversion
- Lac de la Frégate Diversion
- Laforge Diversion
- Manouane Diversion
- Mégiscane Diversion
- Sault aux Cochons Diversion

- Cypress Lake Diversion (with Alberta)
- Pasquia Land Resettlement Diversion (with Manitoba)
- Swift Current Diversion

a. 1509 Istanbul earthquake
b. 1700 Cascadia earthquake
c. 1703 Genroku earthquake
d. Water diversion

103. _____ is the production of food, feed, fiber, fuel and other goods by the systematic raizing of plants and animals.

Chapter 12. Water Pollution

a. Agriculture
b. AL 333
c. AASHTO Soil Classification System
d. AL 129-1

104. The State of _____ is a state located in the southwestern region of the United States. The capital and largest city is Phoenix. The second largest city is Tucson, followed by the four Phoenix-area conurbation cities of Mesa, Glendale, Chandler, and Scottsdale.
a. Kaibab Plateau
b. Arizona
c. AL 129-1
d. AASHTO Soil Classification System

105. In physics, the _____ states that the total amount of energy in an isolated system remains constant, although it may change forms, e.g. friction turns kinetic energy into thermal energy. In thermodynamics, the first law of thermodynamics is a statement of the _____ for thermodynamic systems, and is the more encompassing version of the _____.
a. 1509 Istanbul earthquake
b. 1703 Genroku earthquake
c. Conservation of energy
d. 1700 Cascadia earthquake

106. _____ is the process of improving a structure. Two prominent types of _____s are commercial and residential. The process of a _____, however complex, can usually be broken down into several processes.

a. 1509 Istanbul earthquake
b. 1703 Genroku earthquake
c. 1700 Cascadia earthquake
d. Renovation

107. In physical geography, a _____ is an environment "at the interface between truly terrestrial ecosystems and aquatic systems making them inherently different from each other yet highly dependent on both". In essence, they are ecotones.
a. 1700 Cascadia earthquake
b. 1703 Genroku earthquake
c. 1509 Istanbul earthquake
d. Wetland

108. In physics, _____ is a scalar physical quantity that describes the amount of work that can be performed by a force. _____ is an attribute of objects and systems that is subject to a conservation law. Several different forms of _____ exist to explain all known natural phenomena.
a. AL 129-1
b. AASHTO Soil Classification System
c. AL 333
d. Energy

109. The principal body of law currently in effect is based on the Federal Water Pollution Control Amendments of 1972, which significantly expanded and strengthened earlier legislation. Major amendments were enacted in the Clean Water Act of 1977 enacted by the 95th United States Congress and the _____ of 1987 enacted by the 100th United States Congress.

The Act governs discharges to waters of the United States. Older statutory language used the term 'navigable waters,' but this term was expanded in the 1972 law:

> The term 'navigable waters' means the waters of the United States, including the territorial seas.

a. Flotsam
b. Fish and Wildlife Coordination Act
c. Water Quality Act
d. Jetsam

Chapter 13. Mineral Resources

1. A _____ is a naturally occurring substance formed through geological processes that has a characteristic chemical composition, a highly ordered atomic structure and specific physical properties. A rock, by comparison, is an aggregate of _____s and need not have a specific chemical composition. _____s range in composition from pure elements and simple salts to very complex silicates with thousands of known forms.
    a. 1509 Istanbul earthquake
    b. 1700 Cascadia earthquake
    c. 1703 Genroku earthquake
    d. Mineral

2. _____ is a chemical element in the periodic table that has the symbol Au and atomic number 79. A soft, shiny, yellow, dense, malleable, ductile (trivalent and univalent) transition metal, _____ does not react with most chemicals but is attacked by chlorine, fluorine and aqua regia.
    a. 1703 Genroku earthquake
    b. 1700 Cascadia earthquake
    c. 1509 Istanbul earthquake
    d. Gold

3. A _____ is a bipedal primate belonging to the mammalian species Homo sapiens in the family Hominidae. Compared to other living organisms on Earth, a _____ has a highly developed brain capable of abstract reasoning, language, and introspection.
    a. 1703 Genroku earthquake
    b. Human
    c. 1509 Istanbul earthquake
    d. 1700 Cascadia earthquake

4. _____ is the human modification of natural environment or wilderness into built environment such as fields, pastures, and settlements. The major effect of _____ on land cover since 1750 has been deforestation of temperate regions. More recent significant effects of _____ include urban sprawl, soil erosion, soil degradation, salinization, and desertification.
    a. 1700 Cascadia earthquake
    b. Land use
    c. 1509 Istanbul earthquake
    d. 1703 Genroku earthquake

5. _____ is a chemical element with the symbol Ag and atomic number 47. A soft white lustrous transition metal, it has the highest electrical and thermal conductivity for a metal. It occurs as a free metal as well as various minerals such as argentite and chlorargyrite.
    a. Thorium
    b. Scandium
    c. Sublimation
    d. Silver

6. _____ is the residual semi-solid material left from industrial, water treatment, or wastewater treatment processes.
    a. 1703 Genroku earthquake
    b. 1509 Istanbul earthquake
    c. 1700 Cascadia earthquake
    d. Sludge

7. The _____ is defined as the part of the land adjoining or near the ocean. A coastline is properly a line on a map indicating the disposition of a _____, but the word is often used to refer to the _____ itself. The adjective coastal describes something as being on, near to, or associated with a _____.
    a. 1700 Cascadia earthquake
    b. 1509 Istanbul earthquake
    c. 1703 Genroku earthquake
    d. Coast

8. _____ is the wearing away of land or the removal of beach or dune sediments by wave action, tidal currents, wave currents, or drainage. Waves, generated by storms or fast moving moter craft, cause _____, which may take the form of long-term losses of sediment and rocks, or merely in the temporary redistribution of coastal sediments; erosion in one location may result in accretion nearby.

Chapter 13. Mineral Resources

    a. 1509 Istanbul earthquake
    b. 1700 Cascadia earthquake
    c. 1703 Genroku earthquake
    d. Beach erosion

9. _____ is displacement of solids by the agents of ocean currents, wind, water, or ice by downward or down-slope movement in response to gravity or by living organisms.
    a. AL 129-1
    b. AASHTO Soil Classification System
    c. AL 333
    d. Erosion

10. In physics, _____ is a scalar physical quantity that describes the amount of work that can be performed by a force. _____ is an attribute of objects and systems that is subject to a conservation law. Several different forms of _____ exist to explain all known natural phenomena.
    a. AL 129-1
    b. AL 333
    c. AASHTO Soil Classification System
    d. Energy

11. Consumption of a _____ requires resources and contributes to air and water pollution. In the industrialized world the development of a _____ has become essential for agriculture, transportation, waste collection, information technology, communications that have become prerequisites of a developed society.
    a. AL 129-1
    b. AL 333
    c. AASHTO Soil Classification System
    d. Energy resource

12. _____ is the mineral form of sodium chloride. _____ forms isometric crystals. It commonly occurs with other evaporite deposit minerals such as several of the sulfates, halides and borates. _____ occurs in vast lakes of sedimentary evaporite minerals that result from the drying up of enclosed beds, playas, and seas.
    a. 1703 Genroku earthquake
    b. Halite
    c. 1509 Istanbul earthquake
    d. 1700 Cascadia earthquake

13. _____ is a dietary mineral composed primarily of sodium chloride that is essential for animal life, but toxic to most land plants. _____ flavor is one of the basic tastes, an important preservative and a popular food seasoning.

_____ for human consumption is produced in different forms: unrefined _____ (such as sea _____), refined _____ (table _____), and iodized _____.

    a. 1703 Genroku earthquake
    b. 1700 Cascadia earthquake
    c. 1509 Istanbul earthquake
    d. Salt

14. _____ are sources of water that are useful or potentially useful to humans. It is important because it is needed for life to exist. Many uses of water include agricultural, industrial, household, recreational and environmental activities.
    a. 1700 Cascadia earthquake
    b. 1509 Istanbul earthquake
    c. 1703 Genroku earthquake
    d. Water resources

15. _____ is a fossil fuel formed in swamp ecosystems where plant remains were saved by water and mud from oxidization and biodegradation. It is a sedimentary rock, but the harder forms, such as anthracite _____, can be regarded as metamorphic rocks because of later exposure to elevated temperature and pressure. It is composed primarily of carbon along with assorted other elements, including sulfur.

Chapter 13. Mineral Resources

a. 1509 Istanbul earthquake
b. 1703 Genroku earthquake
c. 1700 Cascadia earthquake
d. Coal

16. An _____ is a volume of rock containing components or minerals in a mode of occurrence that renders it valuable for mining.
a. Ore
b. AASHTO Soil Classification System
c. AL 333
d. AL 129-1

17. _____ is the science and study of the solid matter that constitute the Earth. Encompassing such things as rocks, soil, and gemstones, _____ studies the composition, structure, physical properties, history, and the processes that shape Earth's components.
a. 1509 Istanbul earthquake
b. Glaciology
c. Glacial motion
d. Geology

18. _____ are the hardest natural material known to man and the third-hardest known material. Its hardness and high dispersion of light make it useful for industrial applications and jewelry.
a. Francium
b. Plug-in hybrid electric vehicle
c. Hurricane Mitch
d. Diamonds

19. _____ is the chemical element in the periodic table that has the symbol Al and atomic number 13. It is a silvery and ductile member of the poor metal group of chemical elements. _____ is found primarily as the ore bauxite and is remarkable for its resistance to corrosion (due to the phenomenon of passivation) and its light weight. _____ is used in many industries to make millions of different products and is very important to the world economy.
a. AL 333
b. AL 129-1
c. AASHTO Soil Classification System
d. Aluminum

20. The _____ is used to assess the economic feasibility of a mining operation: the cost of extracting a natural material from its ore is directly related to its concentration, and the cost of extraction must be less than the market value of the material being mined for the operation to be economically feasible
a. 1700 Cascadia earthquake
b. Concentration factor of metal
c. 1703 Genroku earthquake
d. 1509 Istanbul earthquake

21. A _____ is a solid in which the constituent atoms, molecules, or ions are packed in a regularly ordered, repeating pattern extending in all three spatial dimensions. Most metals encountered in everyday life are polycrystals. _____s are often symmetrically intergrown to form _____ twins.
a. 1700 Cascadia earthquake
b. 1509 Istanbul earthquake
c. Crystal
d. 1703 Genroku earthquake

22. _____ rocks form when molten rock, magma, cools and solidifies, with or without crystallization, either below the surface as intrusive, plutonic rocks or on the surface as extrusive, volcanic, rocks.
a. Igneous
b. AASHTO Soil Classification System
c. AL 333
d. AL 129-1

23. _____ is a type of rock best known for sometimes containing diamonds. It is an ultrapotassic, ultramafic, igneous rock composed of olivine, phlogopite, pyroxene and garnet, with a variety of chemically anomalous trace minerals.

Chapter 13. Mineral Resources

a. 1509 Istanbul earthquake
b. 1703 Genroku earthquake
c. 1700 Cascadia earthquake
d. Kimberlite

24. _____ is a chemical element in the periodic table that has the symbol Hg and atomic number 80. A heavy, silvery, transition metal, _____ is one of five elements that are liquid at or near standard room temperature (the others are the metals caesium, francium, and gallium, and the nonmetal bromine).
a. 1700 Cascadia earthquake
b. 1703 Genroku earthquake
c. 1509 Istanbul earthquake
d. Mercury

25. _____ is the process of breaking down rocks, soils and their minerals through direct contact with the atmosphere. _____ occurs without movement. Two main classifications of _____ processes exist. Mechanical or physical _____ involves the breakdown of rocks and soils through direct contact with atmospheric conditions. The second classification, chemical _____, involves the direct effect of atmospheric chemicals in the breakdown of rocks, soils and minerals.
a. 1703 Genroku earthquake
b. Weathering
c. 1700 Cascadia earthquake
d. 1509 Istanbul earthquake

26. A _____, is a fissure in a planet's surface from which geothermally heated water issues. _____s are commonly found near volcanically active places, tectonic plates that are moving apart, ocean basins, and hotspots.
a. 1703 Genroku earthquake
b. 1700 Cascadia earthquake
c. 1509 Istanbul earthquake
d. Hydrothermal vent

27. _____ are a type of hydrothermal vent found on the ocean floor. The vents are formed in fields hundreds of meters wide when superheated water from below the Earth's crust comes through the ocean floor. It can also be known as a Sea Vent. The superheated water is rich in dissolved minerals from the crust, most notably sulfides, which crystallize to create a chimney-like structure around each vent. When the superheated water in the vent comes in contact with the cold ocean water, many minerals are precipitated, creating the distinctive black color.
a. 1703 Genroku earthquake
b. Black smokers
c. 1700 Cascadia earthquake
d. 1509 Istanbul earthquake

28. In plate tectonics, a _____ a linear feature that exists between two tectonic plates that are moving away from each other. These areas can form in the middle of continents but eventually form ocean basins.
a. 1700 Cascadia earthquake
b. 1509 Istanbul earthquake
c. 1703 Genroku earthquake
d. Divergent plate boundary

29. _____ is a theory of geology that has been developed to explain the observed evidence for large scale motions of the Earth's lithosphere. The theory encompassed and superseded the older theory of continental drift.
a. 1703 Genroku earthquake
b. 1509 Istanbul earthquake
c. 1700 Cascadia earthquake
d. Plate tectonics

30. The _____ is a geologic transform fault that runs a length of roughly 800 miles (1,300 km) through California in the United States. The fault's motion is right-lateral strike-slip (horizontal motion.) It forms the tectonic boundary between the Pacific Plate and the North American Plate.
a. 1700 Cascadia earthquake
b. 1509 Istanbul earthquake
c. 1703 Genroku earthquake
d. San Andreas fault

Chapter 13. Mineral Resources

31. In geology, a _____ zone is an area on Earth where two tectonic plates meet and move towards one another, with one sliding underneath the other and moving down into the mantle, at rates typically measured in centimeters per year. An oceanic plate ordinarily slides underneath a continental plate; this often creates an orogenic zone with many volcanoes and earthquakes.
    a. 1700 Cascadia earthquake
    b. 1703 Genroku earthquake
    c. 1509 Istanbul earthquake
    d. Subduction

32. A _____ is an area on Earth where two tectonic plates meet and move towards one another, with one sliding underneath the other and moving down into the mantle, at rates typically measured in centimeters per year. In a sense, _____s are the opposite of divergent boundaries, areas where material rises up from the mantle and plates are moving apart.
    a. 1509 Istanbul earthquake
    b. Subduction zone
    c. 1703 Genroku earthquake
    d. 1700 Cascadia earthquake

33. The term _____ refers to several types of chemical compounds containing sulfur in its lowest oxidation number of −2.
    a. 1509 Istanbul earthquake
    b. 1700 Cascadia earthquake
    c. Sulfide
    d. 1703 Genroku earthquake

34. _____s are planar rock fractures, which show evidence of relative movement. Large _____s within the Earth's crust are the result of shear motion and active _____ zones are the causal locations of most earthquakes. Earthquakes are caused by energy release during rapid slippage along _____s.
    a. 1509 Istanbul earthquake
    b. Fault
    c. 1703 Genroku earthquake
    d. 1700 Cascadia earthquake

35. _____ is a field of study within geology concerned generally with the structures within the crust of the Earth, or other planets, and particularly with the forces and movements that have operated in a region to create these structures.
    a. 1703 Genroku earthquake
    b. 1700 Cascadia earthquake
    c. 1509 Istanbul earthquake
    d. Tectonics

36. _____ occurs typically around intrusive igneous rocks as a result of the temperature increase caused by the intrusion of magma into cooler country rock. The area surrounding the intrusion (called aureoles) where the _____ effects are present is called the metamorphic aureole. Contact metamorphic rocks are usually known as hornfels.
    a. 1703 Genroku earthquake
    b. 1700 Cascadia earthquake
    c. 1509 Istanbul earthquake
    d. Contact metamorphism

37. _____ can be defined as the solid state recrystallisation of pre-existing rocks due to changes in heat and/or pressure and/or introduction of fluids. There will be mineralogical, chemical and crystallographic changes. _____ produced with increasing pressure and temperature conditions is known as prograde _____. Conversely, decreasing temperatures and pressure characterize retrograde _____.
    a. 1703 Genroku earthquake
    b. 1509 Istanbul earthquake
    c. 1700 Cascadia earthquake
    d. Metamorphism

38. _____ is a biological process by which an animal physically develops after birth or hatching, involving a conspicuous and relatively abrupt change in the animal's form or structure through cell growth and differentiation.

Chapter 13. Mineral Resources

a. 1700 Cascadia earthquake
b. Metamorphosis
c. 1509 Istanbul earthquake
d. 1703 Genroku earthquake

39. A biological process is a process of a living organism. _____ are made up of any number of chemical reactions or other events that results in a transformation.

Regulation of _____ occurs where any process is modulated in its frequency, rate or extent.

a. 1509 Istanbul earthquake
b. Biological processes
c. 1703 Genroku earthquake
d. 1700 Cascadia earthquake

40. _____ refers to water-soluble, mineral sediments that result from the evaporation of bodies of surficial water.
a. AL 129-1
b. AASHTO Soil Classification System
c. AL 333
d. Evaporite

41. A _____, in inorganic chemistry, is a salt of phosphoric acid. In organic chemistry it is an ester of phosphoric acid.
a. 1509 Istanbul earthquake
b. Phosphate
c. 1703 Genroku earthquake
d. 1700 Cascadia earthquake

42. A _____ is an accumulation of alluvium or eluvium containing valuable minerals which is formed by deposition of dense mineral phases in a trap site.
a. 1509 Istanbul earthquake
b. Placer
c. 1703 Genroku earthquake
d. 1700 Cascadia earthquake

43. _____ rock is one of the three main rock groups. Rock formed from these covers 75% of the Earth's land area, and includes common types such as chalk, limestone, dolomite, sandstone, and shale.
a. Clasts
b. Sedimentary
c. Sedimentary depositional environment
d. Sedimentary basin

44. A _____ in geology is an intrusive igneous rock body that crystallized from a magma below the surface of the Earth. _____s include batholiths, dikes, sills, laccoliths, lopoliths, and other igneous bodies. In practice, "_____" usually refers to a distinctive mass of igneous rock, typically kilometers in dimension, without a tabular shape like those of dikes and sills.
a. 1700 Cascadia earthquake
b. 1703 Genroku earthquake
c. 1509 Istanbul earthquake
d. Pluton

45. _____ is an aluminium ore. It consists largely of the Al minerals gibbsite, boehmite and diaspore, together with the iron oxides goethite and hematite, the clay mineral kaolinite and small amounts of anatase.
a. 1700 Cascadia earthquake
b. 1703 Genroku earthquake
c. 1509 Istanbul earthquake
d. Bauxite

46. _____ is a surface formation in hot and wet tropical areas which is enriched in iron and aluminium and develops by intensive and long lasting weathering of the underlying parent rock. Nearly all kinds of rocks can be deeply decomposed by the action of high rainfall and elevated temperatures. This gives rise to a residual concentration of more insoluble elements.

Chapter 13. Mineral Resources

a. 1700 Cascadia earthquake
c. 1703 Genroku earthquake
b. 1509 Istanbul earthquake
d. Laterite

47. _____ is a cape on the coast of North Carolina. It is the point that protrudes the farthest to the southeast along the northeast-to-southwest line of the Atlantic coast of North America. Two major Atlantic currents collide just off _____, the southerly-flowing cold water Labrador Current and the northerly-flowing warm water Florida Current (Gulf Stream), creating turbulent waters and a large expanse of shallow sandbars extending up to 14 miles offshore.
a. 1700 Cascadia earthquake
c. Cape Hatteras
b. 1509 Istanbul earthquake
d. 1703 Genroku earthquake

48. Due to shore erosion in the Outer Bank of North Carolina a navagational lighthouse had to be moved leading to the _____.
a. 1509 Istanbul earthquake
c. 1703 Genroku earthquake
b. 1700 Cascadia earthquake
d. Cape Hatteras Lighthouse controversy

49. An _____ is an assessment of the likely influence a project may have on the environment. The purpose of the assessment is to ensure that decision-makers consider _____s before deciding whether to proceed with new projects.
a. Environmental impact
c. AL 333
b. AL 129-1
d. AASHTO Soil Classification System

50. The _____ is an open-pit mine extracting a large porphyry copper deposit southwest of Salt Lake City, Utah, USA, in the Oquirrh Mountains. It is owned by Rio Tinto plc through Kennecott Utah Copper Corporation which operates the mine, a concentrator and a smelter. The mine has been in production since 1906, and has resulted in the creation of a pit over 0.75 miles wide, and covering 1,900 acres.
a. Bingham Mine
c. 1509 Istanbul earthquake
b. 1700 Cascadia earthquake
d. 1703 Genroku earthquake

51. A _____ is a deep valley between cliffs often carved from the landscape by a river. Most were formed by a process of long-time erosion from a plateau level. The cliffs form because harder rock strata that are resistant to erosion and weathering remain exposed on the valley walls.
a. 1703 Genroku earthquake
c. 1509 Istanbul earthquake
b. 1700 Cascadia earthquake
d. Canyon

52. In geography, a _____ is a landscape form or region that receives very little precipitation. They are defined as areas that receive an average annual precipitation of less than 250 mm. A _____ where vegetation cover is exceedingly sparse correspond to the 'hyperarid' regions of the earth, where rainfall is exceedingly rare and infrequent.
a. 1509 Istanbul earthquake
c. 1703 Genroku earthquake
b. 1700 Cascadia earthquake
d. Desert

53. A _____ is a desert surface that is covered with closely packed, interlocking angular or rounded rock fragments of pebble and cobble size. It is thought that they are formed by the gradual removal of the sand, dust and other fine grained material by the wind and intermittent rain.
a. 1700 Cascadia earthquake
c. 1703 Genroku earthquake
b. 1509 Istanbul earthquake
d. Desert pavement

54. _____ is an industrial mining process to extract precious metals and copper compounds from ore.

Chapter 13. Mineral Resources

a. 1703 Genroku earthquake
b. 1700 Cascadia earthquake
c. Heap leaching
d. 1509 Istanbul earthquake

55. _____ is the process of extracting a substance from a solid by dissolving it in a liquid.
   a. 1509 Istanbul earthquake
   b. 1703 Genroku earthquake
   c. 1700 Cascadia earthquake
   d. Leaching

56. _____ is the extraction of valuable minerals or other geological materials from the earth, usually from an ore body, vein, or seam. Any material that cannot be grown from agricultural processes, or created artificially in a laboratory or factory, is usually extracted from the earth by this method.
   a. 1700 Cascadia earthquake
   b. 1509 Istanbul earthquake
   c. 1703 Genroku earthquake
   d. Mining

57. _____ is a type of mining in which soil and rock overlying the mineral deposit are removed. Unless reclaimed, _____ can leave behind large areas of infertile waste rock. In most forms of _____, heavy equipment, such as earthmovers, first remove the overburden - the soil and rock above the deposit.
   a. 1703 Genroku earthquake
   b. 1509 Istanbul earthquake
   c. Surface mining
   d. 1700 Cascadia earthquake

58. _____ is unwanted or undesired material.
   a. 1703 Genroku earthquake
   b. 1509 Istanbul earthquake
   c. 1700 Cascadia earthquake
   d. Waste

59. _____ is a chemical element in the periodic table that has the symbol Cu and atomic number 29. It is a ductile metal with excellent electrical conductivity, and finds extensive use as a building material, as an electrical conductor, and as a component of various alloys.
   a. 1700 Cascadia earthquake
   b. 1703 Genroku earthquake
   c. 1509 Istanbul earthquake
   d. Copper

60. An _____ is traditionally considered any chemical compound that, when dissolved in water, gives a solution with a hydrogen ion activity greater than in pure water, i.e. a pH less than 7.0. That approximates the modern definition of Johannes Nicolaus Brønsted and Martin Lowry, who independently defined an _____ as a compound which donates a hydrogen ion to another compound. Common examples include acetic _____ and sulfuric _____. Acid/base systems are different from redox reactions in that there is no change in oxidation state.
   a. AL 333
   b. AASHTO Soil Classification System
   c. AL 129-1
   d. Acid

61. _____ refers to the outflow of acidic water from abandoned metal mines. However, other areas where the earth has been disturbed may also contribute _____ to the environment
   a. Acid mine drainage
   b. AASHTO Soil Classification System
   c. AL 333
   d. AL 129-1

62. An _____ is an underground layer of water-bearing permeable rock or unconsolidated materials from which groundwater can be usefully extracted using a water well.

Chapter 13. Mineral Resources

a. Aquifer
b. AL 333
c. AL 129-1
d. AASHTO Soil Classification System

63. A _____ is an isolated hill with steep sides and a small flat top, smaller than mesas and plateaus. _____s are prevalent in the western United States and on the Hawaiian Islands, especially around Honolulu.
   a. 1700 Cascadia earthquake
   b. Butte
   c. 1509 Istanbul earthquake
   d. 1703 Genroku earthquake

64. _____ is the natural or artificial removal of surface and sub-surface water from a given area. Many agricultural soils need _____ to improve production or to manage water supplies.
   a. Drainage
   b. 1703 Genroku earthquake
   c. 1509 Istanbul earthquake
   d. 1700 Cascadia earthquake

65. _____ is water located beneath the ground surface in soil pore spaces and in the fractures of geologic formations. _____ is recharged from, and eventually flows to, the surface naturally; natural discharge often occurs at springs and seeps, streams and can often form oases or wetlands.
   a. Groundwater
   b. 1700 Cascadia earthquake
   c. 1703 Genroku earthquake
   d. 1509 Istanbul earthquake

66. _____ are the materials left over after the process of separating the valuable fraction from the worthless fraction of an ore. _____ represent external costs of mining. As mining techniques and the price of minerals improve, it is not unusual for _____ to be reprocessed using new methods, or more thoroughly with old methods, to recover additional minerals.
   a. 1509 Istanbul earthquake
   b. Tailings
   c. 1703 Genroku earthquake
   d. 1700 Cascadia earthquake

67. _____ is a large set of adverse effects upon water bodies such as lakes, rivers, oceans, and groundwater caused by human activities. Although natural phenomena such as volcanoes, algae blooms, storms, and earthquakes also cause major changes in water quality and the ecological status of water, these are not deemed to be pollution. _____ has many causes and characteristics.
   a. 1700 Cascadia earthquake
   b. 1509 Istanbul earthquake
   c. 1703 Genroku earthquake
   d. Water pollution

68. _____ is the introduction of substances or energy into the environment, resulting in deleterious effects of such a nature as to endanger human health, harm living resources and ecosystems, and impair or interfere with amenities and other legitimate uses of the environment.
   a. 1700 Cascadia earthquake
   b. 1509 Istanbul earthquake
   c. 1703 Genroku earthquake
   d. Pollution

69. _____ is a chemical element in the periodic table that has the symbol Cd and atomic number 48. A relatively rare, soft, bluish-white, toxic transition metal, _____ occurs with zinc ores and is used largely in batteries.
   a. 1509 Istanbul earthquake
   b. Cadmium
   c. 1703 Genroku earthquake
   d. 1700 Cascadia earthquake

Chapter 13. Mineral Resources

70. _____ is a national park and wildlife refuge in southwestern Spain. The park, whose biodiversity is unique in Europe, contains a great variety of ecosystems and shelters wildlife including thousands of European and African migratory birds.
    a. 1509 Istanbul earthquake
    b. 1700 Cascadia earthquake
    c. 1703 Genroku earthquake
    d. Donana National Park

71. _____ or the Kingdom of _____ , is a country located in southwestern Europe on the Iberian Peninsula. Its mainland is bordered to the south and east by the Mediterranean Sea except for a small land boundary with Gibraltar; to the north by France, Andorra, and the Bay of Biscay; and to the west by the Atlantic Ocean and Portugal. Spanish territory also includes the Balearic Islands in the Mediterranean, the Canary Islands in the Atlantic Ocean off the African coast, and two autonomous cities in North Africa, Ceuta and Melilla, that border Morocco.
    a. Spain
    b. Andrija Mohorović iÄ‡
    c. Ambulocetus
    d. Amblypoda

72. The term _____ is commonly used to mean the deposition of acidic components in rain, snow, dew, or dry particles. _____ occurs when sulfur dioxide and nitrogen oxides are emitted into the atmosphere, undergo chemical transformations and are absorbed by water droplets in clouds. The droplets then fall to earth as rain, snow, mist, dry dust, hail, or sleet. This increases the acidity of the soil, and affects the chemical balance of lakes and streams.
    a. Acid precipitation
    b. AL 129-1
    c. AL 333
    d. AASHTO Soil Classification System

73. _____ is a layer of gases surrounding the planet Earth and retained by the Earth's gravity, protecting life on Earth by absorbing ultraviolet solar radiation and reducing temperature extremes between day and night.
    a. AL 333
    b. AL 129-1
    c. AASHTO Soil Classification System
    d. Earths atmosphere

74. _____ is a chemical, physical, or biological agent that modifies the natural characteristics of the atmosphere. The atmosphere is a complex, dynamic natural gaseous system that is essential to support life on planet Earth. Stratospheric ozone depletion due to _____ has long been recognized as a threat to human health as well as to the Earth's ecosystems. Worldwide _____ is responsible for large numbers of deaths and cases of respiratory disease.
    a. AL 129-1
    b. Air pollution
    c. AL 333
    d. AASHTO Soil Classification System

75. _____ is a form of extractive metallurgy. The main use of _____ is to produce a metal from its ore.
    a. Smelting
    b. 1700 Cascadia earthquake
    c. 1509 Istanbul earthquake
    d. 1703 Genroku earthquake

76. _____ emission factors are representative values that attempt to relate the quantity of a pollutant released to the ambient air with an activity associated with the release of that pollutant. _____ can be assified as either primary or secondary. Primary ones are substances directly emitted from a process, such as ash from a volcanic eruption or the carbon monoxide gas from a motor vehicle exhaust. The secondary ones are not emitted directly.
    a. AL 129-1
    b. Air pollutant
    c. AASHTO Soil Classification System
    d. AL 333

Chapter 13. Mineral Resources

77. Pollution is the introduction of contaminants into an environment that causes instability, disorder, harm or discomfort to the physical systems or living organisms. Pollution can take the form of chemical substances, or energy, such as noise, heat, or light energy. _____, the elements of pollution, can be foreign substances or energies, or naturally occurring; when naturally occurring, they are considered contaminants when they exceed natural levels.
   a. 1703 Genroku earthquake
   b. 1700 Cascadia earthquake
   c. 1509 Istanbul earthquake
   d. Pollutants

78. _____, is the increase in concentration of a substance, such as the pesticide DDT, that occurs in a food chain as a consequence of:

   - Food chain energetics
   - Low (or nonexistent) rate of excretion/degradation of the substance.

Although sometimes used interchangeably with 'bioaccumulation,' an important distinction is drawn between the two, and with bioconcentration.

   - Bioaccumulation occurs within a trophic level, and is the increase in concentration of a substance in an individuals' tissues due to uptake from food and sediments in an aquatic milieu.
   - Bioconcentration is defined as occurring when uptake from the water is greater than excretion (Landrum and Fisher, 1999)

Thus bioconcentration and bioaccumulation occur within an organism, and _____ occurs across trophic (food chain) levels.

Lipid soluble (lipophilic) substances cannot be excreted in urine, a water-based medium, and so accumulate in fatty tissues of an organism if the organism lacks enzymes to degrade them. When eaten by another organism, fats are absorbed in the gut, carrying the substance, which then accumulates in the fats of the predator. Since at each level of the food chain there is a lot of energy loss, a predator must consume many prey, including all of their lipophilic substances.

   a. 1509 Istanbul earthquake
   b. 1700 Cascadia earthquake
   c. 1703 Genroku earthquake
   d. Biomagnification

79. _____ is either of two distinct practices. One involves creating new land from sea or riverbeds, the other refers to restoring an area to a more natural state.
   a. 1703 Genroku earthquake
   b. 1700 Cascadia earthquake
   c. 1509 Istanbul earthquake
   d. Land reclamation

80. _____ refers to a characteristic of living organisms. It always refers to the interaction of organisms with other organisms and to their collective co-existence, irrespective of whether they are aware of it or not, and irrespective of whether the interaction is voluntary or involuntary.

In the absence of agreement about its meaning, the term '_____' is used in many different senses, referring among other things to:

- attitudes, orientations or behaviours which take the interests, intentions or needs of other people into account;
- common characteristics of people or descriptions of collectivities;
- relations between people generally, or particular associations among people;
- interactions between people;
- membership of a group of people or inclusion or belonging to a community of people;
- co-operation or co-operative characteristics between people;
- relations of dependence;
- the public sector or the need for governance for the good of all, contrasted with the private sector;
- in existentialist and postmodernist thought, relationships between the Self and the Other;
- interactive systems in communities of people, animal or insect populations, or any living organisms.

In one broad meaning, '_____' refers only to society as 'a system of common life', but in another sense it contrasts specifically with 'individual' and individualist theories of society. This is reflected for instance in the different perspectives of liberalism and socialism on society and public affairs.

   a. 1509 Istanbul earthquake
   c. 1703 Genroku earthquake
   b. Social
   d. 1700 Cascadia earthquake

81. In business and government policy, _____ refers to how the organization's actions affect the surrounding community.
   a. 1509 Istanbul earthquake
   c. 1700 Cascadia earthquake
   b. 1703 Genroku earthquake
   d. Social impact

82. _____ is the degradation of land in arid, semi arid and dry sub-humid areas resulting from various climatic variations, but primarily human activities. Current _____ is taking place much faster worldwide than historically and usually arises from the demands of increased populations that settle on the land in order to grow crops and graze animals.
   a. 1703 Genroku earthquake
   c. 1509 Istanbul earthquake
   b. 1700 Cascadia earthquake
   d. Desertification

83. A _____ or medical condition is an abnormal condition of an organism that impairs bodily functions and can be deadly. It is also defined as a way of the body harming itself in an abnormal way, associated with specific symptoms and signs.

In human beings,'_____' is often used more broadly to refer to any condition that causes extreme pain, dysfunction, distress, social problems, and/or death to the person afflicted, or similar problems for those in contact with the person.

   a. Black lung disease
   c. 1700 Cascadia earthquake
   b. Disease
   d. 1509 Istanbul earthquake

Chapter 13. Mineral Resources

84. _____ is technology based on biology, especially when used in agriculture, food science, and medicine.
   a. 1509 Istanbul earthquake
   b. 1703 Genroku earthquake
   c. 1700 Cascadia earthquake
   d. Biotechnology

85. A _____ describes one of a number of pieces of legislation relating to the reduction of smog and air pollution in general. The use of governments to enforce clean air standards has contributed to an improvement in human health and longer life spans.
   a. 1700 Cascadia earthquake
   b. 1703 Genroku earthquake
   c. 1509 Istanbul earthquake
   d. Clean Air Act

86. The _____ are a large group of unicellular microorganisms. Typically a few micrometres in length, _____ have a wide range of shapes, ranging from spheres to rods and spirals. _____ are ubiquitous in every habitat on Earth, growing in soil, acidic hot springs, radioactive waste, water, and deep in the Earth's crust, as well as in organic matter and the live bodies of plants and animals.
   a. Cambodia
   b. Bacteria
   c. Hurricane Iniki
   d. Metabolism

87. _____ is the extraction of specific metals from their ores through the use of bacteria.
   a. 1703 Genroku earthquake
   b. 1700 Cascadia earthquake
   c. 1509 Istanbul earthquake
   d. Bioleaching

88. The _____ is a deep underground gold mine located near Lead, South Dakota. Until it closed in 2002 it was the largest, oldest, and deepest mine in the Western Hemisphere.
   a. 1509 Istanbul earthquake
   b. 1700 Cascadia earthquake
   c. 1703 Genroku earthquake
   d. Homestake Mine

89. _____ is the reprocessing of materials into new products. It prevents useful material resources being wasted, reduces the consumption of raw materials and reduces energy usage, and hence greenhouse gas emissions, compared to virgin production.
   a. 1700 Cascadia earthquake
   b. 1703 Genroku earthquake
   c. 1509 Istanbul earthquake
   d. Recycling

90. For most of the 20th century, the _____ was the primary United States Government agency conducting scientific research and disseminating information on the extraction, processing, use, and conservation of mineral resources.
   a. Andrija Mohorovičić
   b. Amblypoda
   c. U.S. Bureau of Mines
   d. Ambulocetus

91. In physical geography, a _____ is an environment "at the interface between truly terrestrial ecosystems and aquatic systems making them inherently different from each other yet highly dependent on both". In essence, they are ecotones.
   a. 1703 Genroku earthquake
   b. 1700 Cascadia earthquake
   c. 1509 Istanbul earthquake
   d. Wetland

92. An _____ organism is an organism that has an oxygen based metabolism

a. AL 129-1
b. AASHTO Soil Classification System
c. AL 333
d. Aerobic

93. _____ is any water that has been adversely affected in quality by anthropogenic influence.
a. 1700 Cascadia earthquake
b. 1703 Genroku earthquake
c. 1509 Istanbul earthquake
d. Wastewater

94. _____ is a chemical element with the symbol Fe and atomic number 26. _____ is a lustrous, silvery soft metal. _____ and nickel are notable for being the final elements produced by stellar nucleosynthesis, and thus are the heaviest elements which do not require a supernova or similarly cataclysmic event for formation.
a. AASHTO Soil Classification System
b. Iron
c. AL 333
d. AL 129-1

95. _____ is a chemical element in the periodic table that has the symbol Pb and atomic number 82. A soft, heavy, toxic and malleable poor metal, _____ is bluish white when freshly cut but tarnishes to dull gray when exposed to air. _____ is used in building construction, _____-acid batteries, bullets and shot, and is part of solder, pewter, and fusible alloys.
a. 1700 Cascadia earthquake
b. 1703 Genroku earthquake
c. 1509 Istanbul earthquake
d. Lead

Chapter 14. Energy and Resources

1. _____ is an umbrella term that refers to any source of usable energy intended to replace fuel sources without the undesired consequences of the replaced fuels. Typically, official uses of the term, such as qualification for governmental incentives, exclude fossil fuels and nuclear energy whose undesired consequences are high carbon dioxide emissions, the major contributing factor of global warming according to the Intergovernmental Panel on Climate Change, and difficulties of radioactive waste disposal. Over the years, the nature of what was regarded _____ sources has changed considerably, and today because of the variety of energy choices and differing goals of their advocates, defining some energy types as 'alternative' is highly controversial.
   a. AL 333
   b. Alternative energy
   c. AASHTO Soil Classification System
   d. AL 129-1

2. _____ is a fossil fuel formed in swamp ecosystems where plant remains were saved by water and mud from oxidization and biodegradation. It is a sedimentary rock, but the harder forms, such as anthracite _____, can be regarded as metamorphic rocks because of later exposure to elevated temperature and pressure. It is composed primarily of carbon along with assorted other elements, including sulfur.
   a. 1509 Istanbul earthquake
   b. Coal
   c. 1703 Genroku earthquake
   d. 1700 Cascadia earthquake

3. In physics, _____ is a scalar physical quantity that describes the amount of work that can be performed by a force. _____ is an attribute of objects and systems that is subject to a conservation law. Several different forms of _____ exist to explain all known natural phenomena.
   a. AL 129-1
   b. Energy
   c. AASHTO Soil Classification System
   d. AL 333

4. Consumption of a _____ requires resources and contributes to air and water pollution. In the industrialized world the development of a _____ has become essential for agriculture, transportation, waste collection, information technology, communications that have become prerequisites of a developed society.
   a. AASHTO Soil Classification System
   b. Energy resource
   c. AL 333
   d. AL 129-1

5. _____s are the mineralized or otherwise preserved remains or traces of animals, plants, and other organisms. The totality of _____s, both discovered and undiscovered, and their placement in fossiliferous rock formations and sedimentary layers is known as the _____ record.
   a. Fossil
   b. 1703 Genroku earthquake
   c. 1509 Istanbul earthquake
   d. 1700 Cascadia earthquake

6. _____ are hydrocarbons, primarily coal and petroleum, formed from the fossilized remains of dead plants and animals by exposure to heat and pressure in the Earth's crust over hundreds of millions of years. The burning of _____ by humans is the largest source of emissions of carbon dioxide, which is one of the greenhouse gases that enhances radiative forcing and contributes to global warming.
   a. Fossil fuels
   b. 1703 Genroku earthquake
   c. 1509 Istanbul earthquake
   d. 1700 Cascadia earthquake

7. In organic chemistry, a _____ is an organic compound consisting entirely of hydrogen and carbon. With relation to chemical terminology, aromatic _____s or arenes, alkanes, alkenes and alkyne-based compounds composed entirely of carbon or hydrogen are referred to as "Pure" _____s, whereas other _____s with bonded compounds or impurities of sulphur or nitrogen, are referred to as "impure", and remain somewhat erroneously referred to as _____s.

Chapter 14. Energy and Resources

a. 1509 Istanbul earthquake
c. 1703 Genroku earthquake
b. 1700 Cascadia earthquake
d. Hydrocarbon

8. _____ is Solar Radiation emitted from our sun. It has been used in many traditional technologies for centuries, and has come into widespread use where other power supplies are absent, such as in remote locations and in space.
a. 1509 Istanbul earthquake
c. 1700 Cascadia earthquake
b. 1703 Genroku earthquake
d. Solar power

9. _____ describes market relations between prospective sellers and buyers of a good. The model predicts that in a competitive market, price will function to equalize the quantity demanded by consumers and the quantity supplied by producers, resulting in an economic equilibrium of price and quantity.
a. 1509 Istanbul earthquake
c. Demand and supply
b. 1700 Cascadia earthquake
d. 1703 Genroku earthquake

10. An _____ is traditionally considered any chemical compound that, when dissolved in water, gives a solution with a hydrogen ion activity greater than in pure water, i.e. a pH less than 7.0. That approximates the modern definition of Johannes Nicolaus Brønsted and Martin Lowry, who independently defined an _____ as a compound which donates a hydrogen ion to another compound. Common examples include acetic _____ and sulfuric _____. Acid/base systems are different from redox reactions in that there is no change in oxidation state.
a. AASHTO Soil Classification System
c. AL 333
b. Acid
d. AL 129-1

11. The term _____ is commonly used to mean the deposition of acidic components in rain, snow, dew, or dry particles. _____ occurs when sulfur dioxide and nitrogen oxides are emitted into the atmosphere, undergo chemical transformations and are absorbed by water droplets in clouds. The droplets then fall to earth as rain, snow, mist, dry dust, hail, or sleet. This increases the acidity of the soil, and affects the chemical balance of lakes and streams.
a. AL 129-1
c. AASHTO Soil Classification System
b. AL 333
d. Acid precipitation

12. An _____ is any great bottleneck or price rise in the supply of energy resources to an economy. It usually refers to the shortage of oil and additionally to electricity or other natural resources.
a. AL 333
c. AL 129-1
b. AASHTO Soil Classification System
d. Energy crisis

13. An _____ that is used in atomic physics, particle physics and high energy physics is the electronvolt.
a. AL 129-1
c. AASHTO Soil Classification System
b. AL 333
d. Energy unit

14. _____ are the SI unit of energy.
a. 1509 Istanbul earthquake
c. 1703 Genroku earthquake
b. 1700 Cascadia earthquake
d. Joules

15. A _____ is the amount of force required to accelerate a body with a mass of one kilogram at a rate of one meter per second squared.

Chapter 14. Energy and Resources

a. 1703 Genroku earthquake
b. 1509 Istanbul earthquake
c. 1700 Cascadia earthquake
d. Newton

16. _____ is an accumulation of partially decayed vegetation matter. It forms in wetlands.
a. 1700 Cascadia earthquake
b. 1509 Istanbul earthquake
c. 1703 Genroku earthquake
d. Peat

17. _____ is the science and study of the solid matter that constitute the Earth. Encompassing such things as rocks, soil, and gemstones, _____ studies the composition, structure, physical properties, history, and the processes that shape Earth's components.
a. Glacial motion
b. 1509 Istanbul earthquake
c. Glaciology
d. Geology

18. _____ is a hard, compact variety of mineral coal that has a high luster. It has the highest carbon count and contains the fewest impurities of all coals, despite its lower calorific content.
a. AL 333
b. AL 129-1
c. AASHTO Soil Classification System
d. Anthracite

19. _____ is a relatively hard coal containing a tar-like substance called bitumen. It is of higher quality than lignite coal but of poorer quality than anthracite coal.
a. 1700 Cascadia earthquake
b. 1509 Istanbul earthquake
c. 1703 Genroku earthquake
d. Bituminous coal

20. _____ is the lowest rank of coal and used almost exclusively as fuel for steam-electric power generation.
a. Lignite
b. 1703 Genroku earthquake
c. 1700 Cascadia earthquake
d. 1509 Istanbul earthquake

21. _____ is a coal whose properties range from those of lignite to those of bituminous coal and are used primarily as fuel for steam-electric power generation.
a. 1700 Cascadia earthquake
b. 1703 Genroku earthquake
c. Subbituminous coal
d. 1509 Istanbul earthquake

22. _____ is the chemical element in the periodic table that has the symbol S and atomic number 16. It is an abundant, tasteless, odorless, multivalent non-metal. _____, in its native form, is a yellow crystaline solid. In nature, it can be found as the pure element or as sulfide and sulfate minerals.
a. Vinyl
b. Thulium
c. Zinc
d. Sulfur

23. _____ is commonly practiced where a coal seam outcrops a hilly terrain. It removes the overburden above the coal seam and then creates a bench arounf the hill.
a. 1509 Istanbul earthquake
b. 1700 Cascadia earthquake
c. Contour strip mining
d. 1703 Genroku earthquake

24. _____ is the extraction of valuable minerals or other geological materials from the earth, usually from an ore body, vein, or seam. Any material that cannot be grown from agricultural processes, or created artificially in a laboratory or factory, is usually extracted from the earth by this method.

a. Mining
b. 1509 Istanbul earthquake
c. 1703 Genroku earthquake
d. 1700 Cascadia earthquake

25. _____ refers to a method of extracting rock or minerals from the earth by their removal from an open pit or borrow. The term is used to differentiate this form of mining from extractive methods that require tunneling into the earth.
   a. Open-pit mining
   b. AL 333
   c. AASHTO Soil Classification System
   d. AL 129-1

26. _____ is the practice of mining a seam of mineral by first removing a long strip of overlying soil and rock.
   a. 1703 Genroku earthquake
   b. 1509 Istanbul earthquake
   c. 1700 Cascadia earthquake
   d. Strip mining

27. _____ is either of two distinct practices. One involves creating new land from sea or riverbeds, the other refers to restoring an area to a more natural state.
   a. 1700 Cascadia earthquake
   b. Land reclamation
   c. 1509 Istanbul earthquake
   d. 1703 Genroku earthquake

28. _____ is a term used in geology to denote the pressure imposed on a stratigraphic layer by the weight of overlying layers of material.
   a. 1703 Genroku earthquake
   b. Lithostatic pressure
   c. 1509 Istanbul earthquake
   d. 1700 Cascadia earthquake

29. _____ is a strong mineral acid. It is soluble in water at all concentrations. _____ has many applications, and is one of the top products of the chemical industry. Principal uses include ore processing, fertilizer manufacturing, oil refining, wastewater processing, and chemical synthesis.
   a. 1700 Cascadia earthquake
   b. 1703 Genroku earthquake
   c. 1509 Istanbul earthquake
   d. Sulfuric acid

30. _____ is a chemical element in the periodic table that has the symbol C and atomic number 6. An abundant nonmetallic, tetravalent element, _____ has several allotropic forms.
   a. Carbon
   b. 1509 Istanbul earthquake
   c. 1700 Cascadia earthquake
   d. 1703 Genroku earthquake

31. _____ is a chemical compound, normally in a gaseous state, and is composed of one carbon and two oxygen atoms. It is often referred to by its formula CO2. It is present in the Earth's atmosphere at a concentration of approximately .000383 by volume and is an important greenhouse gas due to its ability to absorb many infrared wavelengths of sunlight, and due to the length of time it stays in the atmosphere.
   a. 1703 Genroku earthquake
   b. 1700 Cascadia earthquake
   c. 1509 Istanbul earthquake
   d. Carbon dioxide

32. An _____ is an assessment of the likely influence a project may have on the environment. The purpose of the assessment is to ensure that decision-makers consider _____s before deciding whether to proceed with new projects.
   a. AL 333
   b. AL 129-1
   c. AASHTO Soil Classification System
   d. Environmental impact

Chapter 14. Energy and Resources

33. _____ is the increase in the average temperature of the Earth's near-surface air and oceans in recent decades and its projected continuation. An increase in global temperatures can in turn cause other changes, including sea level rise, and changes in the amount and pattern of precipitation resulting in floods and drought. There may also be changes in the frequency and intensity of extreme weather events.
   - a. 1700 Cascadia earthquake
   - b. 1703 Genroku earthquake
   - c. Global warming
   - d. 1509 Istanbul earthquake

34. A _____ is a building where plants are cultivated.
   - a. Greenhouse
   - b. 1700 Cascadia earthquake
   - c. 1703 Genroku earthquake
   - d. 1509 Istanbul earthquake

35. _____ are gases in an atmosphere that absorb and emit radiation within the thermal infrared range. This process is the fundamental cause of the greenhouse effect.

In our solar system, the atmospheres of Venus, Mars and Titan also contain gases that cause greenhouse effects.

   - a. Greenhouse gases
   - b. Glacier
   - c. General circulation model
   - d. Global warming controversy

36. _____ is any of a number of similar colors evoked by light consisting predominantly of the longest wavelengths of light discernible by the human eye, in the wavelength range of roughly 625-740 nm. Longer wavelengths than this are called infrared, or below _____ and cannot be seen by the naked human eye. _____ is used as one of the additive primary colors of light, complementary to cyan, in RGB color systems.
   - a. 1509 Istanbul earthquake
   - b. 1700 Cascadia earthquake
   - c. Red
   - d. 1703 Genroku earthquake

37. _____ is a layer of gases surrounding the planet Earth and retained by the Earth's gravity, protecting life on Earth by absorbing ultraviolet solar radiation and reducing temperature extremes between day and night.
   - a. AASHTO Soil Classification System
   - b. AL 129-1
   - c. AL 333
   - d. Earths atmosphere

38. _____ is vibration transmitted through a solid, liquid composed of frequencies within the range of hearing and of a level sufficiently strong to be heard. Human ear

For humans, hearing is limited to frequencies between about 20 Hz and 20,000 Hz (20 kHz), with the upper limit generally decreasing with age. Other species have a different range of hearing.

   - a. 1509 Istanbul earthquake
   - b. 1703 Genroku earthquake
   - c. 1700 Cascadia earthquake
   - d. Sound

39. _____ is the third largest island in the world and is located at the centre of Maritime Southeast Asia.
   - a. 1703 Genroku earthquake
   - b. 1509 Istanbul earthquake
   - c. 1700 Cascadia earthquake
   - d. Borneo

Chapter 14. Energy and Resources

40. _____ is a chemical compound with the molecular formula CH_4. It is the simplest alkane, and the principal component of natural gas. Burning one molecule of _____ in the presence of oxygen releases one molecule. _____'s relative abundance and clean burning process makes it a very attractive fuel.
   a. Methane
   b. 1509 Istanbul earthquake
   c. 1703 Genroku earthquake
   d. 1700 Cascadia earthquake

41. _____ is a gaseous fossil fuel consisting primarily of methane but including significant quantities of ethane, butane, propane, carbon dioxide, nitrogen, helium and hydrogen sulfide.
   a. 1700 Cascadia earthquake
   b. 1703 Genroku earthquake
   c. 1509 Istanbul earthquake
   d. Natural gas

42. _____ is a naturally occurring liquid found in formations in the Earth consisting of a complex mixture of hydrocarbons of various lengths.
   a. Petroleum
   b. 1509 Istanbul earthquake
   c. 1703 Genroku earthquake
   d. 1700 Cascadia earthquake

43. In geology, _____ is a naturally occurring aggregate of minerals and/or mineraloids. The Earth's outer solid layer, the lithosphere, is made of _____. In general _____s are of three types, namely, igneous, sedimentary, and metamorphic.

   a. 1703 Genroku earthquake
   b. 1700 Cascadia earthquake
   c. 1509 Istanbul earthquake
   d. Rock

44. In petroleum geology _____ refers to rocks from which hydrocarbons have been generated or are capable of being generated. They form one of the necessary elements of a working hydrocarbon system. They are organic rich sediments that may have been deposited in a variety of environments including deepwater marine, lacustrine and deltaic.
   a. Source rock
   b. 1509 Istanbul earthquake
   c. 1703 Genroku earthquake
   d. 1700 Cascadia earthquake

45. Most often, a _____ refers to an artificial lake, used to store water for various uses. _____s are created first by building a sturdy dam, usually out of cement, earth, rock, or a mixture. Once the dam is completed, a stream is allowed to flow behind it and eventually fill it to capacity.
   a. 1509 Istanbul earthquake
   b. 1700 Cascadia earthquake
   c. 1703 Genroku earthquake
   d. Reservoir

46. A _____ is a naturally occurring substance formed through geological processes that has a characteristic chemical composition, a highly ordered atomic structure and specific physical properties. A rock, by comparison, is an aggregate of _____s and need not have a specific chemical composition. _____s range in composition from pure elements and simple salts to very complex silicates with thousands of known forms.
   a. 1703 Genroku earthquake
   b. 1700 Cascadia earthquake
   c. Mineral
   d. 1509 Istanbul earthquake

47. _____ is the average and variations of weather over long periods of time. _____ zones can be defined using parameters such as temperature and rainfall.

Chapter 14. Energy and Resources

a. 1509 Istanbul earthquake
b. Climate
c. 1703 Genroku earthquake
d. 1700 Cascadia earthquake

48. In geography, a _____ is a type of wetland which is subject to almost continuous inundation. Typically it features grasses, rushes, reeds, typhas, sedges, and other herbaceous plants in a context of shallow water. It is different from a swamp, which has a greater proportion of open water surface, and is generally deeper than a it.
   a. 1700 Cascadia earthquake
   b. 1703 Genroku earthquake
   c. 1509 Istanbul earthquake
   d. Marsh

49. _____ typically refers to a gas produced by the anaerobic digestion or fermentation of organic matter including manure, sewage sludge, municipal solid waste, biodegradable waste or any other biodegradable feedstock, under anaerobic conditions. _____ is comprised primarily of methane and carbon dioxide.
   a. Biogas
   b. 1703 Genroku earthquake
   c. 1509 Istanbul earthquake
   d. 1700 Cascadia earthquake

50. _____ is a solid form of water that contains a large amount of methane within its crystal structure. Originally thought to occur only in the outer regions of the solar system where temperatures are low and water ice is common, extremely large deposits of it have been found under sediments on the ocean floors of Earth.
   a. 1509 Istanbul earthquake
   b. 1703 Genroku earthquake
   c. 1700 Cascadia earthquake
   d. Methane hydrate

51. _____ is a term used in inorganic chemistry and organic chemistry to indicate that a substance contains water. If the water is heavy water, where the hydrogen consists of the isotope deuterium, then the term deuterate may be used in place of _____.
   a. 1700 Cascadia earthquake
   b. 1509 Istanbul earthquake
   c. 1703 Genroku earthquake
   d. Hydrate

52. The _____ is the region around the Earth's North Pole, opposite the Antarctic region around the South Pole. In the northern hemisphere, the _____ includes the _____ Ocean and parts of Canada, Greenland, Russia, the United States, Iceland, Norway, Sweden and Finland. The word _____ comes from the Greek word arktos, which means bear. This is due to the location of the constellation Ursa Major, the "Great Bear", above the _____ region.
   a. AL 129-1
   b. AASHTO Soil Classification System
   c. AL 333
   d. Arctic

53. The _____ in northeastern Alaska, in the North Slope region. It was originally protected in 1960 by order of Fred A. Seaton, the Secretary of the Interior under U.S. President Dwight D. Eisenhower. As part of Alaska National Interest Lands Conservation Act, the refuge was expanded by the United States Congress in 1980 through the lobbying efforts of Olaus and Margaret Murie, with The Wilderness Society.
   a. AL 333
   b. AL 129-1
   c. AASHTO Soil Classification System
   d. Arctic National Wildlife Refuge

54. _____ is a designation for certain protected areas of the United States managed by the United States Fish and Wildlife Service. The system consists of over 500 refuges across the nation.
   a. National Wildlife Refuge
   b. Ambulocetus
   c. Amblypoda
   d. Andrija Mohorovičić

Chapter 14. Energy and Resources

55. _____ transport is a transportation of goods through a pipe. Most commonly, liquid and gases are sent, but pneumatic tubes that transport solid capsules using compressed air have also been used..
   a. 1509 Istanbul earthquake
   b. 1703 Genroku earthquake
   c. Pipeline
   d. 1700 Cascadia earthquake

56. The _____ is a major U.S. oil pipeline connecting oil fields in northern Alaska to a sea port where the oil can be shipped to the Lower 48 states for refining.
   a. 1703 Genroku earthquake
   b. 1509 Istanbul earthquake
   c. 1700 Cascadia earthquake
   d. Trans-Alaska Pipeline

57. _____ includes all non-domesticated plants, animals, and other organisms.
   a. 1700 Cascadia earthquake
   b. 1509 Istanbul earthquake
   c. 1703 Genroku earthquake
   d. Wildlife

58. _____ is a chemical, physical, or biological agent that modifies the natural characteristics of the atmosphere. The atmosphere is a complex, dynamic natural gaseous system that is essential to support life on planet Earth. Stratospheric ozone depletion due to _____ has long been recognized as a threat to human health as well as to the Earth's ecosystems. Worldwide _____ is responsible for large numbers of deaths and cases of respiratory disease.
   a. Air pollution
   b. AL 333
   c. AL 129-1
   d. AASHTO Soil Classification System

59. The _____ is a tributary of the Colorado River, 730 mi long, in the western United States. The _____ Basin covers parts of Wyoming, Utah, and Colorado. The river begins in the Wind River Mountains of Wyoming, and flows through Utah for much of its course, draining the northeastern portion of the state while looping for 40 mi into western Colorado.
   a. Niigata
   b. Green River
   c. High Plains
   d. Lake Louise

60. The _____ is an Eocene geologic formation that records the sedimentation in a series of intermontane lakes. The sedimentary layers were formed in a large area of interconnecting lakes.
   a. 1703 Genroku earthquake
   b. 1700 Cascadia earthquake
   c. 1509 Istanbul earthquake
   d. Green River Formation

61. _____ is a general term applied to a fine-grained sedimentary rock containing significant traces of kerogen that have not been buried for sufficient time to produce conventional fossil fuels. When heated to a sufficiently high temperature a vapor is driven off which can be distilled to yield a petroleum.
   a. Oil shale
   b. AASHTO Soil Classification System
   c. AL 333
   d. AL 129-1

62. _____ is a combination of clay, sand, water, and bitumen. On average bitumen contains 83.2% carbon, 10.4% hydrogen, 4.8% sulphur, 0.94% oxygen, and 0.36% nitrogen.
   a. 1509 Istanbul earthquake
   b. 1703 Genroku earthquake
   c. 1700 Cascadia earthquake
   d. Tar sand

63. _____ is the introduction of substances or energy into the environment, resulting in deleterious effects of such a nature as to endanger human health, harm living resources and ecosystems, and impair or interfere with amenities and other legitimate uses of the environment.

Chapter 14. Energy and Resources

a. 1509 Istanbul earthquake
c. 1703 Genroku earthquake
b. Pollution
d. 1700 Cascadia earthquake

64. _____ is a fine-grained sedimentary rock whose original constituents were clays or muds. It is characterized by thin laminae breaking with an irregular curving fracture, often splintery and usually parallel to the often-indistinguishable bedding plane.
a. 1509 Istanbul earthquake
c. 1703 Genroku earthquake
b. 1700 Cascadia earthquake
d. Shale

65. _____ is one of Canada's prairie provinces. It became a province on September 1, 1905.

_____ is located in western Canada, bounded by the provinces of British Columbia to the west and Saskatchewan to the east, the Northwest Territories to the north, and the U.S. state of Montana to the south.

a. AL 129-1
c. Alberta
b. AASHTO Soil Classification System
d. AL 333

66. The _____ are a large deposit of oil-rich bitumen located in northern Alberta, Canada. These oil sands consist of a mixture of crude bitumen, silica sand, clay minerals, and water.
a. AASHTO Soil Classification System
c. AL 129-1
b. AL 333
d. Athabasca Tar Sands

67. _____ is a country occupying most of northern North America, extending from the Atlantic Ocean in the east to the Pacific Ocean in the west and northward into the Arctic Ocean. It is the world's second largest country by total area, and shares land borders with the United States to the south and northwest.

The land occupied by _____ was inhabited for millennia by various aboriginal peoples.

a. Kingdom of Cambodia
c. Hurricane Mitch
b. Hippocrates
d. Canada

68. _____ is the geological process whereby material is added to a landform. This is the process by which wind and water create a sediment deposit, through the laying down of granular material that has been eroded and transported from another geographical location.
a. 1703 Genroku earthquake
c. 1700 Cascadia earthquake
b. 1509 Istanbul earthquake
d. Deposition

69. _____ is a general term for the plant life of a region; it refers to the ground cover provided by plants, and is, by far, the most abundant biotic element of the biosphere. Primeval redwood forests, coastal mangrove stands, sphagnum bogs, desert soil crusts, roadside weed patches, wheat fields, cultivated gardens and lawns; are all encompassed by the term _____.

a. 1703 Genroku earthquake
c. 1700 Cascadia earthquake
b. 1509 Istanbul earthquake
d. Vegetation

70. A _____ is a bipedal primate belonging to the mammalian species Homo sapiens in the family Hominidae. Compared to other living organisms on Earth, a _____ has a highly developed brain capable of abstract reasoning, language, and introspection.
   a. Human
   b. 1703 Genroku earthquake
   c. 1509 Istanbul earthquake
   d. 1700 Cascadia earthquake

71. A _____ is a body of water, not part of the ocean, that is larger and deeper than a pond.
   a. Lake
   b. 1700 Cascadia earthquake
   c. 1703 Genroku earthquake
   d. 1509 Istanbul earthquake

72. _____ is a chemical compound with the formula SO2. This important gas is the main product from the combustion of sulfur compounds and is of significant environmental concern. Sulphur dioxide is produced by volcanoes and in various industrial processes.
   a. Sulfur dioxide
   b. 1509 Istanbul earthquake
   c. 1700 Cascadia earthquake
   d. 1703 Genroku earthquake

73. An _____ is a natural unit consisting of all plants, animals and micro organisms in an area functioning together with all the non living physical factors of the environment.
   a. Ecosystem
   b. AL 129-1
   c. AL 333
   d. AASHTO Soil Classification System

74. A _____ is a sequence of reactions where a reactive product or by-product causes additional reactions to take place.
   a. 1509 Istanbul earthquake
   b. 1700 Cascadia earthquake
   c. 1703 Genroku earthquake
   d. Chain reaction

75. _____ is a sample of uranium in which the percent composition of uranium-235 has been increased through the process of isotope separation
   a. Enriched uranium
   b. AL 129-1
   c. AL 333
   d. AASHTO Soil Classification System

76. _____ is the splitting of the nucleus of an atom into parts, lighter nuclei, often producing photons, in the form of gamma rays, free neutrons and other subatomic particles as by-products. It produces energy for nuclear power and to drive the explosion of nuclear weapons.
   a. 1509 Istanbul earthquake
   b. 1700 Cascadia earthquake
   c. 1703 Genroku earthquake
   d. Nuclear fission

77. _____ are any of the several different forms of an element each having different atomic mass. _____ of an element have nuclei with the same number of protons but different numbers of neutrons.
   a. AASHTO Soil Classification System
   b. AL 333
   c. AL 129-1
   d. Isotopes

78. In physics, the _____ is a subatomic particle with no net electric charge.
   a. 1700 Cascadia earthquake
   b. 1703 Genroku earthquake
   c. Neutron
   d. 1509 Istanbul earthquake

Chapter 14. Energy and Resources

79. _____ is a chemical element which has the symbol N and atomic number 7 in the periodic table. Elemental _____ is a colorless, odorless, tasteless and mostly inert diatomic gas at standard conditions, constituting 78.08% percent of Earth's atmosphere.
   a. 1700 Cascadia earthquake
   b. Nitrogen
   c. 1509 Istanbul earthquake
   d. 1703 Genroku earthquake

80. _____ is energy released from the atomic nucleus.
   a. Nuclear energy
   b. 1509 Istanbul earthquake
   c. 1703 Genroku earthquake
   d. 1700 Cascadia earthquake

81. _____ is a very coarse-grained igneous rock that has a grain size of 20 mm or more; such rocks are referred to as pegmatitic.
   a. 1703 Genroku earthquake
   b. 1509 Istanbul earthquake
   c. 1700 Cascadia earthquake
   d. Pegmatite

82. _____ is a white/black metallic chemical element in the actinide series of the periodic table that has the symbol U and atomic number 92. When refined, _____ is a silvery white, weakly radioactive metal, which is slightly softer than steel. It is malleable, ductile, and slightly paramagnetic.
   a. AL 129-1
   b. AL 333
   c. AASHTO Soil Classification System
   d. Uranium

83. _____ are a class of astronomical objects. The term is generally used to indicate a diverse group of small celestial bodies that drift in the solar system in orbit around the Sun.
   a. AL 129-1
   b. AASHTO Soil Classification System
   c. AL 333
   d. Asteroids

84. An _____ is a layer of gases that may surround a material body of sufficient mass, by the gravity of the body, and are retained for a longer duration if gravity is high and the _____'s temperature is low. Some planets consist mainly of various gases, and therefore have very deep _____s

The term stellar _____ describes the outer region of a star, and typically includes the portion starting from the opaque photosphere outwards.

   a. AL 129-1
   b. AL 333
   c. AASHTO Soil Classification System
   d. Atmosphere

85. A _____ is a person who practices the vocation of mating carefully selected specimens of the same breed to reproduce specific, consistently replicable qualities and characteristics.
   a. 1700 Cascadia earthquake
   b. 1703 Genroku earthquake
   c. 1509 Istanbul earthquake
   d. Breeder

86. _____ is the capture of the energy of moving water for some useful purpose.
   a. Water power
   b. 1509 Istanbul earthquake
   c. 1703 Genroku earthquake
   d. 1700 Cascadia earthquake

Chapter 14. Energy and Resources

87. _____ consist of two protons and two neutrons bound together into a particle identical to a helium nucleus. _____ are emitted by radioactive nuclei such as uranium or radium in a process known as alpha decay.
    a. AL 333
    b. Alpha particles
    c. AASHTO Soil Classification System
    d. AL 129-1

88. The _____ is the mass of an atom at rest, most often expressed in unified _____ units.[
    a. AL 129-1
    b. AL 333
    c. Atomic mass
    d. AASHTO Soil Classification System

89. In chemistry and physics, the _____ is the number of protons found in the nucleus of an atom. It is traditionally represented by the symbol Z.
    a. AASHTO Soil Classification System
    b. AL 129-1
    c. AL 333
    d. Atomic number

90. _____ are high-energy, high-speed electrons or positrons emitted by certain types of radioactive nuclei such as potassium-40.
    a. 1509 Istanbul earthquake
    b. 1700 Cascadia earthquake
    c. Beta particles
    d. 1703 Genroku earthquake

91. _____ are forms of electromagnetic radiation or light emissions of a specific frequency produced from sub-atomic particle interaction, such as electron-positron annihilation and radioactive decay; most are generated from nuclear reactions occurring within the interstellar medium of space.
    a. 1700 Cascadia earthquake
    b. Gamma Rays
    c. 1703 Genroku earthquake
    d. 1509 Istanbul earthquake

92. The _____ of a quantity, subject to exponential decay, is the time required for the quantity to decay to half of its initial value. The concept originated in the study of radioactive decay, but applies to many other fields as well, including phenomena which are described by non-exponential decays.
    a. 1509 Istanbul earthquake
    b. 1700 Cascadia earthquake
    c. Half-life
    d. 1703 Genroku earthquake

93. _____ is the process in which an unstable atomic nucleus loses energy by emitting radiation in the form of particles or electromagnetic waves.
    a. Radioactive decay
    b. 1509 Istanbul earthquake
    c. 1703 Genroku earthquake
    d. 1700 Cascadia earthquake

94. _____ are waste types containing radioactive chemical elements that do not have a practical purpose. It is sometimes the product of a nuclear process, such as nuclear fission. However, other industries not directly connected to the nuclear industry can produce large quantities of _____.
    a. 1700 Cascadia earthquake
    b. 1509 Istanbul earthquake
    c. 1703 Genroku earthquake
    d. Radioactive waste

95. Radionuclides are often referred to by chemists and physicists as radioactive isotopes or _____, and play an important part in the technologies that provide us with food, water and good health. However, they can also constitute real or perceived dangers.

Chapter 14. Energy and Resources

Naturally occurring radionuclides fall into three categories: primordial radionuclides, secondary radionuclides and cosmogenic radionuclides.

- a. Radioisotopes
- b. 1703 Genroku earthquake
- c. 1700 Cascadia earthquake
- d. 1509 Istanbul earthquake

96. _____ is a chemical element in the periodic table that has the symbol Rn and atomic number 86. A radioactive noble gas that is formed by the decay of radium, _____ is one of the heaviest gases and is considered to be a health hazard.
    - a. Radon
    - b. Ytterbium
    - c. Tantalum
    - d. Selenium

97. The general effects of _____ to the human body are due to its radioactivity and consequent risk of radiation-induced cancer.
    - a. 1700 Cascadia earthquake
    - b. 1509 Istanbul earthquake
    - c. 1703 Genroku earthquake
    - d. Radon emissions

98. _____, as used in physics, is energy in the form of waves or moving subatomic particles emitted by an atom or other body as it changes from a higher energy state to a lower energy state. _____ can be classified as ionizing or non-ionizing _____, depending on its effect on atomic matter. The most common use of the word "_____" refers to ionizing _____. Ionizing _____ has enough energy to ionize atoms or molecules while non-ionizing _____ does not. Radioactive material is a physical material that emits ionizing _____.
    - a. Supercritical fluid
    - b. Supersaturation
    - c. Synthetic aperture radar
    - d. Radiation

99. _____ is unwanted or undesired material.
    - a. 1703 Genroku earthquake
    - b. 1700 Cascadia earthquake
    - c. 1509 Istanbul earthquake
    - d. Waste

100. _____ is a characteristic of a process or state that can be maintained at a certain level indefinitely. The term, in its environmental usage, refers to the potential longevity of vital human ecological support systems.
    - a. 1509 Istanbul earthquake
    - b. 1700 Cascadia earthquake
    - c. 1703 Genroku earthquake
    - d. Sustainability

101. A _____ is a deep valley between cliffs often carved from the landscape by a river. Most were formed by a process of long-time erosion from a plateau level. The cliffs form because harder rock strata that are resistant to erosion and weathering remain exposed on the valley walls.
    - a. 1703 Genroku earthquake
    - b. Canyon
    - c. 1509 Istanbul earthquake
    - d. 1700 Cascadia earthquake

102. The _____ is an electricity-generating nuclear power plant in San Luis Obispo County, California.
    - a. 1703 Genroku earthquake
    - b. Diablo Canyon Nuclear Power Plant
    - c. 1509 Istanbul earthquake
    - d. 1700 Cascadia earthquake

Chapter 14. Energy and Resources

103. _____ is any nuclear technology designed to extract usable energy from atomic nuclei via controlled nuclear reactions. The most common method today is through nuclear fission, though other methods include nuclear fusion and radioactive decay.
   a. 1703 Genroku earthquake
   b. 1700 Cascadia earthquake
   c. 1509 Istanbul earthquake
   d. Nuclear Power

104. A _____ is a facility for the generation of electric power. _____ is also used to refer to the engine in ships, aircraft and other large vehicles.
   a. 1703 Genroku earthquake
   b. 1700 Cascadia earthquake
   c. 1509 Istanbul earthquake
   d. Power station

105. _____ are nuclear reactors that consumes fissile and fertile material at the same time as they creates new fissile material.
   a. 1700 Cascadia earthquake
   b. 1703 Genroku earthquake
   c. 1509 Istanbul earthquake
   d. Breeder reactors

106. _____ is a radioactive, metallic, chemical element. It has the symbol Pu and the atomic number 94. It is the element used in most modern nuclear weapons. The most important isotope of _____ is ^{239}Pu, with a half-life of 24,110 years. It can be made from natural uranium and is fissile.
   a. 1509 Istanbul earthquake
   b. 1700 Cascadia earthquake
   c. Plutonium
   d. 1703 Genroku earthquake

107. _____ is a concept that denotes the precise probability of specific eventualities. Technically, the notion of _____ is independent from the notion of value and, as such, eventualities may have both beneficial and adverse consequences. However, in general usage the convention is to focus only on potential negative impact to some characteristic of value that may arise from a future event.
   a. 1703 Genroku earthquake
   b. 1700 Cascadia earthquake
   c. 1509 Istanbul earthquake
   d. Risk

108. _____ is an abandoned city in northern Ukraine, in the Kiev Oblast near the border with Belarus. The city was evacuated in 1986 due to the disaster at the _____ Nuclear Power Plant, which is located 14.5 kilometers north-northwest.
   a. 1509 Istanbul earthquake
   b. Chernobyl
   c. 1700 Cascadia earthquake
   d. 1703 Genroku earthquake

109. The _____ was a major power plant disaster in 1986. The power plant is located near Pripyat, Ukraine. An explosion at the plant was followed by radioactive contamination of the surrounding geographic area.
   a. 1700 Cascadia earthquake
   b. 1703 Genroku earthquake
   c. Chernobyl nuclear accident
   d. 1509 Istanbul earthquake

110. The _____ was the worst accident in American commercial nuclear power generating history, even though it led to no deaths or injuries to plant workers or members of the nearby community.
   a. 1509 Istanbul earthquake
   b. 1703 Genroku earthquake
   c. 1700 Cascadia earthquake
   d. Three Mile Island accident

Chapter 14. Energy and Resources

111. _____ is a class of diseases in which a group of cells display the traits of uncontrolled growth growth and division beyond the normal limits, invasion intrusion on and destruction of adjacent tissues, and sometimes metastasis spread to other locations in the body via lymph or blood. These three malignant properties of _____s differentiate them from benign tumors, which are self-limited, do not invade or metastasize. Most _____s form a tumor but some, like leukemia, do not.
   a. 1509 Istanbul earthquake
   b. 1703 Genroku earthquake
   c. 1700 Cascadia earthquake
   d. Cancer

112. _____ comprises those aspects of human health, including quality of life, that are determined by physical, chemical, biological, social, and psychosocial factors in the natural environment.
   a. AL 129-1
   b. AASHTO Soil Classification System
   c. AL 333
   d. Environmental health

113. The _____ is one of the largest endocrine glands in the body. This gland is found in the neck inferior to (below) the _____ cartilage (also known as the Adam's apple in men) and at approximately the same level as the cricoid cartilage. The _____ controls how quickly the body burns energy, makes proteins, and how sensitive the body should be to other hormones.
   a. 1700 Cascadia earthquake
   b. 1703 Genroku earthquake
   c. 1509 Istanbul earthquake
   d. Thyroid

114. _____ , officially the Federal Republic of _____ , is a country in Central Europe. It is bordered to the north by the North Sea, Denmark, and the Baltic Sea; to the east by Poland and the Czech Republic; to the south by Austria and Switzerland; and to the west by France, Luxembourg, Belgium, and the Netherlands. The territory of _____ covers 357,021 square kilometers and is influenced by a temperate seasonal climate.
   a. Ambulocetus
   b. Andrija Mohorović iÄ‡
   c. Germany
   d. Amblypoda

115. _____ is the collection, transport, processing, recycling or disposal of waste materials, usually ones produced by human activity, in an effort to reduce their effect on human health or local aesthetics or amenity.
   a. Waste management
   b. 1700 Cascadia earthquake
   c. 1703 Genroku earthquake
   d. 1509 Istanbul earthquake

116. _____ are a major group of living things including familiar organisms such as trees, flowers, herbs, bushes, grasses, vines, ferns, and mosses.
   a. Plants
   b. 1703 Genroku earthquake
   c. 1700 Cascadia earthquake
   d. 1509 Istanbul earthquake

117. _____ is the administrative and technical functions necessary for the treatment, disposal, storage, manipulation, and evacuation of radioactive materials in order to protect the environment and people.
   a. 1509 Istanbul earthquake
   b. Radioactive Waste management
   c. 1703 Genroku earthquake
   d. 1700 Cascadia earthquake

Chapter 14. Energy and Resources

118. The United Mexican States, commonly known as _____, is a federal constitutional republic in North America. It is bordered on the north by the United States; on the south and west by the North Pacific Ocean; on the southeast by Guatemala, Belize, and the Caribbean Sea; and on the east by the Gulf of _____. The United Mexican States are a federation comprising thirty-one states and a federal district, the capital _____ City, whose metropolitan area is one of the world's most populous.
   a. Ambulocetus
   b. Amblypoda
   c. Andrija Mohorović ić
   d. Mexico

119. _____ is a multiprogram science and technology national laboratory managed for the United States Department of Energy by UT-Battelle, LLC. It is located in Oak Ridge, Tennessee, near Knoxville.
   a. AL 333
   b. AASHTO Soil Classification System
   c. AL 129-1
   d. Oak Ridge National Laboratory

120. A _____ is a geological feature that is also known as a Rip in the earth causing magma to flow out and forming an undersea volcano, it also has geological features, a continuous elevational crest for some distance. _____ s are usually termed hills or mountains as well, depending on size.
   a. 1703 Genroku earthquake
   b. 1700 Cascadia earthquake
   c. 1509 Istanbul earthquake
   d. Ridge

121. _____ is Waste containing more than 100 nanocuries of alpha-emitting transuranic isotopes per gram of waste with half-lives greater than 20 years, except for high-level radioactive waste.
   a. 1703 Genroku earthquake
   b. 1700 Cascadia earthquake
   c. 1509 Istanbul earthquake
   d. Transuranic waste

122. The _____ is the portion of Earth between the land surface and the phreatic zone or zone of saturation.
   a. Vadose Zone
   b. 1703 Genroku earthquake
   c. 1700 Cascadia earthquake
   d. 1509 Istanbul earthquake

123. _____ and low level are terms used in classifying levels of description and goals in many fields where systems could be described from different perspectives.

A _____ description is one that describes 'top level' goals, overall systemic features, is more abstracted, and is typically more concerned with the system as a whole, and its goals.

A low level description is one that describes individual components, detail rather than overview, rudimentary functions rather than complex overall ones, and is typically more concerned with individual components within the system and how they operate.

   a. 1703 Genroku earthquake
   b. 1509 Istanbul earthquake
   c. High level
   d. 1700 Cascadia earthquake

124. The _____ is the world's first underground repository licensed to safely and permanently dispose of transuranic radioactive waste that is left from the research and production of nuclear weapons.
   a. 1703 Genroku earthquake
   b. Waste isolation pilot plant
   c. 1700 Cascadia earthquake
   d. 1509 Istanbul earthquake

Chapter 14. Energy and Resources

125. In the terminology of political geography and historiography a national _____ is an administrative political subdivision of a country established by the cognizant government authority holding sovereign power for the territory.

_____s are roughly equivalent to a state, province or county, and may exist either with or without a subnational representative assembly and executive head depending upon the countries constitutional structure.

Â· Benin Â· Bolivia Â· Burkina Faso Â· Cameroon Â· Colombia Â· Côte d'Ivoire Â· El Salvador Â· France Â· Gabon Â· Guatemala Â· Haiti Â· Honduras Â· Nicaragua Â· Niger Â· Peru Â· Paraguay Â· Senegal Â· Uruguay

- Category:_____s of the Duchy of Warsaw
- Category:Administrative divisions

a. 1700 Cascadia earthquake
b. Department
c. 1703 Genroku earthquake
d. 1509 Istanbul earthquake

126. _____ are waste types containing radioactive chemical elements that do not have a practical purpose. It is sometimes the product of a nuclear process, such as nuclear fission. However, other industries not directly connected to the nuclear industry can produce large quantities of _____.
a. 1700 Cascadia earthquake
b. 1509 Istanbul earthquake
c. 1703 Genroku earthquake
d. Nuclear Waste

127. The _____ is a United States federal law enacted in 1982. It established a national program for disposal of highly radioactive wastes, and resulted in the studying of Yucca Mountain as a possible site for long-term disposal of radioactive waste.
a. 1509 Istanbul earthquake
b. 1703 Genroku earthquake
c. Nuclear Waste Policy Act
d. 1700 Cascadia earthquake

128. The _____ is a scientific agency of the United States government. The scientists of the USGS study the landscape of the United States, its natural resources, and the natural hazards that threaten it.
a. Amblypoda
b. Ambulocetus
c. Andrija MohoroviÄ iÄ‡
d. U.S. Geological Survey

129. _____ is a ridge line in Nye County, in the south-central part of the U.S. state of Nevada. It is composed of volcanic material ejected from a now-extinct caldera-forming supervolcano. _____ is most notable as the site of the proposed _____ Repository, a U.S. Department of Energy terminal storage facility for spent nuclear reactor fuel and other radioactive waste.
a. 1703 Genroku earthquake
b. Yucca Mountain
c. 1700 Cascadia earthquake
d. 1509 Istanbul earthquake

130. The United States _____ is a particular type of topography that covers much of the southwestern United States and northwestern Mexico that is typified by elongate north-south trending arid valleys bounded by mountain ranges which also bound adjacent valleys.

Chapter 14. Energy and Resources

a. 1509 Istanbul earthquake
b. 1703 Genroku earthquake
c. Basin and Range
d. 1700 Cascadia earthquake

131. In geology, _____ refers to heat sources within the planet. The planet's internal heat was originally generated during its accretion, due to gravitational binding energy, and since then additional heat has continued to be generated by the radioactive decay of elements such as uranium, thorium, and potassium.
a. 1703 Genroku earthquake
b. 1700 Cascadia earthquake
c. 1509 Istanbul earthquake
d. Geothermal

132. _____ is the use of geothermal heat to generate electricity.
a. 1700 Cascadia earthquake
b. 1703 Genroku earthquake
c. 1509 Istanbul earthquake
d. Geothermal power

133. The _____ is the rate of increase in temperature per unit depth in the Earth. It varies with location and is typically measured by determining the bottom open-hole temperature after the drilling of a borehole.
a. 1703 Genroku earthquake
b. 1509 Istanbul earthquake
c. 1700 Cascadia earthquake
d. Geothermal gradient

134. _____ is a chemical element in the periodic table that has the symbol H and atomic number 1. At standard temperature and pressure it is a colorless, odorless, nonmetallic, univalent, tasteless, highly flammable diatomic gas.
a. 1703 Genroku earthquake
b. 1509 Istanbul earthquake
c. 1700 Cascadia earthquake
d. Hydrogen

135. _____ in the most general terms refers to the movement of currents within fluids. _____ is one of the major modes of Heat and mass transfer. In fluids, convective heat and mass transfer take place through both diffusion and by advection, in which matter or heat is transported by the larger-scale motion of currents in the fluid.
a. 1700 Cascadia earthquake
b. 1703 Genroku earthquake
c. Convection
d. 1509 Istanbul earthquake

136. In vector calculus, the _____ of a scalar field is a vector field which points in the direction of the greatest rate of increase of the scalar field, and whose magnitude is the greatest rate of change.

A generalization of the _____ for functions on a Euclidean space which have values in another Euclidean space is the Jacobian. A further generalization for a function from one Banach space to another is the Fréchet derivative.

a. Gradient
b. 1700 Cascadia earthquake
c. 1509 Istanbul earthquake
d. 1703 Genroku earthquake

137. _____ is a geographical term that is used in various ways among the different branches of geography. In general, a _____ is a medium-scale area of land, Earth or water, smaller than the whole areas of interest, and larger than a specific site or location. A _____ can be seen as a collection of smaller units or as one part of a larger whole.
a. 1700 Cascadia earthquake
b. 1509 Istanbul earthquake
c. Champs-Élysées
d. Region

138. A _____ is a type of hot spring that erupts periodically, ejecting a column of hot water and steam into the air.

Chapter 14. Energy and Resources

a. 1509 Istanbul earthquake
b. 1700 Cascadia earthquake
c. 1703 Genroku earthquake
d. Geyser

139. _____ is water located beneath the ground surface in soil pore spaces and in the fractures of geologic formations. _____ is recharged from, and eventually flows to, the surface naturally; natural discharge often occurs at springs and seeps, streams and can often form oases or wetlands.
a. 1703 Genroku earthquake
b. 1700 Cascadia earthquake
c. 1509 Istanbul earthquake
d. Groundwater

140. _____ is energy transferred from one body or system to another due to a difference in temperature or can be defined as the absolute temperature of an object multiplied by the differential quantity of a system's entropy measured at the boundary of the object.
a. 1509 Istanbul earthquake
b. Heat
c. 1700 Cascadia earthquake
d. 1703 Genroku earthquake

141. A _____ is a machine or device that moves heat from one location to another via work. Most often _____ technology is applied to moving heat from a low temperature heat source to a higher temperature heat sink
a. Heat pump
b. 1703 Genroku earthquake
c. 1700 Cascadia earthquake
d. 1509 Istanbul earthquake

142. A _____ column is a column of rizing air in the lower altitudes of the Earth's atmosphere. _____s are created by the uneven heating of the Earth's surface from solar radiation, and are an example of convection. The Sun warms the ground, which in turn warms the air directly above it.
a. 1509 Istanbul earthquake
b. Thermal
c. 1703 Genroku earthquake
d. 1700 Cascadia earthquake

143. _____ is a temperature change in natural water bodies caused by human influence. The main cause of _____ is the use of water as a coolant, especially in power plants. Water used as a coolant is returned to the natural environment at a higher temperature.
a. 1703 Genroku earthquake
b. 1700 Cascadia earthquake
c. 1509 Istanbul earthquake
d. Thermal pollution

144. _____ is the ongoing effort to provide sustainable energy resources through knowledge, skills, and constructions. When harnessing energy from primary energy sources and converting them into more convenient secondary energy forms, such as electrical energy and cleaner fuel, both emissions and quality are important.
a. AL 129-1
b. AL 333
c. Energy production
d. AASHTO Soil Classification System

145. A _____ is a geological phenomenon which includes a wide range of ground movement, such as rock falls, deep failure of slopes and shallow debris flows. Although gravity's action on an over-steepened slope is the primary reason for a _____, there are other contributing factors affecting the original slope stability.
a. 1509 Istanbul earthquake
b. 1700 Cascadia earthquake
c. 1703 Genroku earthquake
d. Landslide

Chapter 14. Energy and Resources

146. _____ is located in Yellowstone National Park, Wyoming, United States. It was named in 1870 during the Washburn-Langford-Doane Expedition and was the first one in the park to receive a name. An eruption can shoot 3,700–8,400 gallons of boiling water to a height of 106–184 feet lasting from 1.5–5 minutes.
   a. AL 129-1
   b. AL 333
   c. AASHTO Soil Classification System
   d. Old Faithful Geyser

147. A natural resource qualifies as a _____ resource if it is replenished by natural processes at a rate comparable or faster than its rate of consumption by humans or other users. Resources such as solar radiation, tides, and winds are perpetual resources that are in no danger of being used in excess of their long-term availability.
   a. 1700 Cascadia earthquake
   b. Renewable
   c. 1509 Istanbul earthquake
   d. 1703 Genroku earthquake

148. _____ effectively uses natural resources such as sunlight, wind, rain, tides and geothermal heat, which are naturally replenished. _____ technologies range from solar power, wind power, hydroelectricity/micro hydro, biomass and biofuels for transportation.
   a. 1703 Genroku earthquake
   b. 1700 Cascadia earthquake
   c. Renewable energy
   d. 1509 Istanbul earthquake

149. _____ is the flow of air. More generally, it is the flow of the gases which compose an atmosphere; since _____ is not only an Earth based phenomenon.
   a. 1509 Istanbul earthquake
   b. 1700 Cascadia earthquake
   c. 1703 Genroku earthquake
   d. Wind

150. A _____ is a group of wind turbines in the same location used for production of electric power.
   a. 1509 Istanbul earthquake
   b. Wind farm
   c. 1703 Genroku earthquake
   d. 1700 Cascadia earthquake

151. A _____ is a section of land devoted to the production and management of food, either produce or livestock. It is the basic unit in agricultural production.
   a. Farm
   b. 1700 Cascadia earthquake
   c. 1509 Istanbul earthquake
   d. 1703 Genroku earthquake

152. _____ technologies are employed to convert solar energy into usable heat, cause air-movement for ventilation or cooling, or store heat for future use. _____ uses electrical or mechanical equipment, such as pumps and fans, to increase the usable heat in a system. Solar energy collection and utilization systems that do not use external energy, like a solar chimney, are classified as passive solar technologies.
   a. AASHTO Soil Classification System
   b. Active solar
   c. AL 333
   d. AL 129-1

153. In geography, a _____ is a landscape form or region that receives very little precipitation. They are defined as areas that receive an average annual precipitation of less than 250 mm. A _____ where vegetation cover is exceedingly sparse correspond to the 'hyperarid' regions of the earth, where rainfall is exceedingly rare and infrequent.
   a. 1509 Istanbul earthquake
   b. 1703 Genroku earthquake
   c. 1700 Cascadia earthquake
   d. Desert

Chapter 14. Energy and Resources

154. The _____ occupies a significant portion of southern California and smaller parts of southwestern Utah, southern Nevada, and northwestern Arizona, in the United States. Named after the Mohave tribe of Native Americans, it occupies over 22,000 square miles in a typical Basin and Range topography.
  a. 1703 Genroku earthquake
  b. 1509 Istanbul earthquake
  c. 1700 Cascadia earthquake
  d. Mojave Desert

155. _____ technologies convert sunlight into usable heat, cause air-movement for ventilation or cooling, or store heat for future use, without the assistance of other energy sources. Technologies that use a significant amount of conventional energy to power pumps or fans are classified as active solar technologies.
  a. Passive solar
  b. 1700 Cascadia earthquake
  c. 1703 Genroku earthquake
  d. 1509 Istanbul earthquake

156. _____, or PV for short, is a solar power technology that uses solar cells or solar photovoltaic arrays to convert light from the sun directly into electricity.
  a. 1700 Cascadia earthquake
  b. 1509 Istanbul earthquake
  c. 1703 Genroku earthquake
  d. Photovoltaics

157. A _____ is a storm system characterized by a low pressure center and numerous thunderstorms that produce strong winds and flooding rain. _____s feed on heat released when moist air rises, resulting in condensation of water vapour contained in the moist air. They are fueled by a different heat mechanism than other cyclonic windstorms such as nor'easters, European windstorms, and polar lows, leading to their classification as 'warm core' storm systems. Depending on its location and strength, a _____ is referred to by many other names, such as hurricane, typhoon, tropical storm, cyclonic storm, tropical depression, and simply cyclone.
  a. Tropical cyclone
  b. Persia
  c. Khmer Empire
  d. Kenya

158. In meteorology, _____ are an area of low atmospheric pressure characterized by inward spiraling winds that rotate counter clockwise in the northern hemisphere and clockwise in the southern hemisphere of the Earth.
  a. 1700 Cascadia earthquake
  b. Cyclones
  c. 1703 Genroku earthquake
  d. 1509 Istanbul earthquake

159. Hydroelectricity is electricity generated by hydropower. It is the most widely used form of renewable energy. Once a _____ complex is constructed, the project produces no direct waste, and has a considerably different output level of the greenhouse gas carbon dioxide than fossil fuel powered energy plants.
  a. Latin America
  b. Hydroelectric
  c. Japan
  d. Kabul

160. _____ is electricity produced by hydropower. _____ now supplies about 715,000 MWe or 19% of world electricity. It is also the world's leading form of renewable energy, accounting for over 63% of the total in 2005.
  a. 1700 Cascadia earthquake
  b. 1703 Genroku earthquake
  c. 1509 Istanbul earthquake
  d. Hydroelectricity

161. A _____ is a hydropower system; a machine for extracting power from the flow of water.
  a. Water wheel
  b. 1703 Genroku earthquake
  c. 1509 Istanbul earthquake
  d. 1700 Cascadia earthquake

Chapter 14. Energy and Resources

162. The _____ is a bay on the Atlantic coast of North America, on the northeast end of the Gulf of Maine between the Canadian provinces of New Brunswick and Nova Scotia, with a small portion touching the U.S. state of Maine. The _____ is known for its high tidal range and the bay is contested as having the highest vertical tidal range in the world with Ungava Bay in northern Quebec and The Severn Estuary in the UK.
- a. 1700 Cascadia earthquake
- b. 1509 Istanbul earthquake
- c. 1703 Genroku earthquake
- d. Bay of Fundy

163. A _____ is a barrier across flowing water that obstructs, directs or slows down the flow, often creating a reservoir, lake or impoundment.
- a. 1700 Cascadia earthquake
- b. 1703 Genroku earthquake
- c. 1509 Istanbul earthquake
- d. Dam

164. The _____ is a hydroelectric river dam that spans the Yangtze River in Sandouping, Yichang, Hubei, China. It is the largest hydro-electric power station in the world. Except for a planned ship lift, all the original plan of the project was completed on Oct.
- a. Hydroelectricity
- b. 1700 Cascadia earthquake
- c. Three Gorges Dam
- d. 1509 Istanbul earthquake

165. _____ is energy derived by exploiting the rise and fall in sea levels due to the tides.
- a. Tidal power
- b. 1703 Genroku earthquake
- c. 1509 Istanbul earthquake
- d. 1700 Cascadia earthquake

166. _____ is the conversion of wind into more useful forms, usually electricity, using wind turbines.
- a. 1703 Genroku earthquake
- b. 1700 Cascadia earthquake
- c. 1509 Istanbul earthquake
- d. Wind power

167. _____, in the energy production industry, refers to living and recently dead biological material which can be used as fuel or for industrial production. In ecology, _____ refers to the accumulation of life that is possibly living matter.
- a. 1700 Cascadia earthquake
- b. 1509 Istanbul earthquake
- c. 1703 Genroku earthquake
- d. Biomass

168. _____ was the primary source of fuel until the 1800s, when it was displaced by coal and later by oil. _____ is a renewable resource, provided the consumption rate is controlled to sustainable levels.
- a. Firewood
- b. 1700 Cascadia earthquake
- c. 1703 Genroku earthquake
- d. 1509 Istanbul earthquake

169. _____ is the process of completely removing a strip of bark, consisting of Secondary Phloem tissue, cork cambium, and cork, around a tree's outer circumference, causing its death.
- a. Girdling
- b. 1700 Cascadia earthquake
- c. 1703 Genroku earthquake
- d. 1509 Istanbul earthquake

170. _____ is organic matter used as fertilizer in agriculture.
- a. 1700 Cascadia earthquake
- b. 1509 Istanbul earthquake
- c. 1703 Genroku earthquake
- d. Manure

Chapter 14. Energy and Resources

171. _____ defined broadly is solid, liquid, or gas fuel consisting of, or derived from biomass. The more narrow definition used in this article is liquid or gas fuel derived from biomass and used as a fuel in transportation. Biomass used directly as a fuel is commonly called biomass fuel.
   a. Biofuel
   c. 1703 Genroku earthquake
   b. 1509 Istanbul earthquake
   d. 1700 Cascadia earthquake

172. An _____ is the result from the sudden release of stored energy in the Earth's crust that creates seismic waves. At the Earth's surface, _____s may manifest themselves by a shaking or displacement of the ground. An _____ is caused by tectonic plates getting stuck and putting a strain on the ground. The strain becomes so great that rocks give way by breaking and sliding along fault planes.
   a. AL 333
   c. AL 129-1
   b. Earthquake
   d. AASHTO Soil Classification System

173. _____ is the use of a heat engine or a power station to simultaneously generate both electricity and useful heat.
   a. 1700 Cascadia earthquake
   c. 1703 Genroku earthquake
   b. 1509 Istanbul earthquake
   d. Cogeneration

174. The _____ is a diverse scientific, social, and political movement for addressing the concerns of environmentalism. The _____ is represented by a range of organizations, from the large to grassroots. Due to its large membership, varying and strong beliefs, and occasionally speculative nature, the _____ is not always united in its goals.
   a. Environmental movement
   c. Amblypoda
   b. Andrija Mohorović iÄ‡
   d. Ambulocetus

175. In physics, the _____ states that the total amount of energy in an isolated system remains constant, although it may change forms, e.g. friction turns kinetic energy into thermal energy. In thermodynamics, the first law of thermodynamics is a statement of the _____ for thermodynamic systems, and is the more encompassing version of the _____.
   a. 1509 Istanbul earthquake
   c. 1703 Genroku earthquake
   b. 1700 Cascadia earthquake
   d. Conservation of energy

176. _____ is the manner a given entity has decided to address issues of energy development including energy production, distribution and consumption. The attributes of _____ may include legislation, international treaties, incentives to investment, guidelines for energy conservation, taxation and other public policy techniques.
   a. Energy policy
   c. AASHTO Soil Classification System
   b. AL 333
   d. AL 129-1

177. _____ is Chairman and Chief Scientist of the Rocky Mountain Institute, a MacArthur Fellowship recipient (1993), and author and co-author of many books on renewable energy and energy efficiency.

Lovins has worked professionally as an environmentalist and an advocate for a 'soft energy path' for the United States and other nations. He has promoted energy-use and energy-production concepts based on conservation, efficiency, the use of renewable sources of energy, and on generation of energy at or near the site where the energy is actually used.

a. Amazon Rainforest
b. Amblypoda
c. Aung San Suu Kyi
d. Amory Bloch Lovins

Chapter 15. Soils and Environment

1. _____ was the nickname given to a herbicide and defoliant used by the U.S. military in its Herbicidal Warfare program during the Vietnam War.
   a. AL 129-1
   b. AASHTO Soil Classification System
   c. AL 333
   d. Agent Orange

2. _____ is the common name for the group of compounds classified as polychlorinated dibenzodioxins PCDDs. They are members of the family of halogenated organic compounds, have been shown to bioaccumulate in humans and wildlife due to their lipophilic properties, and are known teratogens, mutagens, and suspected human carcinogens.
   a. 1703 Genroku earthquake
   b. Dioxin
   c. 1509 Istanbul earthquake
   d. 1700 Cascadia earthquake

3. There are two distinct views on the meaning of _____. One view is that _____ is part of the fundamental structure of the universe, a dimension in which events occur in sequence, and _____ itself is something that can be measured. A contrasting view is that _____ is part of the fundamental intellectual structure in which _____, rather than being an objective thing to be measured, is part of the mental measuring system.
   a. Time
   b. 1700 Cascadia earthquake
   c. 1703 Genroku earthquake
   d. 1509 Istanbul earthquake

4. _____ is the average and variations of weather over long periods of time. _____ zones can be defined using parameters such as temperature and rainfall.
   a. 1700 Cascadia earthquake
   b. 1509 Istanbul earthquake
   c. 1703 Genroku earthquake
   d. Climate

5. A _____ is an extended period of months or years when a region notes a deficiency in its water supply. Generally, this occurs when a region receives consistently below average precipitation.
   a. 1509 Istanbul earthquake
   b. 1700 Cascadia earthquake
   c. 1703 Genroku earthquake
   d. Drought

6. The _____ has been significantly leached of its mineral and/or organic content, leaving a pale layer largely composed of silicates.
   a. AL 129-1
   b. AASHTO Soil Classification System
   c. AL 333
   d. E horizon

7. An _____ is the result from the sudden release of stored energy in the Earth's crust that creates seismic waves. At the Earth's surface, _____s may manifest themselves by a shaking or displacement of the ground. An _____ is caused by tectonic plates getting stuck and putting a strain on the ground. The strain becomes so great that rocks give way by breaking and sliding along fault planes.
   a. AASHTO Soil Classification System
   b. AL 333
   c. AL 129-1
   d. Earthquake

8. A _____ is a storm system characterized by a low pressure center and numerous thunderstorms that produce strong winds and flooding rain. _____s feed on heat released when moist air rises, resulting in condensation of water vapour contained in the moist air. They are fueled by a different heat mechanism than other cyclonic windstorms such as nor'easters, European windstorms, and polar lows, leading to their classification as 'warm core' storm systems. Depending on its location and strength, a _____ is referred to by many other names, such as hurricane, typhoon, tropical storm, cyclonic storm, tropical depression, and simply cyclone.

Chapter 15. Soils and Environment

a. Tropical cyclone
b. Persia
c. Khmer Empire
d. Kenya

9. _____ is the process of extracting a substance from a solid by dissolving it in a liquid.
   a. 1509 Istanbul earthquake
   b. Leaching
   c. 1703 Genroku earthquake
   d. 1700 Cascadia earthquake

10. The _____ is a soil layer being dominated by the presence of large amounts of organic material in varying stages of decomposition.
    a. AL 129-1
    b. AL 333
    c. AASHTO Soil Classification System
    d. O horizon

11. A _____ is a specific layer in the soil which measures parallel to the soil surface and possesses physical characteristics which differ from the layers above and beneath. Horizon formation is a function of a range of geological, chemical, and biological processes and occurs over long time periods. Soils vary in the degree to which horizons are expressed.
    a. A horizon
    b. 1509 Istanbul earthquake
    c. Soil horizon
    d. 1700 Cascadia earthquake

12. A _____ is an opening in a planet's surface or crust, which allows hot, molten rock, ash, and gases to escape from below the surface. Volcanic activity involving the extrusion of rock tends to form mountains or features like mountains over a period of time.

    _____es are generally found where tectonic plates are diverging or converging.

    a. 1700 Cascadia earthquake
    b. 1509 Istanbul earthquake
    c. Volcano
    d. 1703 Genroku earthquake

13. _____ usually commence with phreatomagmatic eruptions which can be extremely noisy due the rising magma heating water in the ground. This is usually followed by the explosive throat clearing of the vent and the eruption column is dirty grey to black as old weathered rocks are blasted out of the vent. As the vent clears, further ash clouds become grey-white and creamy in colour, with convulations of the ash similar to those of plinian eruptions.
    a. 1703 Genroku earthquake
    b. Vulcanian eruptions
    c. 1509 Istanbul earthquake
    d. 1700 Cascadia earthquake

14. _____ is the process of breaking down rocks, soils and their minerals through direct contact with the atmosphere. _____ occurs without movement. Two main classifications of _____ processes exist. Mechanical or physical _____ involves the breakdown of rocks and soils through direct contact with atmospheric conditions. The second classification, chemical _____, involves the direct effect of atmospheric chemicals in the breakdown of rocks, soils and minerals.
    a. 1700 Cascadia earthquake
    b. 1509 Istanbul earthquake
    c. 1703 Genroku earthquake
    d. Weathering

15. The _____ is the line that separates earth from sky. More precisely, it is the line that divides all of the directions one can possibly look into two categories: those which intersect the Earth, and those which do not.

Chapter 15. Soils and Environment

a. 1509 Istanbul earthquake
b. Horizon
c. 1700 Cascadia earthquake
d. 1703 Genroku earthquake

16. _____ consist of mineral layers which may contain concentrations of clay or minerals such as iron or aluminium, or organic material. In addition, they are defined by having a distinctly different structure or consistence to the A horizon above and the horizons below.
a. 1703 Genroku earthquake
b. 1700 Cascadia earthquake
c. 1509 Istanbul earthquake
d. B horizon

17. _____ is simply named so because they come 'after' A and B within the soil profile. These layers are little affected by soil forming processes, and their lack of pedological development is one of their defining attributes
a. 1700 Cascadia earthquake
b. 1509 Istanbul earthquake
c. 1703 Genroku earthquake
d. C horizon

18. The _____ basically denote the layer of partially-weathered bedrock at the base of the soil profile.
a. 1700 Cascadia earthquake
b. 1703 Genroku earthquake
c. 1509 Istanbul earthquake
d. R horizon

19. The _____ is the clay-enriched horizon at some depth well below the A horizon
a. AASHTO Soil Classification System
b. AL 333
c. AL 129-1
d. Argillic B horizon

20. In geology, _____ are rock s with a grain size of usually no less than 256 mm diameter.
a. 1509 Istanbul earthquake
b. 1700 Cascadia earthquake
c. 1703 Genroku earthquake
d. Boulders

21. _____ is a term used to describe a group of hydrous aluminium phyllosilicate minerals, that are typically less than 2 micrometres in diameter. _____ consists of a variety of phyllosilicate minerals rich in silicon and aluminium oxides and hydroxides which include variable amounts of structural water. _____s are generally formed by the chemical weathering of silicate-bearing rocks by carbonic acid but some are formed by hydrothermal activity.
a. 1700 Cascadia earthquake
b. 1703 Genroku earthquake
c. Clay
d. 1509 Istanbul earthquake

22. _____ are made up of the minerals hydrous aluminium phyllosilicates, sometimes with variable amounts of iron, magnesium, alkali metals, alkaline earths and other cations.
a. 1703 Genroku earthquake
b. 1700 Cascadia earthquake
c. 1509 Istanbul earthquake
d. Clay particles

23. _____s are stones that were frequently used in the pavement of early streets. '_____' is derived from the very old English word 'cob', which had a wide range of meanings, one of which was 'rounded lump' with overtones of large size. 'Cobble', which appeared in the 15th century, simply added the diminutive suffix 'le' to 'cob', and meant a small stone rounded by the flow of water; essentially, a large pebble.
a. 1703 Genroku earthquake
b. 1509 Istanbul earthquake
c. 1700 Cascadia earthquake
d. Cobblestone

24. _____ is a hardened deposit of calcium carbonate. This calcium carbonate cements together other materials, including gravel, sand, clay, and silt. It is found in aridisol and mollisol soil orders. _____ occurs worldwide, generally in arid or semi-arid regions.
- a. 1509 Istanbul earthquake
- b. 1703 Genroku earthquake
- c. 1700 Cascadia earthquake
- d. Caliche

25. _____ is soil or rock derived granular material of a specific grain size. _____ may occur as a soil or alternatively as suspended sediment in a water column of any surface water body. It may also exist as deposition soil at the bottom of a water body.
- a. 1509 Istanbul earthquake
- b. 1700 Cascadia earthquake
- c. 1703 Genroku earthquake
- d. Silt

26. _____ in geology refers to the physical appearance or character of a rock, such as grain size, shape, and arrangement, at both the megascopic or microscopic surface feature level.
- a. Texture
- b. 1700 Cascadia earthquake
- c. 1703 Genroku earthquake
- d. 1509 Istanbul earthquake

27. _____ is determined by how individual soil granules clump or bind together and aggregate.
- a. 1509 Istanbul earthquake
- b. 1700 Cascadia earthquake
- c. 1703 Genroku earthquake
- d. Soil structure

28. A _____ substance is a material with a definite _____ composition. It is a concept that became firmly established in the late eighteenth century after work by the chemist Joseph Proust on the composition of some pure _____ compounds such as basic copper carbonate.
- a. 1509 Istanbul earthquake
- b. 1700 Cascadia earthquake
- c. Chemical property
- d. Chemical

29. _____ involves the change in the composition of rock, often leading to a 'break down' in its form.
- a. 1509 Istanbul earthquake
- b. 1700 Cascadia earthquake
- c. 1703 Genroku earthquake
- d. Chemical weathering

30. _____ is the natural capability of giving life. As a measure, '_____ Rate' is the number of children born per couple, person or population. This is different from fecundity, which is defined as the potential for reproduction (influenced by gamete production, fertilisation and carrying a pregnancy to term.)
- a. 1700 Cascadia earthquake
- b. 1509 Istanbul earthquake
- c. 1703 Genroku earthquake
- d. Fertility

31. A _____ is a substance used in an organism's metabolism which must be taken in from the environment. Non-autotrophic organisms typically acquire _____s by the ingestion of foods. Methods for _____ intake vary, with animals and protists having an internal digestive system, while plants digest _____s externally and then ingested. The effects of _____s are dose-dependent.
- a. 1703 Genroku earthquake
- b. 1509 Istanbul earthquake
- c. 1700 Cascadia earthquake
- d. Nutrient

32. _____ farming is a form of agriculture that excludes the use of synthetic fertilizers and pesticides, plant growth regulators, livestock feed additives, and genetically modified organisms.

Chapter 15. Soils and Environment

a. AL 129-1
b. AASHTO Soil Classification System
c. AL 333
d. Organic

33. _____ is matter that has come from a recently living organism; is capable of decay, or the product of decay; or is composed of organic compounds. The definition of _____ varies upon the subject it is being used for.

a. AL 333
b. Organic matter
c. AASHTO Soil Classification System
d. AL 129-1

34. For morphological image processing operations, see Erosion (morphology)For use of in dermatopathology, see Erosion (dermatopathology) Severe _____ in a wheat field near Washington State University, USA.

Erosion is the removal of solids (sediment, soil, rock and other particles) in the natural environment. It usually occurs due to transport by wind, water, or ice; by down-slope creep of soil and other material under the force of gravity; or by living organisms, such as burrowing animals, in the case of bioerosion.

Erosion is distinguished from weathering, which is the process of chemical or physical breakdown of the minerals in the rocks, although the two processes may occur concurrently.

a. Soil erosion
b. 1509 Istanbul earthquake
c. 1703 Genroku earthquake
d. 1700 Cascadia earthquake

Chapter 15. Soils and Environment

35. An interbasin _____ is a hydrological project undertaken to divert water from one drainage basin into another. This is usually to boost water levels for hydroelectricity, or to supply drinking water nearby.

- Campbell-Heber Diversion
- Coquitlam-Buntzen Diversion
- Kemano Diversion
- Vernon Irrigation District Diversion

- Churchill Diversion-Southern Indian Lake

- Saint John Water Supply

- Bay d'Espoir Diversions
- Deer Lake Diversion
- Smallwood Reservoir-Julian Diversion
- Smallwood Reservoir-Kanairiktok Diversion
- Smallwood Reservoir-Naskaupi Diversion

- Wellington Lake Hydro Project Diversion (with Saskatchewan)

- Ingram Diversion
- Jordan Diversion
- Wreck Cove Diversions

- Long Lake Diversion
- Ogoki Diversion
- Opasatika Diversion
- Root River Diversion

- Barrière Diversion
- Boyd-Sakami Diversion
- Lac de la Frégate Diversion
- Laforge Diversion
- Manouane Diversion
- Mégiscane Diversion
- Sault aux Cochons Diversion

- Cypress Lake Diversion (with Alberta)
- Pasquia Land Resettlement Diversion (with Manitoba)
- Swift Current Diversion

a. 1700 Cascadia earthquake
b. 1509 Istanbul earthquake
c. 1703 Genroku earthquake
d. Water diversion

36. _____ is the production of food, feed, fiber, fuel and other goods by the systematic raizing of plants and animals.

Chapter 15. Soils and Environment 217

   a. AL 129-1
   c. Agriculture
   b. AASHTO Soil Classification System
   d. AL 333

37. _____ is displacement of solids by the agents of ocean currents, wind, water, or ice by downward or down-slope movement in response to gravity or by living organisms.
   a. AL 129-1
   c. AL 333
   b. AASHTO Soil Classification System
   d. Erosion

38. _____ is the substance of which physical objects are composed. _____ can be solid, liquid, plasma or gas. It constitutes the observable universe.
   a. 1509 Istanbul earthquake
   c. 1703 Genroku earthquake
   b. Matter
   d. 1700 Cascadia earthquake

39. _____ is rock that is of a certain particle size range. In geology, _____ is any loose rock that is at least two millimeters in its largest dimension and no more than 75 millimeters.
   a. 1703 Genroku earthquake
   c. 1509 Istanbul earthquake
   b. 1700 Cascadia earthquake
   d. Gravel

40. _____ is the term used for a branch of public policy which encompasses various disciplines which seek to order and regulate the use of land in an efficient and ethical way.
   a. 1703 Genroku earthquake
   c. 1700 Cascadia earthquake
   b. 1509 Istanbul earthquake
   d. Land use planning

41. _____ is a dynamic subject, from the structure of the system itself, to the definitions of classes, and finally in the application in the field. It can be approached from both the pespective of pedogenesis and from soil morphology.
   a. Strip farming
   c. Sulfur cycle
   b. Terrace
   d. Soil classification

42. _____ is the practice and science of classification. Taxonomies, which are composed of taxonomic units known as taxa, are frequently hierarchical in structure, commonly displaying parent-child relationships.
   a. 1509 Istanbul earthquake
   c. 1700 Cascadia earthquake
   b. 1703 Genroku earthquake
   d. Taxonomy

43. The _____ (or _____) is a soil classification system used in engineering and geology disciplines to describe the texture and grain size of a soil. The classification system can be applied to most unconsolidated materials, and is represented by a two-letter symbol. Each letter is described below (with the exception of Pt):

- AASHTO Soil Classification System
- AASHTO
- ASTM International

   a. AL 129-1
   c. AASHTO Soil Classification System
   b. AL 333
   d. Unified soil classification system

Chapter 15. Soils and Environment

44. _____ in chemistry is the intermolecular attraction between like-molecules. It explains phenomena such as surface tension.
   a. 1700 Cascadia earthquake
   b. 1509 Istanbul earthquake
   c. 1703 Genroku earthquake
   d. Cohesion

45. _____ is an effect within the surface layer of a liquid that causes that layer to behave as an elastic sheet. This effect allows insects to walk on water. It allows small metal objects such as needles, razor blades, or foil fragments to float on the surface of water, and causes capillary action.
   a. 1509 Istanbul earthquake
   b. 1700 Cascadia earthquake
   c. 1703 Genroku earthquake
   d. Surface tension

46. The _____ is the surface where the water pressure is equal to atmospheric pressure. A large amount of water within a body of sand or rock below the _____ is called an aquifer, and the ability of rocks to store such groundwater is dependent on their porosity and permeability.
   a. 1700 Cascadia earthquake
   b. 1703 Genroku earthquake
   c. 1509 Istanbul earthquake
   d. Water table

47. _____ is a reaction force applied by a stretched string, rope or a similar object on the objects which stretch it. The direction of the force of it is parallel to the string, towards the string.
   a. Sievert
   b. Thermal energy
   c. Tension
   d. Synthetic aperture radar

48. _____ is a cape on the coast of North Carolina. It is the point that protrudes the farthest to the southeast along the northeast-to-southwest line of the Atlantic coast of North America. Two major Atlantic currents collide just off _____, the southerly-flowing cold water Labrador Current and the northerly-flowing warm water Florida Current (Gulf Stream), creating turbulent waters and a large expanse of shallow sandbars extending up to 14 miles offshore.
   a. 1700 Cascadia earthquake
   b. 1509 Istanbul earthquake
   c. Cape Hatteras
   d. 1703 Genroku earthquake

49. Due to shore erosion in the Outer Bank of North Carolina a navagational lighthouse had to be moved leading to the _____.
   a. 1509 Istanbul earthquake
   b. Cape Hatteras Lighthouse controversy
   c. 1700 Cascadia earthquake
   d. 1703 Genroku earthquake

50. _____ occurs when weight of livestock or heavy machinery compacts the soil, causing it to lose pore space. Affected soils become less able to absorb rainfall, thus increasing runoff and erosion.
   a. 1703 Genroku earthquake
   b. 1509 Istanbul earthquake
   c. 1700 Cascadia earthquake
   d. Soil compressibility

51. _____ is a general term for the plant life of a region; it refers to the ground cover provided by plants, and is, by far, the most abundant biotic element of the biosphere. Primeval redwood forests, coastal mangrove stands, sphagnum bogs, desert soil crusts, roadside weed patches, wheat fields, cultivated gardens and lawns; are all encompassed by the term _____.
   a. 1509 Istanbul earthquake
   b. Vegetation
   c. 1703 Genroku earthquake
   d. 1700 Cascadia earthquake

Chapter 15. Soils and Environment

52. An _____ is traditionally considered any chemical compound that, when dissolved in water, gives a solution with a hydrogen ion activity greater than in pure water, i.e. a pH less than 7.0. That approximates the modern definition of Johannes Nicolaus Brønsted and Martin Lowry, who independently defined an _____ as a compound which donates a hydrogen ion to another compound. Common examples include acetic _____ and sulfuric _____. Acid/base systems are different from redox reactions in that there is no change in oxidation state.
   a. AL 333
   b. AASHTO Soil Classification System
   c. AL 129-1
   d. Acid

53. Rock _____ is the controlled use of explosives to excavate or remove rock. It is a technique used most often in mining and civil engineering such as dam construction.

In 1990, 2.1 million tonnes (2.32 million short tons) of commercial explosives were consumed in the USA, representing an estimated expenditure of 3.5 to 4 billion 1993 dollars on _____.

   a. 1509 Istanbul earthquake
   b. 1700 Cascadia earthquake
   c. 1703 Genroku earthquake
   d. Blasting

54. _____ is deterioration of essential properties in a material due to reactions with its surroundings. In the most common use of the word, this means a loss of an electron of metals reacting with water or oxygen.
   a. 1703 Genroku earthquake
   b. Corrosion
   c. 1509 Istanbul earthquake
   d. 1700 Cascadia earthquake

55. _____ is the most commonly used technique within the science of archaeology. It is the exposure, processing and recording of archaeological remains.
   a. AL 129-1
   b. AASHTO Soil Classification System
   c. AL 333
   d. Excavation

56. _____, symbolically represented as K, is a property of vascular plants, soil or rock, that describes the ease with which water can move through pore spaces or fractures
   a. 1703 Genroku earthquake
   b. 1509 Istanbul earthquake
   c. 1700 Cascadia earthquake
   d. Hydraulic conductivity

57. In geology, _____ is a naturally occurring aggregate of minerals and/or mineraloids.

The Earth's outer solid layer, the lithosphere, is made of _____. In general _____s are of three types, namely, igneous, sedimentary, and metamorphic.

   a. 1703 Genroku earthquake
   b. 1509 Istanbul earthquake
   c. Rock
   d. 1700 Cascadia earthquake

58. _____ is a soil in which there is a high content of expansive clay known as montmorillonite that forms deep cracks in drier seasons or years. Alternate shrinking and swelling causes self-mulching, where the soil material consistently mixes itself.
   a. 1700 Cascadia earthquake
   b. 1703 Genroku earthquake
   c. 1509 Istanbul earthquake
   d. Vertisol

Chapter 15. Soils and Environment

59. _____ is the natural or artificial removal of surface and sub-surface water from a given area. Many agricultural soils need _____ to improve production or to manage water supplies.
   a. 1700 Cascadia earthquake
   b. 1703 Genroku earthquake
   c. 1509 Istanbul earthquake
   d. Drainage

60. _____ is any particulate matter that can be transported by fluid flow and which eventually is deposited as a layer of solid particles on the bed or bottom of a body of water or other liquid.
   a. 1509 Istanbul earthquake
   b. 1700 Cascadia earthquake
   c. 1703 Genroku earthquake
   d. Sediment

61. Most often, a _____ refers to an artificial lake, used to store water for various uses. _____s are created first by building a sturdy dam, usually out of cement, earth, rock, or a mixture. Once the dam is completed, a stream is allowed to flow behind it and eventually fill it to capacity.
   a. 1700 Cascadia earthquake
   b. 1703 Genroku earthquake
   c. Reservoir
   d. 1509 Istanbul earthquake

62. Models of soil erosion play critical roles in soil and water resource conservation and nonpoint source pollution assessments, including: sediment load assessment and inventory, conservation planning and design for sediment control, and for the advancement of scientific understanding. The most widely used soil erosion model is the _____ or one of its derivatives.

The _____ was developed in the United States based on soil erosion data collected beginning in the 1930s by the USDA Soil Conservation Service (now the USDA Natural Resources Conservation Service) .

   a. Ecology
   b. Endemic species
   c. Ecological pyramid
   d. Universal Soil Loss Equation

63. _____ is the introduction of substances or energy into the environment, resulting in deleterious effects of such a nature as to endanger human health, harm living resources and ecosystems, and impair or interfere with amenities and other legitimate uses of the environment.
   a. 1509 Istanbul earthquake
   b. 1703 Genroku earthquake
   c. 1700 Cascadia earthquake
   d. Pollution

64. The outer barrier refers to the string of _____s that divide the lagoons south of Long Island from the Atlantic Ocean.

These islands include Long Beach _____, Jones Beach Island, Fire Island and West Hampton Dunes. The outer barrier extends seventy-five miles 120 km along the south shore of Long Island, New York, from Rockaway Beach on the NYC/Nassau County border from Long Beach _____s western edge, to Suffolk County's east end of Shinnecock Bay.

   a. 1509 Istanbul earthquake
   b. 1700 Cascadia earthquake
   c. 1703 Genroku earthquake
   d. Barrier island

Chapter 15. Soils and Environment

65. The _____ is defined as the part of the land adjoining or near the ocean. A coastline is properly a line on a map indicating the disposition of a _____, but the word is often used to refer to the _____ itself. The adjective coastal describes something as being on, near to, or associated with a _____.
   a. Coast
   b. 1703 Genroku earthquake
   c. 1700 Cascadia earthquake
   d. 1509 Istanbul earthquake

66. _____ in geology is the accumulation of sediment in rivers and nearby landforms. _____ occurs when sediment supply exceeds the ability of a river to transport the sediment.
   a. AL 129-1
   b. AL 333
   c. AASHTO Soil Classification System
   d. Aggradation

67. _____ is the farming practice of ploughing across a slope following its contours. The rows formed have the effect of slowing water run-off during rainstorms so that the soil is not washed away.
   a. Contour plowing
   b. 1703 Genroku earthquake
   c. 1509 Istanbul earthquake
   d. 1700 Cascadia earthquake

68. A _____ is a bipedal primate belonging to the mammalian species Homo sapiens in the family Hominidae. Compared to other living organisms on Earth, a _____ has a highly developed brain capable of abstract reasoning, language, and introspection.
   a. 1509 Istanbul earthquake
   b. 1703 Genroku earthquake
   c. Human
   d. 1700 Cascadia earthquake

69. In agriculture, a _____ is a leveled section of a hilly cultivated area, designed as a method of soil conservation to slow or prevent the rapid surface runoff of irrigation water
   a. Strip farming
   b. Sulfur cycle
   c. Soil classification
   d. Terrace

70. _____ is the uppermost layer of soil, usually the top 2 to 6 inches. It has the highest concentration of organic matter and microorganisms, and is where most of the Earth's biological soil activity occurs. Plants generally concentrate their roots in, and obtain most of their nutrients from this layer. The actual depth of the _____ layer can be measured as the depth from the surface to the first densely packed soil layer known as hardpan.
   a. 1509 Istanbul earthquake
   b. Topsoil
   c. 1703 Genroku earthquake
   d. 1700 Cascadia earthquake

71. _____ is the degradation of land in arid, semi arid and dry sub-humid areas resulting from various climatic variations, but primarily human activities. Current _____ is taking place much faster worldwide than historically and usually arises from the demands of increased populations that settle on the land in order to grow crops and graze animals.
   a. 1703 Genroku earthquake
   b. 1700 Cascadia earthquake
   c. 1509 Istanbul earthquake
   d. Desertification

72. _____ is the artificial application of water to the soil usually for assisting in growing crops. In crop production it is mainly used to replace missing rainfall in periods of drought, but also to protect plants against frost.
   a. AASHTO Soil Classification System
   b. AL 333
   c. AL 129-1
   d. Irrigation

Chapter 15. Soils and Environment

73. _____ is the human modification of natural environment or wilderness into built environment such as fields, pastures, and settlements. The major effect of _____ on land cover since 1750 has been deforestation of temperate regions. More recent significant effects of _____ include urban sprawl, soil erosion, soil degradation, salinization, and desertification.
   a. 1703 Genroku earthquake
   b. 1700 Cascadia earthquake
   c. Land use
   d. 1509 Istanbul earthquake

74. _____ is used to describe the steepness, incline, gradient, or grade of a straight line. A higher _____ value indicates a steeper incline. The _____ is defined as the ratio of the 'rise' divided by the 'run' between two points on a line, or in other words, the ratio of the altitude change to the horizontal distance between any two points on the line.
   a. 1509 Istanbul earthquake
   b. 1700 Cascadia earthquake
   c. 1703 Genroku earthquake
   d. Slope

75. _____ is the increase in the population of cities in proportion to the region's rural population. _____ is studied in terms of its effects on the ecology and economy of a region.
   a. AL 129-1
   b. Urbanization
   c. AASHTO Soil Classification System
   d. AL 333

76. _____ is a layer of gases surrounding the planet Earth and retained by the Earth's gravity, protecting life on Earth by absorbing ultraviolet solar radiation and reducing temperature extremes between day and night.
   a. AL 129-1
   b. AASHTO Soil Classification System
   c. Earths atmosphere
   d. AL 333

77. _____ is a chemical, physical, or biological agent that modifies the natural characteristics of the atmosphere. The atmosphere is a complex, dynamic natural gaseous system that is essential to support life on planet Earth. Stratospheric ozone depletion due to _____ has long been recognized as a threat to human health as well as to the Earth's ecosystems. Worldwide _____ is responsible for large numbers of deaths and cases of respiratory disease.
   a. AASHTO Soil Classification System
   b. AL 129-1
   c. AL 333
   d. Air pollution

78. _____ is a large set of adverse effects upon water bodies such as lakes, rivers, oceans, and groundwater caused by human activities. Although natural phenomena such as volcanoes, algae blooms, storms, and earthquakes also cause major changes in water quality and the ecological status of water, these are not deemed to be pollution. _____ has many causes and characteristics.
   a. 1700 Cascadia earthquake
   b. Water pollution
   c. 1509 Istanbul earthquake
   d. 1703 Genroku earthquake

79. _____ is the geological process whereby material is added to a landform. This is the process by which wind and water create a sediment deposit, through the laying down of granular material that has been eroded and transported from another geographical location.
   a. Deposition
   b. 1700 Cascadia earthquake
   c. 1509 Istanbul earthquake
   d. 1703 Genroku earthquake

80. _____ is the process of a material being more closely packed together.

Chapter 15. Soils and Environment

  a. 1509 Istanbul earthquake
  c. 1703 Genroku earthquake
  b. 1700 Cascadia earthquake
  d. Compaction

81. In geography, a _____ is a landscape form or region that receives very little precipitation. They are defined as areas that receive an average annual precipitation of less than 250 mm. A _____ where vegetation cover is exceedingly sparse correspond to the 'hyperarid' regions of the earth, where rainfall is exceedingly rare and infrequent.
  a. Desert
  c. 1703 Genroku earthquake
  b. 1700 Cascadia earthquake
  d. 1509 Istanbul earthquake

82. _____ is the state of extreme dryness, or the process of extreme drying. A desiccant is a hygroscopic substance that induces or sustains such a state in its local vicinity in a moderately-well sealed container.
  a. 1703 Genroku earthquake
  c. 1700 Cascadia earthquake
  b. Desiccation
  d. 1509 Istanbul earthquake

83. A _____ is a hill of sand built by eolian processes. _____s are subject to different forms and sizes based on their interaction with the wind. Most kinds of _____ are longer on the windward side where the sand is pushed up the _____, and a shorter in the lee of the wind. The trough between _____s is called a slack. A "_____ field" is an area covered by extensive sand _____s. Large _____ fields are known as ergs.
  a. 1509 Istanbul earthquake
  c. 1703 Genroku earthquake
  b. 1700 Cascadia earthquake
  d. Dune

84. _____ is the study of the movement, distribution, and quality of water throughout the Earth, and thus addresses both the hydrologic cycle and water resources.
  a. Hydrology
  c. 1509 Istanbul earthquake
  b. 1703 Genroku earthquake
  d. 1700 Cascadia earthquake

85. The _____ occupies a significant portion of southern California and smaller parts of southwestern Utah, southern Nevada, and northwestern Arizona, in the United States. Named after the Mohave tribe of Native Americans, it occupies over 22,000 square miles in a typical Basin and Range topography.
  a. 1509 Istanbul earthquake
  c. 1703 Genroku earthquake
  b. 1700 Cascadia earthquake
  d. Mojave Desert

86. _____ can be defined as any process that uses microorganisms, fungi, green plants or their enzymes to return the natural environment altered by contaminants to its original condition. _____ may be employed to attack specific soil contaminants, such as degradation of chlorinated hydrocarbons by bacteria. An example of a more general approach is the cleanup of oil spills by the addition of nitrate and/or sulfate fertilisers to facilitate the decomposition of crude oil by indigenous or exogenous bacteria.
  a. Bioremediation
  c. 1700 Cascadia earthquake
  b. 1509 Istanbul earthquake
  d. 1703 Genroku earthquake

87. _____ is the presence of man-made chemicals or other alteration of the natural soil environment. This type of contamination typically arises from the rupture of underground storage tanks, application of pesticides, percolation of contaminated surface water to subsurface strata, leaching of wastes from landfills or direct discharge of industrial wastes to the soil.

a. 1703 Genroku earthquake
c. 1700 Cascadia earthquake
b. 1509 Istanbul earthquake
d. Soil pollution

88. A _____ is a geological phenomenon which includes a wide range of ground movement, such as rock falls, deep failure of slopes and shallow debris flows. Although gravity's action on an over-steepened slope is the primary reason for a _____, there are other contributing factors affecting the original slope stability.
   a. 1700 Cascadia earthquake
   c. 1703 Genroku earthquake
   b. Landslide
   d. 1509 Istanbul earthquake

Chapter 16. Waste as a Resource: Waste Management

1. _____ is unwanted or undesired material.
   - a. Waste
   - b. 1700 Cascadia earthquake
   - c. 1509 Istanbul earthquake
   - d. 1703 Genroku earthquake

2. _____ is the collection, transport, processing, recycling or disposal of waste materials, usually ones produced by human activity, in an effort to reduce their effect on human health or local aesthetics or amenity.
   - a. 1703 Genroku earthquake
   - b. 1700 Cascadia earthquake
   - c. 1509 Istanbul earthquake
   - d. Waste management

3. _____ is a holistic effort to analyze and overcome the power structures that have traditionally thwarted environmental reforms. _____ proponents generally view the environment as encompassing "where we live, work, and play"; thus, the movement seeks to redress inequitable distributions of environmental burdens and access to environmental goods.
   - a. AASHTO Soil Classification System
   - b. AL 129-1
   - c. AL 333
   - d. Environmental justice

4. _____ is waste that poses substantial or potential threats to public health or the environment. Many types of businesses generate _____. Some are small companies that may be located in a community.
   - a. 1509 Istanbul earthquake
   - b. 1700 Cascadia earthquake
   - c. 1703 Genroku earthquake
   - d. Hazardous waste

5. _____ refers to a characteristic of living organisms. It always refers to the interaction of organisms with other organisms and to their collective co-existence, irrespective of whether they are aware of it or not, and irrespective of whether the interaction is voluntary or involuntary.

In the absence of agreement about its meaning, the term '_____' is used in many different senses, referring among other things to:

- attitudes, orientations or behaviours which take the interests, intentions or needs of other people into account;
- common characteristics of people or descriptions of collectivities;
- relations between people generally, or particular associations among people;
- interactions between people;
- membership of a group of people or inclusion or belonging to a community of people;
- co-operation or co-operative characteristics between people;
- relations of dependence;
- the public sector or the need for governance for the good of all, contrasted with the private sector;
- in existentialist and postmodernist thought, relationships between the Self and the Other;
- interactive systems in communities of people, animal or insect populations, or any living organisms.

In one broad meaning, '_____' refers only to society as 'a system of common life', but in another sense it contrasts specifically with 'individual' and individualist theories of society. This is reflected for instance in the different perspectives of liberalism and socialism on society and public affairs.

a. Social
b. 1703 Genroku earthquake
c. 1509 Istanbul earthquake
d. 1700 Cascadia earthquake

6. _____ is the capital and largest urban area of both England and the United Kingdom. An important settlement for two millennia, _____'s history goes back to its founding by the Romans. Since its foundation, _____ has been part of many movements and phenomena throughout history, including the English Renaissance, the Industrial Revolution, and the Gothic Revival.
   a. 1509 Istanbul earthquake
   b. Barcelona
   c. 1700 Cascadia earthquake
   d. London

7. _____ is the branch of logistics that deals with the tangible components of a supply chain. Specifically, this covers the acquisition of spare parts and replacements, quality control of purchasing and ordering such parts, and the standards involved in ordering, shipping, and warehousing the said parts.

_____ is just managing all types of materials in an organization.

   a. 1703 Genroku earthquake
   b. 1700 Cascadia earthquake
   c. 1509 Istanbul earthquake
   d. Materials management

8. _____ is the reprocessing of materials into new products. It prevents useful material resources being wasted, reduces the consumption of raw materials and reduces energy usage, and hence greenhouse gas emissions, compared to virgin production.
   a. 1700 Cascadia earthquake
   b. Recycling
   c. 1509 Istanbul earthquake
   d. 1703 Genroku earthquake

9. _____ is using an item more than once. This includes conventional _____ where the item is used again for the same function, and new-life _____ where it is used for a new function. In contrast, recycling is the breaking down of the used item into raw materials which are used to make new items.
   a. 1700 Cascadia earthquake
   b. 1509 Istanbul earthquake
   c. 1703 Genroku earthquake
   d. Reuse

10. _____ is a kind of air pollution; the word "_____" is a portmanteau of smoke and fog. Classic _____ results from large amounts of coal burning in an area and is caused by a mixture of smoke and sulphur dioxide.
    a. 1509 Istanbul earthquake
    b. 1700 Cascadia earthquake
    c. 1703 Genroku earthquake
    d. Smog

11. The principal body of law currently in effect is based on the Federal Water Pollution Control Amendments of 1972, which significantly expanded and strengthened earlier legislation. Major amendments were enacted in the Clean Water Act of 1977 enacted by the 95th United States Congress and the _____ of 1987 enacted by the 100th United States Congress.

The Act governs discharges to waters of the United States. Older statutory language used the term 'navigable waters,' but this term was expanded in the 1972 law:

   The term 'navigable waters' means the waters of the United States, including the territorial seas.

a. Jetsam
b. Flotsam
c. Fish and Wildlife Coordination Act
d. Water Quality Act

12. _____ is the scientific study of the distribution and abundance of living organisms and how the distribution and abundance are affected by interactions between the organisms and their environment.
    a. Ecology
    b. Universal Soil Loss Equation
    c. Indicator species
    d. Ecological pyramid

13. _____ is the shifting of industrial process from linear systems, in which resource and capital investments move through the system to become waste, to a closed loop system where wastes become inputs for new processes.
    a. AL 333
    b. Industrial ecology
    c. AL 129-1
    d. AASHTO Soil Classification System

14. _____ is a waste type that includes predominantly household waste with sometimes the addition of commercial wastes collected by a municipality within a given area. They are in either solid or semisolid form and generally exclude industrial hazardous wastes.
    a. 1509 Istanbul earthquake
    b. Solid waste
    c. 1703 Genroku earthquake
    d. 1700 Cascadia earthquake

15. _____ is a philosophy that aims to guide people in the redesign of their resource-use system with the aim of reducing waste to zero.
    a. 1700 Cascadia earthquake
    b. 1703 Genroku earthquake
    c. 1509 Istanbul earthquake
    d. Zero waste

16. The _____ is a scientific agency of the United States government. The scientists of the USGS study the landscape of the United States, its natural resources, and the natural hazards that threaten it.
    a. Andrija Mohorovičić
    b. Amblypoda
    c. Ambulocetus
    d. U.S. Geological Survey

17. An _____ is traditionally considered any chemical compound that, when dissolved in water, gives a solution with a hydrogen ion activity greater than in pure water, i.e. a pH less than 7.0. That approximates the modern definition of Johannes Nicolaus Brønsted and Martin Lowry, who independently defined an _____ as a compound which donates a hydrogen ion to another compound. Common examples include acetic _____ and sulfuric _____. Acid/base systems are different from redox reactions in that there is no change in oxidation state.
    a. AL 333
    b. AASHTO Soil Classification System
    c. AL 129-1
    d. Acid

18. The term _____ is commonly used to mean the deposition of acidic components in rain, snow, dew, or dry particles. _____ occurs when sulfur dioxide and nitrogen oxides are emitted into the atmosphere, undergo chemical transformations and are absorbed by water droplets in clouds. The droplets then fall to earth as rain, snow, mist, dry dust, hail, or sleet. This increases the acidity of the soil, and affects the chemical balance of lakes and streams.
    a. AL 129-1
    b. AL 333
    c. AASHTO Soil Classification System
    d. Acid precipitation

19. _____ is a chemical element in the periodic table that has the symbol Cd and atomic number 48. A relatively rare, soft, bluish-white, toxic transition metal, _____ occurs with zinc ores and is used largely in batteries.

Chapter 16. Waste as a Resource: Waste Management

a. 1703 Genroku earthquake
b. 1700 Cascadia earthquake
c. 1509 Istanbul earthquake
d. Cadmium

20. _____ is the aerobic decomposition of biodegradable organic matter, producing compost.
a. Composting
b. 1509 Istanbul earthquake
c. 1703 Genroku earthquake
d. 1700 Cascadia earthquake

21. _____ is a waste treatment technology that involves the combustion of waste at high temperatures.
a. AL 333
b. AL 129-1
c. AASHTO Soil Classification System
d. Incineration

22. _____ is a chemical element in the periodic table that has the symbol Hg and atomic number 80. A heavy, silvery, transition metal, _____ is one of five elements that are liquid at or near standard room temperature (the others are the metals caesium, francium, and gallium, and the nonmetal bromine).
a. 1703 Genroku earthquake
b. Mercury
c. 1509 Istanbul earthquake
d. 1700 Cascadia earthquake

23. _____ is a chemical element which has the symbol N and atomic number 7 in the periodic table. Elemental _____ is a colorless, odorless, tasteless and mostly inert diatomic gas at standard conditions, constituting 78.08% percent of Earth's atmosphere.
a. 1700 Cascadia earthquake
b. 1703 Genroku earthquake
c. 1509 Istanbul earthquake
d. Nitrogen

24. _____ is an uncovered site used for disposal of waste without environmental controls.
a. AL 129-1
b. AASHTO Soil Classification System
c. Open dump
d. AL 333

25. _____ is the chemical element in the periodic table that has the symbol S and atomic number 16. It is an abundant, tasteless, odorless, multivalent non-metal. _____, in its native form, is a yellow crystaline solid. In nature, it can be found as the pure element or as sulfide and sulfate minerals.
a. Vinyl
b. Sulfur
c. Thulium
d. Zinc

26. _____ are a class of astronomical objects. The term is generally used to indicate a diverse group of small celestial bodies that drift in the solar system in orbit around the Sun.
a. Asteroids
b. AL 333
c. AL 129-1
d. AASHTO Soil Classification System

27. An _____ is a layer of gases that may surround a material body of sufficient mass, by the gravity of the body, and are retained for a longer duration if gravity is high and the _____'s temperature is low. Some planets consist mainly of various gases, and therefore have very deep _____s

The term stellar _____ describes the outer region of a star, and typically includes the portion starting from the opaque photosphere outwards.

Chapter 16. Waste as a Resource: Waste Management

a. AL 129-1
b. AL 333
c. Atmosphere
d. AASHTO Soil Classification System

28. A _____ substance is a material with a definite _____ composition. It is a concept that became firmly established in the late eighteenth century after work by the chemist Joseph Proust on the composition of some pure _____ compounds such as basic copper carbonate.
a. 1509 Istanbul earthquake
b. 1700 Cascadia earthquake
c. Chemical
d. Chemical property

29. _____ is a waste that is made from harmful chemicals (mostly produced by large factories.) _____ may fall under regulations such as COSHH in the UK, or the Clean Water Act and Resource Conservation and Recovery Act in the US. _____ may or may not be classed as hazardous waste.
a. Metalloid
b. 1509 Istanbul earthquake
c. Transferability
d. Chemical waste

30. A _____, is a site for the disposal of waste materials by burial and is the oldest form of waste treatment.
a. 1703 Genroku earthquake
b. 1509 Istanbul earthquake
c. 1700 Cascadia earthquake
d. Landfill

31. An _____ is a chemical compound containing an oxygen atom and other elements. Most of the earth's crust consists of them. They result when elements are oxidized by air.
a. AASHTO Soil Classification System
b. Oxide
c. AL 333
d. AL 129-1

32. _____ is a term used to describe a group of hydrous aluminium phyllosilicate minerals, that are typically less than 2 micrometres in diameter. _____ consists of a variety of phyllosilicate minerals rich in silicon and aluminium oxides and hydroxides which include variable amounts of structural water. _____s are generally formed by the chemical weathering of silicate-bearing rocks by carbonic acid but some are formed by hydrothermal activity.
a. 1509 Istanbul earthquake
b. 1703 Genroku earthquake
c. Clay
d. 1700 Cascadia earthquake

33. _____ is water located beneath the ground surface in soil pore spaces and in the fractures of geologic formations. _____ is recharged from, and eventually flows to, the surface naturally; natural discharge often occurs at springs and seeps, streams and can often form oases or wetlands.
a. 1509 Istanbul earthquake
b. 1700 Cascadia earthquake
c. Groundwater
d. 1703 Genroku earthquake

34. _____ is the liquid produced when water percolates through any permeable material. It can contain either dissolved or suspended material, or usually both. This liquid is most commonly found in association with landfills, where rain percolates through the waste and reacts with the products of decomposition, chemicals and other materials in the waste to produce the _____.
a. 1703 Genroku earthquake
b. 1700 Cascadia earthquake
c. 1509 Istanbul earthquake
d. Leachate

35. _____ is a method of controlled disposal of refuse on land. _____ involves natural fermentation brought by microorganisms. It is often employed to reclaim otherwise useless land.

Chapter 16. Waste as a Resource: Waste Management

a. 1703 Genroku earthquake
c. Sanitary landfill
b. 1700 Cascadia earthquake
d. 1509 Istanbul earthquake

36. _____ is a large set of adverse effects upon water bodies such as lakes, rivers, oceans, and groundwater caused by human activities. Although natural phenomena such as volcanoes, algae blooms, storms, and earthquakes also cause major changes in water quality and the ecological status of water, these are not deemed to be pollution. _____ has many causes and characteristics.
   a. 1509 Istanbul earthquake
   c. 1703 Genroku earthquake
   b. 1700 Cascadia earthquake
   d. Water pollution

37. _____ is a quantity expressing the two-dimensional size of a defined part of a surface, typically a region bounded by a closed curve. The term surface _____ refers to the total _____ of the exposed surface of a 3-dimensional solid, such as the sum of the _____s of the exposed sides of a polyhedron. _____ is an important invariant in the differential geometry of surfaces.
   a. Area
   c. AL 333
   b. AASHTO Soil Classification System
   d. AL 129-1

38. _____ is the introduction of substances or energy into the environment, resulting in deleterious effects of such a nature as to endanger human health, harm living resources and ecosystems, and impair or interfere with amenities and other legitimate uses of the environment.
   a. 1700 Cascadia earthquake
   c. Pollution
   b. 1509 Istanbul earthquake
   d. 1703 Genroku earthquake

39. _____ is a sedimentary rock composed largely of the mineral calcite. _____ often contains variable amounts of silica in the form of chert or flint, as well as varying amounts of clay, silt and sand as disseminations, nodules, or layers within the rock. The primary source of the calcite in _____ is most commonly marine organisms. These organisms secrete shells that settle out of the water column and are deposited on ocean floors as pelagic ooze or alternatively is conglomerated in a coral reef.
   a. 1703 Genroku earthquake
   c. 1509 Istanbul earthquake
   b. Limestone
   d. 1700 Cascadia earthquake

40. An _____ is an underground layer of water-bearing permeable rock or unconsolidated materials from which groundwater can be usefully extracted using a water well.
   a. AASHTO Soil Classification System
   c. AL 129-1
   b. AL 333
   d. Aquifer

41. In geology, _____ is a naturally occurring aggregate of minerals and/or mineraloids.

The Earth's outer solid layer, the lithosphere, is made of _____. In general _____s are of three types, namely, igneous, sedimentary, and metamorphic.

   a. 1700 Cascadia earthquake
   c. Rock
   b. 1703 Genroku earthquake
   d. 1509 Istanbul earthquake

Chapter 16. Waste as a Resource: Waste Management

42. A _____ is a bipedal primate belonging to the mammalian species Homo sapiens in the family Hominidae. Compared to other living organisms on Earth, a _____ has a highly developed brain capable of abstract reasoning, language, and introspection.
   a. 1509 Istanbul earthquake
   b. Human
   c. 1703 Genroku earthquake
   d. 1700 Cascadia earthquake

43. _____ is the degradation of land in arid, semi arid and dry sub-humid areas resulting from various climatic variations, but primarily human activities. Current _____ is taking place much faster worldwide than historically and usually arises from the demands of increased populations that settle on the land in order to grow crops and graze animals.
   a. 1703 Genroku earthquake
   b. 1700 Cascadia earthquake
   c. 1509 Istanbul earthquake
   d. Desertification

44. A _____ is a body of water with a current, confined within a bed and banks. _____s are important as conduits in the water cycle, instruments in aquifer recharge, and corridors for fish and wildlife migration.
   a. 1703 Genroku earthquake
   b. 1509 Istanbul earthquake
   c. Stream
   d. 1700 Cascadia earthquake

45. _____ is a layer of gases surrounding the planet Earth and retained by the Earth's gravity, protecting life on Earth by absorbing ultraviolet solar radiation and reducing temperature extremes between day and night.
   a. AL 129-1
   b. AASHTO Soil Classification System
   c. AL 333
   d. Earths atmosphere

46. _____ is a chemical, physical, or biological agent that modifies the natural characteristics of the atmosphere. The atmosphere is a complex, dynamic natural gaseous system that is essential to support life on planet Earth. Stratospheric ozone depletion due to _____ has long been recognized as a threat to human health as well as to the Earth's ecosystems. Worldwide _____ is responsible for large numbers of deaths and cases of respiratory disease.
   a. AL 333
   b. Air pollution
   c. AASHTO Soil Classification System
   d. AL 129-1

47. _____ are dangerous compounds that cause contamination and are dangerous to human health and the environement.
   a. 1700 Cascadia earthquake
   b. 1509 Istanbul earthquake
   c. 1703 Genroku earthquake
   d. Hazardous chemicals

48. The _____ is the portion of Earth between the land surface and the phreatic zone or zone of saturation.
   a. Vadose Zone
   b. 1509 Istanbul earthquake
   c. 1703 Genroku earthquake
   d. 1700 Cascadia earthquake

49. The U.S Environmental Protection Agency defines a _____ as "any substance or mixture of substances intended for preventing, destroying, repelling, or lessening the damage of any pest".
   a. Pesticide
   b. 1700 Cascadia earthquake
   c. 1703 Genroku earthquake
   d. 1509 Istanbul earthquake

50. _____ are artificial channels for water. There are two main types of _____: irrigation _____, which are used for the delivery of water, and waterways, which are transportation _____ used for passage of goods and people, often connected to existing lakes, rivers, or oceans.

a. 1509 Istanbul earthquake
b. 1700 Cascadia earthquake
c. 1703 Genroku earthquake
d. Canals

51. _____ is a neighborhood in Niagara Falls, New York, United States of America. It officially covers 36 square blocks in the far southeastern corner of the city, along 99th Street and Read Avenue. Two bodies of water define the northern and southern boundaries of the neighborhood: Bergholtz Creek to the north and the Niagara River one-quarter mile to the south.
   a. Love Canal
   b. 1700 Cascadia earthquake
   c. 1703 Genroku earthquake
   d. 1509 Istanbul earthquake

52. _____ is a set of massive waterfalls located on the Niagara River, straddling the international border separating the Canadian province of Ontario and the U.S. state of New York. and _____, New York, and renowned both for their beauty and as a valuable source of hydroelectric power.
   a. 1703 Genroku earthquake
   b. 1700 Cascadia earthquake
   c. 1509 Istanbul earthquake
   d. Niagara Falls

53. The _____ is a diverse scientific, social, and political movement for addressing the concerns of environmentalism. The _____ is represented by a range of organizations, from the large to grassroots. Due to its large membership, varying and strong beliefs, and occasionally speculative nature, the _____ is not always united in its goals.
   a. Environmental movement
   b. Amblypoda
   c. Andrija Mohorovičić
   d. Ambulocetus

54. The _____ is an agency of the federal government of the United States charged with protecting human health and with safeguarding the natural environment: air, water, and land.
   a. Andrija Mohorovičić
   b. Amblypoda
   c. Ambulocetus
   d. Environmental Protection Agency

55. The _____ is the list of hazardous waste sites in the United States eligible for long-term remedial action financed under the federal Superfund program. Environmental Protection Agency regulations outline a formal process for assessing hazardous waste sites and placing them on the _____.
   a. 1700 Cascadia earthquake
   b. National Priorities List
   c. 1509 Istanbul earthquake
   d. 1703 Genroku earthquake

56. The _____ enacted in 1976, is a Federal law of the United States It states that RCRA's goals are:to protect the public from harm caused by waste disposal to encourage reuse, reduction, and recycling to clean up spilled or improperly stored wastes.
   a. 1703 Genroku earthquake
   b. 1700 Cascadia earthquake
   c. 1509 Istanbul earthquake
   d. Resource Conservation and Recovery Act

57. The _____ was enacted by the United States Congress in response to the Love Canal disaster. The Act was created to protect people, families, communities and others from heavily contaminated toxic waste sites that have been abandoned. It paid for toxic waste cleanups at sites where no other responsible parties could pay for a cleanup by assessing a tax on petroleum and chemical industries.

Chapter 16. Waste as a Resource: Waste Management

a. 1509 Istanbul earthquake

b. 1700 Cascadia earthquake

c. 1703 Genroku earthquake

d. Comprehensive Environmental Response, Compensation, and Liability Act

58. An _____ is the manufacturing of a good or service within a category.
    a. Industry
    b. AL 129-1
    c. AASHTO Soil Classification System
    d. AL 333

59. An _____ is intended to quantify environmental performance and environmental position. An _____ report ideally contains a statement of environmental performance and environmental position, and may also aim to define what needs to be done to sustain or improve on indicators of such performance and position.
    a. AL 333
    b. AASHTO Soil Classification System
    c. AL 129-1
    d. Environmental audit

60. The _____ was a nuclear reactor accident in the Chernobyl Nuclear Power Plant in the Soviet Union. It was the worst nuclear power plant disaster ever and the only level 7 instance on the International Nuclear Event Scale. It resulted in a severe release of radioactivity into the environment following a massive power excursion which destroyed the reactor.
    a. 1509 Istanbul earthquake
    b. Chernobyl disaster
    c. 1703 Genroku earthquake
    d. 1700 Cascadia earthquake

61. An _____ is an assessment of the likely influence a project may have on the environment. The purpose of the assessment is to ensure that decision-makers consider _____s before deciding whether to proceed with new projects.
    a. AL 333
    b. Environmental impact
    c. AASHTO Soil Classification System
    d. AL 129-1

62. _____ is a concept for disposing of High Level Radioactive Waste from Nuclear reactors. The system seeks to place the waste as much as five kilometers beneath the surface of the Earth and relies primarily on the immense natural geological barrier to do most of the work of confining the waste safely and permanently so that it will never pose a threat to the environment.
    a. 1509 Istanbul earthquake
    b. 1700 Cascadia earthquake
    c. 1703 Genroku earthquake
    d. Deep waste disposal

63. An _____ is the result from the sudden release of stored energy in the Earth's crust that creates seismic waves. At the Earth's surface, _____s may manifest themselves by a shaking or displacement of the ground. An _____ is caused by tectonic plates getting stuck and putting a strain on the ground. The strain becomes so great that rocks give way by breaking and sliding along fault planes.
    a. AASHTO Soil Classification System
    b. Earthquake
    c. AL 333
    d. AL 129-1

64. The _____ was a United States chemical weapons manufacturing center located in the Denver Metropolitan Area in Commerce City, Colorado. The site was operated by the United States Army throughout the later 20th century and was controversial among local residents until its closure.
    a. 1703 Genroku earthquake
    b. 1700 Cascadia earthquake
    c. 1509 Istanbul earthquake
    d. Rocky Mountain Arsenal

65. _____ systems are a diverse group of air pollution control devices that can be used to remove particulates and/or gases from industrial exhaust streams. Recently, the term is used to describe systems that inject a dry reagent or slurry into a dirty exhaust stream to "scrub out" acid gases. _____s are one of the primary devices that control gaseous emissions, especially acid gases.
   a. Scrubber
   b. 1509 Istanbul earthquake
   c. 1703 Genroku earthquake
   d. 1700 Cascadia earthquake

66. _____ is a fossil fuel formed in swamp ecosystems where plant remains were saved by water and mud from oxidization and biodegradation. It is a sedimentary rock, but the harder forms, such as anthracite _____, can be regarded as metamorphic rocks because of later exposure to elevated temperature and pressure. It is composed primarily of carbon along with assorted other elements, including sulfur.
   a. 1703 Genroku earthquake
   b. 1700 Cascadia earthquake
   c. 1509 Istanbul earthquake
   d. Coal

Chapter 17. Air Pollution

1. _____ is a chemical compound with the formula SO2. This important gas is the main product from the combustion of sulfur compounds and is of significant environmental concern. Sulphur dioxide is produced by volcanoes and in various industrial processes.
   a. 1703 Genroku earthquake
   b. Sulfur dioxide
   c. 1700 Cascadia earthquake
   d. 1509 Istanbul earthquake

2. _____ is a layer of gases surrounding the planet Earth and retained by the Earth's gravity, protecting life on Earth by absorbing ultraviolet solar radiation and reducing temperature extremes between day and night.
   a. AASHTO Soil Classification System
   b. AL 129-1
   c. AL 333
   d. Earths atmosphere

3. _____ is a chemical, physical, or biological agent that modifies the natural characteristics of the atmosphere. The atmosphere is a complex, dynamic natural gaseous system that is essential to support life on planet Earth. Stratospheric ozone depletion due to _____ has long been recognized as a threat to human health as well as to the Earth's ecosystems. Worldwide _____ is responsible for large numbers of deaths and cases of respiratory disease.
   a. AASHTO Soil Classification System
   b. AL 129-1
   c. AL 333
   d. Air pollution

4. _____ is the introduction of substances or energy into the environment, resulting in deleterious effects of such a nature as to endanger human health, harm living resources and ecosystems, and impair or interfere with amenities and other legitimate uses of the environment.
   a. 1700 Cascadia earthquake
   b. Pollution
   c. 1509 Istanbul earthquake
   d. 1703 Genroku earthquake

5. _____ is a kind of air pollution; the word "_____" is a portmanteau of smoke and fog. Classic _____ results from large amounts of coal burning in an area and is caused by a mixture of smoke and sulphur dioxide.
   a. 1700 Cascadia earthquake
   b. 1703 Genroku earthquake
   c. Smog
   d. 1509 Istanbul earthquake

6. _____ is the chemical element in the periodic table that has the symbol S and atomic number 16. It is an abundant, tasteless, odorless, multivalent non-metal. _____, in its native form, is a yellow crystaline solid. In nature, it can be found as the pure element or as sulfide and sulfate minerals.
   a. Thulium
   b. Zinc
   c. Sulfur
   d. Vinyl

7. An _____ is traditionally considered any chemical compound that, when dissolved in water, gives a solution with a hydrogen ion activity greater than in pure water, i.e. a pH less than 7.0. That approximates the modern definition of Johannes Nicolaus Brønsted and Martin Lowry, who independently defined an _____ as a compound which donates a hydrogen ion to another compound. Common examples include acetic _____ and sulfuric _____. Acid/base systems are different from redox reactions in that there is no change in oxidation state.
   a. AL 129-1
   b. AASHTO Soil Classification System
   c. AL 333
   d. Acid

8. The term _____ is commonly used to mean the deposition of acidic components in rain, snow, dew, or dry particles. _____ occurs when sulfur dioxide and nitrogen oxides are emitted into the atmosphere, undergo chemical transformations and are absorbed by water droplets in clouds. The droplets then fall to earth as rain, snow, mist, dry dust, hail, or sleet. This increases the acidity of the soil, and affects the chemical balance of lakes and streams.

Chapter 17. Air Pollution

   a. AASHTO Soil Classification System
   b. AL 333
   c. Acid precipitation
   d. AL 129-1

9. _____ is the largest city in the state of California and the American West as well as second largest in the United States. Often abbreviated as L.A. and nicknamed The City of Angels, _____ is rated an alpha world city, has an estimated population of 3.8 million and spans over 498.3 square miles (1,290.6 km who hail from all over the globe and speak 224 different languages. _____ is the seat of _____ County, the most populated and one of the most diverse counties in the United States.
   a. Coachella Valley
   b. 1700 Cascadia earthquake
   c. 1509 Istanbul earthquake
   d. Los Angeles

10. _____ is the geological process whereby material is added to a landform. This is the process by which wind and water create a sediment deposit, through the laying down of granular material that has been eroded and transported from another geographical location.
   a. 1700 Cascadia earthquake
   b. 1509 Istanbul earthquake
   c. 1703 Genroku earthquake
   d. Deposition

11. _____ is a quantity expressing the two-dimensional size of a defined part of a surface, typically a region bounded by a closed curve. The term surface _____ refers to the total _____ of the exposed surface of a 3-dimensional solid, such as the sum of the _____ s of the exposed sides of a polyhedron. _____ is an important invariant in the differential geometry of surfaces.
   a. AASHTO Soil Classification System
   b. AL 129-1
   c. AL 333
   d. Area

12. _____ is a chemical element in the periodic table that has the symbol C and atomic number 6. An abundant nonmetallic, tetravalent element, _____ has several allotropic forms.
   a. 1509 Istanbul earthquake
   b. 1700 Cascadia earthquake
   c. Carbon
   d. 1703 Genroku earthquake

13. _____, with the chemical formula CO, is a colorless, odorless, and tasteless gas. It is the product of the incomplete combustion of carbon-containing compounds, notably in internal-combustion engines. It has significant fuel value, burning in air with a characteristic blue flame, producing carbon dioxide.
   a. 1700 Cascadia earthquake
   b. 1703 Genroku earthquake
   c. 1509 Istanbul earthquake
   d. Carbon monoxide

14. _____ is vibration transmitted through a solid, liquid composed of frequencies within the range of hearing and of a level sufficiently strong to be heard. Human ear

For humans, hearing is limited to frequencies between about 20 Hz and 20,000 Hz (20 kHz), with the upper limit generally decreasing with age. Other species have a different range of hearing.

   a. 1509 Istanbul earthquake
   b. 1703 Genroku earthquake
   c. 1700 Cascadia earthquake
   d. Sound

Chapter 17. Air Pollution

15. In organic chemistry, a _____ is an organic compound consisting entirely of hydrogen and carbon. With relation to chemical terminology, aromatic _____s or arenes, alkanes, alkenes and alkyne-based compounds composed entirely of carbon or hydrogen are referred to as "Pure" _____s, whereas other _____s with bonded compounds or impurities of sulphur or nitrogen, are referred to as "impure", and remain somewhat erroneously referred to as _____s.
    a. 1509 Istanbul earthquake
    b. Hydrocarbon
    c. 1703 Genroku earthquake
    d. 1700 Cascadia earthquake

16. _____ is a triatomic molecule, consisting of three oxygen atoms. It is an allotrope of oxygen that is much less stable than the diatomic species O2. Ground-level _____ is an air pollutant with harmful effects on the respiratory systems of animals. On the other hand, _____ in the upper atmosphere protects living organisms by preventing damaging ultraviolet light from reaching the Earth's surface.
    a. AASHTO Soil Classification System
    b. AL 333
    c. AL 129-1
    d. Ozone

17. _____s, alternatively referred to as _____ matter (PM) or fine particles, are tiny particles of solid or liquid suspended in a gas or liquid. In contrast, aerosol refers to particles and the gas together. Sources of _____ matter can be man made or natural.
    a. 1703 Genroku earthquake
    b. Particulate
    c. 1509 Istanbul earthquake
    d. 1700 Cascadia earthquake

18. _____, a sub-discipline of chemistry, is the study of the interactions between atoms, small molecules, and light.
    a. 1703 Genroku earthquake
    b. 1700 Cascadia earthquake
    c. 1509 Istanbul earthquake
    d. Photochemistry

19. _____ are organic chemical compounds that have high enough vapour pressures under normal conditions to significantly vaporize and enter the atmosphere.
    a. Volatile organic compounds
    b. 1703 Genroku earthquake
    c. 1509 Istanbul earthquake
    d. 1700 Cascadia earthquake

20. A _____ is a chemical substance of two or more different chemically bonded chemical elements, with a fixed ratio determining the composition. The ratio of each element is usually expressed by chemical formula.
    a. 1509 Istanbul earthquake
    b. 1703 Genroku earthquake
    c. 1700 Cascadia earthquake
    d. Chemical compound

21. _____ is the substance of which physical objects are composed. _____ can be solid, liquid, plasma or gas. It constitutes the observable universe.
    a. 1509 Istanbul earthquake
    b. 1700 Cascadia earthquake
    c. 1703 Genroku earthquake
    d. Matter

22. _____ is a chemical element which has the symbol N and atomic number 7 in the periodic table. Elemental _____ is a colorless, odorless, tasteless and mostly inert diatomic gas at standard conditions, constituting 78.08% percent of Earth's atmosphere.
    a. 1700 Cascadia earthquake
    b. 1703 Genroku earthquake
    c. 1509 Istanbul earthquake
    d. Nitrogen

Chapter 17. Air Pollution

23. _____ farming is a form of agriculture that excludes the use of synthetic fertilizers and pesticides, plant growth regulators, livestock feed additives, and genetically modified organisms.
   a. AASHTO Soil Classification System
   b. AL 333
   c. Organic
   d. AL 129-1

24. An _____ is any member of a large class of chemical compounds whose molecules contain carbon.
   a. AL 333
   b. AL 129-1
   c. Organic compound
   d. AASHTO Soil Classification System

25. _____ are chemical compounds that readily transfer oxygen atoms or substances that gain electrons in a redox chemical reaction.
   a. AL 129-1
   b. AASHTO Soil Classification System
   c. Oxidants
   d. AL 333

26. An _____ is a chemical compound containing an oxygen atom and other elements. Most of the earth's crust consists of them. They result when elements are oxidized by air.
   a. AASHTO Soil Classification System
   b. Oxide
   c. AL 333
   d. AL 129-1

27. _____ are tiny particles of solid or liquid suspended in a gas. They range in size from less than 10 nanometres to more than 100 micrometres in diameter.
   a. Particulates
   b. 1700 Cascadia earthquake
   c. 1703 Genroku earthquake
   d. 1509 Istanbul earthquake

28. Pollution is the introduction of contaminants into an environment that causes instability, disorder, harm or discomfort to the physical systems or living organisms. Pollution can take the form of chemical substances, or energy, such as noise, heat, or light energy. _____, the elements of pollution, can be foreign substances or energies, or naturally occurring; when naturally occurring, they are considered contaminants when they exceed natural levels.
   a. 1700 Cascadia earthquake
   b. 1703 Genroku earthquake
   c. 1509 Istanbul earthquake
   d. Pollutants

29. _____ is a fossil fuel formed in swamp ecosystems where plant remains were saved by water and mud from oxidization and biodegradation. It is a sedimentary rock, but the harder forms, such as anthracite _____, can be regarded as metamorphic rocks because of later exposure to elevated temperature and pressure. It is composed primarily of carbon along with assorted other elements, including sulfur.
   a. Coal
   b. 1700 Cascadia earthquake
   c. 1703 Genroku earthquake
   d. 1509 Istanbul earthquake

30. In physics, _____ is a scalar physical quantity that describes the amount of work that can be performed by a force. _____ is an attribute of objects and systems that is subject to a conservation law. Several different forms of _____ exist to explain all known natural phenomena.
   a. Energy
   b. AASHTO Soil Classification System
   c. AL 333
   d. AL 129-1

Chapter 17. Air Pollution

31. Consumption of a _____ requires resources and contributes to air and water pollution. In the industrialized world the development of a _____ has become essential for agriculture, transportation, waste collection, information technology, communications that have become prerequisites of a developed society.
   a. AASHTO Soil Classification System
   b. Energy resource
   c. AL 333
   d. AL 129-1

32. _____s are the mineralized or otherwise preserved remains or traces of animals, plants, and other organisms. The totality of _____s, both discovered and undiscovered, and their placement in fossiliferous rock formations and sedimentary layers is known as the _____ record.
   a. 1700 Cascadia earthquake
   b. 1509 Istanbul earthquake
   c. 1703 Genroku earthquake
   d. Fossil

33. _____ are hydrocarbons, primarily coal and petroleum, formed from the fossilized remains of dead plants and animals by exposure to heat and pressure in the Earth's crust over hundreds of millions of years. The burning of _____ by humans is the largest source of emissions of carbon dioxide, which is one of the greenhouse gases that enhances radiative forcing and contributes to global warming.
   a. 1703 Genroku earthquake
   b. 1700 Cascadia earthquake
   c. 1509 Istanbul earthquake
   d. Fossil fuels

34. _____$_x$ is a generic term for mono-_____ (_____ and _____$_2$.) These oxides are produced during combustion, especially combustion at high temperatures.

At ambient temperatures, the oxygen and nitrogen gases in air will not react with each other.

   a. 1509 Istanbul earthquake
   b. 1700 Cascadia earthquake
   c. 1703 Genroku earthquake
   d. Nitrogen oxides

35. In inorganic chemistry, a _____ is a salt of sulfuric acid
   a. Tungsten
   b. Radon
   c. Xenon
   d. Sulfate

36. _____ is a strong mineral acid. It is soluble in water at all concentrations. _____ has many applications, and is one of the top products of the chemical industry. Principal uses include ore processing, fertilizer manufacturing, oil refining, wastewater processing, and chemical synthesis.
   a. 1509 Istanbul earthquake
   b. 1703 Genroku earthquake
   c. 1700 Cascadia earthquake
   d. Sulfuric acid

37. _____ is the iron-containing oxygen-transport metalloprotein in the red blood cells of vertebrates.

In mammals, the protein makes up about 97% of the red blood cell's dry content, and around 35% of the total content (including water.) _____ transports oxygen from the lungs or gills to the rest of the body where it releases the oxygen for cell use.

   a. 1700 Cascadia earthquake
   b. 1509 Istanbul earthquake
   c. 1703 Genroku earthquake
   d. Hemoglobin

Chapter 17. Air Pollution

38. A _____ is a salt of nitric acid with an ion composed of one nitrogen and three oxygen atoms. In freshwater or estuarine systems close to land, _____ can reach high levels that can potentially cause the death of fish. Water quality may also be affected through ground water resources that have a high number of septic systems in a watershed.
   a. 1700 Cascadia earthquake
   b. 1703 Genroku earthquake
   c. 1509 Istanbul earthquake
   d. Nitrate

39. The chemical compound _____ is an aqueous solution of hydrogen nitrate. It is a highly corrosive and toxic acid that can cause severe burns. Colorless when pure, older samples tend to acquire a yellow cast due to the accumulation of oxides of nitrogen.
   a. 1509 Istanbul earthquake
   b. Nitric acid
   c. 1703 Genroku earthquake
   d. 1700 Cascadia earthquake

40. The _____ is the part of the Earth's atmosphere which contains relatively high concentrations of ozone .
   a. Ozone layer
   b. AASHTO Soil Classification System
   c. AL 333
   d. AL 129-1

41. _____ is a chemical element in the periodic table that has the symbol H and atomic number 1. At standard temperature and pressure it is a colorless, odorless, nonmetallic, univalent, tasteless, highly flammable diatomic gas.
   a. 1700 Cascadia earthquake
   b. 1703 Genroku earthquake
   c. Hydrogen
   d. 1509 Istanbul earthquake

42. _____ is a chemical compound with the formula HF. Together with hydrofluoric acid, it is the principal industrial source of fluorine and hence the precursor to many important compounds including pharmaceuticals and polymers . HF is widely used in the petrochemical industry and a component of many superacids.
   a. 1509 Istanbul earthquake
   b. 1700 Cascadia earthquake
   c. Hydrogen fluoride
   d. 1703 Genroku earthquake

43. _____ is the chemical compound with the formula H2S. This colorless, toxic and flammable gas is responsible for the foul odor of rotten eggs and flatulence. It often results from the bacterial break down of organic matter in the absence of oxygen, such as in swamps and sewers . It also occurs in volcanic gases, natural gas and some well waters.
   a. 1703 Genroku earthquake
   b. 1700 Cascadia earthquake
   c. 1509 Istanbul earthquake
   d. Hydrogen sulfide

44. _____, officially the Republic of _____, is a country in South Asia. It is the seventh-largest country by geographical area, the second-most populous country, and the most populous democracy in the world. Bounded by the Indian Ocean on the south, the Arabian Sea on the west, and the Bay of Bengal on the east, _____ has a coastline of 7,517 kilometers.
   a. Isthmus
   b. Informal sector
   c. India
   d. Imam

45. _____ is the reduced form of fluorine. Both organic and inorganic compounds containing the element fluorine are considered _____s. As a halogen, fluorine forms a monovalent ion. The range of _____s is considerable as fluorine forms compounds with all elements except He, Ne, and Ar. _____s range from severe toxins such as sarin to life-saving pharmaceuticals such as efavirenz and from refractory materials such as calcium _____ to highly reactive sulfur tetrafluoride.

Chapter 17. Air Pollution

a. 1509 Istanbul earthquake
b. 1700 Cascadia earthquake
c. 1703 Genroku earthquake
d. Fluoride

46. _____ are a major group of living things including familiar organisms such as trees, flowers, herbs, bushes, grasses, vines, ferns, and mosses.
    a. 1703 Genroku earthquake
    b. 1700 Cascadia earthquake
    c. 1509 Istanbul earthquake
    d. Plants

47. The term _____ refers to several types of chemical compounds containing sulfur in its lowest oxidation number of −2.
    a. 1700 Cascadia earthquake
    b. 1509 Istanbul earthquake
    c. 1703 Genroku earthquake
    d. Sulfide

48. _____ is the production of food, feed, fiber, fuel and other goods by the systematic raizing of plants and animals.
    a. AL 129-1
    b. AL 333
    c. Agriculture
    d. AASHTO Soil Classification System

49. The Republic of _____, is a country in Southeast Asia. Comprising 17,508 islands, it is the world's largest archipelagic state. With a population of 222 million people in 2006, it is the world's fourth most populous country and the most populous Muslim-majority nation; however, no reference is made to Islam in the Indonesian constitution.
    a. Indonesia
    b. AL 333
    c. AASHTO Soil Classification System
    d. AL 129-1

50. _____ was discovered in 1888 as an ester of isocyanic acid. As a highly toxic and irritating material, it is hazardous to human health.
    a. 1703 Genroku earthquake
    b. 1700 Cascadia earthquake
    c. 1509 Istanbul earthquake
    d. Methyl isocyanate

51. A _____ is an area with a high density of trees, historically, a wooded area set aside for hunting. These plant communities cover large areas of the globe and function as animal habitats, hydrologic flow modulators, and soil conservers, constituting one of the most important aspects of the Earth's biosphere.
    a. 1509 Istanbul earthquake
    b. 1703 Genroku earthquake
    c. 1700 Cascadia earthquake
    d. Forest

52. A _____ is an uncontrolled fire that pops up fire often occurring in wildland areas, but which can also consume houses or agricultural resources. Common causes include lightning, human carelessness, arson, volcano eruption, and pyroclastic cloud from active volcano. Heat waves, droughts, and cyclical climate changes such as El Niño can also have a dramatic effect on the risk of wildfires.
    a. 1509 Istanbul earthquake
    b. 1703 Genroku earthquake
    c. 1700 Cascadia earthquake
    d. Forest fire

53. _____ is the artificial application of water to the soil usually for assisting in growing crops. In crop production it is mainly used to replace missing rainfall in periods of drought, but also to protect plants against frost.
    a. AL 333
    b. AASHTO Soil Classification System
    c. AL 129-1
    d. Irrigation

Chapter 17. Air Pollution

54. _____ refers to the cutting and burning of forests or woodlands to create fields for agriculture or pasture for livestock, or for a variety of other purposes.
   a. 1703 Genroku earthquake
   b. 1700 Cascadia earthquake
   c. 1509 Istanbul earthquake
   d. Slash-and-burn

55. The _____ is a standardized indicator of the air quality in a given location. It measures mainly ground-level ozone and particulates but may also include sulphur dioxide, and nitrogen dioxide. Various agencies around the world measure such indices, though definitions may change between places.
   a. Air Quality Index
   b. AL 333
   c. AASHTO Soil Classification System
   d. AL 129-1

56. _____ describes any of a group of minerals that can be fibrous, many of which are metamorphic and are hydrous magnesium silicates.
   a. Asbestos
   b. AL 129-1
   c. AASHTO Soil Classification System
   d. AL 333

57. In meteorology, an _____ is a deviation from the normal change of a property with altitude. It almost always refers to temperature, i.e., an increase in temperature with height, or to the layer within which such an increase occurs.
   a. AASHTO Soil Classification System
   b. AL 129-1
   c. AL 333
   d. Atmospheric inversion

58. _____, is the increase in concentration of a substance, such as the pesticide DDT, that occurs in a food chain as a consequence of:

- Food chain energetics
- Low (or nonexistent) rate of excretion/degradation of the substance.

Although sometimes used interchangeably with 'bioaccumulation,' an important distinction is drawn between the two, and with bioconcentration.

- Bioaccumulation occurs within a trophic level, and is the increase in concentration of a substance in an individuals' tissues due to uptake from food and sediments in an aquatic milieu.
- Bioconcentration is defined as occurring when uptake from the water is greater than excretion (Landrum and Fisher, 1999)

Thus bioconcentration and bioaccumulation occur within an organism, and _____ occurs across trophic (food chain) levels.

Lipid soluble (lipophilic) substances cannot be excreted in urine, a water-based medium, and so accumulate in fatty tissues of an organism if the organism lacks enzymes to degrade them. When eaten by another organism, fats are absorbed in the gut, carrying the substance, which then accumulates in the fats of the predator. Since at each level of the food chain there is a lot of energy loss, a predator must consume many prey, including all of their lipophilic substances.

Chapter 17. Air Pollution

a. 1700 Cascadia earthquake
c. 1703 Genroku earthquake
b. Biomagnification
d. 1509 Istanbul earthquake

59. _____ is a chemical element in the periodic table that has the symbol Cd and atomic number 48. A relatively rare, soft, bluish-white, toxic transition metal, _____ occurs with zinc ores and is used largely in batteries.
a. 1700 Cascadia earthquake
c. 1703 Genroku earthquake
b. 1509 Istanbul earthquake
d. Cadmium

60. Fly ash is one of the residues generated in the combustion of coal. Fly ash is generally captured from the chimneys of coal-fired power plants, and is one of two types of ash that jointly are known as _____; the other, bottom ash, is removed from the bottom of coal furnaces. Depending upon the source and makeup of the coal being burned, the components of fly ash vary considerably, but all fly ash includes substantial amounts of silicon dioxide (SiO_2) (both amorphous and crystalline) and calcium oxide (CaO.)
a. 1703 Genroku earthquake
c. 1700 Cascadia earthquake
b. Coal ash
d. 1509 Istanbul earthquake

61. In meteorology, an _____ is a deviation from the normal change of an atmospheric property with altitude. It almost always refers to temperature.
a. AASHTO Soil Classification System
c. AL 129-1
b. AL 333
d. Inversion

62. _____ is a chemical element in the periodic table that has the symbol Pb and atomic number 82. A soft, heavy, toxic and malleable poor metal, _____ is bluish white when freshly cut but tarnishes to dull gray when exposed to air. _____ is used in building construction, _____-acid batteries, bullets and shot, and is part of solder, pewter, and fusible alloys.
a. 1509 Istanbul earthquake
c. Lead
b. 1703 Genroku earthquake
d. 1700 Cascadia earthquake

63. _____ is the capital and largest urban area of both England and the United Kingdom. An important settlement for two millennia, _____'s history goes back to its founding by the Romans. Since its foundation, _____ has been part of many movements and phenomena throughout history, including the English Renaissance, the Industrial Revolution, and the Gothic Revival.
a. 1509 Istanbul earthquake
c. Barcelona
b. 1700 Cascadia earthquake
d. London

64. _____ is the interdisciplinary scientific study of the atmosphere that focuses on weather processes and forecasting.
a. 1700 Cascadia earthquake
c. 1509 Istanbul earthquake
b. 1703 Genroku earthquake
d. Meteorology

65. _____ is a physical property of a system that underlies the common notions of hot and cold; something that is hotter has the greater _____. Temperature is one of the principal parameters of thermodynamics.
a. Temperature
c. 1509 Istanbul earthquake
b. 1703 Genroku earthquake
d. 1700 Cascadia earthquake

66. _____, is an increase in temperature with height, or to the layer within which such an increase occurs.

Chapter 17. Air Pollution

a. 1700 Cascadia earthquake
c. 1703 Genroku earthquake
b. 1509 Istanbul earthquake
d. Temperature inversion

67. _____ is the study of Earth's surface features or those of other planets, moons, and asteroids
a. 1700 Cascadia earthquake
c. 1703 Genroku earthquake
b. 1509 Istanbul earthquake
d. Topography

68. _____ refers to the process of breeding such an animal, often with the intention of creating offspring that share the traits of both parent lineages. An outcross is a type of _____ used within a purebred breed to increase the genetic diversity within the breed.
a. 1700 Cascadia earthquake
c. 1703 Genroku earthquake
b. 1509 Istanbul earthquake
d. Crossbreeding

69. The oceanic or limnological _____ is a layer in which active turbulence has homogenized some range of depths. The surface of it is a layer where this turbulence is generated by winds, cooling, or processes such as evaporation or sea ice formation which result in an increase in salinity.
a. 1700 Cascadia earthquake
c. 1509 Istanbul earthquake
b. 1703 Genroku earthquake
d. Mixed layer

70. The _____ is the coastal sediment-filled plain located between the peninsular and transverse ranges in southern California in the United States containing the central part of the city of Los Angeles as well as its southern and southeastern suburbs (both in Los Angeles and Orange counties.) It is approximately 35 miles (56 km) long and 15 miles (24 km) wide, bounded on the north by the Santa Monica Mountains and Puente Hills, and on the east and south by the Santa Ana Mountains and San Joaquin Hills. The Palos Verdes Peninsula, formerly an island, marks the outer edge of the basin along the coast.
a. 1509 Istanbul earthquake
c. 1703 Genroku earthquake
b. Los Angeles Basin
d. 1700 Cascadia earthquake

71. Smog is a kind of air pollution; the word 'smog' is a portmanteau of smoke and fog. Classic smog results from large amounts of coal burning in an area caused by a mixture of smoke and sulfur dioxide. Modern smog does not usually come from coal but from vehicular and industrial emissions that are acted on in the atmosphere by sunlight to form secondary pollutants that also combine with the primary emissions to form _____.
a. 1700 Cascadia earthquake
c. Flue gas stack
b. Photochemical smog
d. 1509 Istanbul earthquake

72. The _____ is the movement of air into and out of buildings, chimneys, flue gas stacks, or other containers, and is driven by buoyancy. Buoyancy occurs due to a difference in indoor-to-outdoor air density resulting from temperature and moisture differences.
a. 1700 Cascadia earthquake
c. 1703 Genroku earthquake
b. 1509 Istanbul earthquake
d. Stack effect

73. An _____ or motor car is a wheeled motor vehicle for transporting passengers, which also carries its own engine or motor. Most definitions of the term specify that _____s are designed to run primarily on roads, to have seating for one to eight people, to typically have four wheels, and to be constructed principally for the transport of people rather than goods. However, the term '_____' is far from precise, because there are many types of vehicles that do similar tasks.

a. Automobile
b. AL 129-1
c. Feebate
d. AASHTO Soil Classification System

74. _____ is radiant energy emitted by the sun from a nuclear fusion reaction that creates electromagnetic energy. The spectrum of _____ is close to that of a black body with a temperature of about 5800 K. About half of the radiation is in the visible short-wave part of the electromagnetic spectrum. The other half is mostly in the near-infrared part, with some in the ultraviolet part of the spectrum.
a. 1703 Genroku earthquake
b. 1509 Istanbul earthquake
c. 1700 Cascadia earthquake
d. Solar radiation

75. _____, as used in physics, is energy in the form of waves or moving subatomic particles emitted by an atom or other body as it changes from a higher energy state to a lower energy state. _____ can be classified as ionizing or non-ionizing _____, depending on its effect on atomic matter. The most common use of the word "_____" refers to ionizing _____. Ionizing _____ has enough energy to ionize atoms or molecules while non-ionizing _____ does not. Radioactive material is a physical material that emits ionizing _____.
a. Supersaturation
b. Radiation
c. Synthetic aperture radar
d. Supercritical fluid

76. A _____ is an urban area with a high population and a particular administrative, legal, or historical status.

Large industrialized cities generally have advanced systems for sanitation, utilities, land usage, housing, and transportation and more. This close proximity greatly facilitates interaction between people and firms, benefiting both parties in the process.

a. 1509 Istanbul earthquake
b. 1700 Cascadia earthquake
c. City
d. 1703 Genroku earthquake

77. The United Mexican States, commonly known as _____, is a federal constitutional republic in North America. It is bordered on the north by the United States; on the south and west by the North Pacific Ocean; on the southeast by Guatemala, Belize, and the Caribbean Sea; and on the east by the Gulf of _____. The United Mexican States are a federation comprising thirty-one states and a federal district, the capital _____ City, whose metropolitan area is one of the world's most populous.
a. Amblypoda
b. Ambulocetus
c. Mexico
d. Andrija Mohorovičić

78. _____ is the capital city of Mexico. It is the most important economic, industrial and cultural center in the country, and the most populous city with over 8,836,045 inhabitants in 2008. Greater _____ incorporates 59 adjacent municipalities of Mexico State and 1 municipality of the state of Hidalgo, according to the most recent definition agreed upon by the federal and state governments.
a. Mexico City
b. 1703 Genroku earthquake
c. 1509 Istanbul earthquake
d. 1700 Cascadia earthquake

Chapter 17. Air Pollution

79. _____ are requirements that set specific limits to the amount of pollutants that can be released into the environment. Many _____ focus on regulating pollutants released by automobiles and other powered vehicles but they can also regulate emissions from industry, power plants, small equipment such as lawn mowers and diesel generators. Frequent policy alternatives to _____ are technology standards (which mandate the use of a specific technology) and emission trading.
   a. AASHTO Soil Classification System
   b. AL 129-1
   c. AL 333
   d. Emissions standards

80. _____, is an occupational lung disease caused by the inhalation of coal dust, characterized by formation of nodular fibrotic changes in lungs.
   a. 1509 Istanbul earthquake
   b. Black lung disease
   c. 1703 Genroku earthquake
   d. 1700 Cascadia earthquake

81. _____ is a class of diseases in which a group of cells display the traits of uncontrolled growth growth and division beyond the normal limits, invasion intrusion on and destruction of adjacent tissues, and sometimes metastasis spread to other locations in the body via lymph or blood. These three malignant properties of _____s differentiate them from benign tumors, which are self-limited, do not invade or metastasize. Most _____s form a tumor but some, like leukemia, do not.
   a. 1700 Cascadia earthquake
   b. 1509 Istanbul earthquake
   c. Cancer
   d. 1703 Genroku earthquake

82. _____ comprises those aspects of human health, including quality of life, that are determined by physical, chemical, biological, social, and psychosocial factors in the natural environment.
   a. AL 333
   b. AL 129-1
   c. AASHTO Soil Classification System
   d. Environmental health

83. _____ is an intermediate in the oxidation or combustion of methane as well as other carbon compounds. It can be found in the smoke from forest fires, in automobile exhaust, and in tobacco smoke. In the atmosphere, it is produced by the action of sunlight and oxygen on atmospheric methane and other hydrocarbons.
   a. 1700 Cascadia earthquake
   b. Formaldehyde
   c. 1703 Genroku earthquake
   d. 1509 Istanbul earthquake

84. _____ refers to chemical or biological contaminants in indoor air. Indoor Air Quality may be compromised by microbial contaminants, chemicals, any mass or energy stressor that can induce health effects.
   a. AL 129-1
   b. Exhaust gas
   c. Indoor air pollution
   d. AASHTO Soil Classification System

85. _____ is a disease of uncontrolled cell growth in tissues of the lung. This growth may lead to metastasis, which is invasion of adjacent tissue and infiltration beyond the lungs. The vast majority of primary _____s are carcinomas of the lung, derived from epithelial cells.
   a. 1509 Istanbul earthquake
   b. Lung cancer
   c. 1703 Genroku earthquake
   d. 1700 Cascadia earthquake

Chapter 17. Air Pollution

86. _____ is a province located in the central part of Canada, the largest by population and second largest, after Quebec, in total area. _____ is bordered by the provinces of Manitoba to the west and Quebec to the east, and the U.S. states of Minnesota, Michigan, Ohio, Pennsylvania, and New York to the south. Most of _____'s borders with the United States are natural, starting at the Lake of the Woods and continuing through four of the Great Lakes: Superior, Huron, Erie, and _____, then along the Saint Lawrence River near Cornwall.
- a. Andrija Mohorovičić
- b. Amblypoda
- c. Ambulocetus
- d. Ontario

87. _____ is a chemical element in the periodic table that has the symbol Rn and atomic number 86. A radioactive noble gas that is formed by the decay of radium, _____ is one of the heaviest gases and is considered to be a health hazard.
- a. Radon
- b. Tantalum
- c. Ytterbium
- d. Selenium

88. The general effects of _____ to the human body are due to its radioactivity and consequent risk of radiation-induced cancer.
- a. 1509 Istanbul earthquake
- b. Radon emissions
- c. 1703 Genroku earthquake
- d. 1700 Cascadia earthquake

89. _____ is a form of extractive metallurgy. The main use of _____ is to produce a metal from its ore.
- a. Smelting
- b. 1703 Genroku earthquake
- c. 1509 Istanbul earthquake
- d. 1700 Cascadia earthquake

90. A _____ or medical condition is an abnormal condition of an organism that impairs bodily functions and can be deadly. It is also defined as a way of the body harming itself in an abnormal way, associated with specific symptoms and signs.

In human beings,'_____' is often used more broadly to refer to any condition that causes extreme pain, dysfunction, distress, social problems, and/or death to the person afflicted, or similar problems for those in contact with the person.

- a. 1509 Istanbul earthquake
- b. 1700 Cascadia earthquake
- c. Black lung disease
- d. Disease

91. A _____ uses cyclonic action to separate dust particles from the gas stream.
- a. 1700 Cascadia earthquake
- b. 1703 Genroku earthquake
- c. 1509 Istanbul earthquake
- d. Centrifugal collector

92. _____ is a reduction technique used in most gasoline and diesel engines.It works by recirculating a portion of an engine's exhaust gas back to the engine cylinders. Intermixing the incoming air with recirculated exhaust gas dilutes the mix with inert gas, lowering the adiabatic flame temperature and in diesel engines reducing the amount of excess oxygen. Because nitrogen oxide and nitrogen dioxide formation progresses much faster at high temperatures, it serves to limit the generation of nitrogen oxide and nitrogen dioxide. nitrogen oxide and nitrogen dioxide is primarily formed when a mix of nitrogen and oxygen is subjected to high temperatures

Chapter 17. Air Pollution

    a. Exhaust gas recirculation
    c. AL 333
    b. AL 129-1
    d. AASHTO Soil Classification System

93. The _____ cation is a positively charged polyatomic cation and is formed by protonation of ammonia. It is also a general name for positively charged or protonated substituted amines and quaternary cations.
    a. AL 129-1
    c. Ammonium
    b. AASHTO Soil Classification System
    d. AL 333

94. _____, sometimes, is an inorganic chemical compound commonly used as a fertilizer. It contains 21% nitrogen as ammonia and 24% sulfur as sulfate. Its molecular formula is closely related to Mohr's salt an _____ analogue with an iron atom within the compound.
    a. AL 129-1
    c. AL 333
    b. AASHTO Soil Classification System
    d. Ammonium sulfate

95. _____ is the chemical element in the periodic table that has the symbol Ca and atomic number 20. It has an atomic mass of 40.078. _____ is a soft grey alkaline earth metal that is used as a reducing agent in the extraction of thorium, zirconium and uranium. _____ is also the fifth most abundant element in the Earth's crust.
    a. Calcium
    c. 1509 Istanbul earthquake
    b. 1700 Cascadia earthquake
    d. 1703 Genroku earthquake

96. _____ is the chemical compound. This white material crystallizes in cubes like rock salt. CaS has been studied as a component in a process that would recycle gypsum, a product of flue gas desulfurization.
    a. 1700 Cascadia earthquake
    c. 1509 Istanbul earthquake
    b. 1703 Genroku earthquake
    d. Calcium sulfide

97. A _____ is a device used to reduce the toxicity of emissions from an internal combustion engine.
    a. 1703 Genroku earthquake
    c. 1509 Istanbul earthquake
    b. 1700 Cascadia earthquake
    d. Catalytic converter

98. _____ breaks down the coal into its components, usually by subjecting it to high temperature and pressure, using steam and measured amounts of oxygen. It is also a possibility for future energy use, as the produced syngas can be cleaned-up relatively easily leading to cleaner burning than burning coal directly.
    a. 1700 Cascadia earthquake
    c. Coal gasification
    b. 1703 Genroku earthquake
    d. 1509 Istanbul earthquake

99. _____ , officially the Federal Republic of _____ , is a country in Central Europe. It is bordered to the north by the North Sea, Denmark, and the Baltic Sea; to the east by Poland and the Czech Republic; to the south by Austria and Switzerland; and to the west by France, Luxembourg, Belgium, and the Netherlands. The territory of _____ covers 357,021 square kilometers and is influenced by a temperate seasonal climate.
    a. Ambulocetus
    c. Germany
    b. Andrija Mohorovi Ä iÄ‡
    d. Amblypoda

100. The mineral _____ is iron disulfide, FeS2. It has isometric crystals that usually appear as cubes. Its metallic luster and pale-to-normal, brass-yellow hue have earned it a nickname due to many miners mistaking it for the real thing.

Chapter 17. Air Pollution

a. Pyrite
c. 1703 Genroku earthquake
b. 1700 Cascadia earthquake
d. 1509 Istanbul earthquake

101. _____ is a process that converts carbonaceous materials, such as coal, petroleum, or biomass, into carbon monoxide and hydrogen by reacting the raw material at high temperatures with a controlled amount of oxygen. The resulting gas mixture is called synthesis gas or syngas and is itself a fuel. _____ is a very efficient method for extracting energy from many different types of organic materials, and also has applications as a clean waste disposal technique.
   a. Gasification
   c. 1703 Genroku earthquake
   b. 1509 Istanbul earthquake
   d. 1700 Cascadia earthquake

102. A _____ describes one of a number of pieces of legislation relating to the reduction of smog and air pollution in general. The use of governments to enforce clean air standards has contributed to an improvement in human health and longer life spans.
   a. 1700 Cascadia earthquake
   c. 1509 Istanbul earthquake
   b. 1703 Genroku earthquake
   d. Clean Air Act

103. _____ is the current state-of-the art technology used for removing sulfur dioxide from the exhaust flue gases in power plants that burn coal or oil to produce steam for the steam turbines that drive their electricity generators.
   a. Photochemical smog
   c. Flue gas desulfurization
   b. 1700 Cascadia earthquake
   d. 1509 Istanbul earthquake

Chapter 18. Global Climate Change

1. _____ is the average and variations of weather over long periods of time. _____ zones can be defined using parameters such as temperature and rainfall.
   a. 1700 Cascadia earthquake
   b. Climate
   c. 1509 Istanbul earthquake
   d. 1703 Genroku earthquake

2. _____ refers to the variation in the Earth's global climate or in regional climates over time. It describes changes in the variability or average state of the atmosphere over time scales ranging from decades to millions of years. These changes can be caused by processes internal to the Earth, external forces or, more recently, human activities.
   a. 1509 Istanbul earthquake
   b. 1703 Genroku earthquake
   c. Climate change
   d. 1700 Cascadia earthquake

3. _____ seeks to integrate various fields of academic study to understand the Earth as a system. It looks at interaction between the the atmosphere, hydrosphere, lithosphere and biosphere.

In 1996, the American Geophysical Union, in cooperation with the Keck Geology Consortium and with support from five divisions within the National Science Foundation, convened a workshop 'to define common educational goals among all disciplines in the Earth sciences.' In its report, participants noted that, 'The fields that make up the Earth and space sciences are currently undergoing a major advancement that promotes understanding the Earth as a number of interrelated systems.' Recognizing the rise of this systems approach, the workshop report recommended that an _____ curriculum be developed with support from the National Science Foundation.

   a. AL 129-1
   b. Earth system science
   c. AASHTO Soil Classification System
   d. AL 333

4. An _____ is a period of long-term reduction in the temperature of Earth's climate, resulting in an expansion of the continental ice sheets, polar ice sheets and mountain glaciers .
   a. AL 333
   b. AASHTO Soil Classification System
   c. Ice Age
   d. AL 129-1

5. The _____ was a period of cooling occurring after a warmer era known as the Medieval climate optimum. It is generally agreed that there were three minima, beginning about 1650, about 1770, and 1850, each separated by slight warming intervals.
   a. Little Ice Age
   b. 1700 Cascadia earthquake
   c. 1703 Genroku earthquake
   d. 1509 Istanbul earthquake

6. _____ is any of a number of similar colors evoked by light consisting predominantly of the longest wavelengths of light discernible by the human eye, in the wavelength range of roughly 625-740 nm. Longer wavelengths than this are called infrared, or below _____ and cannot be seen by the naked human eye. _____ is used as one of the additive primary colors of light, complementary to cyan, in RGB color systems.
   a. 1700 Cascadia earthquake
   b. 1703 Genroku earthquake
   c. 1509 Istanbul earthquake
   d. Red

7. _____ is a layer of gases surrounding the planet Earth and retained by the Earth's gravity, protecting life on Earth by absorbing ultraviolet solar radiation and reducing temperature extremes between day and night.
   a. AL 333
   b. AL 129-1
   c. AASHTO Soil Classification System
   d. Earths atmosphere

Chapter 18. Global Climate Change

8. _____ is present in a low concentration on earth. It is essential to photosynthesis in plants and other photoautotrophs, and is also a prominent greenhouse gas.
   a. AL 333
   b. Atmospheric carbon dioxide
   c. AASHTO Soil Classification System
   d. AL 129-1

9. _____ is a chemical element in the periodic table that has the symbol C and atomic number 6. An abundant nonmetallic, tetravalent element, _____ has several allotropic forms.
   a. 1703 Genroku earthquake
   b. 1700 Cascadia earthquake
   c. Carbon
   d. 1509 Istanbul earthquake

10. _____ is a chemical compound, normally in a gaseous state, and is composed of one carbon and two oxygen atoms. It is often referred to by its formula CO2. It is present in the Earth's atmosphere at a concentration of approximately .000383 by volume and is an important greenhouse gas due to its ability to absorb many infrared wavelengths of sunlight, and due to the length of time it stays in the atmosphere.
   a. 1703 Genroku earthquake
   b. 1700 Cascadia earthquake
   c. 1509 Istanbul earthquake
   d. Carbon dioxide

11. _____ is the science and study of the solid matter that constitute the Earth. Encompassing such things as rocks, soil, and gemstones, _____ studies the composition, structure, physical properties, history, and the processes that shape Earth's components.
   a. Geology
   b. 1509 Istanbul earthquake
   c. Glaciology
   d. Glacial motion

12. The _____ in stratigraphy, Chronostratigraphy, paleontology and other natural sciences refers to the entirety of the layers of rock strata -- depositions laid down in volcanism or by weathering detritus (clays, sands etc.) including all its fossil content and the information it yields about the history of the Earth: its past climate, geography, geology and the evolution of life on its surface. According to the Law of Superposition (first proposed in the mid-seventeenth century by the Danish naturalist Nicolas Steno) sedimentary and volcanic rocklayers are deposited on top of each other.
   a. 1703 Genroku earthquake
   b. 1509 Istanbul earthquake
   c. Geologic record
   d. 1700 Cascadia earthquake

13. _____ occurs when snow falls on a glacier, is compressed, and becomes part of a glacier that winds its way toward a body of water.
   a. 1509 Istanbul earthquake
   b. 1703 Genroku earthquake
   c. 1700 Cascadia earthquake
   d. Blue ice

14. In computer science, _____ computing (RTC) is the study of hardware and software systems that are subject to a '_____ constraint'--i.e., operational deadlines from event to system response. By contrast, a non-_____ system is one for which there is no deadline, even if fast response or high performance is desired or preferred. The needs of _____ software are often addressed in the context of _____ operating systems, and synchronous programming languages, which provide frameworks on which to build _____ application software.
   a. 1700 Cascadia earthquake
   b. Real-time
   c. 1703 Genroku earthquake
   d. 1509 Istanbul earthquake

15. _____ is any particulate matter that can be transported by fluid flow and which eventually is deposited as a layer of solid particles on the bed or bottom of a body of water or other liquid.

252 Chapter 18. Global Climate Change

a. 1703 Genroku earthquake
b. 1700 Cascadia earthquake
c. 1509 Istanbul earthquake
d. Sediment

16. A _____ is an approximately circular depression in the surface of a planet, moon or other solid body in the Solar System, formed by the hyper-velocity impact of a smaller body with the surface. Impact _____s typically have raised rims, and they range from small, simple, bowl-shaped depressions to large, complex, multi-ringed, impact basins.

a. 1700 Cascadia earthquake
b. 1509 Istanbul earthquake
c. 1703 Genroku earthquake
d. Crater

17. An _____ is a layer of gases that may surround a material body of sufficient mass, by the gravity of the body, and are retained for a longer duration if gravity is high and the _____'s temperature is low. Some planets consist mainly of various gases, and therefore have very deep _____s

The term stellar _____ describes the outer region of a star, and typically includes the portion starting from the opaque photosphere outwards.

a. Atmosphere
b. AASHTO Soil Classification System
c. AL 333
d. AL 129-1

18. _____ are a class of computer-driven models for weather forecasting, understanding climate and projecting climate change.

a. 1509 Istanbul earthquake
b. Global Circulation Models
c. 1703 Genroku earthquake
d. 1700 Cascadia earthquake

19. A _____ uses mathematical language to describe a system. _____s are used not only in the natural sciences and engineering disciplines (such as physics, biology, earth science, meteorology, and electrical engineering) but also in the social sciences (such as economics, psychology, sociology and political science); physicists, engineers, computer scientists, and economists use _____s most extensively.

Eykhoff (1974) defined a _____ as 'a representation of the essential aspects of an existing system (or a system to be constructed) which presents knowledge of that system in usable form'.

a. 1703 Genroku earthquake
b. Mathematical model
c. 1700 Cascadia earthquake
d. 1509 Istanbul earthquake

20. The _____ is the set of all extant phenomena in a given atmosphere at a given time. The term usually refers to the activity of these phenomena over short periods, as opposed to the term climate, which refers to the average atmospheric conditions over longer periods of time.

a. 1509 Istanbul earthquake
b. 1700 Cascadia earthquake
c. 1703 Genroku earthquake
d. Weather

21. _____ is a class of diseases in which a group of cells display the traits of uncontrolled growth growth and division beyond the normal limits, invasion intrusion on and destruction of adjacent tissues, and sometimes metastasis spread to other locations in the body via lymph or blood. These three malignant properties of _____s differentiate them from benign tumors, which are self-limited, do not invade or metastasize. Most _____s form a tumor but some, like leukemia, do not.

Chapter 18. Global Climate Change

a. 1509 Istanbul earthquake
b. 1700 Cascadia earthquake
c. 1703 Genroku earthquake
d. Cancer

22. A _____ or medical condition is an abnormal condition of an organism that impairs bodily functions and can be deadly. It is also defined as a way of the body harming itself in an abnormal way, associated with specific symptoms and signs.

In human beings,'_____' is often used more broadly to refer to any condition that causes extreme pain, dysfunction, distress, social problems, and/or death to the person afflicted, or similar problems for those in contact with the person.

a. 1700 Cascadia earthquake
b. 1509 Istanbul earthquake
c. Disease
d. Black lung disease

23. _____ is a chemical element which has the symbol N and atomic number 7 in the periodic table. Elemental _____ is a colorless, odorless, tasteless and mostly inert diatomic gas at standard conditions, constituting 78.08% percent of Earth's atmosphere.

a. 1700 Cascadia earthquake
b. 1703 Genroku earthquake
c. 1509 Istanbul earthquake
d. Nitrogen

24. _____$_x$ is a generic term for mono-_____ (_____ and _____$_2$.) These oxides are produced during combustion, especially combustion at high temperatures.

At ambient temperatures, the oxygen and nitrogen gases in air will not react with each other.

a. 1509 Istanbul earthquake
b. 1703 Genroku earthquake
c. 1700 Cascadia earthquake
d. Nitrogen oxides

25. The _____ is the lowest portion of Earth's atmosphere. It is the densest layer of the atmosphere and contains approximately 75% of the mass of the atmosphere and almost all the water vapor and aerosols.

a. 1509 Istanbul earthquake
b. Troposphere
c. 1703 Genroku earthquake
d. 1700 Cascadia earthquake

26. _____ is the gas phase of water. _____ is one state of the water cycle within the hydrosphere. _____ can be produced from the evaporation of liquid water or from the sublimation of ice. Under normal atmospheric conditions, _____ is continuously evaporating and condensing.

a. 1509 Istanbul earthquake
b. 1700 Cascadia earthquake
c. Water vapor
d. 1703 Genroku earthquake

27. _____ is a chemical, physical, or biological agent that modifies the natural characteristics of the atmosphere. The atmosphere is a complex, dynamic natural gaseous system that is essential to support life on planet Earth. Stratospheric ozone depletion due to _____ has long been recognized as a threat to human health as well as to the Earth's ecosystems. Worldwide _____ is responsible for large numbers of deaths and cases of respiratory disease.

a. AL 129-1
b. AL 333
c. AASHTO Soil Classification System
d. Air pollution

Chapter 18. Global Climate Change

28. _____ is the increase in the average temperature of the Earth's near-surface air and oceans in recent decades and its projected continuation. An increase in global temperatures can in turn cause other changes, including sea level rise, and changes in the amount and pattern of precipitation resulting in floods and drought. There may also be changes in the frequency and intensity of extreme weather events.
   a. 1700 Cascadia earthquake
   b. 1703 Genroku earthquake
   c. 1509 Istanbul earthquake
   d. Global warming

29. _____ is an umbrella term for a variety for different diseases affecting the heart. As of 2007, it is the leading cause of death in the United States, England, Canada and Wales, killing one person every 34 seconds in the United States alone.

Coronary artery disease is a disease of the artery caused by the accumulation of atheromatous plaques within the walls of the arteries that supply the myocardium.

   a. 1509 Istanbul earthquake
   b. 1700 Cascadia earthquake
   c. 1703 Genroku earthquake
   d. Heart Disease

30. An _____ is a chemical compound containing an oxygen atom and other elements. Most of the earth's crust consists of them. They result when elements are oxidized by air.
   a. AL 129-1
   b. AL 333
   c. AASHTO Soil Classification System
   d. Oxide

31. _____ is the introduction of substances or energy into the environment, resulting in deleterious effects of such a nature as to endanger human health, harm living resources and ecosystems, and impair or interfere with amenities and other legitimate uses of the environment.
   a. 1700 Cascadia earthquake
   b. 1703 Genroku earthquake
   c. 1509 Istanbul earthquake
   d. Pollution

32. _____ is the gas phase component of a another state of matter which does not completely fill its container. It is distinguished from the pure gas phase by the presence of the same substance in another state of matter. Hence when a liquid has completely evaporated, it is said that the system has been completely transformed to the gas phase.
   a. 1703 Genroku earthquake
   b. 1700 Cascadia earthquake
   c. Vapor
   d. 1509 Istanbul earthquake

33. _____ are compounds containing chlorine, fluorine and carbon only, that is they contain no hydrogen. They were formerly used widely in industry, for example as refrigerants, propellants, and cleaning solvents. Their use has been regularly prohibited by the Montreal Protocol, because of effects on the ozone layer.
   a. 1703 Genroku earthquake
   b. 1700 Cascadia earthquake
   c. Chlorofluorocarbons CFCs
   d. 1509 Istanbul earthquake

34. _____ is a self-propagating wave in space with electric and magnetic components.
   a. AASHTO Soil Classification System
   b. AL 129-1
   c. Electromagnetic radiation
   d. AL 333

35. _____ is a chemical compound with the molecular formula CH_4. It is the simplest alkane, and the principal component of natural gas. Burning one molecule of _____ in the presence of oxygen releases one molecule. _____'s relative abundance and clean burning process makes it a very attractive fuel.

Chapter 18. Global Climate Change

    a. 1703 Genroku earthquake   b. 1700 Cascadia earthquake
    c. 1509 Istanbul earthquake   d. Methane

36. _____ is Solar Radiation emitted from our sun. It has been used in many traditional technologies for centuries, and has come into widespread use where other power supplies are absent, such as in remote locations and in space.
    a. 1700 Cascadia earthquake   b. 1703 Genroku earthquake
    c. 1509 Istanbul earthquake   d. Solar power

37. In physics, _____ is a scalar physical quantity that describes the amount of work that can be performed by a force. _____ is an attribute of objects and systems that is subject to a conservation law. Several different forms of _____ exist to explain all known natural phenomena.
    a. AL 333   b. AL 129-1
    c. AASHTO Soil Classification System   d. Energy

38. A _____ is a building where plants are cultivated.
    a. Greenhouse   b. 1703 Genroku earthquake
    c. 1509 Istanbul earthquake   d. 1700 Cascadia earthquake

39. The _____ refers to the change in the steady state temperature of a planet or moon by the presence of an atmosphere containing gas that absorbs and emits infrared radiation. Greenhouse gases, which include water vapor, carbon dioxide and methane, warm the atmosphere by efficiently absorbing thermal infrared radiation emitted by the Earth's surface, by the atmosphere itself, and by clouds. As a result of its warmth, the atmosphere also radiates thermal infrared in all directions, including downward to the Earth's surface.
    a. General circulation model   b. Radiative forcing
    c. Glacier   d. Greenhouse effect

40. _____, as used in physics, is energy in the form of waves or moving subatomic particles emitted by an atom or other body as it changes from a higher energy state to a lower energy state. _____ can be classified as ionizing or non-ionizing _____, depending on its effect on atomic matter. The most common use of the word "_____" refers to ionizing _____. Ionizing _____ has enough energy to ionize atoms or molecules while non-ionizing _____ does not. Radioactive material is a physical material that emits ionizing _____.
    a. Supersaturation   b. Synthetic aperture radar
    c. Supercritical fluid   d. Radiation

41. _____ is the branch of logistics that deals with the tangible components of a supply chain. Specifically, this covers the acquisition of spare parts and replacements, quality control of purchasing and ordering such parts, and the standards involved in ordering, shipping, and warehousing the said parts.

_____ is just managing all types of materials in an organization.

    a. Materials management   b. 1509 Istanbul earthquake
    c. 1703 Genroku earthquake   d. 1700 Cascadia earthquake

42. _____ is Earth's southernmost continent, overlying the South Pole. It is situated in the southern hemisphere, almost entirely south of the Antarctic Circle, and is surrounded by the Southern Ocean. At 14.4 million km Since there is little precipitation, except at the coasts, the interior of the continent is technically the largest desert in the world.

a. Extratropical
b. Antarctica
c. Ediacaran biota
d. Extratropical cyclone

43. _____ is a theory of geology that has been developed to explain the observed evidence for large scale motions of the Earth's lithosphere. The theory encompassed and superseded the older theory of continental drift.
    a. 1509 Istanbul earthquake
    b. 1703 Genroku earthquake
    c. 1700 Cascadia earthquake
    d. Plate tectonics

44. _____ is a physical property of a system that underlies the common notions of hot and cold; something that is hotter has the greater _____. Temperature is one of the principal parameters of thermodynamics.
    a. 1509 Istanbul earthquake
    b. 1700 Cascadia earthquake
    c. 1703 Genroku earthquake
    d. Temperature

45. _____ is the term used to encompass a multitude of environmental and ecological changes that have been noticed, measured and studied on Earth. It encompasses the study of climate change, species extinction, land use change, changes in the carbon cycle and hydrologic cycle.
    a. 1700 Cascadia earthquake
    b. Global change
    c. 1509 Istanbul earthquake
    d. 1703 Genroku earthquake

46. The average atmospheric temperature of the world overall is rizing, which is known as _____.
    a. 1509 Istanbul earthquake
    b. 1703 Genroku earthquake
    c. 1700 Cascadia earthquake
    d. Global temperature change

47. An _____ is a mass of glacier ice that covers surrounding terrain and is greater than 19,305 mile². The only current _____s are in Antarctica and Greenland. _____s are bigger than ice shelves or glaciers. Masses of ice covering less than 50,000 km² are termed an ice cap. An ice cap will typically feed a series of glaciers around its periphery. Although the surface is cold, the base of an _____ is generally warmer. This process produces fast-flowing channels in the _____.
    a. AL 333
    b. AL 129-1
    c. AASHTO Soil Classification System
    d. Ice sheet

48. _____ is a field of study within geology concerned generally with the structures within the crust of the Earth, or other planets, and particularly with the forces and movements that have operated in a region to create these structures.
    a. 1509 Istanbul earthquake
    b. Tectonics
    c. 1703 Genroku earthquake
    d. 1700 Cascadia earthquake

49. The _____ is the second-to-latest interglacial era of the Ice Age. It began about 131,000 years ago. Changes in orbital parameters from today, greater obliquity and eccentricity, and perihelion, known as the Milankovitch cycle, probably led to greater seasonal temperature variations in the Northern Hemisphere, although global annual means temperatures were probably similar to those of the Holocene.
    a. AL 333
    b. AL 129-1
    c. AASHTO Soil Classification System
    d. Eemian period

50. The _____ stadial was a brief cold climate period following the Bölling/Allerød interstadial at the end of the Pleistocene between approximately 12,700 to 11,500 years Before Present, and preceding the Preboreal of the early Holocene.

Chapter 18. Global Climate Change

a. Younger Dryas
b. 1509 Istanbul earthquake
c. 1703 Genroku earthquake
d. 1700 Cascadia earthquake

51. _____ cycles are the collective effect of changes in the Earth's movements upon its climate.
a. 1509 Istanbul earthquake
b. Milankovitch
c. 1703 Genroku earthquake
d. 1700 Cascadia earthquake

52. _____ are the collective effect of changes in the Earth's movements upon its climate, named after Serbian civil engineer and mathematician Milutin Milankoviæ.
a. Milankovitch cycles
b. 1703 Genroku earthquake
c. 1509 Istanbul earthquake
d. 1700 Cascadia earthquake

53. The thermohaline circulation is sometimes called the _____, the great ocean conveyor, or the global conveyor belt. On occasion, it is used to refer to the meridional overturning circulation The term MOC, however, is more accurate and well defined, as it is difficult to separate the part of the circulation which is actually driven by temperature and salinity alone as opposed to other factors such as the wind.
a. East Australian Current
b. Atmospheric circulation
c. Eastern boundary currents
d. Ocean conveyor belt

54. _____ are changes in the amount of solar radiation emitted by the Sun. There are periodic components to these variations, the principal one being the 11-year solar cycle (or sunspot cycle), as well as aperiodic fluctuations. Solar activity has been measured via satellites during recent decades and through 'proxy' variables in prior times.
a. General circulation model
b. Glacier
c. Greenhouse effect
d. Solar variations

55. Technically, an _____ is a suspension of fine solid or liquid droplets in a gas. Contrast with a smoke which is a suspension of solid particles in a gas. In general conversation, _____ usually refers to an _____ spray can or the output of such a can.
a. AL 129-1
b. AL 333
c. Aerosol
d. AASHTO Soil Classification System

56. _____ effects, processes, objects, or materials are those that are derived from human activities, as opposed to those occuring in natural environments without human influences.
a. AL 333
b. AL 129-1
c. AASHTO Soil Classification System
d. Anthropogenic

57. In climate science, _____ is (loosely) defined as the change in net irradiance at the tropopause. 'Net irradiance' is the difference between the incoming radiation energy and the outgoing radiation energy in a given climate system and is thus measured in Watts per square meter. The change is computed based on 'unperturbed' values, as defined by the Intergovernmental Panel on Climate Change (IPCC) as the measured difference relative to a base period.
a. Glacier
b. Global warming controversy
c. Greenhouse effect
d. Radiative forcing

58. _____s, alternatively referred to as _____ matter (PM) or fine particles, are tiny particles of solid or liquid suspended in a gas or liquid. In contrast, aerosol refers to particles and the gas together. Sources of _____ matter can be man made or natural.

a. Particulate
b. 1509 Istanbul earthquake
c. 1703 Genroku earthquake
d. 1700 Cascadia earthquake

59. _____ are tiny particles of solid or liquid suspended in a gas. They range in size from less than 10 nanometres to more than 100 micrometres in diameter.
   a. 1700 Cascadia earthquake
   b. 1703 Genroku earthquake
   c. 1509 Istanbul earthquake
   d. Particulates

60. The _____, is an island country located in Southeast Asia with Manila as its capital city. The _____ comprises 7,107 islands in the western Pacific Ocean, sharing maritime borders with Indonesia, Malaysia, Palau, the Republic of China, and Vietnam. The _____ is the world's 12th most populous country with a population of 90 million people.
   a. 1700 Cascadia earthquake
   b. Philippine Islands
   c. Philippines
   d. 1509 Istanbul earthquake

61. A _____ is an opening in a planet's surface or crust, which allows hot, molten rock, ash, and gases to escape from below the surface. Volcanic activity involving the extrusion of rock tends to form mountains or features like mountains over a period of time.

_____es are generally found where tectonic plates are diverging or converging.

   a. Volcano
   b. 1703 Genroku earthquake
   c. 1700 Cascadia earthquake
   d. 1509 Istanbul earthquake

62. _____ is the substance of which physical objects are composed. _____ can be solid, liquid, plasma or gas. It constitutes the observable universe.
   a. 1700 Cascadia earthquake
   b. 1703 Genroku earthquake
   c. 1509 Istanbul earthquake
   d. Matter

63. _____ climate is the average weather for a region above the tree line. The climate becomes colder at high elevations—this characteristic is described by the lapse rate of air: air will tend to get colder as it rises, since it expands.
   a. AASHTO Soil Classification System
   b. AL 129-1
   c. Alpine
   d. AL 333

64. _____ is a cape on the coast of North Carolina. It is the point that protrudes the farthest to the southeast along the northeast-to-southwest line of the Atlantic coast of North America. Two major Atlantic currents collide just off _____, the southerly-flowing cold water Labrador Current and the northerly-flowing warm water Florida Current (Gulf Stream), creating turbulent waters and a large expanse of shallow sandbars extending up to 14 miles offshore.
   a. Cape Hatteras
   b. 1703 Genroku earthquake
   c. 1509 Istanbul earthquake
   d. 1700 Cascadia earthquake

65. Due to shore erosion in the Outer Bank of North Carolina a navagational lighthouse had to be moved leading to the _____.
   a. 1700 Cascadia earthquake
   b. 1509 Istanbul earthquake
   c. 1703 Genroku earthquake
   d. Cape Hatteras Lighthouse controversy

Chapter 18. Global Climate Change

66. _____ is displacement of solids by the agents of ocean currents, wind, water, or ice by downward or down-slope movement in response to gravity or by living organisms.
 a. Erosion
 b. AL 333
 c. AASHTO Soil Classification System
 d. AL 129-1

67. _____ is a global coupled ocean-atmosphere phenomenon. The Pacific ocean signatures, are important temperature fluctuations in surface waters of the tropical Eastern Pacific Ocean.
 a. AASHTO Soil Classification System
 b. AL 333
 c. AL 129-1
 d. El Nino

68. _____ form at high latitudes where temperatures remain cold enough during the summer to keep the previous winter's snow from melting allowing snow and ice to accumulate. It is a glacier that spreads out from a central mass of ice.
 a. Global warming controversy
 b. General circulation model
 c. Radiative forcing
 d. Continental glacier

69. _____ can refer to: a period of time; a distinctive historical period or era, a unit of the geologic time scale, less than a period and greater than an age, or a phase in the development of the universe with distinctive properties.
 a. Epoch
 b. AL 333
 c. AASHTO Soil Classification System
 d. AL 129-1

70. The Laurentian _____ are a group of five large lakes in North America on or near the Canada-United States border. They are the largest group of fresh water lakes on Earth.
 a. 1509 Istanbul earthquake
 b. Great Lakes
 c. 1703 Genroku earthquake
 d. 1700 Cascadia earthquake

71. The _____ is a vast body of ice covering roughly 80% of the surface of Greenland. It's almost 2,400 kilometres long in a north-south direction, and its greatest width is 1,100 kilometres at a latitude of 77° N, near its northern margin. It sheet covers 1.71 million km², or roughly 80% of the surface of Greenland. The thickness is generally more than 2 km and over 3 km at its thickest point.
 a. Greenland ice sheet
 b. 1703 Genroku earthquake
 c. 1700 Cascadia earthquake
 d. 1509 Istanbul earthquake

72. An _____ is a dome-shaped ice mass that covers less than 50,000 km² of land area. Masses of ice covering more than 50,000 km² are termed an ice sheet.
 a. AL 333
 b. AL 129-1
 c. AASHTO Soil Classification System
 d. Ice cap

73. An _____ is a geological interval of warmer global average temperature that separates glacials, or ice ages. The current Holocene _____ has persisted since the Pleistocene, about 11,400 years ago.
 a. AL 129-1
 b. AASHTO Soil Classification System
 c. AL 333
 d. Interglacial

74. A _____ is a body of water, not part of the ocean, that is larger and deeper than a pond.
 a. Lake
 b. 1509 Istanbul earthquake
 c. 1703 Genroku earthquake
 d. 1700 Cascadia earthquake

Chapter 18. Global Climate Change

75. The _____ on the geologic timescale had been intended to cover the world's recent period of repeated glaciations. The _____ follows the Pliocene and is followed by the Holocene. The _____ is the third epoch of the Neogene period or 6th epoch of the Cenozoic era. The end of the _____ corresponds with the end of the Paleolithic age used in archaeology. The _____ is divided into the Early _____, Middle _____ and Late _____, and numerous faunal stages.
   a. 1703 Genroku earthquake
   b. 1700 Cascadia earthquake
   c. Pleistocene
   d. 1509 Istanbul earthquake

76. In geology, a _____ is a depression with predominant extent in one direction. The terms U-shaped and V-shaped are descriptive terms of geography to characterize the form of _____s. Most _____s belong to one of these two main types or a mixture of them, at least with respect of the cross section of the slopes or hillsides.
   a. 1703 Genroku earthquake
   b. 1700 Cascadia earthquake
   c. Valley
   d. 1509 Istanbul earthquake

77. _____

African Economic Community map

Although it has abundant natural resources, _____ remains the world's poorest and most underdeveloped continent, due largely to the effects of: tropical diseases, the slave trade, corrupt governments, failed central planning, the international trade regime and geopolitics; as well as widespread human rights violations, the negative effects of colonialism, despotism, illiteracy, superstition, tribal and military conflict. According to the United Nations' Human Development Report in 2003, the bottom 25 ranked nations were all African nations.

Widespread poverty, illiteracy, malnutrition and inadequate water supply and sanitation, as well as poor health, affect a large majority of the people who reside in the African continent.

   a. AL 129-1
   b. Africa
   c. AASHTO Soil Classification System
   d. AL 333

78. In meteorology, an _____ is a large volume of air having fairly uniform characteristics of temperature, atmospheric pressure, and water vapor content.
   a. AL 333
   b. AL 129-1
   c. AASHTO Soil Classification System
   d. Air mass

79. _____ have an extremely low yearly precipitation, receiving much less rain or snowfall annually than would satisfy the climatological demand for evaporation and transpiration.
   a. AL 129-1
   b. AASHTO Soil Classification System
   c. AL 333
   d. Arid lands

80. _____ are artificial channels for water. There are two main types of _____: irrigation _____, which are used for the delivery of water, and waterways, which are transportation _____ used for passage of goods and people, often connected to existing lakes, rivers, or oceans.
   a. 1703 Genroku earthquake
   b. Canals
   c. 1509 Istanbul earthquake
   d. 1700 Cascadia earthquake

Chapter 18. Global Climate Change

81. In geography, a _____ is a landscape form or region that receives very little precipitation. They are defined as areas that receive an average annual precipitation of less than 250 mm. A _____ where vegetation cover is exceedingly sparse correspond to the 'hyperarid' regions of the earth, where rainfall is exceedingly rare and infrequent.
   a. 1509 Istanbul earthquake
   b. Desert
   c. 1700 Cascadia earthquake
   d. 1703 Genroku earthquake

82. _____ is the degradation of land in arid, semi arid and dry sub-humid areas resulting from various climatic variations, but primarily human activities. Current _____ is taking place much faster worldwide than historically and usually arises from the demands of increased populations that settle on the land in order to grow crops and graze animals.
   a. 1700 Cascadia earthquake
   b. 1509 Istanbul earthquake
   c. 1703 Genroku earthquake
   d. Desertification

83. A _____ is a bipedal primate belonging to the mammalian species Homo sapiens in the family Hominidae. Compared to other living organisms on Earth, a _____ has a highly developed brain capable of abstract reasoning, language, and introspection.
   a. 1700 Cascadia earthquake
   b. 1703 Genroku earthquake
   c. 1509 Istanbul earthquake
   d. Human

84. _____ is a neighborhood in Niagara Falls, New York, United States of America. It officially covers 36 square blocks in the far southeastern corner of the city, along 99th Street and Read Avenue. Two bodies of water define the northern and southern boundaries of the neighborhood: Bergholtz Creek to the north and the Niagara River one-quarter mile to the south.
   a. 1700 Cascadia earthquake
   b. 1703 Genroku earthquake
   c. 1509 Istanbul earthquake
   d. Love Canal

85. _____ is the northern continent of the Americas, situated in the Earth's northern hemisphere and almost totally in the western hemisphere. It is bordered on the north by the Arctic Ocean, on the east by the North Atlantic Ocean, on the southeast by the Caribbean Sea, and on the south and west by the North Pacific Ocean; South America lies to the southeast. _____ covers an area of about 24,709,000 square kilometers, about 4.8% of the planet's surface or about 16.5% of its land area.
   a. 1703 Genroku earthquake
   b. 1700 Cascadia earthquake
   c. 1509 Istanbul earthquake
   d. North America

86. _____ is any product of the condensation of atmospheric water vapor that is deposited on the earth's surface. It occurs when the atmosphere becomes saturated with water vapour and the water condenses and falls out of solution. Air becomes saturated via two processes, cooling and adding moisture.
   a. 1509 Istanbul earthquake
   b. 1700 Cascadia earthquake
   c. 1703 Genroku earthquake
   d. Precipitation

87. The _____ is the world's largest hot desert, and second largest desert after Antarctica. At over 9,000,000 square kilometres, it is almost as large as the United States, and is larger than Australia. It's name derives from the Arabic word "çahra"; to refer to the Sahara as the '_____' is a pleonasm.
   a. Sahara Desert
   b. 1509 Istanbul earthquake
   c. 1700 Cascadia earthquake
   d. 1703 Genroku earthquake

Chapter 18. Global Climate Change

88. _____ generally describes climatic regions that receive low annual rainfall and have predominantly shrub or short-grass vegetation.
   a. 1509 Istanbul earthquake
   b. 1700 Cascadia earthquake
   c. 1703 Genroku earthquake
   d. Semi-arid

89. _____ is one of two regressive evolution processes associated with the loss of equilibrium of a stable soil. Degradation is an evolution, different of natural evolution, related to the locale climate and vegetation. It is due to the replacement of the primitive vegetation by a secondary vegetation. This replacement modifies the humus composition and amount, and impacts the formation of the soil. It is directly related to human activity.
   a. Soil degradation
   b. 1703 Genroku earthquake
   c. 1700 Cascadia earthquake
   d. 1509 Istanbul earthquake

90. _____ is a general term for the plant life of a region; it refers to the ground cover provided by plants, and is, by far, the most abundant biotic element of the biosphere. Primeval redwood forests, coastal mangrove stands, sphagnum bogs, desert soil crusts, roadside weed patches, wheat fields, cultivated gardens and lawns; are all encompassed by the term _____.
   a. 1509 Istanbul earthquake
   b. 1703 Genroku earthquake
   c. 1700 Cascadia earthquake
   d. Vegetation

91. An _____ is traditionally considered any chemical compound that, when dissolved in water, gives a solution with a hydrogen ion activity greater than in pure water, i.e. a pH less than 7.0. That approximates the modern definition of Johannes Nicolaus Brønsted and Martin Lowry, who independently defined an _____ as a compound which donates a hydrogen ion to another compound. Common examples include acetic _____ and sulfuric _____. Acid/base systems are different from redox reactions in that there is no change in oxidation state.
   a. AL 333
   b. AL 129-1
   c. Acid
   d. AASHTO Soil Classification System

92. _____ is the production of food, feed, fiber, fuel and other goods by the systematic raizing of plants and animals.
   a. AL 129-1
   b. AASHTO Soil Classification System
   c. AL 333
   d. Agriculture

93. _____ are made up of dust and occurs primarily in the Dust Bowl or America. They cause the sky to look very dark. or black.
   a. 1703 Genroku earthquake
   b. 1509 Istanbul earthquake
   c. 1700 Cascadia earthquake
   d. Black blizzards

94. _____ is the conversion of forested areas to non-forest land use such as arable land, pasture, urban use, logged area or wasteland. _____ results from removal of trees without sufficient reforestation and results in declines in: habitat and biodiversity, wood for fuel and industrial use and decline in quality of life.
   a. 1509 Istanbul earthquake
   b. Deforestation
   c. 1703 Genroku earthquake
   d. 1700 Cascadia earthquake

95. The _____ was a series of catastrophic dust storms causing major ecological and agricultural damage to American and Canadian prairie lands in the 1930s, caused by decades of farming techniques that promoted erosion coupled with severe drought.

Chapter 18. Global Climate Change

a. 1509 Istanbul earthquake
c. 1703 Genroku earthquake
b. 1700 Cascadia earthquake
d. Dust Bowl

96. A _____ is a meteorological phenomenon common in arid and semi-arid regions. Such a storm may result from the passage of a gust front or simply a substantial increase in wind velocity over a wider region. In all instances, the ground must be very dry and loosely consolidated.
    a. 1700 Cascadia earthquake
    c. 1509 Istanbul earthquake
    b. 1703 Genroku earthquake
    d. Dust storm

97. _____ is the artificial application of water to the soil usually for assisting in growing crops. In crop production it is mainly used to replace missing rainfall in periods of drought, but also to protect plants against frost.
    a. Irrigation
    c. AL 333
    b. AASHTO Soil Classification System
    d. AL 129-1

98. _____ is the process in which trees are cut down usually as part of a timber harvest. _____ can also remove wood for forest management goals. _____ is controversial due to its environmental and aesthetic impacts.
    a. 1509 Istanbul earthquake
    c. Logging
    b. 1703 Genroku earthquake
    d. 1700 Cascadia earthquake

99. _____ occurs when plants are exposed to livestock grazing for extended periods of time, or without sufficient recovery periods.
    a. AL 333
    c. AL 129-1
    b. AASHTO Soil Classification System
    d. Overgrazing

100. In biology a _____ is the collection of inter-breeding organisms of a particular species; in sociology, a collection of human beings. A _____ shares a particular characteristic of interest, most often that of living in a given geographic area. In taxonomy _____ is a low-level taxonomic rank.
    a. Metapopulation
    c. 1700 Cascadia earthquake
    b. 1509 Istanbul earthquake
    d. Population

101. _____ is the change in population over time, and can be quantified as the change in the number of individuals in a population per unit time. The term _____ can technically refer to any species, but almost always refers to humans, and it is often used informally for the more specific demographic term _____ rate, and is often used to refer specifically to the growth of the population of the world.
    a. 1703 Genroku earthquake
    c. 1509 Istanbul earthquake
    b. Population growth
    d. 1700 Cascadia earthquake

102. A _____ is any disturbed state of an astronomical body's atmosphere, especially affecting its surface, and strongly implying severe weather. It may be marked by strong wind, thunder and lightning, heavy precipitation, such as ice, or wind transporting some substance through the atmosphere.
    a. 1700 Cascadia earthquake
    c. 1509 Istanbul earthquake
    b. 1703 Genroku earthquake
    d. Storm

103. _____ is the flow of air. More generally, it is the flow of the gases which compose an atmosphere; since _____ is not only an Earth based phenomenon.

a. 1700 Cascadia earthquake
b. 1509 Istanbul earthquake
c. 1703 Genroku earthquake
d. Wind

104. _____ processes pertain to the activity of the winds and more specifically, to the winds' ability to shape the surface of the Earth and other planets.
   a. AL 333
   b. Eolian
   c. AASHTO Soil Classification System
   d. AL 129-1

105. A _____ is a severe winter storm condition characterized by low temperatures, strong winds, and heavy blowing snow. They are formed when a high pressure system, also known as a ridge, interacts with a low pressure system; this results in the advection of air from the high pressure zone into the low pressure area.
   a. 1703 Genroku earthquake
   b. 1700 Cascadia earthquake
   c. Blizzard
   d. 1509 Istanbul earthquake

106. The _____ is the broadest level of ecological study, the global sum of all ecosystems. From the broadest biophysiological point of view, the _____ is the global ecological system integrating all living beings and their relationships, including their interaction with the elements of the lithosphere, hydrosphere, and atmosphere. This _____ is postulated to have evolved, beginning through a process of biogenesis or biopoesis, at least some 3.5 billion years ago.
   a. Biosphere
   b. 1703 Genroku earthquake
   c. 1509 Istanbul earthquake
   d. 1700 Cascadia earthquake

107. Mean _____ is the average height of the sea, with reference to a suitable reference surface.
   a. 1700 Cascadia earthquake
   b. 1703 Genroku earthquake
   c. 1509 Istanbul earthquake
   d. Sea level

108. _____ is an increase in sea level. Multiple complex factors may influence such changes.
   a. Sea level rise
   b. 1703 Genroku earthquake
   c. 1509 Istanbul earthquake
   d. 1700 Cascadia earthquake

109. _____ is a fossil fuel formed in swamp ecosystems where plant remains were saved by water and mud from oxidization and biodegradation. It is a sedimentary rock, but the harder forms, such as anthracite _____, can be regarded as metamorphic rocks because of later exposure to elevated temperature and pressure. It is composed primarily of carbon along with assorted other elements, including sulfur.
   a. 1509 Istanbul earthquake
   b. 1700 Cascadia earthquake
   c. 1703 Genroku earthquake
   d. Coal

110. The _____ is an international environmental treaty produced at the United Nations Conference on Environment and Development, informally known as the Earth Summit, held in Rio de Janeiro in 1992. The treaty aimed at reducing emissions of greenhouse gas in order to combat global warming.
   a. 1509 Istanbul earthquake
   b. Framework Convention on Climate Change
   c. 1703 Genroku earthquake
   d. 1700 Cascadia earthquake

Chapter 18. Global Climate Change

111. In organic chemistry, a _____ is an organic compound consisting entirely of hydrogen and carbon. With relation to chemical terminology, aromatic _____s or arenes, alkanes, alkenes and alkyne-based compounds composed entirely of carbon or hydrogen are referred to as "Pure" _____s, whereas other _____s with bonded compounds or impurities of sulphur or nitrogen, are referred to as "impure", and remain somewhat erroneously referred to as _____s.
- a. 1700 Cascadia earthquake
- b. Hydrocarbon
- c. 1703 Genroku earthquake
- d. 1509 Istanbul earthquake

112. _____ (æ—¥æœ¬ Nihon or Nippon making it an archipelago. The largest islands are HonshÅ«, HokkaidÅ, KyÅ«shÅ« and Shikoku, together accounting for 97% of _____'s land area. Most of the islands are mountainous, many volcanic; for example, _____'s highest peak, Mount Fuji, is a volcano.
- a. Kenya
- b. Kabul
- c. Java
- d. Japan

113. _____ (äº¬éƒ½ KyÅ to

The new city, Heian-kyÅ, became the seat of Japan's imperial court in 794, beginning the Heian period of Japanese history. In Japanese, the city has been called Kyo, Miyako or Kyo no Miyako. In the 11th century, the city was renamed _____.

- a. Kyoto
- b. Kampala
- c. Lao
- d. Katanga Province

114. A _____ is a cultural and social community. In as much as most members never meet each other, yet feel a common bond, it may be considered an imagined community. One of the most influential doctrines in Western Europe and the Western hemisphere since the late eighteenth century is that all humans are divided into groups called _____s.
- a. Nation
- b. 1703 Genroku earthquake
- c. 1509 Istanbul earthquake
- d. 1700 Cascadia earthquake

115. The term _____ is commonly used to mean the deposition of acidic components in rain, snow, dew, or dry particles. _____ occurs when sulfur dioxide and nitrogen oxides are emitted into the atmosphere, undergo chemical transformations and are absorbed by water droplets in clouds. The droplets then fall to earth as rain, snow, mist, dry dust, hail, or sleet. This increases the acidity of the soil, and affects the chemical balance of lakes and streams.
- a. AL 333
- b. AASHTO Soil Classification System
- c. Acid precipitation
- d. AL 129-1

116. _____s are the mineralized or otherwise preserved remains or traces of animals, plants, and other organisms. The totality of _____s, both discovered and undiscovered, and their placement in fossiliferous rock formations and sedimentary layers is known as the _____ record.
- a. 1703 Genroku earthquake
- b. Fossil
- c. 1509 Istanbul earthquake
- d. 1700 Cascadia earthquake

117. _____ is a gaseous fossil fuel consisting primarily of methane but including significant quantities of ethane, butane, propane, carbon dioxide, nitrogen, helium and hydrogen sulfide.
- a. 1703 Genroku earthquake
- b. 1700 Cascadia earthquake
- c. 1509 Istanbul earthquake
- d. Natural gas

118. _____ is vibration transmitted through a solid, liquid composed of frequencies within the range of hearing and of a level sufficiently strong to be heard. Human ear

For humans, hearing is limited to frequencies between about 20 Hz and 20,000 Hz (20 kHz), with the upper limit generally decreasing with age. Other species have a different range of hearing.

- a. 1700 Cascadia earthquake
- b. 1509 Istanbul earthquake
- c. 1703 Genroku earthquake
- d. Sound

119. _____ is a triatomic molecule, consisting of three oxygen atoms. It is an allotrope of oxygen that is much less stable than the diatomic species O2. Ground-level _____ is an air pollutant with harmful effects on the respiratory systems of animals. On the other hand, _____ in the upper atmosphere protects living organisms by preventing damaging ultraviolet light from reaching the Earth's surface.
- a. Ozone
- b. AL 333
- c. AASHTO Soil Classification System
- d. AL 129-1

120. The _____ is the part of the Earth's atmosphere which contains relatively high concentrations of ozone.
- a. AASHTO Soil Classification System
- b. AL 129-1
- c. AL 333
- d. Ozone layer

Chapter 19. Geology, Society, and the Future

1. _____ is the geological process whereby material is added to a landform. This is the process by which wind and water create a sediment deposit, through the laying down of granular material that has been eroded and transported from another geographical location.
    a. 1509 Istanbul earthquake
    b. 1703 Genroku earthquake
    c. Deposition
    d. 1700 Cascadia earthquake

2. A _____ is any disturbed state of an astronomical body's atmosphere, especially affecting its surface, and strongly implying severe weather. It may be marked by strong wind, thunder and lightning, heavy precipitation, such as ice, or wind transporting some substance through the atmosphere.
    a. Storm
    b. 1703 Genroku earthquake
    c. 1509 Istanbul earthquake
    d. 1700 Cascadia earthquake

3. _____ is a class of diseases in which a group of cells display the traits of uncontrolled growth growth and division beyond the normal limits, invasion intrusion on and destruction of adjacent tissues, and sometimes metastasis spread to other locations in the body via lymph or blood. These three malignant properties of _____s differentiate them from benign tumors, which are self-limited, do not invade or metastasize. Most _____s form a tumor but some, like leukemia, do not.
    a. Cancer
    b. 1509 Istanbul earthquake
    c. 1703 Genroku earthquake
    d. 1700 Cascadia earthquake

4. The term _____ refers to any substance, radionuclide or radiation which is an agent directly involved in the promotion of cancer or in the facilitation of its propagation.
    a. 1509 Istanbul earthquake
    b. 1703 Genroku earthquake
    c. Carcinogens
    d. 1700 Cascadia earthquake

5. _____ is a measure of the number of deaths in some population, scaled to the size of that population, per unit time.
    a. 1700 Cascadia earthquake
    b. 1509 Istanbul earthquake
    c. 1703 Genroku earthquake
    d. Mortality rate

6. _____ comprises those aspects of human health, including quality of life, that are determined by physical, chemical, biological, social, and psychosocial factors in the natural environment.
    a. AL 129-1
    b. AL 333
    c. AASHTO Soil Classification System
    d. Environmental health

7. _____ is the study of the adverse effects of chemicals on living organisms. It is the study of symptoms, mechanisms, treatments and detection of poisoning, especially the poisoning of people.
    a. Toxicology
    b. 1509 Istanbul earthquake
    c. 1703 Genroku earthquake
    d. 1700 Cascadia earthquake

8. A _____ is a poisonous substance produced by living cells or organisms.
    a. Toxin
    b. 1703 Genroku earthquake
    c. 1700 Cascadia earthquake
    d. 1509 Istanbul earthquake

9. In medicine, a _____ is a disease that is long-lasting or recurrent. The term chronic describes the course of the disease, or its rate of onset and development. A chronic course is distinguished from a recurrent course; recurrent diseases relapse repeatedly, with periods of remission in between.

a. 1509 Istanbul earthquake
b. 1703 Genroku earthquake
c. Chronic disease
d. 1700 Cascadia earthquake

10. A _____ or medical condition is an abnormal condition of an organism that impairs bodily functions and can be deadly. It is also defined as a way of the body harming itself in an abnormal way, associated with specific symptoms and signs.

In human beings,'_____' is often used more broadly to refer to any condition that causes extreme pain, dysfunction, distress, social problems, and/or death to the person afflicted, or similar problems for those in contact with the person.

a. 1700 Cascadia earthquake
b. 1509 Istanbul earthquake
c. Black lung disease
d. Disease

11. _____ is water that has a high mineral content. This content usually consists of high levels of metal ions, mainly calcium and magnesium in the form of carbonates, but may include several other metals as well as bicarbonates and sulfates.

a. Hard water
b. 1700 Cascadia earthquake
c. 1509 Istanbul earthquake
d. 1703 Genroku earthquake

12. _____ is an umbrella term for a variety for different diseases affecting the heart. As of 2007, it is the leading cause of death in the United States, England, Canada and Wales, killing one person every 34 seconds in the United States alone.

Coronary artery disease is a disease of the artery caused by the accumulation of atheromatous plaques within the walls of the arteries that supply the myocardium.

a. Heart disease
b. 1700 Cascadia earthquake
c. 1509 Istanbul earthquake
d. 1703 Genroku earthquake

13. _____ is the term used to describe types of water that contain few or no calcium or magnesium ions. The term is usually relative to hard water, which does contain significant amounts of such ions.

a. 1509 Istanbul earthquake
b. 1703 Genroku earthquake
c. 1700 Cascadia earthquake
d. Soft water

14. A _____ is a political association with effective sovereignty over a geographic area and representing a population. These may be nation _____s, sub-national _____s or multinational _____s. A _____ usually includes the set of institutions that claim the authority to make the rules that govern the exercise of coercive violence for the people of the society in that territory, though its status as a _____ often depends in part on being recognized by a number of other _____s as having internal and external sovereignty over it.

a. 1509 Istanbul earthquake
b. State
c. 1700 Cascadia earthquake
d. Extraterritoriality

15. The _____ of America is a federal constitutional republic comprising fifty states and a federal district. The country is situated mostly in central North America, where its forty-eight contiguous states and Washington, D.C., the capital district, lie between the Pacific and Atlantic Oceans, bordered by Canada to the north and Mexico to the south. The state of Alaska is in the northwest of the continent, with Canada to its east and Russia to the west across the Bering Strait.

a. AASHTO Soil Classification System
c. AL 333

b. United States
d. AL 129-1

16. An interbasin _____ is a hydrological project undertaken to divert water from one drainage basin into another. This is usually to boost water levels for hydroelectricity, or to supply drinking water nearby.

- Campbell-Heber Diversion
- Coquitlam-Buntzen Diversion
- Kemano Diversion
- Vernon Irrigation District Diversion

- Churchill Diversion-Southern Indian Lake

- Saint John Water Supply

- Bay d'Espoir Diversions
- Deer Lake Diversion
- Smallwood Reservoir-Julian Diversion
- Smallwood Reservoir-Kanairiktok Diversion
- Smallwood Reservoir-Naskaupi Diversion

- Wellington Lake Hydro Project Diversion (with Saskatchewan)

- Ingram Diversion
- Jordan Diversion
- Wreck Cove Diversions

- Long Lake Diversion
- Ogoki Diversion
- Opasatika Diversion
- Root River Diversion

- Barrière Diversion
- Boyd-Sakami Diversion
- Lac de la Frégate Diversion
- Laforge Diversion
- Manouane Diversion
- Mégiscane Diversion
- Sault aux Cochons Diversion

- Cypress Lake Diversion (with Alberta)
- Pasquia Land Resettlement Diversion (with Manitoba)
- Swift Current Diversion

a. 1509 Istanbul earthquake
c. 1703 Genroku earthquake
b. Water diversion
d. 1700 Cascadia earthquake

17. _____ is the production of food, feed, fiber, fuel and other goods by the systematic raizing of plants and animals.
   a. AL 333
   b. AL 129-1
   c. Agriculture
   d. AASHTO Soil Classification System

18. _____ refers to a member of any human group whose adult males grow to less than 150 cm in average height or less than 155 cm. A member of a slightly taller group is termed pygmoid. The best known _____ are the Aka, Efe and Mbuti of central Africa.
   a. 1509 Istanbul earthquake
   b. Pygmies
   c. 1703 Genroku earthquake
   d. 1700 Cascadia earthquake

19. _____ is the science and study of the solid matter that constitute the Earth. Encompassing such things as rocks, soil, and gemstones, _____ studies the composition, structure, physical properties, history, and the processes that shape Earth's components.
   a. Glaciology
   b. 1509 Istanbul earthquake
   c. Glacial motion
   d. Geology

20. _____ (æ—¥æœ¬ Nihon or Nippon making it an archipelago. The largest islands are HonshÅ«, HokkaidÅ, KyÅ«shÅ« and Shikoku, together accounting for 97% of _____'s land area. Most of the islands are mountainous, many volcanic; for example, _____'s highest peak, Mount Fuji, is a volcano.
   a. Kabul
   b. Java
   c. Kenya
   d. Japan

21. A _____ substance is a material with a definite _____ composition. It is a concept that became firmly established in the late eighteenth century after work by the chemist Joseph Proust on the composition of some pure _____ compounds such as basic copper carbonate.
   a. 1509 Istanbul earthquake
   b. Chemical property
   c. 1700 Cascadia earthquake
   d. Chemical

22. The _____ is the second-longest named river in North America, with a length of 2320 miles from Lake Itasca to the Gulf of Mexico. It drains most of the area between the Rocky Mountains and the Appalachian Mountains, except for the areas drained by Hudson Bay via the Red River of the North, the Great Lakes and the Rio Grande.
   a. 1703 Genroku earthquake
   b. Mississippi River
   c. 1700 Cascadia earthquake
   d. 1509 Istanbul earthquake

23. The _____ is an agency of the federal government of the United States charged with protecting human health and with safeguarding the natural environment: air, water, and land.
   a. Andrija MohoroviÄiÄ‡
   b. Ambulocetus
   c. Amblypoda
   d. Environmental Protection Agency

24. _____ is a disease of uncontrolled cell growth in tissues of the lung. This growth may lead to metastasis, which is invasion of adjacent tissue and infiltration beyond the lungs. The vast majority of primary _____s are carcinomas of the lung, derived from epithelial cells.

Chapter 19. Geology, Society, and the Future

a. 1509 Istanbul earthquake
b. 1703 Genroku earthquake
c. Lung cancer
d. 1700 Cascadia earthquake

25. _____ is a chemical element in the periodic table that has the symbol Rn and atomic number 86. A radioactive noble gas that is formed by the decay of radium, _____ is one of the heaviest gases and is considered to be a health hazard.
a. Selenium
b. Ytterbium
c. Tantalum
d. Radon

26. The general effects of _____ to the human body are due to its radioactivity and consequent risk of radiation-induced cancer.
a. 1700 Cascadia earthquake
b. 1703 Genroku earthquake
c. 1509 Istanbul earthquake
d. Radon emissions

27. The _____ is a physiographic subprovince of the New England Uplands section of the New England province of the Appalachian Highlands. The prong consists of mountains comprised of crystalline metamorphic rock.

The _____ stretches from near Reading, Pennsylvania, through northern New Jersey and southern New York, reaching its northern terminus in Connecticut.

a. 1509 Istanbul earthquake
b. 1700 Cascadia earthquake
c. 1703 Genroku earthquake
d. Reading Prong

28. The _____ is the movement of air into and out of buildings, chimneys, flue gas stacks, or other containers, and is driven by buoyancy. Buoyancy occurs due to a difference in indoor-to-outdoor air density resulting from temperature and moisture differences.
a. 1700 Cascadia earthquake
b. 1703 Genroku earthquake
c. 1509 Istanbul earthquake
d. Stack effect

29. _____ is the flow of air. More generally, it is the flow of the gases which compose an atmosphere; since _____ is not only an Earth based phenomenon.
a. Wind
b. 1700 Cascadia earthquake
c. 1703 Genroku earthquake
d. 1509 Istanbul earthquake

30. _____ is vibration transmitted through a solid, liquid composed of frequencies within the range of hearing and of a level sufficiently strong to be heard. Human ear

For humans, hearing is limited to frequencies between about 20 Hz and 20,000 Hz (20 kHz), with the upper limit generally decreasing with age. Other species have a different range of hearing.

a. 1509 Istanbul earthquake
b. 1703 Genroku earthquake
c. 1700 Cascadia earthquake
d. Sound

31. _____ may refer to either the private sector or the public sector. In the public sector it generally refers to a government's use and creation of the laws, regulations, and other policy mechanisms concerning environmental issues and sustainability. In the private sector it usually refers to the compliance with those tools, or the independent development of self-regulation and rule-making that may go beyond what is required by governments.
   a. AASHTO Soil Classification System
   b. AL 129-1
   c. AL 333
   d. Environmental Policy

32. An _____ is an assessment of the likely influence a project may have on the environment. The purpose of the assessment is to ensure that decision-makers consider _____s before deciding whether to proceed with new projects.
   a. AL 333
   b. AASHTO Soil Classification System
   c. AL 129-1
   d. Environmental impact

33. An _____ is an assessment of the likely influence a project may have on the environment. It is the process of identifying, predicting, evaluating and mitigating the biophysical, social, and other relevant effects of development proposals prior to major decisions being taken and commitments made, to ensure that decision-makers consider environmental impacts before deciding whether to proceed with new projects.
   a. AL 333
   b. AASHTO Soil Classification System
   c. Environmental Impact Report
   d. AL 129-1

34. The _____ is a United States environmental law that was signed into law on January 1, 1970 by U.S. President Richard Nixon. The law applies only to federal agencies and the programs they fund. Essentially it requires that, prior to taking any "major" or "significant" action, the agency must consider the environmental impacts of that action.
   a. 1509 Istanbul earthquake
   b. 1703 Genroku earthquake
   c. National Environmental Policy Act
   d. 1700 Cascadia earthquake

35. _____ is the process of breaking a complex topic or substance into smaller parts to gain a better understanding of it. The technique has been applied in the study of mathematics and logic since before Aristotle, though _____ as a formal concept is a relatively recent development.

As a formal concept, the method has variously been ascribed by Ibn al-Haytham, Descartes (Discourse on the Method), Galileo, and Isaac Newton, as a practical method of physical discovery.

   a. AL 333
   b. Analysis
   c. AASHTO Soil Classification System
   d. AL 129-1

36. The _____ is a division of the White House that coordinates federal environmental efforts in the United States and works closely with agencies and other White House offices in the development of environmental and energy policies and initiatives.
   a. 1703 Genroku earthquake
   b. Council on Environmental Quality
   c. 1700 Cascadia earthquake
   d. 1509 Istanbul earthquake

37. The _____ is part of the current San Luis National Wildlife Refuge. The site gained national attention during the later half of the 20th century due to selenium toxicity and rapid die off of migratory waterfowl, fish, insects, plants and algae within the _____.

Chapter 19. Geology, Society, and the Future

a. 1509 Istanbul earthquake
b. 1703 Genroku earthquake
c. Kesterson Reservoir
d. 1700 Cascadia earthquake

38. Most often, a _____ refers to an artificial lake, used to store water for various uses. _____s are created first by building a sturdy dam, usually out of cement, earth, rock, or a mixture. Once the dam is completed, a stream is allowed to flow behind it and eventually fill it to capacity.
   a. Reservoir
   b. 1700 Cascadia earthquake
   c. 1703 Genroku earthquake
   d. 1509 Istanbul earthquake

39. _____ refers to the area of the Central Valley of California that lies south of the Sacramento-San Joaquin Delta in Stockton. Although most of the valley is rural, it does contain major urban cities such as Stockton, Fresno, Modesto, Bakersfield, and Merced.
   a. 1703 Genroku earthquake
   b. 1509 Istanbul earthquake
   c. 1700 Cascadia earthquake
   d. San Joaquin Valley

40. In geology, a _____ is a depression with predominant extent in one direction. The terms U-shaped and V-shaped are descriptive terms of geography to characterize the form of _____s. Most _____s belong to one of these two main types or a mixture of them, at least with respect of the cross section of the slopes or hillsides.
   a. 1703 Genroku earthquake
   b. 1700 Cascadia earthquake
   c. 1509 Istanbul earthquake
   d. Valley

41. One of the basic reasons for _____ is to keep variables in different parts of the program distinct from one another. Since there are only a small number of short variable names, and programmers share habits about the naming of variables (e.g., i for an array index), in any program of moderate size the same variable name will be used in multiple different scopes. The question of how to match various variable occurrences to the appropriate binding sites is generally answered in one of two ways: static _____ and dynamic _____.
   a. 1509 Istanbul earthquake
   b. Scoping
   c. 1703 Genroku earthquake
   d. 1700 Cascadia earthquake

42. _____ is the artificial application of water to the soil usually for assisting in growing crops. In crop production it is mainly used to replace missing rainfall in periods of drought, but also to protect plants against frost.
   a. Irrigation
   b. AL 333
   c. AL 129-1
   d. AASHTO Soil Classification System

43. _____ is the process of extracting a substance from a solid by dissolving it in a liquid.
   a. 1703 Genroku earthquake
   b. 1509 Istanbul earthquake
   c. 1700 Cascadia earthquake
   d. Leaching

44. _____ is a chemical element in the periodic table that has the symbol Se and atomic number 34. It is a toxic nonmetal that is chemically related to sulfur and tellurium. It occurs in several different forms but one of these is a stable gray metallike form that conducts electricity better in the light than in the dark and is used in photocells.
   a. Silver
   b. Terbium
   c. Silicon
   d. Selenium

Chapter 19. Geology, Society, and the Future

45. _____ is the degree to which a substance is able to damage an exposed organism. _____ can refer to the effect on a whole organism, such as a human, bacterium, or plant, as well as the effect on a substructure of the organism, such as a cell or an organ such as the liver. By extension, the word may be metaphorically used to describe toxic effects on larger and more complex groups, such as the family unit or society at large.
   a. 1700 Cascadia earthquake
   b. Toxicity
   c. Acute exposure
   d. 1509 Istanbul earthquake

46. _____, is the increase in concentration of a substance, such as the pesticide DDT, that occurs in a food chain as a consequence of:

   - Food chain energetics
   - Low (or nonexistent) rate of excretion/degradation of the substance.

Although sometimes used interchangeably with 'bioaccumulation,' an important distinction is drawn between the two, and with bioconcentration.

   - Bioaccumulation occurs within a trophic level, and is the increase in concentration of a substance in an individuals' tissues due to uptake from food and sediments in an aquatic milieu.
   - Bioconcentration is defined as occurring when uptake from the water is greater than excretion (Landrum and Fisher, 1999)

Thus bioconcentration and bioaccumulation occur within an organism, and _____ occurs across trophic (food chain) levels.

Lipid soluble (lipophilic) substances cannot be excreted in urine, a water-based medium, and so accumulate in fatty tissues of an organism if the organism lacks enzymes to degrade them. When eaten by another organism, fats are absorbed in the gut, carrying the substance, which then accumulates in the fats of the predator. Since at each level of the food chain there is a lot of energy loss, a predator must consume many prey, including all of their lipophilic substances.

   a. 1700 Cascadia earthquake
   b. 1509 Istanbul earthquake
   c. 1703 Genroku earthquake
   d. Biomagnification

47. The _____ is an agency under the U.S. Department of the Interior and oversees water resource management, specifically as it applies to the oversight and/or operation of numerous water diversion, delivery, storage and hydroelectric power generation projects it built throughout the western United States.
   a. Andrija Mohorovičić
   b. Ambulocetus
   c. Amblypoda
   d. Bureau of Reclamation

48. _____ are sources of water that are useful or potentially useful to humans. It is important because it is needed for life to exist. Many uses of water include agricultural, industrial, household, recreational and environmental activities.
   a. Water Resources
   b. 1700 Cascadia earthquake
   c. 1703 Genroku earthquake
   d. 1509 Istanbul earthquake

Chapter 19. Geology, Society, and the Future

49. _____ is the human modification of natural environment or wilderness into built environment such as fields, pastures, and settlements. The major effect of _____ on land cover since 1750 has been deforestation of temperate regions. More recent significant effects of _____ include urban sprawl, soil erosion, soil degradation, salinization, and desertification.
   a. 1700 Cascadia earthquake
   b. 1703 Genroku earthquake
   c. 1509 Istanbul earthquake
   d. Land use

50. _____ is the term used for a branch of public policy which encompasses various disciplines which seek to order and regulate the use of land in an efficient and ethical way.
   a. Land use planning
   b. 1509 Istanbul earthquake
   c. 1703 Genroku earthquake
   d. 1700 Cascadia earthquake

51. _____ is the capital and the most populous city of Colorado, in the United States. _____ is a consolidated city-county located in the South Platte River Valley on the High Plains just east of the Front Range of the Southern Rocky Mountains. The _____ downtown district is located immediately east of the confluence of Cherry Creek with the South Platte River, approximately 15 miles east of the foothills of the Rocky Mountains.
   a. Denver
   b. 1703 Genroku earthquake
   c. 1509 Istanbul earthquake
   d. 1700 Cascadia earthquake

52. In physics, _____ is a scalar physical quantity that describes the amount of work that can be performed by a force. _____ is an attribute of objects and systems that is subject to a conservation law. Several different forms of _____ exist to explain all known natural phenomena.
   a. Energy
   b. AL 129-1
   c. AASHTO Soil Classification System
   d. AL 333

53. Consumption of a _____ requires resources and contributes to air and water pollution. In the industrialized world the development of a _____ has become essential for agriculture, transportation, waste collection, information technology, communications that have become prerequisites of a developed society.
   a. AASHTO Soil Classification System
   b. AL 129-1
   c. AL 333
   d. Energy resource

54. A _____ is a bipedal primate belonging to the mammalian species Homo sapiens in the family Hominidae. Compared to other living organisms on Earth, a _____ has a highly developed brain capable of abstract reasoning, language, and introspection.
   a. 1509 Istanbul earthquake
   b. 1703 Genroku earthquake
   c. 1700 Cascadia earthquake
   d. Human

55. A _____ is a body of water, not part of the ocean, that is larger and deeper than a pond.
   a. 1703 Genroku earthquake
   b. 1700 Cascadia earthquake
   c. 1509 Istanbul earthquake
   d. Lake

56. _____ is one of the five Great Lakes of North America, and the only one in the group located entirely within the United States. It is bounded, from west to east, by the U.S. states of Wisconsin, Illinois, Indiana, and Michigan. The lake is slightly larger than the country of Croatia.

a. 1700 Cascadia earthquake
b. 1703 Genroku earthquake
c. 1509 Istanbul earthquake
d. Lake Michigan

57. A _____ is a naturally occurring substance formed through geological processes that has a characteristic chemical composition, a highly ordered atomic structure and specific physical properties. A rock, by comparison, is an aggregate of _____s and need not have a specific chemical composition. _____s range in composition from pure elements and simple salts to very complex silicates with thousands of known forms.
    a. Mineral
    b. 1700 Cascadia earthquake
    c. 1509 Istanbul earthquake
    d. 1703 Genroku earthquake

58. _____ is a national park located largely in Mariposa and Tuolumne Counties, California, United States. It is one of the largest and least fragmented habitat blocks in the Sierra Nevada, and the park supports a diversity of plants and animals. The park has an elevation range from 2,000 to 13,114 feet.
    a. 1509 Istanbul earthquake
    b. 1700 Cascadia earthquake
    c. 1703 Genroku earthquake
    d. Yosemite National Park

59. _____ is the degradation of land in arid, semi arid and dry sub-humid areas resulting from various climatic variations, but primarily human activities. Current _____ is taking place much faster worldwide than historically and usually arises from the demands of increased populations that settle on the land in order to grow crops and graze animals.
    a. 1509 Istanbul earthquake
    b. 1703 Genroku earthquake
    c. Desertification
    d. 1700 Cascadia earthquake

60. _____ is a cape on the coast of North Carolina. It is the point that protrudes the farthest to the southeast along the northeast-to-southwest line of the Atlantic coast of North America. Two major Atlantic currents collide just off _____, the southerly-flowing cold water Labrador Current and the northerly-flowing warm water Florida Current (Gulf Stream), creating turbulent waters and a large expanse of shallow sandbars extending up to 14 miles offshore.
    a. 1509 Istanbul earthquake
    b. 1700 Cascadia earthquake
    c. 1703 Genroku earthquake
    d. Cape Hatteras

61. Due to shore erosion in the Outer Bank of North Carolina a navagational lighthouse had to be moved leading to the _____.
    a. 1509 Istanbul earthquake
    b. 1700 Cascadia earthquake
    c. 1703 Genroku earthquake
    d. Cape Hatteras Lighthouse controversy

62. A _____ is an area with a high density of trees, historically, a wooded area set aside for hunting. These plant communities cover large areas of the globe and function as animal habitats, hydrologic flow modulators, and soil conservers, constituting one of the most important aspects of the Earth's biosphere.
    a. 1703 Genroku earthquake
    b. 1700 Cascadia earthquake
    c. 1509 Istanbul earthquake
    d. Forest

63. A _____ is a landform created by running water eroding sharply into soil, typically on a hillside. They resemble large ditches or small valleys, but are metres to tens of metres in height and width. When the _____ formation is in process, the water flow rate can be substantial, which causes the significant deep cutting action into soil.
    a. 1509 Istanbul earthquake
    b. Gully
    c. 1703 Genroku earthquake
    d. 1700 Cascadia earthquake

Chapter 19. Geology, Society, and the Future

64. A _____ is a geological phenomenon which includes a wide range of ground movement, such as rock falls, deep failure of slopes and shallow debris flows. Although gravity's action on an over-steepened slope is the primary reason for a _____, there are other contributing factors affecting the original slope stability.
   a. 1700 Cascadia earthquake
   b. 1703 Genroku earthquake
   c. 1509 Istanbul earthquake
   d. Landslide

65. _____ is the process in which trees are cut down usually as part of a timber harvest. _____ can also remove wood for forest management goals. _____ is controversial due to its environmental and aesthetic impacts.
   a. 1700 Cascadia earthquake
   b. 1703 Genroku earthquake
   c. 1509 Istanbul earthquake
   d. Logging

66. _____ is displacement of solids by the agents of ocean currents, wind, water, or ice by downward or down-slope movement in response to gravity or by living organisms.
   a. AASHTO Soil Classification System
   b. AL 129-1
   c. Erosion
   d. AL 333

67. _____ is a body of law, which is a system of complex and interlocking statutes, common law, treaties, conventions, regulations and policies which seek to protect the natural environment which may be affected, impacted or endangered by human activities.
   a. AL 333
   b. AL 129-1
   c. AASHTO Soil Classification System
   d. Environmental law

68. _____, a form of alternative dispute resolution (ADR) or 'appropriate dispute resolution', aims to assist two (or more) disputants in reaching an agreement. The parties themselves determine the conditions of any settlements reached-- rather than accepting something imposed by a third party. The disputes may involve (as parties) states, organizations, communities, individuals or other representatives with a vested interest in the outcome.
   a. Flotsam
   b. Jetsam
   c. Fish and Wildlife Coordination Act
   d. Mediation

69. _____ is one of the largest investor-owned energy companies in the United States. The company provides a wide range of energy-related products and services to its customers.
   a. Andrija Mohorovičić
   b. Ambulocetus
   c. Consolidated Edison Company
   d. Amblypoda

70.

The _____ (Morone saxatilis) is a typical member of the Moronidae family in shape, having a streamlined, silvery body marked with longitudinal dark stripes running from behind the gills to the base of the tail. Maximum size is 200 cm and maximum scientifically recorded weight 57 kg.

_____ have been introduced to the Pacific Coast of North America and into many of the large reservoir impoundments across the United States by state game and fish commissions for the purposes of recreational fishing and as a predator to control populations of gizzard shad.

Chapter 19. Geology, Society, and the Future

    a. 1703 Genroku earthquake
    b. 1700 Cascadia earthquake
    c. Striped bass
    d. 1509 Istanbul earthquake

71. _____ is a characteristic of a process or state that can be maintained at a certain level indefinitely. The term, in its environmental usage, refers to the potential longevity of vital human ecological support systems.
    a. 1509 Istanbul earthquake
    b. 1703 Genroku earthquake
    c. 1700 Cascadia earthquake
    d. Sustainability

72. In biology a _____ is the collection of inter-breeding organisms of a particular species; in sociology, a collection of human beings. A _____ shares a particular characteristic of interest, most often that of living in a given geographic area. In taxonomy _____ is a low-level taxonomic rank.
    a. Metapopulation
    b. 1700 Cascadia earthquake
    c. 1509 Istanbul earthquake
    d. Population

73. The term _____ commonly refers to the total number of living humans on Earth at a given time. As of May 31, 2009, the Earth's population is estimated by the United States Census Bureau to be 6,792,467,727. The _____ has been growing continuously since the end of the Black Death around 1400.
    a. World Population
    b. Ambulocetus
    c. Andrija Mohorovičić
    d. Amblypoda

ANSWER KEY

Chapter 1

1. d	2. d	3. b	4. b	5. d	6. a	7. d	8. a	9. c	10. d
11. d	12. c	13. c	14. c	15. d	16. d	17. d	18. a	19. d	20. a
21. b	22. b	23. a	24. a	25. c	26. b	27. d	28. b	29. b	30. d
31. b	32. c	33. d	34. b	35. a	36. a	37. a	38. b	39. b	40. b
41. b	42. d	43. d	44. d	45. d	46. d	47. d	48. d	49. a	50. d
51. d	52. d	53. b	54. d	55. d	56. d	57. a	58. d	59. a	60. d
61. d	62. c	63. d	64. d	65. d	66. c	67. a	68. c	69. b	70. d
71. a	72. b	73. d	74. d	75. d	76. b	77. d	78. d	79. b	80. b
81. a	82. d	83. b	84. c	85. d	86. d	87. d	88. d	89. d	90. c
91. c	92. d	93. d	94. d	95. d	96. c	97. d	98. b	99. d	100. d
101. b	102. c	103. d	104. d	105. b	106. d	107. a	108. b	109. a	110. b
111. a	112. d	113. d	114. d	115. d	116. a	117. d			

Chapter 2

1. d	2. d	3. a	4. d	5. d	6. d	7. b	8. d	9. d	10. c
11. d	12. c	13. a	14. d	15. d	16. d	17. d	18. c	19. d	20. a
21. d	22. d	23. d	24. b	25. b	26. c	27. d	28. b	29. d	30. b
31. c	32. d	33. d	34. d	35. a	36. d	37. a	38. c	39. a	40. d
41. a	42. c	43. c	44. c	45. d	46. c	47. d	48. d	49. b	50. c
51. d	52. c	53. d	54. b	55. d	56. c	57. d	58. d	59. d	60. d
61. d	62. c	63. b	64. d	65. c	66. a	67. c	68. a	69. c	70. d
71. d	72. d	73. d	74. d	75. a	76. d	77. d	78. d	79. d	80. a
81. b	82. a	83. b	84. d	85. d	86. d	87. c	88. d	89. a	90. d
91. d	92. b	93. c	94. b	95. c	96. b	97. c	98. d	99. d	100. a
101. d	102. a	103. a	104. d						

Chapter 3

1. b	2. d	3. a	4. b	5. a	6. d	7. c	8. d	9. b	10. d
11. a	12. a	13. a	14. a	15. d	16. d	17. d	18. b	19. a	20. c
21. a	22. b	23. d	24. a	25. b	26. d	27. d	28. c	29. a	30. a
31. d	32. d	33. a	34. d	35. b	36. d	37. d	38. a	39. c	40. c
41. b	42. d	43. d	44. d	45. b	46. d	47. d	48. a	49. d	50. a
51. d	52. d	53. a	54. b	55. a	56. d	57. b	58. c	59. b	60. d
61. c	62. d	63. c	64. d	65. d	66. c	67. a	68. d	69. a	70. d
71. d	72. d	73. d	74. d	75. c	76. a	77. a	78. a	79. c	80. b
81. d	82. d	83. d	84. b	85. b	86. d	87. a	88. c	89. d	90. c
91. d	92. d	93. b	94. d	95. c	96. c	97. d	98. a	99. c	100. b
101. b	102. a	103. b	104. d	105. d	106. c	107. b	108. b	109. b	110. a
111. b	112. d	113. a	114. b	115. d	116. d	117. c	118. a	119. b	120. d
121. a	122. a	123. d	124. d	125. d	126. d	127. d	128. b	129. c	130. d
131. b	132. d	133. a	134. d	135. d	136. a	137. b	138. d	139. b	140. b
141. d	142. b	143. d	144. d	145. a	146. a	147. c	148. a	149. d	150. d
151. d	152. d	153. d	154. d	155. c	156. d	157. d	158. b	159. c	

Chapter 4

1. b	2. d	3. b	4. c	5. d	6. d	7. d	8. c	9. b	10. c
11. d	12. b	13. d	14. c	15. d	16. b	17. a	18. d	19. d	20. d
21. d	22. d	23. d	24. d	25. b	26. d	27. a	28. a	29. a	30. d
31. b	32. a	33. a	34. d	35. d	36. b	37. c	38. d	39. a	40. a
41. a	42. d	43. b	44. a	45. d	46. d	47. b	48. d	49. d	50. d
51. d	52. d	53. a	54. d	55. d	56. d	57. a	58. c	59. d	60. d
61. b	62. d	63. d	64. c	65. b	66. c				

Chapter 5

1. d	2. a	3. b	4. a	5. c	6. c	7. d	8. d	9. d	10. c
11. b	12. d	13. a	14. a	15. c	16. b	17. b	18. b	19. c	20. d
21. a	22. b	23. a	24. b	25. d	26. d	27. b	28. a	29. a	30. b
31. d	32. d	33. d	34. d	35. d	36. c	37. b	38. b	39. d	40. d
41. d	42. d	43. c	44. c	45. d	46. c	47. c	48. b	49. b	50. b
51. d	52. d	53. c	54. d	55. a	56. b	57. d	58. b	59. d	60. d
61. c	62. a	63. a	64. d	65. d	66. a	67. d	68. c	69. d	70. a
71. c	72. c	73. b	74. b	75. c	76. d	77. d	78. b	79. d	80. b
81. d	82. b	83. d	84. a	85. d	86. d	87. b	88. c	89. d	90. d
91. b	92. a	93. c	94. a	95. b	96. c	97. a	98. b	99. d	100. d
101. a	102. b	103. a	104. a	105. a	106. a	107. b	108. d	109. d	110. c
111. d	112. d	113. d	114. a	115. b	116. c				

Chapter 6

1. c	2. a	3. d	4. d	5. d	6. b	7. c	8. c	9. d	10. d
11. a	12. a	13. d	14. a	15. a	16. a	17. d	18. d	19. c	20. d
21. d	22. a	23. b	24. d	25. d	26. c	27. d	28. d	29. b	30. c
31. c	32. d	33. d	34. d	35. d	36. d	37. c	38. d	39. a	40. d
41. a	42. c	43. a	44. c	45. d	46. d	47. d	48. d	49. c	50. a
51. d	52. d	53. d	54. d	55. d	56. c	57. c	58. d	59. a	60. c
61. c	62. b	63. c	64. b	65. c	66. a	67. b	68. d	69. d	70. b
71. d	72. d	73. c	74. d	75. a	76. d	77. d	78. a	79. d	80. d
81. a	82. d	83. d	84. a	85. b	86. d	87. d	88. d	89. d	90. d
91. d	92. b	93. a							

Chapter 7

1. d	2. d	3. c	4. d	5. d	6. d	7. d	8. a	9. c	10. b
11. b	12. d	13. a	14. d	15. d	16. d	17. a	18. a	19. d	20. a
21. d	22. a	23. d	24. d	25. d	26. d	27. c	28. d	29. d	30. d
31. a	32. b	33. d	34. d	35. d	36. a	37. d	38. a	39. b	40. c
41. a	42. d	43. a	44. a	45. d	46. d	47. d	48. b	49. d	50. d
51. d	52. a	53. d	54. c	55. c	56. d	57. d	58. d	59. c	60. d
61. a	62. b	63. c	64. d	65. b	66. b	67. a	68. b	69. b	70. b
71. d	72. d	73. d							

ANSWER KEY

Chapter 8

1. d	2. d	3. d	4. c	5. c	6. b	7. a	8. a	9. a	10. d
11. d	12. c	13. d	14. a	15. a	16. c	17. c	18. d	19. c	20. d
21. a	22. d	23. d	24. d	25. b	26. d	27. d	28. b	29. d	30. c
31. d	32. a	33. d	34. c	35. c	36. d	37. d	38. b	39. a	40. d
41. d	42. c	43. c	44. d	45. b	46. a	47. d	48. d	49. b	50. d
51. a	52. d	53. c	54. d	55. b	56. a	57. b	58. d	59. d	60. a
61. d	62. a	63. d	64. b	65. d	66. d	67. c	68. d		

Chapter 9

1. d	2. a	3. c	4. d	5. d	6. d	7. d	8. b	9. a	10. c
11. b	12. a	13. d	14. a	15. a	16. d	17. b	18. b	19. d	20. d
21. c	22. c	23. d	24. c	25. d	26. b	27. d	28. a	29. c	30. c
31. c	32. d	33. d	34. d	35. d	36. b	37. d	38. d	39. a	40. a
41. d	42. d	43. d	44. d	45. d	46. d	47. c	48. d	49. a	50. d
51. c	52. c	53. b	54. c	55. d	56. d	57. d	58. d	59. d	60. d
61. d	62. c	63. a	64. b	65. d	66. a	67. d	68. a	69. d	70. d
71. d	72. d	73. d	74. d	75. b					

Chapter 10

1. d	2. c	3. d	4. d	5. d	6. b	7. c	8. d	9. d	10. c
11. b	12. b	13. b	14. d	15. c	16. a	17. a	18. b	19. d	20. d
21. b	22. d	23. b	24. b	25. a	26. d	27. d	28. a	29. d	30. a
31. b	32. b	33. c	34. a	35. d	36. c	37. d	38. b	39. d	40. d
41. a	42. d	43. d	44. d	45. b	46. d	47. d	48. a	49. d	50. d
51. c	52. b	53. d	54. a	55. a	56. a	57. a	58. d	59. d	60. b
61. b	62. b	63. a	64. d	65. d	66. a	67. b	68. d	69. d	70. b
71. a	72. a	73. d	74. c	75. b	76. d	77. a	78. b	79. c	80. c
81. d	82. d	83. d	84. d	85. d	86. d	87. c	88. d	89. d	90. d

Chapter 11

1. c	2. c	3. d	4. d	5. c	6. a	7. a	8. d	9. b	10. b
11. d	12. b	13. d	14. c	15. d	16. c	17. c	18. a	19. a	20. d
21. d	22. c	23. c	24. d	25. d	26. c	27. d	28. d	29. d	30. c
31. a	32. c	33. a	34. d	35. d	36. d	37. a	38. d	39. b	40. b
41. d	42. b	43. d	44. d	45. d	46. a	47. b	48. b	49. d	50. c
51. c	52. d	53. d	54. d	55. c	56. d	57. d	58. d	59. d	60. a
61. d	62. c	63. d	64. b	65. a	66. d	67. d	68. c	69. a	70. c
71. c	72. b	73. a	74. c	75. a	76. c	77. d	78. d	79. a	80. d
81. d	82. d	83. d	84. d	85. d	86. d	87. a	88. c	89. d	90. a
91. d	92. d	93. c	94. d	95. d	96. c	97. c	98. c	99. a	100. a
101. d	102. b	103. c	104. d	105. c	106. d	107. b	108. c	109. d	110. a
111. a	112. d	113. d	114. d						

Chapter 12

1. c	2. a	3. a	4. d	5. d	6. c	7. d	8. b	9. d	10. d
11. b	12. a	13. a	14. d	15. c	16. b	17. d	18. a	19. c	20. c
21. d	22. d	23. d	24. c	25. d	26. d	27. d	28. d	29. d	30. d
31. d	32. a	33. d	34. b	35. a	36. d	37. c	38. a	39. b	40. d
41. c	42. d	43. d	44. d	45. a	46. d	47. c	48. b	49. c	50. d
51. d	52. d	53. b	54. b	55. a	56. d	57. d	58. d	59. d	60. a
61. d	62. d	63. d	64. d	65. d	66. a	67. d	68. d	69. d	70. c
71. c	72. c	73. c	74. d	75. d	76. c	77. d	78. d	79. d	80. b
81. a	82. d	83. d	84. d	85. d	86. b	87. b	88. d	89. d	90. d
91. d	92. d	93. b	94. d	95. d	96. c	97. a	98. d	99. d	100. d
101. d	102. d	103. a	104. b	105. c	106. d	107. d	108. d	109. c	

Chapter 13

1. d	2. d	3. b	4. b	5. d	6. d	7. d	8. d	9. d	10. d
11. d	12. b	13. d	14. d	15. d	16. a	17. d	18. d	19. d	20. b
21. c	22. a	23. d	24. d	25. b	26. d	27. b	28. d	29. d	30. d
31. d	32. b	33. c	34. b	35. d	36. d	37. d	38. b	39. b	40. d
41. b	42. b	43. b	44. d	45. d	46. d	47. c	48. d	49. a	50. a
51. d	52. d	53. d	54. c	55. d	56. d	57. c	58. d	59. d	60. d
61. a	62. a	63. b	64. a	65. a	66. b	67. d	68. d	69. b	70. d
71. a	72. a	73. d	74. b	75. a	76. b	77. d	78. d	79. d	80. b
81. d	82. d	83. b	84. d	85. d	86. b	87. d	88. d	89. d	90. c
91. d	92. d	93. d	94. b	95. d					

Chapter 14

1. b	2. b	3. b	4. b	5. a	6. a	7. d	8. d	9. c	10. b
11. d	12. d	13. d	14. d	15. d	16. d	17. d	18. d	19. d	20. a
21. c	22. d	23. c	24. a	25. a	26. d	27. b	28. b	29. d	30. a
31. d	32. d	33. c	34. a	35. a	36. c	37. d	38. d	39. d	40. a
41. d	42. a	43. d	44. a	45. d	46. c	47. b	48. d	49. a	50. d
51. d	52. d	53. d	54. a	55. c	56. d	57. d	58. a	59. b	60. d
61. a	62. d	63. b	64. d	65. c	66. d	67. d	68. d	69. d	70. a
71. a	72. a	73. a	74. d	75. a	76. d	77. d	78. c	79. b	80. a
81. d	82. d	83. d	84. d	85. d	86. a	87. b	88. c	89. d	90. c
91. b	92. c	93. a	94. d	95. a	96. a	97. d	98. d	99. d	100. d
101. b	102. b	103. d	104. d	105. d	106. c	107. d	108. b	109. c	110. d
111. d	112. d	113. d	114. c	115. a	116. a	117. b	118. d	119. d	120. d
121. d	122. a	123. c	124. b	125. b	126. d	127. c	128. d	129. b	130. c
131. d	132. d	133. d	134. d	135. c	136. a	137. d	138. d	139. d	140. b
141. a	142. b	143. d	144. c	145. d	146. d	147. b	148. c	149. d	150. b
151. a	152. b	153. d	154. d	155. a	156. d	157. a	158. b	159. b	160. d
161. a	162. d	163. d	164. c	165. a	166. d	167. d	168. a	169. a	170. d
171. a	172. b	173. d	174. a	175. d	176. a	177. d			

ANSWER KEY

Chapter 15

1. d	2. b	3. a	4. d	5. d	6. d	7. d	8. a	9. b	10. d
11. c	12. c	13. b	14. d	15. b	16. d	17. d	18. d	19. d	20. d
21. c	22. d	23. d	24. d	25. d	26. a	27. d	28. d	29. d	30. d
31. d	32. d	33. b	34. a	35. d	36. c	37. d	38. b	39. d	40. d
41. d	42. d	43. d	44. d	45. d	46. d	47. c	48. c	49. b	50. d
51. b	52. d	53. d	54. b	55. d	56. d	57. c	58. d	59. d	60. d
61. c	62. d	63. d	64. d	65. a	66. d	67. a	68. c	69. d	70. b
71. d	72. d	73. c	74. d	75. b	76. c	77. d	78. b	79. a	80. d
81. a	82. b	83. d	84. a	85. d	86. a	87. d	88. b		

Chapter 16

1. a	2. d	3. d	4. d	5. a	6. d	7. d	8. b	9. d	10. d
11. d	12. a	13. b	14. b	15. d	16. d	17. d	18. d	19. d	20. a
21. d	22. b	23. d	24. c	25. b	26. a	27. c	28. c	29. d	30. d
31. b	32. c	33. c	34. d	35. c	36. d	37. a	38. c	39. b	40. d
41. c	42. b	43. d	44. c	45. d	46. b	47. d	48. a	49. a	50. d
51. a	52. d	53. a	54. d	55. b	56. d	57. d	58. a	59. d	60. b
61. b	62. d	63. b	64. d	65. a	66. d				

Chapter 17

1. b	2. d	3. d	4. b	5. c	6. c	7. d	8. c	9. d	10. d
11. d	12. c	13. d	14. d	15. b	16. d	17. b	18. d	19. a	20. d
21. d	22. d	23. c	24. c	25. c	26. b	27. a	28. d	29. a	30. a
31. b	32. d	33. d	34. d	35. d	36. d	37. d	38. d	39. b	40. a
41. c	42. c	43. d	44. c	45. d	46. d	47. d	48. c	49. a	50. d
51. d	52. d	53. d	54. d	55. a	56. a	57. d	58. b	59. d	60. b
61. d	62. c	63. d	64. d	65. a	66. d	67. d	68. d	69. d	70. b
71. b	72. d	73. a	74. d	75. b	76. c	77. c	78. a	79. d	80. b
81. c	82. d	83. b	84. c	85. b	86. d	87. a	88. b	89. a	90. d
91. d	92. a	93. c	94. d	95. a	96. d	97. d	98. c	99. c	100. a
101. a	102. d	103. c							

Chapter 18

1. b	2. c	3. b	4. c	5. a	6. d	7. d	8. b	9. c	10. d
11. a	12. c	13. d	14. b	15. d	16. d	17. a	18. b	19. b	20. d
21. d	22. c	23. d	24. d	25. b	26. c	27. d	28. d	29. d	30. d
31. d	32. c	33. c	34. c	35. d	36. d	37. d	38. a	39. d	40. d
41. a	42. b	43. d	44. d	45. b	46. d	47. d	48. b	49. d	50. a
51. b	52. a	53. d	54. d	55. c	56. d	57. d	58. a	59. d	60. c
61. a	62. d	63. c	64. a	65. d	66. a	67. d	68. d	69. a	70. b
71. a	72. d	73. d	74. a	75. c	76. c	77. b	78. d	79. d	80. b
81. b	82. d	83. d	84. d	85. d	86. d	87. a	88. d	89. a	90. d
91. c	92. d	93. d	94. b	95. d	96. d	97. a	98. c	99. d	100. d
101. b	102. d	103. d	104. b	105. c	106. a	107. d	108. a	109. d	110. b
111. b	112. d	113. a	114. a	115. c	116. b	117. d	118. d	119. a	120. d

Chapter 19

1. c	2. a	3. a	4. c	5. d	6. d	7. a	8. a	9. c	10. d
11. a	12. a	13. d	14. b	15. b	16. b	17. c	18. b	19. d	20. d
21. d	22. b	23. d	24. c	25. d	26. d	27. d	28. d	29. a	30. d
31. d	32. d	33. c	34. c	35. b	36. b	37. c	38. a	39. d	40. d
41. b	42. a	43. d	44. d	45. b	46. d	47. d	48. a	49. d	50. a
51. a	52. a	53. d	54. d	55. d	56. d	57. a	58. d	59. c	60. d
61. d	62. d	63. b	64. d	65. d	66. c	67. d	68. d	69. c	70. c
71. d	72. d	73. a							

www.ingramcontent.com/pod-product-compliance
Lightning Source LLC
Chambersburg PA
CBHW080545230426
43663CB00015B/2715